Betrayal in Mexico

*A True Story of Romance
& Adventure in the
Early Days of Exotic
Puerto Vallarta*

LOUIS E. BITTRICH
AND THERESIA J. LEWIS

R&E Publishers
Saratoga, California

R & E Publishers
P.O. Box 2008, Saratoga, CA 95070
Tel: (408) 866-6303   Fax: (408) 866-0825

Book Design by Diane Parker

Bittrich, Louis E.
    Betrayal in Mexico: a true story of romance & adventure in the early days of exotic Puerto Vallarta / Louis E. Bittrich and Theresia J. Lewis
        p. cm.
    ISBN 1-56875-072-2: $14.95
    1. Americans--Mexico--Puerto Vallarta--Fiction. 2. Women--Mexico--Puerto Vallarta--Fiction. 3. Puerto Vallarta (Mexico)--Fiction.
I. Lewis, Theresia J. II. Title.
PS3552.I775B48 1994
813'.54--dc20
                                       94-4054
                                          CIP

Some of the names have been changed, for reasons
that will become clear as you read my story.
But all the events happened exactly
as I have described them.

1

I let out a whoop of laughter, but nobody heard. Could it have been only six weeks ago? I saw myself peering through the heavy crystal doors of the Banco de Guadalajara. The taxi driver brought me to the best bank in the city, as I had asked. It was two o'clock in the afternoon and they were closed, but I was determined to do my business that day.

The guards were preening. They knew how handsome they were in their uniforms, and they were anxious to make an impression on the interesting foreign lady, even if she was acting strangely. Even if she was taller than they were. I've found that my height does not deter the typical Mexican *machismo* for a moment. In fact, some men even act as if it adds to the challenge.

"¿Qué se le ofrece, señorita?" What can we do for you?

"Nice touch," I thought. I loved being called *'señorita'*! I smiled sweetly and swept past them, my silk skirt swirling softly around my legs, and my high heels clicking on the polished marble floor. I was dressed for the occasion. Nothing left to chance. I had even added some modest diamond jewelry, so that I would be taken seriously.

I approached the official who looked most *simpatico*, leaned over and looked straight into his brown eyes. *"Necesito el baño y unas tijeras, por favor."* I smiled again as he considered the strange request.

"The rest room is to the right and down that hallway," he answered in Spanish, "but was it scissors you said?"

I suppose he figured that since I was so obviously out of place, so clearly blonde, and perhaps rather eccentric, that I had gotten the word wrong. I assured him that it was scissors I needed. He handed them over and I promised to return soon.

In the rest room, I struggled out of my girdle, and began cutting away the very small stitches I had made, to form a sort of money belt. It was a trick I had learned from my mother. I had $60,000—in $500-bill notes, so I wouldn't look as if I was pregnant with an ox. I felt flushed as I returned to the desk of Pascual Morán. At the exchange rate of 12.5 to one, back in 1964, I was almost a millionaire in pesos!

I hadn't stolen the money, exactly. Bob had offered it to me, sort of flung it at me, figuratively, during one of our fights. It was clear from the way he said it that he never expected me to take him up on it.

But I was out of there the very next day.

"I would like to open an account in your bank. Please forgive the late hour, but I didn't want to carry so much money around any longer." I blinked my eyes demurely, and handed over the total amount, in the large bills. Pascual sat down very quickly. Then, recovering immediately, he began to draw up the necessary papers.

SIX WEEKS LATER

"Oww!" I yelled. "What's going on up there, anyway?" My head glanced off the ceiling in the back of the station wagon. All in one graceless movement, I twisted around and lunged protectively toward my babies in the crib behind me. "Where are we?" I asked Helen. "I must have dozed."

I looked into little Buster's huge, dark eyes. They seemed mildly amused, as if to ask, "What's all the fuss about?" His brother had not even looked up from his toys.

"We're in a ditch—" Helen was laughing uncontrollably, bent double over the steering wheel. "We're in a ditch!" she shrieked. "What do you call it, a *vado*? No, that's one of those—"

"I can see that, *gringa*!" I said to my sister sarcastically. The humor in this situation was lost on me. Suppose we had broken an axle? How would I even know what a broken axle looked like? "But where—?"

"I think we're still a couple of hours away from Hermosillo. You know, the cats were getting fidgety, and I was trying to pour them some water in their little dish. Then Kaiser dived up in front, stuck his big paws between me and the wheel, and—"

The joke vanished from her eyes. "Oh God, Theresa, the cats!" She grabbed the door handle and was out of the car in a sprint, before I completely understood.

Then she was back, poking her head in the door. "Kaiser!" I yelled. I grabbed his collar and held him back. Poor guy, it was almost too much excitement for his adolescent German enthusiasm.

"Don't you worry, Theresa, I'll find the cats. They can't be far." My eyes were beginning to mist over and I felt silly.

"Theresa." She drew herself up to her big sisterly stance. "Look. You can see for miles. They've got to be out there somewhere. I'm just afraid they'll get their collars hung up on one of those little bushes." She yelled a quick "be right back" over her shoulder, and her short, wiry body disappeared over the first rise.

I looked out over the parched land, choked with wild grass and low scrub. Up to the point where the Sierra Madre rose purple in the distance, nothing broke up the monotony of the desert, not even the fluffy backs of two frightened Persian cats. "Surely the sun will pick up the rhinestones on their collars," I thought. "Lucky we got them up like that."

"What you got there, Bear?" I asked, singing it out like an idiot. "Your plastic beads? That's pretty!" I don't know if I was trying to reassure my baby or myself with the stupid smile on my face.

"Well, really, Lewis, you've done it this time." I almost turned around. My husband's exasperated voice seemed so close to my ear. "How are you going to make it through the Mexican desert in July? You don't know anything about cars. You don't even know how to pay a traffic ticket! Stupid rich—"

"I don't need you to tell me that, Bob Lewis!" I was standing in the middle of our bedroom in California, screaming. "I'll find somebody else to help me out. I don't need you!" I slammed some shoes into my suitcase, as if it was really his face I was aiming for.

"You'll hate Mexico. Let me tell you about Tijuana. Mazatlán. That country is poor. They're all thieves and losers." He was waving his arms with frustration. No argument seemed to be working. I smiled coolly, which made him even angrier.

"It's filthy down there. A big Dutch broad like you will never be able to stand it." There he thought he had me. Everything depended on his picture of me as the slightly dopey, innocent foreign student he had found four years before. But I was not stupid, just unused to American ways.

Already I had been a career girl in Spain for five years. And now, I was ready and determined to strike out on my own again. "I suppose you think you could help me out down there?" I chided. "You can't even speak Spanish. And you're too old to learn."

He threw up his hands. "OK, so I lied. Will I ever hear the end of that?"

"Thirty-eight years old! Ha! Ten years . . . and on an official document too! You're closer to my father's age." I pinned him with what I hoped was my fiercest look. "If my father only—"

"Oh, not that again."

"If my father only knew our story, he would send his men all the way from Holland to get you."

"Come off it, Terry—"

"They'd cut your neck and bury you under the Golden Gate Bridge!" Perhaps American television was having its way with me. I don't know why I liked that image so much, or how I thought my father was going to do that. He may have been rich, but he had no Mafia connections, nor any others in the underworld that I knew of.

I shook away the ugly memories of strident voices, and looked out over the arid Desierto de Altar for any sign of Helen or a spoiled feline. Nothing. "It's for you I'm doing this," I said, turning once again to the babies. "You know it, don't you? Just wait till you feel that warm sea water running through your little toes!" I grabbed Buster and hugged him through the bars of the crib.

"Cookie, cookie," shouted Bear and crawled over to the edge of the friendly prison for his hug. A little blond, brown-eyed kid of almost two now, he could walk, of course, but there didn't seem to be much point to that in their cramped playpen in the rear of the station wagon. I dug through bags and cases beside the bars and came up with a couple of their favorite treats.

Kneeling there, hanging on to the bars together, the two brothers hardly looked as if they belonged to the same nation, let alone the same family. Buster resembled his father exactly, dark skin, dark hair. "You'll fit right in around here without any trouble," I chuckled to myself. "And you, my little Dutch boy," I said, mussing Bear's white hair. "You don't look a bit like your daddy, do you?"

"Daddy?" he said.

"Yes, Daddy," I sighed.

"You want a divorce?" the strident tone continued. "Why don't you go back to Holland where you belong? I can take care of the kids here. These are American kids."

I put Kaiser on a leash and got out of the car to stretch my legs. But the voices pursued me.

"You must be crazy to want to live in Mexico. THINK! You can have all the money you want here. Anything. Look around you."

I looked around at our beautiful house on the heights above the bay. All the lights of San Francisco were just beginning to come up. A breeze brought a soft caress and a hint of pine and eucalyptus to the redwood deck where I was standing. Will I miss this house? How elegant I thought it was when Bob first showed it to me. But no more.

A sweet-looking deer walked out of the forest and looked at me tentatively. But I would not be charmed. "Sell this house on the mountain!" I screamed. "I don't want it! All I smell are the skunks and those damned trees that remind me of my father's pharmacy."

"Oh, I get it. All you want is to be a colonial madame again. A house filled with little dark servants running around doing errands for Terry. Useless errands that—" he sputtered. "The big white lady in the grand house in the tropics." His lips curled. "Get realistic! You won't even have electricity in that place."

"I love it down there. I want to go back to the sun. Don't you understand?"

"I can see the picture. Just like your beautiful dark grandmother, sitting on the veranda all day long, while her personal servant combs her long black hair with an ivory comb. Let's face it, kid, those headhunters in Indonesia—"

"Yes, I had a black grandmother! But at least I know where mine came from!" A pretty low blow, I guess, but he was starting to tamper with one of my favorite childhood dreams. Those memories were precious.

Bob Lewis does have all kinds of dark blood, as well as white—Negro, Indian, Cuban, French. But prejudice is not one of my shortcomings. I could hardly afford it. My family is the same. I am one of the pale ones. But when we would get together in Rotterdam after the war, we had black, brown, red, pale skins, all in the same room. We used to call ourselves the Zebras.

I found myself slumped on the gritty soil, against the back wheel of the station wagon. The U-Haul was tipped precariously into a Mexican ditch that was beginning to look familiar. I must have been thrashing around a bit, because there was Kaiser, offering me big, slobbery kisses of consolation. "It's OK, my boy," I assured him. "We're free."

I grabbed his leash and ran him around the car and the trailer a few times, to make him happy, and to clear my head. It was too much trouble to get shoes on the boys. Besides, they didn't need "bathroom stops," as the mounds of disposable diaper boxes in the back of the car demonstrated.

I peeked in and saw Buster, my baby of nearly a year, already asleep, and Bear beginning to nod. They can make it to Hermosillo, I decided. I opened all the car doors and checked to make sure the air was circulating as well as it could on a July day in Sonora.

About thirty minutes later, Helen appeared. Her way of walking told me that she had had no luck. "We'd better forget about the cats," I said. "It's getting too hot for the babies. We need to go." She looked sick. What she had done wasn't exactly dangerous. We had been driving pretty slowly through the desert, so we wouldn't overheat the car. And the traffic was limited to an occasional goat or *burro* or jackrabbit. Still, it was foolish, and she knew it. The highway, really a narrow lane of potholes, sloped down from the center on both sides, and one had to pay constant attention. The road from Tucson to Hermosillo may be fine now, but this was 1964.

"I'll drive for a while. Don't worry about it," I consoled her. And we were off. The wind, though it was warm, felt good once again on our faces. I hiked up the skirt of my spaghetti-strap sundress, to get more of a breeze on my legs, and wished it was possible to wear shorts in Mexico. But no woman who wanted to be regarded as a lady would dare to do that yet, for a good many years.

The steady hum of the engine brought back the unwelcome voices. "Well, all right," I thought, "what else have I got to do?" Helen was already asleep in the back seat. I surrendered. "Perhaps if I let all the echoes play out, I can get rid of them once and for all."

Bob was preaching again, his finger poking at the air: ". . . and I'm stuck with a crazy Dutch bitch who's pregnant all the time . . . and now a father-in-law who wants to kill me and bury me under the Golden Gate Bridge. Maybe I should let you go. . . ."

"*¡Perfecto!*" I shouted triumphantly. "You just tell that Natalie of yours to get her . . . self over to the notary tomorrow for the papers." Ice dripped from every syllable at the mention of his secretary, and I saw him flinch. Secretly I had to admit he was being pretty reasonable about the whole thing, even if much of it was out of guilt.

Several months before I had been a bouncy little newlywed, happy and relatively carefree among the fashionable set in the San Francisco bay area. I had just returned from Holland. It was my father's seventieth birthday, and I had gone home, to celebrate and to show off my darling babies. My parents were starting to come around—though they would never bring themselves to admit out loud that I had moved to America permanently.

From Rotterdam, I telephoned my husband every other day. So in love. Of course, there in Berkeley, it was past midnight, but he never seemed to mind. He was still awake.

We had the house, I had all my beautiful china, my crystal, my silver, my oriental rugs. My father had even shipped me my beloved piano, over the sea from Europe, through the Panama Canal. I had been pregnant most of the time, and I had no friends, and most of my evenings were spent waiting in front of the television for Bob Lewis to come home from work. But I didn't see it that way then.

My dream life was just barely touched one day, when I saw a doctor and found out I needed to have a cyst removed. It seemed like a harmless enough operation. Perhaps it could even be burned off. I just needed to talk to Bob. To have him near by.

I drove my sporty little Jaguar across the bay bridge, excited to surprise him with a visit, perhaps a lunch date, in the middle of the day.

When I got to the insurance office, the doorman said, "I'm sorry, Mrs. Lewis, your husband is gone for the day." Well, I was disappointed. But since I had driven all the way into the city, why not make use of the time? A couple of months earlier Bob's secretary had given birth to a baby, and he had urged me to play the gracious lady and send her a nice gift, which I had done. I still had her mailing address in the pocket of my coat.

"I know, I'll pay a visit to Natalie. Perhaps she and I can become friends."

Imagine my surprise when I drove up to the apartment building and saw Bob's car parked in front. But I had an explanation for everything. "Probably planning to work late. And I wasn't home to receive his call."

I pushed the button of the elevator and looked forward to a pleasant cocktail hour.

They had started ahead of me.

Natalie answered the door, flustered. Behind her, looking very much at home on the sofa, and surrounded by Heineken beer bottles, was my husband. As interesting as the look on his face was, that wasn't what caught my eye. It was the two-month-old baby comfortably resting in his arms, a dead ringer for my dark-eyed husband.

I'm not sure what I did then. I wasn't used to swearing back then, but I think I must have let out a string of obscenities that surprised everyone. I only remember Natalie trying to hide behind that beautiful mane of wavy red hair, cowering beside the sofa, and looking as if she wanted to crawl inside it.

Outside the building, I marched straight for Bob's car, took out my set of keys, and drove off. The next thing I knew, I was crawling out of a huge bank of dense bushes in Golden Gate Park. I had not buried my husband there, but I sure had disposed of his car! It was well hidden.

I took a cab back to Natalie's, retrieved my own car, blustering all the way home. "Goddam Jaguar, I've always hated it. Never could get my body into the damn thing. Seems like I've always been pregnant."

The light began to dawn. "This was an awfully nice birthday present. Almost too expensive, now that I think of it. I wonder which girl this one was a pay-off for?" I guess I was a pretty stupid Dutch broad after all. Twenty-nine years old, and I couldn't spot an infidelity when it walked up and laughed in my face.

I made plans to return to Holland for a divorce. It took the police three days to find his car.

The station wagon and U-Haul approached yet another Mexican *vado*.

Yes, Helen was right. The word on the road signs referred to a dip in the road like this one, not to the ditches on either side. During the rainy season, the water rushed off the mountains so fast that everything was swept before it. And the road would have been washed out too, if it hadn't simply accommodated nature and inclined toward the bottom of the dry creek bed and then up the bank on the other side. We were lucky, I suppose, that the day was dry. But it still took careful maneuvering sometimes, to make sure the trailer hitch did not scrape the road, or even snap off, as we hit bottom.

Could anything be farther from Holland than this place, in every way? Rotterdam last year was—well, Rotterdam. Chilly, grey, Dutch. I can't say I really felt American yet, but I had had a taste of the open West, and I did not feel Dutch any longer either.

When I arrived, I could not tell my parents the whole story. But of course, they made plans anyway for me to move immediately into their house with my babies. My father had always hated Bob. And now he disapproved of me. He was retired and bored. My mother was drinking too much. And when she wasn't drinking, she was shopping. Neither activity interested me much. I returned to San Francisco for Christmas.

My husband was a perfect gentleman. Charming, enthusiastic, and repentant. We planned to start all over again with a second honeymoon in Guadalajara.

And there I fell in love. Not with Bob, but with Mexico. I had no idea! Here was a beautiful, sophisticated city, high up in a tropical mountain range that reminded me so much of Indonesia, where I grew up as a child. We spent three weeks there, and my love affair grew with each day. We drove out to Lake Chapala, and enjoyed the picturesque villages along the shore. We browsed through one intriguing shop after another in Tlaquepaque, on the edge of Guadalajara. There were palm trees, flowers everywhere. Paradise was so close to me there in California, and I didn't even know it!

We returned, and Bob Lewis continued on his best behavior. For a while. Then gradually, my evenings began to get longer again in front of the television. Dinners began to be delayed or canceled much more frequently. It became pretty clear to me what my life would be. I knew I was the third wife, but I had always sympathized with his side of the stories. Now I began to understand the former Mrs. Lewises.

In May, just six weeks ago, when Bob sold his ranch for $60,000, I saw my chance. I withdrew the money from the bank, and boarded a plane for Guadalajara. I wanted nothing more from my parents. But I thought it was only fair that my husband should set me up in paradise.

Later on, when he moved to Puerto Vallarta, I got to know Pascual, the banker who lent me the scissors that day. We had many a good laugh over that scene!

The babies were stirring in the far back of the station wagon. Helen sent back a bottle and some fruit juice, and that seemed to satisfy them. We could still wait until Hermosillo. The heat made everyone drowsy, and soon again, I was the only one awake in the car.

"UN SOLO CARRIL," announced the sign just before one of the rare bridges on the high desert of Sonora. "So what else is new?" I asked myself. "Since we crossed the border, there hasn't been room for much more than one lane." But it seemed to be a good omen. At least it was a bridge, and not a dip. Perhaps it indicated that we were finally nearing a town.

The rule on these narrow bridges was that both cars would rush forward, and whoever thought he would reach it first blinked his lights to show he had the right-of-way. A chancy arrangement at best. Luckily, there was still no traffic on the road.

I tugged at the bodice of my sundress, making a mental note that a loose cotton blouse would be better for traveling the next few days.

"Yes, Bob, I'm leaving you all alone here in your playground, old man. You can tell your errand girl—what's her name?"

"You know very well—"

"Yes. Natalie. That's right. You tell her to get her . . . boobs on over to the notary and get me my permission to take the kids to Mexico."

This last item of official nonsense was a gift from Marlon Brando to all of us. Ever since he kidnapped his son and took him off to Mexico a few years before, it had become illegal for an American child to cross the border without the written consent of both parents. Can you believe it?

Therefore, though the voices being exorcised on this long desert drive were loud voices, there were also plenty of soft ones too. I had to stay friendly with Bob to get the permission. And he was good about it. Although I suspect he secretly never thought I would go through with my plans.

When he finally stood in the driveway on that last morning, he had tears in his eyes.

"Terry, are you sure you want to rush into this? If you want to change your mind, I forgive you."

"Forgive? You forgive me? For what?"

"Well, you want to take my boys away—"

"*Your* boys! Now you think of that—" My temper was starting to flare again. But there was no point. I was almost off.

"You're making my old age miserable. This is the age when a man starts thinking about retiring, not about raising a new family." It was hard to stay mad at him when he sounded so ridiculous. "How did I know I'd get stuck with a woman who got pregnant, and stayed pregnant all the time? What could I do?"

"Go find yourself a calendar, Bob. I didn't have Bear for a year and a half after we were married."

"Just kiss him goodbye, and let's get going," added Helen, irritated with all this dialogue, which she'd heard before.

"Well, if you're still there at Christmas time, perhaps I'll drop down to see you and the kids," called my husband, as I pulled away from my American life. I was cutting the umbilical cord. I left him standing there, the empty house, empty of family at least, behind him.

"Hey, everybody, wake up! It's Hermosillo!"

The town wasn't especially important for us, but the joy I felt was due to reaching a destination—any kind of destination in the interior of my new country. The feeling doubled when I saw a row of palm trees along the road, the first sign of the lush tropics that I knew were ahead. "We're heading south," I reassured myself, and smiled a broad smile to no one in particular. My joy tripled when I spotted over on the left side, nestled in some large shade trees, a small hotel. It had a swimming pool.

"Come on, boys!" I parked the car in a large open space, grabbed my papers, and in moments we were all checked in.

In a flash we had our swimming suits on and were sitting up to our chins in the cool water of the pool. I had been concerned about our becoming dehydrated, especially the babies. Crossing the desert in July is foolish enough, I suppose, but we had also been sitting beside the road for an hour, while my sister went searching for the cats. Here was the perfect solution. Now we could relax.

Helen came out of the room a few moments later, strolling at a more leisurely pace. "You sure didn't take any chances with that trailer, did you?"

"Plenty of room," I laughed. "Plenty of room to spare."

The night before in Los Angeles we had learned our lesson. We were tired from the trip, anxious to get to bed, and I had pulled the car quickly into the parking place in front of the motel room. The next morning, we loaded up the car. I got in and backed straight out.

Suddenly, it became painfully clear to us that nobody had taught us how to back up a trailer!

There wasn't enough room to maneuver by going straight. I turned the steering wheel slightly. The trailer veered the wrong way and headed for a shiny new Buick. I pulled back into the parking place and started all over again. The trailer ended up even more crooked. I turned the steering wheel the other direction. The trailer was even more askew than before. Whatever I did, I angled into bigger trouble. Helen got in and tried it, but with no better luck.

Finally a nice-looking gentleman saw our predicament and offered to help us out. In a couple of moments the station wagon and U-Haul were out into the parking lot, aimed frontwards toward the exit. It looked so easy. I don't know what he did.

"It's really not so difficult," he explained, smiling. "Just be sure to go slowly, and turn the steering wheel the opposite way from what seems natural." A broad, friendly grin came over his face. I wished we could take him with us.

"How far are you all going?" he asked.

"Puerto Vallarta." Helen and I answered at the same time, neither of us daring to look him in the eye.

"Mexico? You're going another thousand miles with this thing and you don't—" He stopped, probably at a loss how to continue politely. He looked a little helpless, and grinned again. "Well, just remember, the opposite of what you think it should be. Good luck!" He waved goodbye and looked relieved to be getting into the safety of his own car, driving off in a different direction.

"Don't worry," I consoled Helen. "I'll fix it so we just don't have to back it up any more." And so we did. From then on, whenever the Lewis caravan stopped for a restaurant or a hotel, there was always plenty of room around, on all sides, and a clear exit toward the front.

I had startled everyone when I checked into the hotel, speaking good Spanish. By the time we were comfortably at home in the pool, the word apparently had spread. The family simply had to find out more about us. A plump *señora* with a very pleasant smile started toward us with a tray of drinks. Fruit juice for all, including her.

"*Muchas gracias, señora. Muy amable,*" I said. How gracious the Mexican people are! I must admit I could have put away a martini or two, but perhaps a lady doesn't ask for such things in Mexico. At least away from the larger cities. Anyhow, she was kind to think of us. And also bursting with curiosity.

"You have come through the wide *desierto* today?" she asked, with a look of shocked disbelief. "But, *los niños*—"

"Don't worry about the boys," I assured her. "They did fine." They were giggling and splashing contentedly in the clear blue water. She would have a difficult time claiming they had been mistreated in any way. They were becoming little Mexicans already on the first day! We laughed and got acquainted, and she told me all about her sons and daughters. Ten of them already, though she couldn't have been more than thirty-five years old.

"But how are you going to drive to Puerto Vallarta?" she asked, concerned. "Don't you know that there is no road?"

The man at the border had had the same question, and the same genuine concern for two ladies, two babies, two cats, one German shepherd, and a trailer full of Lord knows what.

"*¡Ay, señora!* What can I do for you?" He peered into the windows, and Kaiser let out a low, menacing sound of warning. But the man won him over, and the rest of us too, as he showed how typically Mexican he was—that is, how unable he was to resist babies.

"*¡ Qué bonito!* A cute little blondie! *Sí, señora*, you have those big blue eyes... this is your baby."

Could you call it flirting? A little bit, perhaps, but it was much more genuine interest, a natural friendliness. "Now, where did this dark baby come from?" He glanced down at the papers.

"*Es mío,*" I said proudly.

"Ah, this one is yours too? A little dark one?"

He seemed to want to talk, but he could see also that we were in a hurry, especially when he heard our destination. Our papers were in order. Quickly he stamped them and directed us through the maze with a flourish.

"*¡Pásele, señora, pásele!* Right this way." The men (there were several by this time) didn't even look through our things.

Back out onto the streets of Mexicali, we were officially in Mexico. "Well, we made it! Where are the *mariachis*?" I shouted gaily to anyone who would listen.

I got my first taste of potholes, but certainly not the last. Big potholes. Some looked as if they could swallow up the Chevy and the U-Haul both. We bumped along slowly and carefully through the sprawling border town. People strolled or scurried along through the whirlwinds of dust, oblivious to the fact that a new adventure was starting for us.

"So this is a border town," I mused, grabbing the steering wheel with both hands. "Well, I think the people are charming. I wonder what Bob was talking about?"

I have held that opinion of the Mexican people—all but half a dozen of them, who will have a large role in this story—ever since.

"*Humilde*" is a word I have tried many times to explain to my American friends. There does not seem to be a good translation for it in English, but the word characterized my new countrymen very well: modest, gentle, sincere. I admit that is certainly not a description of the typical Hollywood Mexican. That's our problem. And yes, there is also the strutting *machismo* that is part of every Mexican male's façade. That, unfortunately, is his problem. But when we get past that, the people are charming.

Humilde. I never regretted the next fifteen years of my life.

2

Tepic. An ancient colonial city and now the bustling capital of the state of Nayarit, and for our small caravan, the end of the line. When Cortés arrived here in 1542, all he found was a small Indian village. Still, that was eighty years before the Pilgrims stepped ashore at the Plymouth Rock.

We drove slowly past the old cathedral, its Gothic towers seeming strangely out of place, and followed the signs reading *'AEROPUERTO.'* It was 2:30 in the afternoon, and it was simply too much to think of loading into yet another hotel and loading up the car again the next morning. There was quite enough loading and unloading ahead of us anyway, since, as our friends had been quick to tell us, we could only make the last leg of our journey by small plane. The car and the trailer would have to wait here until Helen could drive them back to California.

We pulled up at the office and Helen ran in, while I changed the babies' diapers and started gathering up their toys. Big drops of summer rain were starting to plop on the windshield. Later on, I wouldn't even pay attention to such an everyday afternoon event during the rainy season. But today, I was concerned. I looked out the window of the car. Big black clouds were banking up over the mountains. The wind had started up.

Helen was back, poking her head inside the car window. "He says we can't go. There's going to be a storm."

The wind was gusting already, and I looked around, more in anger at the elements, than in despair. "Of course we can fly. Go tell him we aren't afraid of a little storm."

Helen didn't look as if she would be able to convey that message with much conviction. "Here, finish this." I got out of the car and walked toward the office. A handsome young man in a tight-fitting blue uniform came striding out to greet me.

"*Mire, señora*. Look! The clouds are growing darker and darker. We cannot fly."

"Does it frighten you?"

"Me? Of course not. But a lady! And with two babies, and her sister....And all this luggage....You say everything in the trailer goes?"

He was shaking his head sadly. He was partly in earnest. But I have done this kind of "horse trading" enough in different parts of the world to know that he was also trying to raise his price.

"Everything." I tossed my head dramatically. I know how to play the game too. "Of course, if you don't want my business, I can find someone else who can—"

"All right, *señora*." He was laughing. We both knew the script well; however, he could afford to be cheerful, for he had won this round in the game. "But you should know, the only planes in Tepic right now are mine. We can work something out. *Me llamo Antonio.* Tony," he added, offering to shake hands.

Two other pilots joined him on the pavement in front of the office. He leaned over and muttered something to them in a low voice. Most likely something like "here's a gutsy lady"—or words to that effect—for their slow stares were full of admiration and curiosity. I had posed myself against the car door, for maximum theatrical effect, and they took their time looking over my long, slim body. It helps to be a sporty blonde in Mexico.

"*¡Andale, ándale!*" called the first pilot, and the loading began. Not one of them could have been even twenty-five years old yet, but it didn't occur to me to be frightened. I knew that Mexico was honeycombed with hundreds of small airports and small aircraft. That's what makes drug trafficking so easy. Many kids here start their love affair with flying when they are sixteen.

We started unpacking all the household goods from the trailer. Helen would go in one plane with little Bob, or "Buster," and most of the luggage and boxes. I would take Al, my firstborn, whom we called "Bear," and the German shepherd, and whatever was left to be packed. The rain was starting to come down in torrents, and the sky grew darker and darker. We almost had to stop and renegotiate the deal when they discovered my gas ice box in the trailer. But I smiled my helpless female smile, he shrugged good-naturedly, and they continued loading.

When they finished, Helen went to put the car away in a storage area, and I watched, as the pilot walked around each plane, shaking his head. He was not smiling now, and I felt this was a new game.

"*Señora*," he said, the rainwater running down his face in little rivulets, "these planes are too small. We will not get off the ground in this storm."

"We've got to. We're all loaded."

"*Señora*, there's a lot of thunder up there in those clouds—"

"Well, if you have to dive, just dive," I said, sticking out my chin bravely.

Out of the corner of my eye I saw him raise his finger to the side of his temple and with a gleam in his eye to his *compañeros*, he moved it slowly round in a circle. I recognized the international sign. '*Loco.*'

"We can wait a while. This storm will be over soon, won't it?" I asked. I started to dig in my purse significantly.

He nodded ascent. "Well, perhaps. But we can't do it with just two planes. We'll need to divide your things. Put most of the luggage into a third one."

I handed him an extra $50. His eyes grew bright. That was a lot of money in a provincial Mexican capital in those days. "*¡Sí, señora!* Right away." He whistled to the two other pilots, and the rearranging began. With the next lull in the storm, we were taking off down the runway, heading straight into the mountains.

Only then did I realize how headstrong, perhaps foolish, I had been. My fears grew when I saw my strong-jawed pilot cross himself and kiss his thumb, as he took the plane up over the first range and into the thick black clouds. I lost no time in following his lead. I crossed myself, and made the sign of the cross over Bear's forehead. I hoped the effect would splash off on Kaiser. I felt too silly to give him a separate sign.

Lightning crashed on all sides, and the thunder was deafening. "So you are a good Catholic?" I yelled above the din.

"At times like this, *señora*." The gleam in his eye had not disappeared. "Nobody else but a beautiful blonde American lady could get me up in this storm today."

"Are you afraid?" I challenged.

I hadn't thought so. But I looked at him closely again. I could see that his eyes were full of the devil, not of fear.

"Only for you, *señora*."

Then I understood. He hadn't really been fearful of the thunderstorm, but only of having a hysterical lady on his hands, when he would have other things to think about. He had a healthy respect for the weather, to be sure. I had sensed that when I first spoke to him. It must have been what made me know that it was all right to go ahead with our plans.

"Don't worry about us. We'll behave ourselves," I assured him and smiled.

I didn't feel as brave as I sounded. Especially a moment later, when the plane hit a maverick air current, and we dived out of the clouds and toward the trees. *"Ave María, ave María,"* I started, remembering my own Catholic upbringing. And the plane leveled off momentarily. "Whoooa!" I shouted on the next plunge. I must have grabbed my boy awfully tightly, for he let out a little squeak and looked deep into my eyes for consolation.

"That's OK, Bear," I yelled cheerfully. "Isn't this fun?"

I don't know whether the pilot stayed close to the jungle because it was safer for him, or easier in the storm, or simply because he could not climb above the threatening black clouds. And I didn't want to ask. On another day, perhaps I could have enjoyed the dense carpet of tropical foliage beneath us—the lacy palm fronds, the brighter green of the broad banana leaves, the tangled vines, that gave it all the appearance of virgin territory—as if no human being had even come this way. But this afternoon, in the buffeting winds, I only had the time and energy to help my man Tony stay aloft above the trees, which I did mainly by pushing my heels nearly through the floor of his small plane.

After about fifteen minutes, and several more dives, I was ready to call the whole thing off. I picked up my stomach up off the floor and started to say, "Perhaps we should turn back after all."

But just then Tony took the plane up yet another mountainside and turned to me. "Just over this last ridge, and we're there!"

I sat back and started worrying about the landing. I had landed at the Puerto Vallarta airport once before, of course. Back in May. But then I was in a large plane. What a difference that makes! In a commercial airliner, the passenger is protected, isolated, removed from the elements. He looks out at the scenery, and it almost resembles a map, a view from space. I had never before this flight had a sense that I could reach out and grab a banana or a coconut as we passed by! "Now this was real flying," I thought proudly.

Of course, the reality of it would have been even stronger if I had landed only a year before. John Huston, who lived in our house later on in the '70's, used to describe the airport when he first came down to scout locations for his film, *Night of the Iguana*. "We would come in and circle this field," he said. "Nothing but grass! The only thing that gave us a hint of an airport was a small *palapa* hut and a row of lights—rag wicks burning kerosene in some coconut shells. Now that's primitive!"

In fact, it was John we had to thank for as much progress as we had by 1964. His film—and the famous love affair of Richard Burton and Elizabeth Taylor behind the scenes—had put Puerto Vallarta on the map. By the time we dived down out of the clouds, there was a small, paved landing strip, large enough to be used by Mexicana Airlines on their runs from Guadalajara to Los Angeles.

The wheels of my plane squealed playfully on the pavement. We had arrived.

"¡Gracias a Dios!" Tony and I echoed each other at almost the same moment. Perhaps the weight of the luggage was more of a concern to him than he had let on. Helen's plane, and then the third, followed shortly after.

Fabulous young man. "Come on," I said. "I'll buy you a drink. I think we all need it."

Tony was laughing. "No bar at this airport," he shrugged.

All the taxis in town—three—were there to greet us. How did they know? We loaded up as much as we could for one trip, and I told the pilots they didn't have to wait for us to come back for our next load. They could leave our things there for us on the grass. I grabbed Tony's hand and pressed it hard. We had been through a powerful experience together, and I felt that we were friends. I would miss him. All three men waved good-bye as Helen and I and the babies and the dog piled into the creaking cars, by now close to scraping the ground, and set out for one of Puerto Vallarta's well-known and oldest hotels, the Rosita.

The career of its owner, Don Luis, is perhaps typical of many sharp businessmen in a fast-growing tourist center. Today a large hotel of more than a hundred rooms sprawls along the beach, occupying five buildings and including several apartments. When I arrived in 1964, he and his family were the hardworking owners and operators of a modest eighteen-room establishment.

It was a delightful place, a system of breezeways and clean, bright rooms clustered around a central patio area. Delicate, lacy grills made of thinly-sliced native jungle trees and parasite vines decorated the walkways and divided off a cozy separate area for the restaurant.

What the old-timers knew was that only twenty years before, the land where we stood had been the city dump. Don Luis, as the official caretaker of the dump, in charge of land fill, had found his job a bit slow. His quick young mind hit upon a way he could supplement his income and make his life more interesting, by selling water. Water that tasted so sweet that people would rather pay for what he sold, than take their own water free from the Rio Cuale, which ran through the center of town.

Every morning he loaded his *burros* with jugs, and set off toward the natural springs of the mountains. The water dripped slowly into his urns, filtered through charcoal, and then ran out into many containers, ready to be sold. The women of the town came to rely on the purity of the water of Luis, and gradually he began to make money.

And the land filled in gradually as well. He and his sons built two or three rooms at first, then a few more, to provide places of rest for the smattering of visitors to the town. In came the rich big game hunters who flew in to try their luck in the mountains, and the men who arrived from the interior to negotiate for sugar cane, brought down by *burro* from the town of El Tuito, just above.

Now Don Luis greeted me at the door, rather surprised to see that this time I was accompanied by two small babies, and that they were mine. He and his daughters, after a quick flurry of activity, left us alone comfortably in our room. We slept very well that night.

But I was too eager to sleep for long. Enough is enough!

I arose with the dawn at 4:30, and while Helen and the boys slept, I started out along the Malecón, the beachfront promenade, and quickly became familiar again with the town which was to become so much a part of my life. At the corner where the road curves in front of the Hotel Oceano, still asleep in the early morning hush of July, I turned back. Finally I settled down in the sand at the foot of a tall, elegant coconut palm and gazed out into the incredible Bahía de Banderas, the "bay of banners."

The first time I saw this bay, back in May, I was looking down out of my plane window upon the full, magnificent stretch of it, from Punta de Mita on the north to the southern tip at Cabo Corrientes. Ninety miles of sparkling white sand beaches formed an almost perfect horseshoe.

"Where are we?" I asked a couple of Canadian stewardesses who had become new friends.

"Puerto Vallarta. Don't you know it?"

"No," I replied. "I've never heard of it."

It's almost unthinkable nowadays, but the sleepy village was still mostly a secret from the outside world back then. I thought I was leaving Guadalajara only briefly and returning almost immediately. I had deposited my money in the bank, I was on my way back to San Francisco to collect my children and my things, and shortly I would be a new citizen of the "City of Roses." I had no idea that my plane would stop at Paradise on the way back to California.

"You really should stay a day or so. It's one of our favorite places," exclaimed one of the girls. "Why don't you stay at the hotel with us?"

The Bahía de Banderas was beckoning. I didn't have to be talked into it.

The stewardesses stretched out on the colorful "party" beach with the odd name, Playa de los Muertos, the "beach of the dead." Aided by some strange concoctions they were calling *coco locos*, the girls lost no time in reaching a state of semi-consciousness in the hot morning sun. They seemed determined to look as if the place had been named for them.

But I was restless as usual. A man approached, not young, not old, and introduced himself as Tiburón. 'The Shark.' On a leather string around his neck, he had a big, mean-looking tooth, which he claimed was from a shark. It probably was.

He also proudly sported a mean-looking scar on his shoulder, which he said was from a dangerous battle with a shark. It probably was not. But this little Indian was colorful, and I became even more interested when he indicated that he had horses for rent.

"*Buenos días*. You. *Gringa*. Dollars?" he asked, gesturing vaguely in the direction of a few skeletal horses in a bamboo pen. He looked a little desperate—I think because he had already exhausted his supply of English words. I answered him in his own language, and he looked relieved, though still a bit confused. Soon I realized that my Castilian Spanish, perfected during my years in Spain, was also difficult for him. As we rode and talked together the rest of that day, I listened carefully to his slang words and expressions and started picking up the Mexican way of speaking.

Before we set out, however, I went to my room and changed into my jodhpurs and boots. When I reappeared, though the sight of a woman in riding pants, flared wide at the thighs, must have seemed comical to my country guide, he was smart enough to hide it, and we set off toward the village. Tiburón rode behind, clad in a faded black swimming suit, stretched-out T-shirt that kept slipping over his shoulder, and a large straw hat. With a funny little hand-woven leather whip, he occasionally nudged my scrawny horse, when the poor beast started acting sleepy. I rode slightly ahead, surprised that this raggedy creature, his mane all tangled in knots and his tail thick with burrs, could move forward at all.

Our route took us leisurely toward the center of the village. Pausing beside the Rio Cuale, I was fascinated to watch a group of fishermen's wives kneeling at the bank, laughing and gossiping, and scrubbing their clothes. It is a sight I have often seen since, and I have never stopped marveling that their shirts are as white as any that come back sealed in plastic from the most careful modern laundry.

Farther up the river toward the mountains, some *burros* stood patiently while construction workers loaded them down with large round boulders from the river bed.

We continued across the bridge, rode past the market and into the little plaza in front of the parish church, dedicated to the Virgin of Guadalupe, Mexico's most revered patron saint. Tiburón proudly pointed to the top of the tower, in the shape of a large filigree crown.

"*La corona de la Virgen*," he beamed. "Twenty thousand people came to help put the bell up into the steeple." His arms spread wide and his eyes grew large. I think I was getting the special tour, and I was appreciative, though my wooden saddle was becoming a bit uncomfortable. I was happy at least that I had changed out of my swimming suit.

Our way wound onto the Malecón, a rather grand cobblestone boulevard, with the sea on the left and a row of small buildings opposite, mostly fishermen's houses overlooking the calm blue water.

"*¡Ay! Miren a la gringa,*" the little kids said in loud whispers, not knowing whether to gape at my blonde hair or at my riding breeches.

"*¡Hola, muchachos!*" I answered, smiling into their dark eyes, and thought how much fun my own boys would have growing up here, running freely on the waterfront.

The front doors were wide open, and I looked curiously into the houses. Though the rooms were crowded, they seemed bright and airy. Still, it was hard to imagine there could be room for a typical large Mexican family. Pleasant-looking women smiled up at me shyly as we passed. The rhythm of their hands continued, *smack! smack!* as they fashioned the large, flat tortillas for the day's main meal. A small fire burned in the little wood stove in the corner. Every house was the same.

Behind, beside, everywhere, the flowers bloomed abundantly— bougainvilleas in all shades of pink and purple, and hibiscus, and the bright yellow cups-of-gold. Every step of the way the beauty of the place, the tantalizing odors of the food being prepared, tempted me to stop.

But I had already asked my sharkish guide to conclude his tour on the hill up above the beach, so we continued to ride.

We crossed the river again and started up into the mountains. Here at the head of the bay, the steep Sierra Madre range hugs Puerto Vallarta with a tight embrace, coming practically down to the water's edge and leaving room for no more than two or three streets behind the Malecón. We climbed carefully and slowly up the slippery paths, choked by the lush vegetation of a tropical jungle.

Suddenly we reached a small clearing high above the Playa de los Muertos, and the vista opened out upon the whole bay below. My breath came fitfully, as if it was I who had climbed up the side of this mountain, and not my poor old nag. I knew my reaction was not from exertion, but excitement.

"*¡Ay, Tiburón, qué magnífico!*" I exclaimed, unable to fill my eyes fast enough. "It's impossible! How is it that the world doesn't know about a place so beautiful?"

"But *señora*, even the whales come here to make love! They spew and mate, and clash their bellies together in the air," he exclaimed, gesturing out beyond the Islas Marietas and laughing slyly.

I looked down at the picturesque village, the church steeple pointing to heaven, like the finger of God warning his people to heed his Ten Commandments. Little houses tumbled against each other around the church, and then more sparsely up the mountainside.

My gaze swept the whole panorama of the coast, up and down, north and south, along the gleaming white beaches, with dense jungle beyond. But my attention kept coming back to the widest part of the beach, a deserted strip about half way from the village to the airport. Behind the dazzling sand were several acres of tall, stately coconut palm trees. I would look away, but the place always drew my eyes back, like a magnet.

"What is that beach over there?" I asked my guide, who was yawning.

"That? Oh, that's the Playa de las Glorias."

"'Heaven'? I can believe it," I said, shaking my head in wonder. "I've got to go down there."

"What? But *señora*, it's—" He was looking at the sun. The smell of homemade tortillas was drifting up, even to where we stood, and his stomach was echoing what he already knew from observation.

"I'm not really hungry, are you?"

"¡Ay—!" he sighed, fidgeting. "That's two hours—"

Poor man. I could see the intense struggle going on between his comfort and his pocketbook. I was paying by the hour. Finally I took pity on him.

"OK. You take me back right now, and then meet me again after *siesta*. I'll be waiting right down there in front of the El Dorado," I said, pointing to the thatched roof of a restaurant on the beach below.

"Or rather, make that 3:30," I continued. "I'm anxious to get going." I didn't need to make it too easy. After all, I was paying the man, and I had to see that beach. It was calling out to me! "And get us some better horses!" I added.

As we picked our way carefully down the mountainside and then all through lunch, my thoughts were whirring inside my skull. No, not really thoughts, for there was no content. They were just currents of excitement. Snatches of little fears. "What if it's not—?" "I've got to—" "But I can't really—" "Will it be—?"

I don't know what I wanted. I know I didn't want lunch. I didn't want to wait for Tiburón. I wanted to be there. I wanted it to be mine.

But I did wait for my guide, and he did return dutifully at the appointed time with some sleeker animals. We rode quickly through the town, and then along the beach. We must have been a rare sight: a big blonde Dutchwoman in pants and an eager, overaged beach boy tagging along.

Some of his buddies whistled and hooted to him. *"¡Ay, cabrón!* Where are you going so fast?" they shouted. "So you take on the tall ones too, eh? Are you going to fuck her on the beach?" Screams of laughter. *"¡Ay, mamacita!* Where can I get one like that?"

I bit the inside of my cheeks hard, pretending that I couldn't understand Spanish. Truly, I didn't know enough of the right words at that time to answer them the way I wanted to. Tiburón had enough decency to look embarrassed, and he jabbed both our horses with his little whip so that we moved on quickly.

We came to another sort of stream or drainage ditch that was wide enough at the beach to be an obstruction, and we turned inland a bit until it was easier to cross, and then continued along the highway, perhaps a hundred yards inland from the water.

Soon the palms were towering in front of us. We approached the property from the narrow airport road, and then followed a winding dirt pathway toward an old pick-up truck near the beach. A small stream, choked with fat summer reeds, angled off to the right. I was immediately struck by how well-kept this property was. There were only the tall, stately trees, no flowers; but without care, palm trees can easily become shaggy and forlorn looking, with their dead yellow fronds bunching down from the top.

We rode farther down the path, and a building I had not seen from the hill gradually became visible. It was a *palapa*, a low hut with a roof of tightly woven palm branches. The style is typical on this part of the Pacific coast; but this one was bigger than a hut, for it was a place of business. Its foundation was a concrete slab about the size of a comfortable middle-class house in the States. Supporting the roof were posts of coconut trunks, that had been choked by thick, ropy 'strangler vines,' their hairy roots making them look like strange insects clinging to the sand.

An older man sat on a large tree trunk, chopping coconuts with a *machete*, and several young people sprawled beside him, laughing and enjoying the warm breeze drifting through the shade of the tropical shelter.

Tiburón rode straight up to the group. When he spoke to this man, his attitude became deferential. *"Buenas tardes, don Cloro,"* he said, holding his straw hat in his hand. "There is someone here who wants to meet you."

"*Don* Cloro?" I thought. "Even an old beachcomber rates a term of respect here—" The thought vanished when I felt myself pinned by the man's shrewd eyes. He seemed to look deep inside me, with a look that was suspicious, but not unfriendly. Then he spoke to Tiburón.

"*Y esto. . .¿es hombre o mujer?*" He glanced briefly at my riding trousers, and his lips curled at the *macho* joke he was sharing with the guide about my sex. Even so, his green eyes sparkled, and stayed on mine. I felt I was included too. There was nothing cruel in the man's attitude.

"This is a lady, don Cloro!" Tiburón's voice pretended amazement. "And she speaks Spanish," he added in a warning tone.

"*Buenas tardes, señor.* This is the most beautiful beach I have ever seen," I said smiling, and jumped off my horse. I was telling the truth. It was not a deliberate attempt to appeal to his pride, or perhaps I should say it was at least not a deceitful remark.

I think I won him over in that instant. Cloro continued to proceed cautiously, as was his nature, but from that moment I felt we were partners of some sort.

Tiburón dismounted and tied up both our horses. The sea pulled me forward, and I could not resist walking toward the waves, lapping placidly now in the heat of the summer afternoon. The sand was thick and luxurious beneath my feet—about fifty yards of it to the water. How fortunate the man was to have this place! In town the beach was rather narrow, and littered in some places with large boulders.

I looked back. My shark was heavy in conversation with don Cloro. I had seen that look before. I had had it myself, when, as a Spanish tour guide I had escorted some group or other into an expensive souvenir shop, counting up in my head the commissions I expected to make.

I studied the older man. Probably in his late fifties, he had a comfortable, generous face—maybe he had even been handsome in his youth. This was a face that had seen much, lived much. His grey hair was cropped short, and he had a stubble of perhaps three days on his cheeks, but his shirt and khaki pants had been freshly ironed. How could I approach this man? Exactly what did I want to ask him?

Some of the young guys and girls had drifted off toward the long canoes that seemed to be carved out of single logs. My eyes strayed along the beach and spotted another building beyond the brook, low under the palms. It was a small house. Cinderblock walls arose from a concrete slab and supported the asbestos roof. There were openings in the walls, not windows, where bamboo sticks were set into the mortar to prevent intruders, but it did have a door. It was perfect!

I took a deep breath and strolled back calmly to the little tavern. It would not be good to appear too eager. Cloro was playing the game too. Chipping away at the coconuts, he had not missed a beat, though he had obviously been watching my every move at the water's edge.

"Do you live in that house?" I asked as I approached.

"Me? No, *señora*. My wife would never stay in such a place. We live in town."

"Who's it for, then?" The questions came tumbling out, one after the other. "Did you build it?"

Since he had his choice of questions, he answered the easier one.

"Yes, *señora*, I am a builder. I built this *palapa*. And my house in town too." His green eyes were laughing at me. He knew I didn't really want to know about his construction business. I saw in the middle of his bright eyes, toward the pupils, there were small circles of clear blue. It made him seem even jollier and full of fun.

Later I learned that he had wondered at first if I was a sort of American agent checking up on some of the expensive homes being built in Mexico with laundered money, or on some other kind of black market deals. In Cloro's position, one could not be too careful. My continental Spanish and my enthusiastic curiosity had betrayed me. Lucky I was not an agent—I would not have had much success!

But those suspicions were well masked behind his laughing eyes. *"¿Coco loco?"* he offered, before I could think how to rephrase my question and get the information I wanted.

"Gracias," I smiled. "'Crazy coconuts'? Well, why not?" I rationalized to myself. "My Canadian girlfriends certainly acted as if they were enjoying them. It will probably bring me closer into his confidence."

I watched as he took his *machete* and chopped the tops cleanly off two more coconuts, taking care to hold them upright, so that the milk did not spill out. Into each, he poured a jigger of rum, then gin, then vodka, and my eyes grew wider with each step. Then he added a sticky-looking purple syrup and some ice and stirred them briefly. The final touch indicated that we were at the "down-home" end of Puerto Vallarta. At the elegant Los Muertos beach, the drinks came topped with an exotic tropical flower. Here at Las Glorias, my host stuck in a couple of spears of palm leaf, which stabbed the air at a rakish angle, and handed me one of the fuzzy coconuts.

"Gracias." The drink was sweet and the breeze was pleasant. "This is the life, isn't it?" I said to myself, my mind racing ahead. "It's going to be my life. It's got to be." I had forgotten about Guadalajara already.

"Does anyone live in that house?" I insisted.

"I built it for some *gringo*. He likes to come here and fish and watch the sea. He doesn't come here much."

"A *gringo*? Where is he from?"

"Up north somewhere. Maybe California," he added, pretending disinterest. The coconut chips were flying. The best ones he saved to use as spoons later, to scoop out the meat of the coconuts. "Where do you come from?" He looked up. He was changing the subject, but it led just where I wanted to go.

"I'm from California too. Perhaps I could find this man and ask him if I could buy his place."

Silence. There was a constant, but subdued activity over at the dugout canoes, but I was only half aware of it. They were young people having a good time on a late spring afternoon. Cloro squinted out to sea and his brown face became a map of wrinkles. But still he said nothing.

"Actually, I'm not an American. I was born in Indonesia."

"Indonesia?" He stumbled over the word a little. "Where is that?"

"It's a country in the southeast of Asia."

Cloro's face was blank.

"It's a large country. As big as Mexico."

Now he looked at me as if he had caught me in a lie. "It's where?" It was incredible to him that somewhere there was a country of that size and he had never heard of it.

"You know in the war, the Americans fought both the Germans and the Japanese? It's over there by Japan." I grabbed a stub of a palm branch for a pointer and enthusiastically set about drawing a map in the sand. Cloro shrugged and offered me another drink, and I accepted. We were getting on well. Perhaps another *coco loco* would make the geography lesson more interesting. He measured out a drink while I drew in the sand. He hadn't touched his.

"And Tiburón?" I offered boldly. My guide had been staying off to the side, showing that he knew his place. With a jerk of his head Cloro motioned him silently toward the inside, and Tiburón went in and got himself a Coke.

We were settled again. I pointed out Japan and Australia, and the large sweep of the Pacific. "And here's Indonesia, under China." The mention of China struck a more familiar chord than Japan had. For according to the local lore, the Chinese had landed often on this coast, centuries before, perhaps even at Punta de Mita, out there at the tip of the bay. Some evidence had been found, though nobody knew much about it.

"And you see, my mother was Dutch. I lived in Holland for a while after the war." A look into his eyes showed that I had lost him again. "I'll tell you about Holland some other time," I said gently. "And I'll draw you another map."

I understood perfectly. This man was one of the shrewdest traders on the coast. Several years back, he had even been mayor of Puerto Vallarta. Yet his formal education had not gone beyond the fourth grade. He had never before needed to know where Indonesia was, so why should he?

"Could I see the house? I think I would like to buy it if the man will sell."

"Can't."

My heart sank. What did he mean? Can't see it? Can't buy it? Why not? Had he only been leading me on?

"*No se puede.* You know about our revolution? You Americans know about Pancho Villa, I think." My geography lesson had had no effect. I was an American again. "He invaded you Americans up in New Mexico. In a Roys-Rolls."

"A what?"

"You know," he said frowning. "That word is too difficult." He wiped the sweat off his forehead. "He shot thirty-six *gringos.*" His face brightened. It was my turn for a history lesson. The gist of it was that after the Mexican revolution, the great land holdings of the wealthy were divided among the farmers. But according to the new constitution, no one could own land along the coastline or the borders.

"And you? Don't you own this land?"

"No, *señora.* It is a lease from the government."

"And the man from California?"

"A lease from me."

"Then I could get a lease too?"

He nodded hesitantly.

"May we take a look at it?" My persistence was paying off—with perhaps a little help from two friendly *coco locos.* He got up and eyed me with some respect. I was talking business with him and drinking with him like an equal, not like some pushy American female who should have stayed off the beach in pants.

We strolled over toward the little house. It was very primitive; but what I saw there was a dream house. "And this is the well?" I asked. "It doesn't look finished."

"It isn't. The *gringo* uses water from the river. You could wash and bathe there too."

"But I couldn't do that. I have two little children. You'll have to finish it."

"*¡Dos hijos!*" The calm mask dissolved. I think I finally managed to surprise him. "But *señora,* you can't—" He glanced over toward the large dugout canoes. The hour of *siesta* was long over, and the young men and women were arranging themselves, preparing to leave.

Suddenly I understood. "Those girls are—"

"*Putas.*" He looked up at me almost shyly, expecting me to be horrified.

I laughed. "But my babies aren't even two years old. They won't understand about whores!" I tried to assure him. "Don't worry about it. I'm not." Every country approaches some subjects conservatively, and then has other areas that are no problem for them, but might be for us. Still, it would take me a while to get used to Mexico.

And Cloro a while to get used to me. He continued to study me carefully, not knowing what to make of me.

"But I really must have the well," I continued. "We can live here without electricity, but I've got to have *agua!*"

"Well, if you can make the other arrangements with the *gringo*, perhaps I can do something for you."

Tiburón was now making signals, politely trying to suggest that it was getting late. "Doña Theresa," he said, with a slight bow of the head, "the horses must go back. It's a long ride." I agreed, secretly pleased that I had been elevated to *'doña.'*

"Meet me this evening in town," offered Cloro, as we started back toward his *palapa.* "I will find you on the Malecón, and I will bring the name of this man in California."

"Thank you." I extended my hand. "What time?"

"About eight o'clock. Go to El Patio. The owner there is also *una holandesa.* I will find you."

Another Dutch woman in Puerto Vallarta? I was intrigued.

I was in the bar at El Patio at quarter to eight. Connie Gutiérrez, the Dutch woman, was not there. Her name betrayed the fact that years before she had fallen in love here in this sleepy village and married a Mexican, and then later opened this restaurant. Though I didn't meet her that night, there was still plenty there to occupy my attention.

In the evenings, all of Mexico lives outdoors. I was fascinated with the scene across from me. The whole town had come out to the Malecón to enjoy the cooler air and watch the sunset. Mothers strolled leisurely up and down the boulevard with their babies and small children, lovers attempted to steal a glance or two, hawkers were selling all kinds of food from greasy little carts, while flies buzzed around fiercely.

I looked beyond the broad sidewalk, down to the sea. At the water's edge were the village fishermen, tending to their boats, fixing their nets. Dressed only in little shorts and sandals, their bellies almost black from the sun, they were busy all up and down the beach, laughing and drinking tequila straight out of the bottle. Others were here in the bar with me.

I looked around and saw that I was the only woman in the room. "Yes, I will learn a lot here," I thought, but more with eagerness than concern.

Cloro Palacios strolled in at quarter to nine, not even aware that he was late. Another Mexican habit I would have to learn to live with. "Promptness" is a concept that carries no meaning at all for these people.

He handed over a scruffy little piece of paper on which was written "Gene LaPorte," with a San Francisco address.

"San Francisco—that's perfect! That's where I live!" I took that as a sign that the little house on Playa de las Glorias was meant for me. Things were working out so easily, as if they had been specially prepared.

"You see, I'm used to you people from California," he said, leaning back comfortably in his chair. He had changed his shirt, but he had the same *huaraches* on his dirty feet. Those handmade leather sandals with soles from tire treads were to be found everywhere along the coast, as I would later discover.

"I worked for a man from Los Angeles. Tall man. He came here to make a movie. Lots of Americans." He began to tell me stories of helping John Huston to build the set and the actors' quarters for *Night of the Iguana* a couple of years before. The director had chosen the site of Mismaloya, a rocky point that reached out into the sea five or six miles down the coast. It was quite a project. The jungle had to be cleared. Everything had to be brought in by small boats—all the building materials at first, then later the filming equipment, the actors, the technicians, the caterers, everything.

Opportunity had presented itself to Cloro in several ways. His supply canoes were kept busy day and night. And then he also ran a profitable business on the side, buying whiskey cheaply from the ships passing down the coast, and then selling it to the Hollywood people at inflated American prices.

Of course, I didn't learn all this that first night at El Patio. He didn't know me well enough yet to tell me all of it. But he did keep me interested with stories about the glamorous Ava Gardner and the off-camera fireworks between Richard Burton and the beautiful woman with the violet eyes.

We knew already that evening that we shared great hopes for the future. But neither of us had any idea how Puerto Vallarta would soon explode into a major tourist center, partly on account of the stories going round the world at that moment about those very people.

Everything that happened to me from then on seemed to move at double speed.

I left Cloro, with his promise that the well would have a pump by the time I returned. When I got back to San Francisco, I called on Gene LaPorte, and he was delighted to have someone stay in his little house. We settled on a rent of $50 a month, and he agreed to buy a gas refrigerator for me, if I could bring it down in the trailer.

I gave away the boys' winter clothes, I bought plastic containers for preserving food, for carrying water, washing clothes, doing housework, in every conceivable size and shape. And I packed the trailer.

And in no time, here it was, an early morning in July, and here I was sitting happily under a palm tree on the Bahía de Banderas, the bay of my future.

3

"¡Pescado!"

The word broke in pleasantly as I floated into a sleepy morning awareness. I stretched long and luxuriously to greet another new day. I had not been sound asleep. Likely the fisherman's call of fresh fish had been intruding on my consciousness for several moments, as he neared my little beach house. I could see him in my imagination, the day's catch suspended from a long pole over both shoulders, banging loudly on the pole with his fillet knife.

"¡Pescado!"

There was the insistent breakfast call again. It was my own personal wake-up call. I inhaled deeply. The moist odors of the jungle pushed through the small barred windows next to me, proclaiming the freshness of the mountains, of newborn flowers, combined with the rot of overripe things. Nature was full with the promise of life and its indifference toward decay and death.

Again I stretched and yawned. The banging of the knife was now very close. If I wanted this man's fish for my breakfast, delivered directly almost to my door, I had to get up soon.

I threw my legs over the edge of my cot and slipped into a swimming suit. Quickly I looked in on the babies, comfortably contorted in their own bed. Lupita's eyes opened and she looked up, but I put a finger over my mouth and then waved to her. She knew by the sign that all was well and that she should sleep a little longer while I went down to the beach.

"Another glorious day!" At the doorway I sighed a deep sigh of content, and congratulated myself once again for being here. The rays of a new sun darted between thick fronds, and the whole Pacific coast sprang into lush green life. A pungent aroma drifted down from the charcoal factories in the hills just above me. I reached for a basket to carry the fish and stepped outside, and began weaving between the slender palm trunks toward the water.

"Good catch, Felipe?" I called out to the boy in front of me.

"Sí, señora. Much better than yesterday."

"¡Bien!"

I bought a couple of fish from him and sent him smiling on his way. My eye caught a dark flurry of activity further along the water's edge. A small group of Felipe's buddies had landed in their small boats and were dividing up the catch, even selling some of their fish right there.

Their arrival had been no secret from the pelicans, who darted and swooped, grabbing off here a small fish, there a big piece cut off by a fisherman and tossed away. I had spent many an hour in the early morning sun, watching them dive like that. Their large beaks snapped easily over a prize. Once they had a mouthful, their ugly grey crops pouched below their beaks and swelled along their necks, as the lumps of fish slid toward their stomachs. Sometimes a stiff chunk went in sideways and seemed to get stuck in their throats. How patiently the birds dealt with it, arching and bobbing their long necks. The sight was fascinating to me. They seemed to be a holdover from some prehistoric age.

I looked again at the scene from a distance; but today the warm water of the Pacific was calling out to me. I left the heady smell of the coconut forest behind. My feet crunched through the thin dry crust of morning sand, and underneath it felt damp and cool, as I made my way to the water. The last few steps became a running dive. In the calm swell of the sea, I glided and rolled, letting the salty water bring to me the full sense of liberation that I had found in my new life.

A breeze carried the sound of the church bell from the village. Six o'clock. I knew what the scene was like in the town. Meat, poultry, and vegetable stalls were opening in the *mercado*, and the vendors were beginning to set up their displays.

Scarred house shutters were banging open on the Malecón and the street behind, one by one. Little children and dogs and chickens were scampering in front of the brooms of countless *abuelas*, the grandmothers, who swept the dirt floors carefully and removed scattered bedding from the couches, mats, and benches for the day. The *señoras* had already been up an hour at least, to put the corn on the stove to boil. By now the smell filled the rooms, waking the rest of the family. In a short time they would pound the grain, grinding it with water and lime into a *masa*, the precious cornmeal from which they lovingly formed their tortillas.

I glanced back over the gentle waves toward my own house. A man on a beautiful horse was riding up, and Lupita appeared at the doorway to receive a jug of foaming milk, fresh from the udder and still warm, from the handsome man with a large *sombrero*. "What could be more ideal?" I thought. "For days I never have to go to town!"

The milkman arrived daily on horseback, my breakfast was delivered by the fishermen. We had coconuts and guavas, even bananas and mangos, picked on our walks through the forests, the last couple of days.

A large wave rolled up and I dove into it, swimming quickly out to sea until I was breathing deeply. Then I slid over on my back and swam leisurely toward home. Lupita would be putting the milk on the stove to boil for pasteurizing, and starting in to get the babies up. She could handle everything.

There was nothing I was needed, for I knew Lupita's love for the boys and the consoling comfort of her ample bosom could solve any problem that came up. But I just wanted to be there when they woke up. And I knew Lupita had put on my *cafe con leche*.

"Good coffee, Lupita," I said when we were all seated at the small table.

She smiled with pride. "*Gracias, señora.*"

Almost the first thing I did after bringing my things over from the hotel in Cloro's truck was to look for a maid to help me with the house and the children. I found two girls, Lupe and Consuela, who stayed with me from then on. Lupe lived in. Her complexion was not good in those years, and her face was rather plain, but my boys adored her.

"Well, boys, what'll we do today?" I asked, knowing the answer already.

"Swim," shouted Bear. "Swim, swim!" He danced around the room poking at the air with a hard roll and crumbling pieces of it on the floor. His brother let out a squeal of anticipation too.

"OK, are you ready? I'll race you to the water!"

Later on, at the water's edge, the boys romped with the maids and I just sat and gloried in the happy sight of it. Kaiser, my German shepherd, had a hard time deciding whether he wanted to stay there with me on the side, or join in the fun.

A large iguana scurried farther up a tall palm tree nearby, its long tail hanging far down behind him. Another prehistoric creature.

The moment I saw this place, my little corner of the tropics, I knew I had to have it. I don't know whether I understood it at the time in this way, but I just wanted to give my boys the freedom I had felt as I was growing up in Indonesia. I wanted them to have space—a life in the outdoors that they could not have had if they had stayed tied to the TV in a closed house up in San Francisco.

I wanted a daily schedule to be something totally unknown to them, at least at their age. I wanted them to feel the luscious sand in their toes, to be able to run as far as they could see and as fast as they wanted to, without danger. I wanted them to feel the sun on their backs, on their legs, and even on their little rumps.

It would have horrified their father, but diapers were the first thing that went. They seemed somehow out of place in paradise. When nature called, they felt the warm urine just slide down their legs without a thought. Even young Buster soon learned to scoop out a small hole at the water's edge to do his business. When he was through he made a half-hearted attempt to cover it, but usually the waves carried the turds away immediately, and he ran laughingly into the water to clean himself up.

Part of this freedom was to be mine too. I had been so closed in between those four walls for four years, ever since I got married. Now I felt a great urge to be outdoors too, to explore my own soul. And where else would I have given them and myself such luxury?

In a few days, my new stall boy Guilberto was to bring a beautiful white pony for Bear, and a horse for me, so that we could ride everywhere, and feel the wind in our hair. Where in America could I have kept horses right outside the door, and had two maids and a stall boy, on my income?

I believe there is a big difference for children between being brought up in an apartment building in a big city and being brought up on the land. Our way of life may have looked primitive to outsiders, but in important ways it was rich.

The boys were now totally absorbed in their games, which they were able to create endlessly in the surf and the sand. I decided to take some time with my garden.

I had already made several improvements around Gene LaPorte's house. The walls were being whitewashed with a dazzling white, and I had found a carpenter to make me some shutters for the windows. While he was there, I had him build a small patio with a roof of palm leaves. Inside hung some short drapes of a nubby local cloth with an Indian pattern—though in our deserted stretch of the beach, we rarely felt the need to close them. *Equipales*, those typically Mexican barrel chairs made from leather and thin strips of wood, I had scattered around the room.

Since we had no electricity, there were several kerosene lanterns in case we wanted to read at night to pass the time. Usually, however, the sun and the day's exercise made me tired enough to go to sleep early.

I grabbed some fertilizer and the bucket and shovel I had brought down from California. All the plastics I had packed! Too much, really. As Cloro and I took some of the things off the truck we were both amazed at what I had thought was necessary. Those American trash cans with tightly sealed little hoods with a swinging door, for example—as if the Mexicans hadn't yet figured out how to confront trash! The Dutchman always comes out, I guess. I wanted everything clean.

On the other hand, many of those things I really did need, and good plastic was not easy to find in Mexico in those years. I had to have something to seal the powdered milk for the babies. I had bought all plastic dishes and lots of plastic glasses, so we wouldn't have to worry about them on the beach. Since the humidity was fierce, especially in the summertime, I knew I would use all the cookie and cracker containers that I packed. And I even used all the trash cans. In fact, many times I came to wish that the Mexicans had some just like them, for publicly they are a very messy people. They think nothing of cluttering up their gorgeous natural landscapes with complete disregard.

I had already started flower beds all around the house, and some lemon and avacado trees. It was astounding how quickly things grew in this fertile soil. I suppose I should have remembered it from my childhood in the tropics, but kids don't think of such things at that age.

Now as the boys and I walked through the forests in the nearby mountains, I found the profusion of flowers and trees incredible. Of course the neat rows of pineapple plants were man-made. But who had planted the lush mangos and papayas so far inland? Were these secret gardens of the Indians of long ago?

I asked Cloro about it one day, relaxing at his tavern next door. His answer was less romantic, but no less amazing. Yes, I had heard birds everywhere in these forests, from the seaside to deep in the mountains. "It's simple," he explained. "Along comes a bird, picks up a seed from here, picks up a seed from over there, and soon the whole mountain is full of wild trees." Their beaks, their droppings always have whole seeds as well as those they have digested. The earth is so fertile, the air is so warm, the rainfall so abundant, especially in this season, that plants spring up in the tropical forest almost overnight. They seem to grow almost as you watch them. Men may clear a path for themselves through the jungle with machetes, but it will also disappear again in a few days.

It happened in my garden, as well as in the jungle. Later, whenever I gave a large cocktail party and served martinis with a twist of lemon, as my Mexican friends liked them, I knew the guests would spit the seeds out in my gardens beside the walkways, and I'll be damned, a couple of months later I would be weeding out little lemon trees from between my flowers! If the kids dropped the pit of a mango, the same thing. Bananas and bamboo traveled underground and then just shot up, a yard or more in a day sometimes.

Now that's almost instant gratification for a gardener! And I was out there puttering around every day, determined to have a real Dutch garden.

We had already started to lose track of time. I didn't realize it was Sunday that day, until I looked around at the people beginning to arrive on my beach as the sun rose higher. Of course, it was not "my" beach, for no beach is private in Mexico. The whole length of the seashore from California to Guatemala, and on the Gulf of Mexico side too, is for all the people. A nice idea, I think.

On Sundays the *rancheros* came as usual, riding tall on their beautiful horses. But they did not come alone to sip a *coco loco* and talk business with Cloro or to laugh with the whores. They led a stately parade through the sand along the beach from town. Their whole family came walking behind, all their little children, their mothers, perhaps their grandmothers, sisters and brothers, mostly barefoot, and seemingly unaware that the walk was a mile and a half each way. And central to the procession, of course, was *la mamá*, the rancher's wife, equally as dignified, carrying a gorgeous basket of food on her head.

On weekdays, at about four o'clock in the afternoon after *siesta*, the *señoras* bathed and dressed themselves and their children and then took the fresh evening air of the Malecón for a few hours, while their husbands finished working. There were few radios and no television to offer entertainment in those days. But Sunday's picnic outing was the highlight of the week, and the whole family was together.

In fact, it was the men who frolicked easily in the water with their small children, while the women sat off to the side, gossiping in the cool shade of the palms. The fathers laughed and played gently and lovingly with all the kids on the beach, including mine. For those special Sunday hours, they entirely forgot their *macho* images.

When the sun was high and everyone was hungry, the mothers opened their baskets and spread out a feast, always centered around hot tortillas and chicken. Then all took their *siesta* as they wished.

Often I noticed the women, full of curiosity, glancing sideways over at me while

I shuffled around with my wheelbarrow, moving the earth around, and planting my flowers. They just shook their heads. "In this cursed heat," their eyes seemed to say. "That woman must be out of her mind. She'll learn *pronto* that she has to sit and rest."

But I couldn't rest. Oh, I stayed out of the sun in the heat of the day, sure. Otherwise, I had to build. I had to fix my place and make it pretty. I was restless.

For hours every day, I sat talking with Cloro under his *palapa* roof, learning all the secrets of the place. This man was a real wheeler-dealer! To look at him sitting relaxed in these casual surroundings, his sweaty old straw hat cocked to one side, one would hardly guess that he had already probably concluded several business deals that day, usually by exchanging only a word on the street, leaning his head out of his truck, or chatting in the private back room of his beachfront *palapa*. That was about as formal as business meetings were in those days. A man's word and a handshake were enough.

Besides his tavern and his construction affairs, I soon learned that he was also the loan shark of the beach, sometimes lending cash at high rates of interest, at other times just giving it away if he thought the need was urgent. Often he knew he would not be repaid for a long time. Or payment came back to him in trade, as corn, pigs, chickens, or a day's labor. I don't know how he kept track of all his varied accounts.

Sometimes with the cash came a gentle lecture.

"Two thousand pesos!" he teased the sad-eyed young woman standing in the sun, surrounded by several little children. "What would a pretty young girl like you do with so much money?"

She whispered in his ear.

"OK. *Está bien*. But this is only an advance. You get that old man of yours to pay me back when he can." He let out an impatient sputter. "You know, you really are lazy bitches. After all these little *niños*, don't you know how to take care of such things before you make love?" He grabbed one of the little boys as he went flying by, and gave him a hug.

"But we were walking way out there along the beach, and the moon—"

"And now poor Pepe has another mouth to feed," he growled.

After she left with her money, I couldn't resist: "I think you made her too sad, Cloro. 'Poor Pepe' was out there too, wasn't he? Why didn't he do something to take care of it?"

"Doña Theresa, you don't understand. That is the job for the woman."

"You're right, I don't understand."

"The woman has the children, so the woman knows what to do."

"Well I know one thing they could do. 'Poor Pepe' could have his balls fixed, if they don't want any more children."

Cloro threw his arms in the air, pretending to be horrified, and went off to mix some drinks for the rowdy crowd in the corner. You can imagine how far I got with him on that subject—though I did bring it up again now and then over the years. To judge from the local gossip, he himself had been quite a *macho* stud when he was young. And a drunk too, according to the stories. But I never ever saw him take a drink now.

Odd for a tavern owner. Or perhaps not really. Sometimes he served me a *coco loco* with the *rancheros*, sometimes he would mix up a special one when we just sat alone and enjoyed the breeze, while the kids played in the surf nearby.

"¡Arriba
abajo
al centro
pa' dentro!"

he used to toast, with coconut milk for himself, straight. "Up, down, in the middle, and into your belly!"

I got a grand education.

He sat on his coconut trunk and saw me watching his boys climb high up in the trees, with huge *machetes*. "They will trim the branches and then lower the fruit down on a rope, if it is ready," he instructed. "When it just drops, the nut splits open and then the milk is lost."

He had already taught me to appreciate the delicious sweet juice of the coconut, even without the addition of liquor. "Drink one of these every day, and you'll never be sick with the worms," he said. "Look around. We all do it." I suppose I had noticed several boys pushing tiny carts up and down the beach, heavily overloaded with coconuts, but I had only half wondered how so many of them could make money at it.

If somehow the worms did succeed in entering our body around the nails of our bare feet, there was the local herb *peperesina*, that we used for treatment. Although there was a *farmacia* in the village, most Mexicans had little use for it, for their knowledge of herbs had been with them far longer than the pharmacy. For a toothache, oil of cloves worked like a charm. And the local lore even taught a bit of elementary chemistry: since the sting of a jellyfish is highly acidic, it can easily be neutralized by applying urine, which is alkaline.

A sure sign of trust came the day Cloro offered to teach me how to split coconuts with a *machete*.

"How do you know so much about raising coconuts?" I asked one day, sliding down from the hard bench onto the warm sand. It seemed that whenever I sat on that rough furniture out of the palm trunks, I found just the place where some woody part or other stuck uncomfortably up my rear end.

"*Señora,* this beach is mine." He gestured proudly. "I planted all these trees." I looked at him in surprise.

Thoughtfully, he took off the tattered old straw hat he always wore and wiped his forehead. "I got the papers in 1948, but the land was given to me already. From the revolution. Each farmer got seven *hectáreas*. What could I do in this sand? I could not plant corn."

"But how did you know what to do?" I asked again.

"We all know about our country's famous coconut plantations. Especially down by Manzanillo," he shrugged. "We just know it." He showed me how he had planted each tree at least twenty feet from the next, to give the roots space to mature. If they grow closer, like the ones in town, they will never bear fruit. Even so, it's seven long years before the first small coconut comes.

They are not just used for food. In the corner was a stack of coconuts. "Those I save for their precious copra," he explained. "The meat gives an oil, that we sell to the factories." He nodded in the direction of the high mountains. "There they make our good soaps."

One day after I returned from the market, I exploded into the little tavern on the beach, bursting with enthusiasm.

"Cloro, I've got it!" I yelled. "You know, what this town needs are some good, plump chickens! Clean, like we have in America. I'm going to start a chicken farm!"

"I don't think that's a good idea," he mumbled, barely looking up from his work.

"What do you mean? You know what they look like, those scrawny things, hanging up over the counters." I have a strong stomach, but it was difficult to push out of my mind the picture of a few filthy yellow chicken carcasses hanging upside down, their eyes staring out at me from their shrunken heads. The proud red crowns were now wilted and dusty, and their grotesque, long nails were still caked with dirt and shit from the chicken yards. Puerto Vallarta needed me!

Surely once I started my business, the local restaurants, especially those catering to tourists, would be proud to advertise that their chickens came from an American-style chicken farm!

"Theresa, it will never work," he said calmly, as if he were trying to explain something to a child. "Don't spend money on it."

"But listen to me," I insisted. "I know you would all love a chicken with more meat on it."

No encouragement.

"You are an old country man, from the coast. You don't know what the *gringos* do in the States. Think of the eggs—"

He shook his head.

"In America we've got white chickens, not brown. With white eggs. They're bigger. I could supply all the restaurants."

"But white chickens are not good for us here. We've always—"

"You mean I can't do it here?" I cut him off almost defiantly. The hard-headed Dutchman was coming out.

"Now, doña Theresa—" I was *doña* again. "You may do it, of course."

His face brightened momentarily. "Perhaps you do need a little something under the table until your papers come through." I couldn't work legally without papers, which could take months, even years. Meanwhile, almost anything could be handled in Mexico with the aid of a bribe to the authorities. A *mordida*, a little "bite." Thus invited to join an enterprise as a sort of "business partner," any official was happy to turn a blind eye, and life went on.

"You'll see. We'll be fabulously successful!"

Cloro threw up his hands and shot me a sly smile, still shaking his head.

I threw myself into my plans wholeheartedly. I made a trip over the mountains to Guadalajara to search for a supplier. I found a man who promised to send along all the chickens I wanted, as soon as I was ready. Meanwhile, I bought every book I could find on the subject. I hired another local boy, Carlos, to help me with the business. I studied every night by the light of my kerosene lamps.

Together with Guilberto, the three of us started building a coop according to my fevered specifications. We laid out the foundations, snaking along through the palm trees next to my house. With Cloro's truck, we hauled the mortar and the posts and the support beams, and we set them in the sand next to the spots where they would stand. Bear and Buster scurried around, trying to help in any way they could.

I quickly became an even rarer species of creature on the local entertainment scene. The *rancheros* made it their business to ride past slowly every day. They watched my ass bobbing up and down, while I washed countless buckets of the salty sand with fresh water, to prepare it for mixing with mortar. They chuckled when several times I nearly got myself or my shoes stuck in concrete. And they nodded a grudging approval as the staples started going in. I can swing a mean hammer.

"*Miren a la gringa*," they said, jabbing each other in amusement. "Look at her!" But the tone was really one of amazement, not cruelty. They knew their women would never be seen doing this kind of manual labor in the sun alongside two young boys. It was their job to stay dainty and feminine, and to keep their skin white, so that they avoided any suspicion of Indian blood in their veins. For, since the time of the *conquistadores*, it was the dark-skinned Indians who did the menial work for the conquerors. Still, the look in these men's eyes was admiring. Perhaps they wished secretly that their own women had a little more ambition.

On Sundays the women themselves came, and shook their heads even more, and sat farther back in the shade of the palm trees.

Soon the posts were in place. We started to staple the chicken wire onto the posts, and my excitement mounted. About halfway around the area, we ran out of staples.

"Well, I guess it's time to go to town and order my chickens anyway," I said to myself. There were no telephones in those days. We had to go in to Puerto Vallarta to use the telegraph or a two-way radio to communicate with the outside world.

I threw a dress on over my swimming suit, put some shorts on the boys, and we piled into Cloro's truck. We always went dressed that way, so that any time the urge struck us, we were ready to jump into the sea. Later on, as the town expanded and the hotels sprouted along the beach between us and the village, we could almost make our way to town from swimming pool to swimming pool.

"Look, boys," I said, pointing to a building on the next street with a little red flag out in front. There was a crowd, for the red flag meant that someone had slaughtered a cow. There was to be beef that day in Puerto Vallarta.

We stopped first at the post office, at the curve of the Malecón, across from the Hotel Oceano.

Part of the morning ritual when we checked our mail was also to decide which of our favorite food carts to stop at. In front of the post office on the left side, a shriveled little man sold delicious pickled pig's skin and pig's feet on crunchy *tostados,* deep-fried tortilla chips. He had been there at the same spot for as long as anyone could remember. On the other side of the bank, there was another little cart with fresh cherry clams and oysters, spiced to perfection.

My *gringo* boys, born in San Francisco, had quickly become *aficionados* too, and it was no easier for them to choose than it was for me.

We went to the telegraph office and ordered a thousand baby chicks. I was thrilled with the anticipation. Then we stopped at the hardware store on the Malecón and picked up enough staples for the rest of the job.

"Hey Terry, how's the chicken business? How about a drink?"

I looked down the street toward the friendly voice. And there was Connie Gutiérrez, hanging out the window of her El Patio Restaurant, as she loved to do, greeting everybody in town as they walked by.

"*Hola*, Connie! Sounds good to me," I yelled. I turned to the boys. "You boys can play on the sidewalk here, but stay where I can see you. Or else you can go down to the water right there in front. OK?" They were easy to please. In fact, they had already found some friends.

Connie and I sank into the cool interior of her place. She was an adventurous lady. A Canadian of Dutch descent (Cloro had gotten it a little mixed up), she had come down from Canada about ten years before. She and her husband had opened the restaurant, but now she was running it alone as a saucy merry widow.

"Do you ever think this place is too small, Connie? How did you happen to stay here?"

"Oh, Terry—my husband was a big game hunter all up and down the coast. A lot of good deer, even mountain cats up in the jungle."

"Mountain cats?"

"Sure. Like little tigers. Those mountains have lots of game. Men came in here by plane from all over. Palamero used to tell me that when the little *rancheros* would see his plane—" She let out a hoot of laughter. "He would circle the field out there two or three times, and they would all run out and cut the grass real fast. And he'd keep circling and circling, and they were cutting the grass and cutting, and then *zup*! he would dive in there and have himself a ball for a couple of days."

"There wasn't even a landing strip?"

"Honey, you know when Tennessee Williams used to come in at night, if they didn't have the coconuts with the kerosene, or if there was a storm, they just pulled some cars and trucks around and turned on the headlights so the plane could land."

She got up to serve some beers to another table, still chuckling. With her open, freckled face and extravagant flowing dresses, I thought she herself could have been a character in one of Tennessee Williams' plays. In fact, an attractive widow who is left with a restaurant, and who likes everybody, especially the men—who knows, she could have been the model for the Ava Gardner character in *Night of the Iguana*? Her droopy eyes showed the toll that drink was beginning to take, though she was a nice drunk. Years later, she quit alcohol altogether, just like Cloro.

"Yeah, Terry. You know, that bridge on the way out to your place was new just this year. That's progress! Before they finished it, all the taxis had to go through the river to get to the airport. If the river was high, we'd put a couple of planks out and the tourists just stepped over on the boards and the big boulders. And if it was too high," she slapped her thigh and belted out another hearty laugh, "you just missed your plane! You had to stay another day."

I got up to check on the kids while Connie served a young couple who just sat down. The boys were totally absorbed in some game with little sticks in the sand.

"You want boondocks? I've got one for you," Connie laughed when she came back to the table. "That sweet *padre* Aldana at the Guadalupe church. You know him?"

I nodded my head yes.

"You know, he's been trying for a couple of years to bring in the tourists and make them a part of it. He started giving some of his services in English. But it was so hard for him." She shook her head. "Poor guy, he was really trying."

She noticed that the young American couple was trying to listen to the story without appearing to be rude. Connie shoved her chair back, and included them. "You have to know that in Spanish, the word for 'potato' is *papa*. But it's also the word for 'pope,'" she explained.

I started giggling. I could see what was coming.

"Well, last year, when Pope John died, the *padre* was doing one of his English Sundays. And in the middle of the mass, somebody handed him a note to read to us. His face got real solemn, and he looked out with tears in his eyes, and he said to us in English, 'Ladies and gentlemen, I have very sad news. We are all in mourning for the loss of our special friend. I must tell you, the potato is dead.'"

Connie was screaming with laughter. Well, we all were.

What a perfect Puerto Vallarta story! A major "jet-set" attraction now as I write this, and not twenty-five years ago it was only a sleepy fishing village, hardly on the map.

I loved chatting with Connie, but my half-finished chicken coop was pulling me away. I was driven!

I collected my kids, and we started along the beach toward the truck, and home to Playa de las Glorias. But not before the boys had stopped to look at nearly every snack, every food stand along the waterfront.

It was always easy for them to talk me into making a supper out of it. At the first little cart was fresh corn on the cob from the market, steaming hot. While we watched, the lady sprinkled on lemon and powdered Chihuahua cheese, sour cream and *chiles*, salt and pepper. Mmmm!

At another cart we smelled the *chorizos*, spicy smoked pork sausages. My American boys grabbed onto those things as if they were hot dogs or hamburgers. Down the line were fresh roasted peanuts too.

I headed for my favorite *tacos de tripa*, with chopped onions, hot sauce, and *cilantro*, a popular Mexican spice, like parsley. There was an American couple standing beside the cart, about to bite into their first one. Usually the *norteamericanos* loved them, until the hot sauce began to take its full effect! Or was it that they finally realized to their horror, after consulting their phrase books, that they had been eating chopped intestines? I vowed to myself that I would not spoil this couple's enjoyment. They were having too much fun.

Another surprise like that was *tortillas de caveza*. Broiled in oil, in a big frying pan over charcoal, and in the open air of the street the aroma it is delicious! Again, a real favorite among Americans until they found out that *caveza* means "head," and that the meat on their innocent-looking tortilla was—yes, from the cheeks and the nose and the lips and the eyes and the brains.

The boys and I didn't want to leave without dessert. They headed for the *camotes*, sweet potatoes in brown sugar, while I stopped for my favorite *flan*, found everywhere in Mexico, even if it is really a French custard. We ate a whole satisfying meal without leaving the Malecón.

By the next morning we were finished with the wire, and before we knew it, the chicks arrived. How I love chickens! And there's nothing better than a good cock fight! Perhaps, I thought, we can branch out later with fighting cocks. But for now, we were in the food business. I had studied everything I could get my hands on. I had even learned how to inject the birds against disease.

Every morning I walked through the coop with my first cup of coffee, talking to my new babies, and making sure Carlos was attending to everything, keeping everything clean. The chicks had already grown quite a bit larger than when they arrived. In ten weeks from delivery, they would be ready for market.

Then one evening in about the fourth week, I was strolling along beside the water, returning from town, when Carlos started running toward me from far down the beach. He was almost in tears.

"*¡Señora, señora!*" He was trying to get his breath. "*¡Dios mío!* We have troubles!"

My mind immediately flashed on my boys. I felt sure they were safe with Lupita and Guilberto, but still, with the sea on one side and the small stream in back, not to mention the road to the airport, there was always a chance of a sudden accident.

"What's happened to them?" I asked in anguish.

Carlos' voice was no less anguished. "It's the chicken fever."

My mind whirred. At least it wasn't the boys. But what could be wrong?

"They're all dead. *Lo siento.* I'm sorry, *señora.*"

"Nonsense. All dead, you say?"

He nodded his head in despair.

"But how could this be your fault? What do you mean, you're sorry?"

We ran toward the coop, and there they were, the corpses of my proud little beauties, strewn everywhere about the pen. For certain, they were dead.

"I know you fed them every day," I moaned. "Didn't you give them enough water? Did some animal get in here?"

"No, *señora.* It's the chicken disease. Maybe I should have said something."

"What?" My temper was rising. "You knew about it?" I surveyed my investment of thousands of dollars, scattered all over the ground, and looked again at the simple peasant boy. "What are you talking about?"

"I could have told you, but I was so sure that with these—"

"Told me what?"

"All the chickens in Puerto Vallarta have been dying. It's the chicken disease."

"And why didn't you say something?"

"Well, *señora,* those chickens were all brown ones."

"And—?"

He shone with a full-toothed smile now, sure of his logic, and relieved of all blame. "Well, I was sure ours wouldn't die. Because you can see—ours are all white!"

With a thud, I sat down on the sand amid a thousand dead birds.

4

My head kept floating up and over to the side of my left shoulder.

"Cloro!" I whispered in a confidential, frantic tone. "Cloro, watch out!"

I blinked my eyes hard, trying to focus in on the danger that was coming toward us fast. "Cloro, now WATCH OUT!"

It was coming closer.

Cloro took my arm. *"Tranquila, Theresa, tranquila.* Don't worry about it. It's OK." He gave my arm a squeeze.

"But Cloro, do you see it?"

"Yeah, Theresa, yeah."

"That wave is coming, Cloro. Let's get the hell out of here!"

It was like a bad dream. You know you've got to run, but your legs don't work. Why didn't anybody else see it?

"Cloro, that wave is reeeally coming, man!"

It was mounting higher and higher. It threatened to swamp the whole pitiful little *palapa* where we were sitting. Why wasn't he worried?

"Don't you see it, Cloro?"

He nodded and squeezed me by the shoulders. The other guys in the place were just sitting there too, staring out to sea.

"WHOOA!!" I arched back and fell off the bench into the sand. Then before I knew it, I was running through the palms behind.

That rollercoaster ride began innocently enough. I was out in my garden one afternoon, playing the hardworking Dutch lady, when I was attracted by loud radio music down at Cloro's tavern.

"Well, a girl's got to have some fun, too," I told myself, and threw down the trowel. "This will keep."

The *mariachi*-style music got louder and more insistent as I made my way through the cool, dark shade of the palms toward the *palapa*. It was the one kind of music you could be sure to find, on the radio or in any village square in Mexico. These people, more than almost any other, love their *fiestas.* And right in the midst of every celebration will be the *mariachi* musicians, singing and playing their guitars and violins and trumpets. Lovers sometimes hired them to help serenade their ladies in the middle of the night. I've heard that the strange word is related in some way to "marriage."

Here on Cloro's beach, it was not a love scene, and certainly not a marriage, but many of the same urges were working. The little whores were laughing and screaming and dancing in the sun. Their faces were all painted like bright advertisements, and their little asses were wiggling and squirming across the sand in short nylon skirts, skin tight. And the boys were squirming even more, watching them. All of them were drinking tequila straight.

Cloro saw me come up, but the *rancheros* hardly noticed. And the girls never missed a beat. As I approached, I took the trouble to walk a big circle around the large dugout canoes that were beached a short distance from the *palapa*. The little "love rooms," as Cloro called them. Because every once in a while, a young man would pick out a particular girl that teased his itch, and start dancing with her. Usually the dance was short. Quickly they tumbled into the bottom of a canoe, where they could finish their ritual in private.

Or as much privacy as a public beach afforded—as my own boys grew older, they got as good an education out here on the beach as they did in school.

"*Hola*, Cloro! Gimme some of that tequila too," I called, pointing to the little glasses toppled over beside some of the men.

"The men are drinking *ricilla*, Theresa. I don't think—"

"Oh, come on, Cloro. You've seen me with a *coco loco* or two. What is that stuff anyhow?"

"Well, perhaps it wouldn't hurt anything." He handed me a small *copita* of the liquor. "But slowly!" he warned.

That afternoon as we talked, I found out about another of Cloro's professions, which I had only guessed at. The man was *the* moonshiner of the whole damn bay! *Ricilla* is a fresh drink made from the native maguey plant, the same "century plant" as they use to make tequila. But there is something about the quick process of distilling it—I wasn't really following the whole explanation—that makes it illegal. So often, when the "love rooms" were not otherwise occupied, Cloro and his boys took them out along the coast to find the secret home brew up in the jungles, and do their trading.

Hearing his stories was like being dropped forty years back into the Chicago of the bootleggers! Cloro's men knew by sight all the boats in the area. Since they had no motors and fished mostly with nets, the neighbors' boats always had to stay close to the shore. It was those that were unfamiliar, and farther out, that everyone kept a sharp lookout for.

They set off down the beach toward Mismaloya and the wild mountains above it, carrying a load of empty gallon bottles. When the coast was clear (literally!), Cloro gave a little sign. Once their contact was made, he and his buddies quickly drove the canoes onto the sand, and his *compañeros* came out of hiding with full bottles of their white lightning.

The Mexicans loved the stuff. Each time he went out, Cloro bought about a hundred bottles or so, and paid cash. Then he slipped quietly back into Puerto Vallarta and made a huge profit, serving it in his tavern. It was risky, though. Sometimes he got caught, and then the *mordida* had to be paid, the "bite" from official Mexico, which ate up his profits. But mostly he was left alone. As Cloro saw it, he was bolstering the economy of the area and avoiding taxes—two things he was proudest of.

"You're quite a businessman, Cloro," I remarked. He smiled broadly at the compliment, exposing teeth yellowed from long years of smoking. "How did you ever get started with something like that?"

"Ay, Theresa! I have seven children. In the early years, what was I to do? They gave me this land, but the big men kept the best for themselves after the revolution." He took a long, slow drag on his cigarette. "The little guys are always just barely hanging on at the bank. All I could do was plant my coconuts and wait for them to grow. Seven long years before the fruit comes!"

The first night we met, he had already told me about selling whiskey to John Huston's crew. Apparently he had been smuggling it into town long before that. After all, there was no highway south of Tepic. If the villagers were to enjoy any "luxury," it had to be brought in by sea. His enterprise soon spread in all directions: transporting sugar across the mountain trails to Mascota by *burro*, bringing lumber down secretly from the forests above Yelapa, trading cigarettes or whatever a passing ship carried that was in demand. He even made money from his truck, since it was one of only four or five in the town. He seemed to know everybody up and down the coast, and high up into the mountains. The connections he had made while mayor of Puerto Vallarta had been invaluable.

As I started on my second little *copita* of the stuff, I gradually discovered that *ricilla* was not only illegal, it was a hallucinatory potion.

"Look at the sea, Cloro, it's red today. Why is it red?" I asked.

"Theresa, the sea is like a woman. She bleeds, the sea bleeds. Look there at the little red *organismos*—" he said, pointing to the plankton. "They make the sea red."

"You Mexicans! You like to compare everything to a woman!"

"It's because we love you women, Theresa. We love all women!" He looked out at the young girls still dancing on the beach. "We like to have many women. But Theresa, they cost so much," he lamented, shaking his head sheepishly and making a little circular sign with his thumb and forefinger.

I had a feeling he wasn't just talking about the price of a whore.

"My wife thinks that you are my lover, Theresa! What do you think of that?"

I knew that had to happen. Already the first night on the Malecón, I could see it coming. The townspeople strolled past and looked at us with more than the usual interest. In Mexico, it is near impossible for a man simply to be friends with a woman, without sex. Or so they think. Perhaps Cloro's earlier reputation had something to do with it too.

"What do you think, Theresa," he panted, with an exaggerated leer in his eyes and his eyebrows arched, "wouldn't you really rather have me as your lover than one of those handsome younger men?"

I lowered my voice to a sexy hush. "I don't know, Cloro. . .I can't tell." I cocked my head provocatively to one side and stared up at him shyly and seductively. "You have to be the one. You have to make the decision."

I never could have refused him straight out. I loved the man dearly, but not that way. We both knew—and even his wife knew, I'm sure—that we would never be lovers. But an innocent little drama in the heat of the afternoon? What could it hurt? And it certainly was pure flirtation. I could never go to bed with a man who has dirty toenails!

Then at about that time, the first big wave rolled in and threatened to wipe out the entire beach. The next thing I knew, I was running through the palms by myself. I wasn't aware of it at the time, but of course my dear Cloro still kept a close eye on me, to be sure I was all right.

It wasn't till I was in bed that night that I suddenly made the connection. "A smuggler—of course! No wonder I feel so close to him. I'm the daughter of a real pro myself!" As I lay there, waiting for sleep to come, my mind turned back to the dark days of my childhood during the war.

It's never any trouble for me to conjure up the picture of my mother being beaten in the concentration camp where we were prisoners, her frail body wracked and all but unconscious, slumped over in a pool of her own blood. In fact, the trouble is to stifle that image when it comes, unbidden, even now.

Two days before, the Japanese officers had come swaggering through each of the cramped barracks where we slept, barking orders: "Need women to sew! Sew fast! Who can sew?" As the armies of occupation were stretching out farther and farther away from the Japanese homeland in those long early months of 1943, they needed their ships to carry armaments and military provisions only. Uniforms, also being used up too fast, were to be provided by their pitiful prisoners. There was a truckload of military green material at the gate.

"You sew?" demanded an officer, making his way through block number nine, the mean cow shed that we shared with women and children from about forty other families. He poked the bayonet of his rifle into the sides of the women as he went. "You sew?"

They looked around at each other cautiously. Apparently what the soldiers wanted was fairly simple: a supply of jungle caps with flaps of material sticking down the back to protect their tender Nipponese necks from the hot tropical sun. "Show me, who can sew?" the man said, raising his own hand to indicate what he wanted from us.

Some of the women got up from their tiny bamboo benches and showed interest. It was evident that some work was going to be required of everybody. At least, they reasoned, if they were sewing, they were better off than the ones who had to go into the mountains every day to cut wood to keep the cooking fires going in the big oil drums. Out there in the jungle, it was hard work, and they were bitten daily by mosquitoes and snakes, and Lord knows what else.

Some of them raised their hands.

One woman pointed to Dido, my mother, and said, "That woman is an excellent seamstress." The others were startled, but said nothing.

The proud commander immediately strode up to her and drew himself up to his full height. At five foot seven, my mother was taller than many of our Japanese guards. That probably made them angry to begin with.

"You sew?" he screamed into her face. "Why not put your hand up like the others?"

She hesitated only slightly, and then made the move that plunged her headlong into the next three years, the next feverish chapter of her life. She spat in the commander's face. "I'll never work for you goddam Jap sonsabitches! I am loyal to my queen."

Perhaps the officer didn't understand all the words, but the tone of voice was clear enough, and the saliva in his face was unmistakable. He exploded with anger.

"Take her!" he barked, screaming some sort of war cry to his sergeant. "Take that daughter of a Dutch whore colonist to the middle of the camp for everybody to see. She will not sew the uniforms."

He hit her hard on the face two or three times with the front and back of his hand. The women in the barracks were so stunned that no one made a move to help her. There was little they could have done anyway. With his heavy boot, he stomped down violently on her bare feet and then shoved her, doubled over in pain, toward the sergeant.

The junior officer grabbed her arms behind her and pushed her out of the barracks, prodding her in her skinny ass with his knee, when she could not walk fast enough to suit him. They came to the open, sandy space in the middle of the camp, where every morning we had *Appel*, or roll call. He threw her onto the ground in the hot sun and ripped open the top of her faded dress.

"Mama! Mama!" we yelled. Helen and I, and our little sister, ran alongside, crying and screaming and trying to hang onto our mother, but the Jap soldiers slapped us and flung us away. Some of the women rushed up and dragged us aside and hid our faces in their skirts.

Out came the knotted cat-o'-nine-tails. The little man lashed at her poor white back, over and over and over, welt rising upon welt, with blood oozing from every wound.

"What does the woman say now?" blustered the commander, certain of his triumph. He had taken up his favorite post, striding back and forth on a raised platform above the parade ground, where he could survey the whole raggedy crowd and not get his boots dirty. He was waving his ceremonial sword.

My mother said nothing.

"Tie her up!" he screamed, his face red with rage. "All women shall see what happens to those that don't sew for our emperor, son of the sun god!"

The soldiers brought a large bamboo pole, about four inches around. They strapped her to it by the wrists and ankles, with the rod fastened snug behind her knees, so that it was impossible to sit or crouch. All she could do was kneel there, with no water and no food, her naked back exposed to the hot sun, ready for the next beating. She knelt like that for two days.

Morning and evening, the whole camp—two thousand women from all the barracks surrounding that parade ground—were called out to witness the next beatings, the torture of Dido, the "Dutch whore" who would not sew for the Japanese. If she lost consciousness, the whip brought her back.

The three of us girls were made to stand in front and see everything. At least my fourth sister, weak and dying of polio in the barracks, was spared the sight. We pleaded with them, we wept to ourselves to see her back, ripped open by the whip and buzzing with flies, a single wound from her shoulder blades to her waist.

The women gathered round and stared out of runny, hollow eyes, their own tropical wounds festering, their heads shaved on account of lice. Some of them hissed or shouted, "Don't be stubborn, Dido. They'll kill you!"

Perhaps it was hatred that kept her going. She knew she was losing the best years of her young life, being boxed in by these Oriental torturers, high in the mountains of Java, not knowing where my father was, or even if he was alive.

The commander gave orders for a scaffold to be built. She was to be beheaded the next day, as an example to the whole camp.

At *Appel* the next morning, the runty little Jap commander strode out to the platform and enthroned himself on a small stool, with his knees spread wide. Between them he held his samurai sword straight up at attention. "Bring her here!" he barked to the junior officers.

My mother was untied, and she simply collapsed onto the ground, a little heap of bones and flesh. The officers prodded a couple women into service, and slowly, feebly, she was helped to the scaffold for the execution.

The commander rose to his feet to give the order. And then something happened which I have never been able to explain for certain. Was it to demoralize the others in the camp? Was it admiration for her courage? Whatever his reason, he suddenly gave orders for her to be released!

"Let this woman be an example," he snarled, his lips curling in a sneer. "She does not have to sew, or do any work for the camp. Take her away."

The women buzzed with excitement, but had no courage to cheer. They carried Dido back to her bamboo bunk, barely alive, but still defiant. The woman who had betrayed her was ostracized. All my mother asked for at that moment was iodine. "Pour it over me," she commanded. "We've got to take care of the wounds."

And thus began my mother's new career as "ace" smuggler, the strength of block number nine.

Around the perimeter of the camp was a broad drainage ditch, which carried off the water from the monsoon rains and the excrement of two thousand sick prisoners—at least those who could still walk to the latrines. At each of the corners of the camp was a tall patrol tower, where soldiers sat at night with searchlights and machine guns. The ditch was flanked, both inside and outside, by barbed wire. And then beyond that was the *kadek*, a high fence of tightly woven bamboo, which shut out the outside world.

Each night my mother went into the shit ditch, sometimes up to her neck and dog-paddling to avoid the searchlights, through both barbed-wire barricades, to the *kadek*. Breathlessly she scratched and repeated the password in an Indonesian dialect, which she knew: "You fool! Where are you, you fool?"

And then she waited in silence.

When the one on the other side was sure it was safe, he scratched and identified himself as the "fool," and they began their bargaining.

Unlike Cloro, Dido did not deal in luxuries. Or rather, the luxuries went in the other direction. Since the Japanese were not particularly interested in keeping their prisoners alive, the food was meager and deliberately oversalted, so that it irritated, rather than helped our diseased condition. Almost all the women in camp were swollen and suffering from dysentery, edema, and beriberi.

But several in our bunkhouse had items of value, and we all shared the secret results of my mother's smuggling. For a special piece of clothing or jewelry, a hand-worked towel or tablecloth, even an odd gold filling, she was able to barter for eggs, sugar, sometimes bananas. It was this food that kept us alive.

All day long the women in the bunkhouse talked in whispers and kept down the noise of their children's play, so that Dido could get her sleep. And most of the night she was in the ditch, and at the *kadek*, avoiding the searchlights. Every precaution was taken. If a piece of jewelry could be divided into pieces for several transactions, it was. If there was any chance that the "fool" on the other side could get hold of a valuable item and run with it, it was tied to a strong string and held close until a bargain was struck.

Every morning shortly before daylight, Dido returned to the barracks with the profits of her trading. She tied her trousers at the ankles like "harem pants," so that if necessary, she could run as fast as possible and keep her hands free.

Whatever she brought back was divided fairly among all the women and children in our building. Much as she might have been tempted to give her own children special treatment, there were never any complaints. All of us shared equally, even if it was only a piece of a hard-boiled egg, or a teaspoonful of sugar. We even ate the shells of the eggs, for the calcium.

One night the "fool" on the other side was aptly named. He hadn't had the sense to boil the eggs.

On her way back, a searchlight came dangerously close, and my mother dropped the precious eggs into her pants and started to run faster. Immediately she felt the slime of the egg whites oozing down the whole length of her legs. Did she perhaps let out a little cry of surprise? At any rate, the Japs somehow became suspicious, and in an instant they were searching everywhere through the camp.

My mother ducked around a corner and skidded into the infirmary, where the doctors, two Dutch homosexuals, had their quarters. Smelling vile as she did, she jumped quickly into bed with one of them, locked his throat in a death grip, and planted on his startled mouth a lingering kiss which I'm sure he never forgot!

Their embrace lasted until the searching noises died down and the danger was past. Then she slipped quietly away as deftly as she had entered.

Another time, as we all stood at attention on the sweltering ground in the middle of the compound for roll call, a small Indonesian man passed by the gate and pointed his finger in our direction.

"There she is," he said. "That's the woman who does the smuggling."

When I think about it even now, I get the same sick shivers down the whole length of my body, with waves of nausea and diarrhea. We froze. And without moving or speaking, all of us watched his finger as it slowly swept along the files of gaunt women. It seemed like forever, but finally the finger passed by my mother's determined face and came to rest on that of a woman two rows down, the mother of seven children.

She was taken screaming, as we all knew she would be, to the "pig's pit," a kind of well about ten feet deep and less than a yard in diameter. It was covered by woven bamboo matting and then with dirt. A prisoner could only stand or squat there in the semi-darkness; it was not wide enough to lie down in or sit comfortably. What torture it must have been to fall exhausted against the sides of the pit, never able to get the weight off her excruciatingly tired legs! Camp food was passed to her in a dirty cup once a day during the week or ten days of her ordeal.

Dido found she was good at her specialized "profession," but it was taking its toll, along with her worry about us girls, especially my little sister with polio. After three years of this life, she barely weighed seventy pounds.

It was probably just as well that there wasn't more to our skinny bodies in those years. We were crowded so cruelly into the barracks that each of us had only 42 centimeters of space on a bamboo bunk for sleeping. That's about the width of the pillow on your bed—the shorter dimension, not the longer one.

Next to us lay Nel from Delden, filled with fluid and sprawling over the bunks on both sides of her. She was dying of dysentery and beriberi. Nel was so puffed up in the last year of her life that she must have weighed 350 pounds. I still have a mental picture of my mother bent over her cot, talking softly to her and bathing her with a rag torn from her dress. The woman's huge tits made an indelible impression on me. My mother would lift up first one, all covered with stretch marks, and then the other, and carefully she dried the tender skin underneath. Wherever she handled the woman, the light pressure from her fingers left deep dents in Nel's skin that would remain for hours afterward.

She was a Jewish lady, but she had been "saved" for this final episode by some bit of Dutch blood in her veins. Otherwise as a Jew, she would have been executed immediately. By the time we knew her, she was no longer able to move from her bed. Even the Japs left her alone. Diarrhea and urine and blood poured out of her, through the bamboo and onto the dirt and the flies below, and we did what we could to cover it up.

There was one well for two thousand women in the camp. We girls took turns standing in line sometimes for three hours in the sun, waiting our time to get a little bucket of water so my mother could bathe Nel from Delden.

Most of the women avoided her. She was an ugly sight, with her flushed face and reddish curls sticking straight out from her head. She complained always that her nerves were raw, that the pain was unbearable, and she cussed out everybody who irritated her. Even the soldiers usually steered clear. But my mother had compassion and was good to her, even though it meant sharing our meager space with a giant "bunkmate."

Smoking was her one pleasure. "Helen," she would say, "run get me a Lucky Strike, won't you?"

And my sister, who was ten years old, became a good thief. Somehow, she always managed to find paper somewhere, and a bit of grass. She rolled a big fat cigarette for the woman and snuck into the kitchen to light it with a piece of charcoal. Then, sucking furiously to keep it alive, she had to run all the way back to the barracks before it was smoked out.

"Ahhh! This is a Lucky!" sighed Nel, and puffed happily for a while. We could almost see her body relax a little under the mounds of flesh, easing her closer toward death. In return for the favor, my sister got Nel's portion of food, which the woman couldn't keep down by then. Helen has been a chain smoker ever since.

Years later we found out another reason for my mother's close attentiveness, and at the same time, the others' fearful shyness of her. Grotesque as she was, Nel was a clever woman! Under her huge body, which the Nips no longer required at roll call, she hid a small radio.

When Dido returned at night from her smuggling, before anyone else was up, she was able to follow the war reports. By 1944, as the Americans were beginning to drive back the enemy, my mother's news was often good.

But good news was not an unmixed blessing for us. Even without the radio, we would always have known when our torturers had lost a battle. For they came through each time and grabbed off women at random to be executed.

Nel from Delden held on until MacArthur landed on New Guinea. Spirits were high in the camp, even though the Japs had just beheaded twelve to fifteen of us in revenge. We knew it was the beginning of the end for us. My mother went through the camp, humming the Dutch national anthem, and it caught on like fire. But Nel's heart gave out and she died.

The radio was carefully buried with her. They hated to have to do it, but it was too risky to keep it in camp without its human cover. Perhaps the women had plans to retrieve it later, but the monsoon rains quickly soaked the grave and ruined the radio forever.

My mother continued through the camp praying to her favorite Saint Theresa, filling the women with hope at the recent news, and at the same time trying to keep them peaceful and quiet so the Japs would not take more reprisals. "Don't get panicky now," she would say. "We're almost there!"

"But the radio—"

"It doesn't matter. MacArthur is coming here next!"

Dido Bruins was good to everyone. I am proud that she is still remembered by people in Holland, who lived through that terrible time with us. I think it was our beloved Santa Theresa that kept us alive, who restored our riches to us after the war.

She and Dido must have had an interesting partnership, because my mother was a tough broad.

She had another special secret that we kids found out about only later. Somehow, although we were hardly able to bring anything along with us to the concentration camp, I managed to have my favorite rag doll with me. Every day as I played the simple games with the other children in the sun and the mud, the doll dragged along behind me, my constant companion. When she got tattered, my mother mended her with great tenderness. Though its expression, even its features, were almost invisible by now, she was my special friend, who never left my sight—nor my mother's.

A couple of years later, on the boat back to Holland, Dido took the doll and gathered us around her. Slowly, ecstatically, she slit open the cloth skin of the doll. She unfolded the stuffing carefully, placing each piece of cotton batting in her lap with her bony fingers. And gradually she revealed the secret of the doll.

Smiling, she placed a fortune of small, but exquisite stones in my father's trembling hand, one by one. There were diamonds, sapphires, emeralds, rubies, from her dowry, and from our earlier days of wealth in Indonesia.

Tears were pouring from my father's eyes. "You're as slick as a Dutch eel," he whispered proudly.

With that treasure, we got a new start for ourselves in war-ravaged Europe.

It was difficult now, in the warmth of the Mexican summer, to realize that we were the same people from that mountain camp in Java, far away and long ago.

The next afternoon in my new Mexican paradise turned dark and stormy. It was hard to shake off the evil thoughts.

"We're going to La Isla tonight," I told Kaiser, grabbing him by his sturdy neck and hugging him close.

It was a night club not far behind my house, recently opened up by an elegant homosexual from Mexico City. Puerto Vallarta was still a small country town, and a lot of people didn't like him because they saw only his perversity. But I thought he was OK, and besides, I needed to have some fun. "Live while you can," my father often told me while we were growing up in Holland. He was always fearful that the Russians would show up any day on our doorstep.

I got out the small dugout canoe made from a single cedar tree, and Kaiser and I made our way through the purple and white water lilies that clogged the small stream behind our house. Sounds of romantic Spanish love songs drifted toward us across the moonlit water, promising both happiness and sadness.

The club was no more than a couple of brick walls and a *palapa* roof which reached up to a beautiful point, but it offered me relief on some lonely nights. I can't say that I really missed Bob Lewis. I had a fair idea what he would be doing that night in San Francisco, and even if I had been there, it probably wouldn't have been with me that he was doing it. But still, I did have a longing for romance. In those early days, I found it in the songs at La Isla.

I had to be careful not to start feeling low or drinking too much, however. A couple of times, paddling back from the shanty, Kaiser and I did a complete rollover into the little river. Then, full of mud and water lilies, we had to paddle and push our tiny craft back home upside down.

I was never afraid for myself or my children on those warm, magical evenings. The Mexicans, my Lupita and Guilberto especially, were so warm, so used to huge families with many brothers and sisters, that I knew my boys were surrounded by love and compassion.

And I was never bothered as I made my way back through the dense palm grove. Well, not by men, anyhow. Sometimes when I met a cow or a bull, roaming free along the beach in search of a delicious young palm leaf, I had to play matador in order to get home. I ran from tree to tree, my heart beating fast, hoping my legs would carry me through the thick sand.

There were not many car owners in the village at that time, but I got to know them all rather intimately as well, since the lot next to mine was the local lovers' lane.

Once again content, I fell onto my cot each night and drifted off to sleep, listening to the sound of the little sand crabs scuttling across my floor to find a midnight snack for themselves.

Sometimes it was my turn to cheer Cloro.

"I have just been to the novena for my grandson," he announced sadly one day when I walked into the tavern. He sat there, barely focusing on a two-day-old newspaper.

"A novena? What do you mean?"

"For us it is nine days of prayers for the dead. He—" His voice trailed off, his eyes were red from exhaustion and mourning.

"I'm sorry, Cloro. I had not heard," I said.

"He was an angel. He is in heaven now with the Holy Virgin."

I did not know this little boy, but I was sure that he and Cloro had a special fondness for each other. All the children loved him, mine included. As they grew older, they were always jumping onto the back of his truck, riding with him on his errands, eating with him at his house in town. Kids hung on him like extra parts of his body.

"I don't know what to do, Theresa," he lamented. "My sons are no good. They all drink too much. They beat up their wives." He grabbed his *machete* and began hacking sturdily on the shell of a coconut. "And my lazy daughters all married lazy bastards," he said, punctuating the words with chips flying everywhere. "They stay home all day. If they're not praying, they're getting fat and fucking and getting more children."

I knew their life was dull. Like everyone else in town, Cloro and his wife Nemecia had always lived in a small house by the Rio Cuale, where they got their water, where she washed their clothes, and where they all bathed. As each child married and moved out of the house, he had built another house nearby for them. He would have given anything to have his kids finish high school. He even could have afforded the university. But they showed no interest. The men's jobs were unimportant and uninteresting. The women cleaned their bare little houses, made their corn tortillas, cooked their little chickens, and had babies. That was their life. That was all there was.

"Well, I have a new plan to make us some money," I said brightly.

"Oh no," he replied immediately, and flinched. But he couldn't keep the flicker of a smile from slipping out of the corner of his mouth. "Are we going to be ranchers again?"

"*¡Cómo no!* Of course! Well, farmers actually."

"Theresa, you don't know anything about farming in Mexico. We don't do it here like they do it in—well, in your country, near Spain."

"That's what I mean. You only have corn and beans here. And sometime a little squash. But look around you. The American tourists want salads, with lettuce and tomatoes. Maybe cucumbers."

"We have that."

"Yes, but you have to fly it in. That's so expensive."

He nodded his head.

"Don't you think the hotels will pay us a good price, especially if the money is still a lot less than they've been paying?" My enthusiasm was boundless. "This one is sure to work," I smiled.

"So you're going to grow tomatoes?"

"Yes. Tomatoes and lettuce and cucumbers. Good American vegetables. I have all this chicken shit already—it makes great fertilizer."

Why I thought I needed to fertilize the jungle, I don't remember. It was a question I guess I hadn't asked myself. But I'm embarrassed to admit that it was even worse than that. "Besides," I continued, bright-eyed, "I know what the Indians did on Cape Cod when they planted their corn."

Cloro looked up, feigning interest.

"They put a fish head into each hole with a kernel of the seed corn. And the vegetables grew bigger and more beautiful."

Cloro screwed his face up into a question mark.

"Well, look at all the sailfish and marlin down by the Rosita! They just throw them back into the sea once they've weighed them and taken the pictures!" I almost shouted. "They're just going to waste! We can have Super-Vegetables!"

Cloro shook his head sadly.

"Well, can I borrow your truck anyway?" I asked, sorry that I could not convince him, but eager to show him and make him admit how clever I was.

Once again Terry Lewis was providing the local entertainment, this time for the lunch crowd at El Patio, on the Malecón opposite the spot where the sportfishing boats came in. There at the water's edge hung the huge fish, the proud prizes of a day or two before, now decaying in the hot sun until someone got around to throwing them back into the sea.

Carlos and I pulled up to the spot every morning and wrestled the carcasses into Cloro's pick-up truck. I got the same friendly conversation, but no more invitations from Connie those days. I don't think she wanted to entertain anyone who smelled like me!

When we had loaded the truck, then I climbed in and drove back over the rough cobblestones of town, to our new vegetable farm. Poor Carlos had to sit behind, so the rotting pieces wouldn't slip out the back. We dug trenches in the sand, a foot and a half deep, and the length of the fish, and buried them, to give them time to decompose further.

I was glad I chose a spot some distance from my house, because about three weeks later, the air above the little mounds was black with insects. We must must have carried back a cargo of unseen maggots along with the dead fish. They had sprouted—or whatever maggots do—in due time, and now the newborn flies were enjoying their first breaths of relatively fresh air.

"Oh well," I told myself, "the birds and the wind will carry them away soon enough. It's the price you have to pay when you make a contribution to the Mexican economy."

Finally I felt we must be ready to plant. The rains were continuing strong, but they wouldn't last forever. In our part of the Pacific, just as suddenly as it starts to pour every afternoon in June, it dries up in November like the high Sonora desert. Of course, that's great for the tourists who want a winter tan, but not so good for a budding vegetable farmer.

We staked out careful long rows in the sand, mixed in our remains of chicken and fish, and gently planted the seeds: tomatoes, lettuce, cucumbers.

In three or four days the little seedlings were already above ground, and we were ecstatic! Again I began to visit my babies each morning with the first cup of coffee. But this time there was not much more for me and Carlos to do than to encourage them to grow. About then, luckily, I got a call which took my mind off it.

'Call,' of course, did not mean telephone call in Puerto Vallarta in 1964. There was no such thing.

A boy came up to my house and said someone was asking for me on one of the radios in town. Filled with curiosity and a little bit of anxiety, I followed him back. It was from San Francisco.

"Halllooooo!" said the voice. "Is it Terry Loooooois?"

"Yeeeeessss! Who is it?"

Then of course, the stupid radio faded out. Sometimes these simple conversations took several hours, going back and forth. And even then I was never entirely sure of what I heard.

It was Gene LaPorte. "I'm comminnggg!"

"Whheennn?"

Interference. Static.

"Can you pick me up?"

"Yes. But whheenn?"

"The sixteeennnth!"

Or was it the fifteenth? Maybe the thirteenth? We lost contact. Shit.

It happened almost every time I talked to the outside world, to Bob, and later to my investors. And usually about the time I was getting the arrival information. I used to go to the airport every day, so I'd be sure not to miss them.

Gene LaPorte was a top executive with Union Carbide, an elegant man just slightly younger than my father. Tall, slim, white-skinned and handsome, he must have fit in beautifully in the Nob Hill section of San Francisco where he lived. The mystery was why he, a man who couldn't even change a tire, wanted a bare little shack without water or electricity, on an uninhabited beach on the Bahía de Banderas. Although he got to be a friend over the years, I never was able to answer that question to my satisfaction.

I wasn't sure how to prepare for him this time. Would he want to stay in his house? What would he think of my improvements? The moment I spotted his kind face and silver hair moving above the other passengers at the customs area, I felt at ease.

With his first visit he established a pattern that continued over several visits. He took a modest room with a little ceiling fan at the Hotel Rosita. Sometimes, he rented a fishing boat and went out onto the bay. But mostly he walked over the beach to us and was content to sit with my kids and me, and watch the sunset and the dolphins playing.

He could have had anything: an air-conditioned suite at the Tropicana, or a luxurious second home in Gringo Gulch, the American colony hugging the hills that rose sharply in the center of town above the Rio Cuale. And he could have had it rather cheaply. Ten thousand meant nothing to this guy. But what he really wanted was to have peace, to get away from everybody. He sat there quietly with us, sometimes with Cloro, not understanding a word of Spanish, and he was happy.

"The house looks wonderful, Terry," he said immediately when he walked in. I had recently added windows and a new door, and gotten a couple of bright things from the market to put on my walls. I wasn't actually paying the fifty-dollar rent to Gene. As we had agreed, I spent the money for improvements, and kept the receipts to show him. I was proud of the job, but I was also a little sad. Did he wish he could stay here now himself?

He never put any pressure on me of that kind. But as he was preparing to leave for California, he surprised me by saying, "You're such a great decorator, Terry. Why don't you build me a new place back behind here? A little guest house for me to use when I come down?"

I was flattered, both because of his praise, and also because he had become so comfortable with my little family and wanted to be with us on his vacations. He had a wife, but it was the kids and me that he wanted to share his special time with. And we were beginning to love him like another grandfather.

"Of course," I agreed. "But you must let Cloro be the one to do the building."

"That's what I meant. You can deal with him in Spanish, can't you?" he smiled, his curious blue eyes twinkling at the corners. And then he was off again to his other life in the corporate world.

The late September days stretched out, and my vegetables did too, at an alarming rate! At first I was proud to see how fertile my little farm was. Then I began to be concerned at the sprawl, and finally, I was just plain horrified.

My plants grew and grew. And grew. And they ripened slowly. And they continued to grow. At last, when I could wait no longer, I called in the buyers I had negotiated with.

They shook their heads in utter disbelief at the grotesque, elephantine sight in front of them. There were vines everywhere. The tomatoes were the size of softballs, soggy and meatless. The cucumbers had grown over a foot in length, but on the inside they were nothing but seeds. Nobody would want them for salads or pickles. The lettuce heads were enormous. Frothy, shapeless masses of green, or tan where the sun had burned them at the edges. Stalks had already started to shoot up where they were going to seed.

Can a garden get too much nourishment, too much water? *¡Claro que sí!* Take my word for it.

I gave everything away to the poor. They barely wanted it.

I was crushed. Perhaps I was not cut out to be a businesswoman after all.

5

I sat sadly in the moonlight, watching the calm breakers tug at the beach. How could I have thought I was a farmer? Why didn't I listen to the real farmer, Cloro?

I had watched him with his coconuts. Each tree had a coconut with a little "apple" hidden inside, and that apple was the seed. Cloro could look at a coconut and feel it, and say, "This one is *el macho*." Then he would put it aside in a special place until the first small leaves peeked shyly out of the shell, and a new tree was being born. He was always right.

He planted the little seedlings about a yard apart, to give them plenty of sunlight, and then when they had grown to about four feet high, he sold them to a nursery, since his own land was covered as much as he wanted by that time.

I was feeling sorry for myself a little bit, but it was much too beautiful to let the mood take hold for long. I watched the night fishermen down the beach, standing patiently waist-deep in the surf. They had set small kerosene fires burning in half coconut shells on the sand, to twinkle in the night air and, they hoped, to attract fish toward the shore. The oily smoke also kept away mosquitoes and *jejenes*, the irritating little gnats of summer.

Some men used home-made nets, which they tossed skillfully over the gentle swell and then pulled back slowly toward themselves with lines about twenty feet in length. Others had a rod and reel, country-Mexican style.

Zzzz-zzz! went the line into the low breakers. And then with slow jerks, they tugged easily so that the sinker skittered across the bottom of the sea, with luck attracting a fast strike from the deep. As they gathered in the line, it was usually wound around the ever-present Tecate beer can, fastened to the base of the rod, its familiar red, black, and silver design scarred deeply from the gouges of many a triple fish hook.

When they had gotten enough for themselves and their families, they often built cooking fires right on the beach and began their supper. Their naked bodies, clothed only in underwear or a loose cloth around their loins, shone gold in the night.

Sometimes they came up smiling to my door. And on those lucky nights, in exchange for some salt and pepper and a squeeze of lime, the boys and I were able to share a late supper with them.

I started thinking about the little house Gene LaPorte wanted, and suddenly, my whole future came to me in a flash. Of course! It was so obvious. Why hadn't I seen it?

Cloro and I had talked a few times about the beauty of this place, and how ripe it was for discovery in a big way. He admitted that he had never believed in the future of Mexico. Official Mexico, that is—the government, where corruption appeared to be an unavoidable way of life. But he had a great deal of faith in the future of his beloved Bahía de Banderas area. After all, he had already contributed his time and energy as mayor some years back. And he believed in the huge profits that would come to Puerto Vallarta from the tourists, once they discovered it. And I did too.

When I was in Spain, I had seen Torremolinos and other fishing villages on the Costa del Sol suddenly mushroom into fabulous international resorts, almost overnight it seemed. Of course, Brigitte Bardot had made an important contribution by bringing the world's attention to Torremolinos. But didn't we have Richard Burton and Elizabeth Taylor bringing publicity to our own village?

Up until now, since there was no highway into the place, Puerto Vallarta had been the secret hideaway of a few select millionaires, who anchored their yachts in the bay for a while on the way down the Pacific Coast, or who flew in from the interior for a few days' hunting in the mountains.

But Cloro and I both felt that the village was about to explode into international fame at any time. We were just down the coast, and within easy reach of the free-spending Hollywood jetsetters. The charm of the place was irresistible. As soon as people heard about it, they would all want to come down. And they were all going to need a place to stay.

There were a few hotels in town already, but not nearly enough to take care of an explosion! And many of the tourists I saw walking up and down the beach in front of my house seemed vaguely dissatisfied with their experience. Of course they stopped to talk and we got acquainted. A blonde with two cute baby boys is a powerful magnet on a Mexican beach.

Mostly they found the Hotel Rosita uncomfortable and the service bad, by their American standards. At the other end of the beach, the Posada Vallarta was much more elegant, but it was way out by the airport, and isolated from the village. Guests from the Rosita walked out past my place, to get away from the squalor of the town. Guests from the Posada walked in toward town past my place, to find some action. The visitors at both hotels seemed bored and at loose ends.

What they needed was a place that was exotic and unusual, but still comfortable, where they could feel entirely at home and want to stay. What they needed was a resort where they would be received personally and entertained by a hostess who cared about them. (I always felt that was my strong point as a tour guide in Spain. I could see what my charges wanted, and deliver it to them.) What these people needed was Terry Lewis, international hostess of the future!

I could hardly wait until Cloro came to work at his tavern the next morning.

"Hey, Cloro!" I yelled.

"Theresita!" he said fondly. "*¿Qué tal?*"

"I have a great idea. You're going to love it!"

"*¡Ay, Theresa!* How come you don't have a husband? A girl like you, so young—and your beautiful blonde hair—"

"Get serious, Cloro. I want to talk business."

Just the slightest flicker of a shadow passed over his brow. An unconscious reflex that expressed something like, "not again!" But what he said out loud was: "Well, in that case, how about a *cerveza*?"

Beer at that hour of the morning? Well, why not? It will come in handy in a moment for a toast to our new venture.

I suppose I have no shame. Anyone with any sense would have been embarrassed to approach this wary man with a third business proposition. But of course if she had sense, she should already have been embarrassed to be seen hauling dead fish in old pick-up trucks, or surrounding herself with chicken wire and chicken shit on a beautiful beach in a Pacific paradise. I guess I must have hit the nail on the head. I had no sense.

But I did have my mother's persistence. And I was determined to do something with myself. I couldn't just sit and watch sunsets. What made me really happy was to have a project I could really jump into with all my energies.

"This is it, Cloro. I've really got it this time!" I exclaimed as he handed me the dark bottle. "This is the perfect property for a big tourist hotel."

I braced myself for a barrage of skepticism. But instead, from the moment I began describing my dream of a tropical paradise, he was with me. We both knew that it was a perfect solution for us, and that we were both perfectly prepared to carry it out beautifully.

He hesitated only briefly. "I don't want to disturb my trees, Theresa," he warned.

"I don't either, Cloro. That's the beauty of it! Wait a moment. I'll be right back."

I ran back to my little house for my Frank Lloyd Wright books. It was odd that in going through every room back in San Francisco, and leaving behind nearly all of my things, I had chosen to bring along those books. I rushed back to the *palapa* with them.

"Look here, Cloro. It's a bungalow that Frank Lloyd Wright wanted to build on a hill in the Arizona desert."

We both bent over the sketch, while I pointed out the special features of the building. It was small and round, almost an Indian design, with a pointed ceiling open at the very top, so that the fresh air was drawn in from outdoors and the hot air rose and escaped through the covered hole in the roof. The name of the architect was not familiar to my new partner, but as a builder he could see the practicality of the design immediately.

"I don't want a big box made of glass and stucco for my hotel. I think we should have individual bungalows, just like this," I exclaimed. I looked up and down the expanse of his property on the water's edge, my enthusiasm about to pop right out of my chest. "We'll scatter them all through here, all along the edge of the sand. They'll be nestled deep in here, below the palm trees, and we won't have to cut down one of them!"

I ran past the dugout canoes and did what must have looked like a strange native dance, as I dragged my bare foot behind me through the sand. "COME ON!" I shouted. I was drawing out a huge circle, right where I thought the first bungalow should be.

Cloro would not deign to run, as he made his way over to see what was going on, but he was clearly moving a good deal faster than he usually did with his curious, open-footed shuffle.

"Here's the door, looking right out on the water," I said, marking off the doorposts with my toe. "OK. You come in here, and there should be a lot of room for the bed, and a chest. But also a little sitting area. Here. We don't need walls inside. Everything should be open. But perhaps a curtain to separate the areas in case—"

I was running back and forth inside my magic circle, and talking, sometimes to Cloro, mostly to myself. He stood back, amused.

"How big do you think this is? About seven meters?" I asked. "Is that big enough?"

I didn't wait for an answer. "—and a kitchenette. Because the Americans like to make a bit of breakfast for themselves sometimes."

I looked up. He was beaming too. "Oh, Cloro, this is it! This is it!" I grabbed him around the shoulders and we did a little jig in the morning sun.

The next step was to find an architect who could do everything I wanted.

Many mornings during the last few months, when I had gone to the village to check for mail at the post office or to conduct my business at the bank, I had afterwards joined the crowd at the Oceano Hotel, where the action was. A Mexican man may have his coffee at home the first thing in the morning, but his real breakfast comes later, with his colleagues. At about ten o'clock, the lawyers, the engineers, the doctors, the architects of Puerto Vallarta are gathered there at the hotel for a hearty meal of fresh fruit, eggs, beans, tortillas, coffee, and fried bananas, and of course their famous hot sauce with freshly ground *chiles.*

I was often the only woman in the room. That is, unless the other woman was one half of a rich American couple, discussing the details of designing and building their new vacation home in Gringo Gulch.

It was at the Oceano that I met my dear friend Doctor Calderón, and the newspaper editor, Rafael de la Cruz. And there also that I met Guillermo Wulff, the main engineer on the *Night of the Iguana* project, whose fights with John Huston are well documented in the director's biography.

A big part of their problem had been the way Mexico was used to doing business. Cloro's arrangements with me, for example, and mine with Gene LaPorte, had been concluded by a simple handshake. Many of Cloro's daily business dealings of all kinds were transacted and settled orally, and still in terms of guesstimates. And all of us from outside had learned, when first stepping onto Mexican soil, that time and deadlines mean nothing.

As was to be expected, the same casual business atmosphere held forth here at the Oceano. It was our living room, in a way.

With the music blaring all around us, mothers with nursing children hanging off their tits and asking us for a dollar, with blind beggars leaning in the open windows from the sidewalk, many a major construction deal was negotiated at those low tables. Millions of dollars were exchanged. Luxury homes were designed on hotel napkins. And I was about to add my deal to the list.

The man I wanted was Luis Alvarez, a white-skinned Mexican with very light hair and an almost European look. He was soft and pleasant, a dreamer and a poet at heart, I think. I had often heard the other men tease him in a friendly way about his singing and playing the guitar at parties. When we talked at the Oceano, it had been about how much we loved and respected the ideas of Frank Lloyd Wright. He had some of the same books I had. He had studied architecture, but not finished his degree.

I had a strange relationship with all these professional men. They were my buddies. I knew that if I was going to be operating with them daily on business terms, that I couldn't also be screwing them, as some of my friends were. And so I kept myself at a slight distance, remaining a person they had to respect.

Not that we didn't have fun! And not that they stopped trying to get me into bed! Their *macho* egos would not have allowed that for a moment. But we had a flirtation only, and a real friendship. Often, they said, the only one they had ever had with a woman.

And when I was in trouble and needed them later, they were all there for me with their support.

We worked hard to build up Puerto Vallarta, and we played hard too. We met here at the Oceano many mornings. Sometimes on the weekends, we partied all afternoon at the El Dorado over at the Playa de los Muertos. Long hours passed, playing the violin and guitar, singing, eating, drinking, reading poetry, and trying to con the Americans into building their million-peso homes, to keep these same architects and engineers and lawyers in business.

In the evenings, there was the town's first discotheque, which had just opened up when the owner of La Margarita restaurant put in a big new sound system. That wild American music! It was an incredible revelation to us, who were on a solid diet of the *mariachi*. How we danced to the new songs! And in the early hours of the morning, we went spinning home, still humming the haunting new tunes like "Yesterday." There was little else to do in Puerto Vallarta besides work and drink and go to the beach and dance.

And screw. When someone's new house construction began to lag, we at the Oceano braced ourselves for the all-too-familiar refrain, sung in the whining nasal tones of a Yankee female:

"Oh honey, I know you've got to go back. But I feel I should stay just a bit longer, and see to the details!"

We didn't have to look over, to know that the eyelashes were working overtime. "You go on ahead up to Dallas. I can take care of things down here, OK?"

All eyes at the Oceano met over eggs and coffee, and brows raised ever so slightly. We all knew that those details she was about to see to were more likely to be found on the architect, than in the fabric shops of Guadalajara.

Cloro and I began checking around and discovered that to build a project like ours on the *ejido*, or public land leased from the government like his palm grove, we needed special permission of the agricultural administration in Mexico City. So off we went.

What a trip! The view of the mountains and then of Guadalajara and Mexico City from the air, and afterwards the luxury of the grand hotels—they were almost too much for Cloro.

And what a pair! Tall, slim, blonde, I loped along in front, with long strides, always in a hurry to cut through the bureaucratic jungles and get to the next office, so that we could return to the coast and start building. Shuffling along behind me, dirty huaraches still on his feet, came my partner, his sharp eyes darting hesitantly in all directions.

"*¡VAMONOS, Cloro!* Come on, man, LET'S GO!" I shouted over my shoulder, above the frenzy of activity and the traffic noises of the Paseo de la Reforma. But he remained standing at the edge of the curb, untutored in the mysteries of traffic signals.

"Theresa, we have to wait a little," he choked, in a tone of voice that was new to me.

I grabbed his hand and hustled us both across the street, almost on a run. I was never ashamed or embarrassed to have him next to me. He had taught me a lot about his world, now it was my turn.

"That's too modern for me, Theresa," he sighed. He let go of my arm reluctantly. He felt relieved, but only temporarily, until the next city problem came up.

I just purely adored him, like a father or a favorite uncle. Everyone stared in the elegant hotel dining rooms when I cut up his meat for him. But I figured he had to learn. Better they stare at that scene for a short time while he learned, than stare forever when he used a tortilla as a fork or a spoon, as everyone on the coast did!

We visited all the offices. We got our permission. We got all the forms signed. We got them notarized. An official at the American embassy recommended a lawyer in Puerto Vallarta who could draw up the papers for the Palacios Corporation, as we intended to call it.

They were relatively painless, those first few hours with official Mexico. How little I realized that they were the first of hundreds, probably thousands of hours with lawyers, notaries, bureaucrats over the next several years!

But I was too engrossed in our exciting project to be the least bit suspicious. We flew back as soon as we were finished, stopping in Guadalajara briefly to order our cement.

The roads into Puerto Vallarta were little more than jungle pathways. How do you ship a heavy load of cement, enough to lay the bricks for maybe eight good-sized bungalows, over those primitive mountains? Cloro knew. He arranged for delivery by truck overland to Tepic, and then to the coast at the small fishing village of San Blas. I paid cash in advance. From San Blas the final leg of the journey was by canoe. The shipment would arrive in a week.

Back home, we got busy with our lawyer, Lic. Palomo, a nice young man, eager to assist the *gringos* of Puerto Vallarta with any legal details, and part them from their cash. *'Licenciado'* was a title he and all the lawyers wore proudly, like *'doctor.'* Cloro was to be the president of our tiny corporation, with a 51% share. And I was right in there with my 49. It was his land, my capital. His knowledge of the construction business, my knowledge of the tourist business. We were a good team.

The lawyer's fee was a shocking $2,000.

But I was ecstatic. I set my friend Luis Alvarez to work, to think about a restaurant with a nice bar, a swimming pool, and a long, elegant entrance driveway of cobblestones, leading up to the office.

The next morning, with a small stake and a piece of string four meters long, we made eight perfect circles in the sand, scattered seemingly at random beneath the palm trees.

We had been warned by the local *maritima* agency that all buildings had to be a certain distance inland from the high water mark. And we knew that the palm trees also needed their space to grow properly. Still, we were able to lay out our bungalows with a diameter of eight meters or twenty-six feet, a modest but comfortable space for our future guests.

Each building had a concrete foundation, to be covered with the beautiful red Mexican tile for easy maintenance. The rest was to be made of bricks, which we contracted for, just above our property in the hills. Since even the roofs were designed as corbeled brick domes, which gave them the appearance of a honeycomb inside, I was excited to see the finished product. The Mexicans are outstanding bricklayers.

But the first load of cement didn't arrive at the end of the first week, or even the second.

"Will everything be three weeks late?" I groaned. "Or worse?"

"No se preocupe, doña Theresa," said Cloro. "Don't worry." (Oh-oh. I was *doña* again. That was not a good sign.) "You just tell me when you want to have this hotel finished, and I will be sure it is ready." His perfect confidence was catching. I relaxed.

The next day ten *campesinos* showed up to assist the bricklayers. If there was one thing we had in abundance, it was sand. But it couldn't be used as it was, loaded with salt. For the mortar to hold, every grain of sand had to be washed in the fresh water stream at the back of the lot.

Once again my ass was bobbing up and down on the beach, as I jumped in and matched the men, bucket for bucket. Once again the *rancheros* sat on their proud horses and enjoyed the entertainment, imported straight from Holland.

As they were watching me, I was keeping an eye on my workers. They had to be watched, said Cloro, or they'd get bored and start slacking off. If the sand was not right, the concrete would crumble and eventually the walls would collapse. I'm proud to say we made those buildings so strong that when the time finally came for tearing them down, those bastards had to dynamite them!

The men continued to be amazed. A Mexican woman would not work like that. The Mexican woman is a lazy cow, basically. In Puerto Vallarta in those days, she went to church every day, washed clothes and gossiped at the river, and generally stayed close to home. Of course, even if she had a desire to get out and work, her husband would not have allowed her to do it. But mostly, she had no such desires anyway.

The longer I lived there, the more convinced I became: it's the Latin women who hold the men back. They refuse to live on the farms, for example. They whine and insist on being close to their families in town. You can see it for yourself, as you fly over the vast countryside of Mexico. There are no farmhouses on the land, as there are in Europe or America. The poor *ranchero* must walk, sometimes three or four hours out and three or four hours back, to get to his seven *hectáreas* of farmland. After that, how much energy is left to work the land?

The women are not industrious as we are. It would never have occurred to the women I saw, most of them, to say, "This afternoon I'm going to sew a dress." Or paint the bedroom. Or work in the garden. Or fix a window. They wouldn't have known where to start. They had no idea what a nail or a hammer is.

The Dutch women at least have gardens, the French women do, the Indonesians and the Chinese do. But the Mexican bitches were proud to be lazy. They used to look at me and shrug. "We are not *machos*," they said. "Why grow your own vegetables when you can go to the store and buy them?" And they dismissed the subject from their minds.

They took showers that lasted sometimes an hour. Some of this was understandable, of course. If they had half a dozen small children or more, the shower was maybe the only place where they could be alone! They spent hours on their hair and make-up, preparing for their evening walk on the Malecón. Their money went for comic books of the latest romances. (I am writing this mostly in the past tense, but the situation is no different today. Their heroes are now the actors and actresses of the television soap operas, which completely absorb them all day long.)

Those in a little better situation had a maid to help them with the housekeeping drudgery. Did that free them up to do something with themselves? Would they work in a hospital, start a Red Cross chapter, care for orphaned children or earthquake victims? No. Those dedicated little housewives spent the afternoons, and late into the evenings, playing canasta. Every day they played. Unless they were shopping for clothes or shoes, thirty pairs and more.

Unfortunately they had no one to serve as a model, no one to show them what an independent woman could be, like Madame Sadat did for the Egyptian women.

For a short time, there was doña Carmen, the flamboyant wife of President López-Portillo. And the Mexican women loved her! Her picture was up on the kitchen wall of every house in every *pueblo* or village. What a gorgeous sight after mousy little Ester Echeverría, who always sounded like she had been sucking on a lemon!

Doña Carmen was like a tiger. Tall, high heels, big dark eyes painted black, with long eyelashes and wild dark hair, she was seen everywhere. A striking figure, always on the move. *La tigra*, they called her. This handsome woman, her large breasts almost bursting out of fashionable low-cut dresses, how she lifted up the spirits of Mexico—the men of course, but the women too! We were all shocked when her lousy husband dumped this wife of thirty years at about the same time he dumped on Mexico, and showed up in Portugal with his young female Minister of Tourism.

Perhaps I felt so strongly about the subject because when I suddenly found myself a new employer, I was always having to compete with these lazy wives for the attention of my workers. They were always bothering their husbands on some pretext or other, always asking for them, interfering in some way because of family matters. The daughter was having a baby, or another one was hurt, or the wife was sick, or somebody else needs him. He was always pulled apart. The women took no responsibility, made no attempt to solve the problems themselves.

I felt sorry for the *rancheros* and the other workers. I know that if I have to, I can work like a man, to help my man when he needs it. And if I don't have to, so much the better. But I feel I can do almost anything a man can do. (Maybe I should make an exception with electrical work—or maybe if I studied it and tried seriously to understand it? Who knows?) Anyhow, I think this is true of most American women. But the Mexican woman? No. She has no interest. She's the one who drags her husband down.

I felt bad sometimes for the children too. Once we got into our construction in a big way, every day about two o'clock, when the sun was high, here came a tiny parade of barefoot boys along the beach. They had been kept out of school, and had walked the two miles or so from town, so they could bring their fathers' lunches. On their heads were several little enamel pots, stacked one on top of each other, to keep the food warm, just as I used to see them in Indonesia. The men began heating up tortillas and beans over small wood fires under the coconut trees, and the odor was tantalizing.

The boys surely didn't feel sorry for themselves, though. And often I had trouble getting my own kids home for lunch, since they much preferred hanging around the pots, eating with the bricklayers and their helpers.

Mexican men have a such kindness and a patience with children. Right away they showed my boys how to scoop up *frijoles*, the refried beans, and a bit of meat with a hot tortilla. From the earliest days, Bear and Buster were known as the beloved *gringuitos de las Glorias*. They adored squatting there on the sand beside the men, just like the sons who had walked from town.

And after the sons left, and the *siesta* began in earnest, Bear and Buster would have gladly followed the men into the canoes with the whores too, if they hadn't been gently shoved aside!

"What does that word *gringo* mean, Cloro?" I asked one day, to break up the monotony of the bucket brigade.

"Well, that's an American. Like you."

"I know that. But it's a funny word. I don't remember it in Spain."

"Oh, sure. I know. It's from the soldiers. Your soldiers." He laughed and rubbed the stubble on his face. "When General—" He stumbled on the name Pershing. "When he came into our country to fight us and try to kill Pancho Villa, that's what we called them. The green coats."

He laughed at his joke through yellowed teeth.

"We used to yell, 'Green Coats, Go Home! *Greencoats*, Go Home!'" Was I getting the straight story here? I guess I'll never know. "That's what we call all *norteamericanos*," he concluded. Then he shrugged and went back to work chuckling.

The site of an American construction project is alive with huge cranes, earth-moving equipment, and a steady convoy of trucks coming in and out. In Puerto Vallarta in 1964, we had only shovels and strong backs. And instead of horsepower, each working architect and engineer had his own *burro* man.

These gentle creatures stood by patiently, nibbling at a bunch of grass from time to time, their long ears at attention, while men piled on what seemed to be impossible loads. Sometimes on half a dozen *burros* at once. In a place where the road was always threatening to turn into a path or shoot up a mountainside, they were the perfect solution for hauling.

For many a Mexican, the curious animals were almost part of the family, especially the cute little babies with their large, soulful eyes. It was the job of the kids to make trips up into the mountains for grass and bring it back down.

Architects who weren't building on a beachfront property like us would get the word to their *burro* man, "Hey, bring me a load of sand!" And off he went to the river. He shoveled the sand into large saddlebags of jute, dripping wet, and by the time they reached the house being built, the sand was already sieved automatically, and dry.

These were good times for the worker who had several *burros* living outside his bedroom window, because in the early Sixties every architect had two or three houses under construction. There was work for his men every day of the year.

Cloro and Luis Alvarez shared the duties of overseeing the work at Las Glorias, and making sure it was done right. Luis was not a pusher, but more of an artist and a dreamer. Many a time I had to give him a ride back into town in the truck when he was stuck out there with us, or even lend him money to pay his workers on another project.

There were no building inspectors or even plumbers who knew what they were doing in those days, so the architect was the supreme boss on any project. In actuality, though, it was Cloro who kept us moving. And I may have been owner and consultant at the "design conferences" in his *palapa*, but on the site next door I was the go-fer.

Out came the string and the stake. "Dig so wide and so deep," we'd say, "and pour the rocks and cement right in here." Then I stayed around to make sure it was done, while Cloro went on to the next task. In no time I got so I could measure sand and wood better than material for a dress. Square meters? No problem.

When the first load of bricks came in, it was an exciting day. Beautiful, hand-made clay bricks, fired to a dark orange-red in the mountain furnaces above us. Five thousand of them made an impressive stack. The go-fer checked them in.

"Cloro, how many bricks did you say we asked for in that first order?"

"Five thousand."

"That's what I thought. There are only 4500 in that pile over there."

He walked over and inspected it thoughtfully. Unfortunately for the brickmakers, the pile had been stacked rather neatly, so the bricks were easy to count.

"You're right," he admitted, shoving back his straw hat and wiping his forehead. "But, *no te preocupes*," he continued, without losing his composure, "don't worry. I'm sure they couldn't get them all on the cart. The rest will be here tomorrow."

And so they were. After Puerto Vallarta knew that I was checking every order, we had no more problems of that sort.

But we did also have to make an adjustment in the way he usually dealt with his carpenters. Once the bricklayers began working, the walls shot up fast. In no time, the first building was at the window level, and we were ready to start putting in the woodwork.

The first thing one bright morning, we were standing back, proudly admiring the shells of our bungalows in their varying stages of completion. It looked as if someone had tossed a bunch of squatty, giant coffee mugs onto the sand.

"What have you heard from don Pedro?" I asked, impatient to get on to the next step.

"Well, doña Theresa, you have to understand that a carpenter in Mexico is an artist. When he wants to work, he works."

I didn't like the sound of that. We had already placed an order for our custom-made doors and windows, with some decorative designs that I thought were truly exquisite. The down payment had been made, and a somewhat abstract due date mentioned.

"*Lo sé*," I fumed. "I know that. You told me he's an artist. That's what we're paying him for, isn't it? His artistry? What's the progress on the windows?"

"Well, *señora*, sometimes he drinks a little."

From "Theresa" to *"doña Theresa"* to *"señora."* The news must really be bad.

Slowly I wormed the story out of him. Cloro's friend the carpenter had spent the whole downpayment in a *cantina*, providing drinks and women for everyone. Now he had no money to buy the wood.

"Es un borracho," Cloro shrugged. "He's a drunk."

"You mean he hasn't even started our window frames?" I was livid.

"Señora, there really is a better way. We can have the most beautiful cedar for the same price."

"What do you mean?"

"If we want to do the carpentry work ourselves."

"This had better be good," I pouted, calming down a little.

Actually, I was relieved that the talk was moving in another direction. Don Pedro was Cloro's friend, promises had been made and broken, we would probably never see the windows or the money again; but somehow all of this was tied up with the famed Mexican *machismo*, and I was glad of a chance to get off the subject and avoid the possibility of an insult or a confrontation.

"Good cedar?" I asked. I knew that pine was less than worthless for building on the beach. Termites got in and wrecked it in a flash. "I want good wood. This place is going to stand for the next two hundred years!"

"The best."

"How do we get cedar like that?"

"Well, there is the Mexican way, and then there is the better way." He was talking politics again, and he was on solid ground.

"If we ask the forestry service for the permissions to cut the trees, it will take four months for the papers. Perhaps three, with a juicy *mordida* to the commissioner."

"Three months!" I groaned.

"¡Paciencia!" he grinned, and continued. "Get ready for a trip up into the mountains. But this time, no children and no maids. It's going to be a difficult trip, by horseback. We're going to Chacala," he announced. "I know the mayor. I am *compadre*, the godfather to his children." His face was filled with excited anticipation as he strode off.

"Put on your man's pants," he called over his shoulder.

And then he disappeared inside his "office," the back room of the *palapa*.

The next morning the dew had not even burned off the small tufts of hardy beach grass when we began the first leg of our journey.

In one of Cloro's larger canoes, fitted out with a ten-horsepower outboard motor and four rowers besides, we headed straight out across the bay toward its southern tip, at Yelapa. In a relatively short time we were there. We rode in on a big wave, and at once the beach was crowded with smiling young men, pulling our canoe up onto the sand.

"Hola, Cloro! *¡Buenos días!"* Special handshakes all around. Cloro was a big shot at this end of the bay too.

There were a few, probably standard, jokes about moonshine and *federales*, and then he turned to me.

"This is doña Theresa," he told them. *"Es holandesa."* Blank looks all around, as he must have expected. "She comes from . . . she is not American. . . . It's by Spain."

"Ah, sí—" All heads bobbed up and down amiably.

"We need horses. We are going up to Chacala."

"Hey, man, anything!" More happy smiles. "You need a guide? OK."

Three scrawny little mountain ponies were led out. What the hell! I slung my long legs over one of them, and we were off, almost straight up the mountainside.

If I had thought before that my beach place was paradise, I was not prepared for this.

We made our way slowly, mostly following alongside a rushing torrent of cold water, which fell headlong out of the mountains toward the sea. In some places, it was almost choked off with huge boulders, bigger even than some of the houses in the villages below us. The waterfalls were spectacular.

There was something of a path through this lush green jungle, although the recent summer rains had almost completely closed it in. Cloro and Nardo, our guide, were constantly at work with their *machetes* to clear our way, chopping off bamboo and cane stalks already grown thick, baby mango and papaya trees, dozens of varieties of small ferns. Innumerable plants, in such prodigality—just the ones they were chopping away would bring a fortune in any American greenhouse!

When the path took us a bit away from the stream, we heard the rich sounds of the jungle: the buzzing and chirping of thousands of insects, the screeching of parrots and parakeets, as they dived through the thick vines and trees high above us. Bright feathers of yellow and gold and several shades of green shouted out their exotic beauty to the intruders on horseback below.

We stopped to have a bite to eat and water our horses at the stream, and I squinted into the jungle, trying to comprehend the savage profusion of it. Nardo showed me a huge "paper tree," the *papillo*, whose bark peels off easily in paper-thin slices. And his finger continued above to where, blending into the branches, a boa constrictor lay napping lazily in the afternoon sun. Taking my cue from the men, I remained calmness itself on the outside, but I must say I did not feel it.

We rode for ten hours, mounting higher and higher. Finally, in a clearing ahead, I spotted our destination, the village of Chacala. The mayor, who didn't seem at all surprised to have visitors, was already rushing out to greet us with a big smile. How do they know these things? Had we been preceded by jungle drums? I hadn't heard any.

Esteban proved to be the mayor of three disgusting little houses of wattle and daub construction, with the usual *palapa* roofs. But he couldn't have been a more gracious host. He and Cloro exchanged generous *abrazos* and kisses. I was next, and he wasn't sure how to deal with me, so he shook my hand with great energy, and started to lead us through the squalor toward his house. I felt his hands rough and sturdy from hard work with the earth.

As we paused to dodge goats and chickens and pigs at the front doorway, Cloro tried to explain me to the mayor.

"This is my friend, the *señora*," he began. *"Esta señora. . .no sé. . .viene de allá. . .de—"* He stumbled over the word 'Indonesia.' I was clearly a problem.

"She, uh . . . she comes from way over the sea—"

"Ah, sí—" began Esteban.

"No, she's not an American. She comes from WAY back, man. That must be a big ocean over there."

Esteban was trying to understand. "And that's where she's from," continued Cloro, feeling he was losing ground. "Oh, forget it—" he declared with finality. "I don't know where the hell she's from."

The conversation ended the way it usually did. We all smiled helplessly.

The population of Chacala was growing. Naked children ran up and tugged on our clothes. The women, who had never been out of the village, never seen a white woman, and certainly not one in pants, stared openly. A few scrawny *burros* tied to a stump at the edge of the clearing were rubbing against the trees and scratching.

One of the women suddenly made a dive for a chicken which would soon be *sopa* for the special company this evening.

We entered the mayor's house and squatted on the dirt floor. Out came the bottle of *ricilla*, saved specially for such occasions. I knew enough by now to treat this drink with respect, and to take it slowly.

Over in the corner of the room, Esteban's heavy wife stood at her *comal*, the flat earthenware griddle over a charcoal fire, preparing the tortillas for our evening meal. The aroma of the cornmeal, blending with the steamy broth from the chicken soup, was heavenly!

Before we knew it, as the sky began shading toward coral and the chickens found their high tree branches to roost for the night, we were settling down for supper. Our hostess bought out her homemade *salsa picante* and refried beans. Several children joined us around this simple Mexican feast, exactly like thousands of others that had been served on that spot for centuries. It was perfect. We were loud in our expression of gratitude.

When we had finished the meal, out came the bottle again. After another small *copita*, I was ready to call it a night.

"Cloro, do you think there's a place where I could lie down for a little nap?" I asked, trying to stifle the visions that were fighting to surface in my brain.

Esteban's wife took me gently by the arm and led me toward the back, to a rough bamboo frame, covered with corn husks. It was probably the place of honor, though I wasn't sure what to think about the corn husks. They looked prickly and rough. But I was in no mood to figure out things like that.

Generally when I entered a room in Mexico, especially one as primitive as this one, I checked around for the usual hiding places of scorpions. They especially liked to build nests in the corners, where the wood pieces join together, or in wood piles. But that night I didn't check anything. And I didn't feel anything— mosquitoes, fleas, nothing. I fell into bed, still dressed in my jodhpurs, and was delighted to find that the corn husks were silky soft on my sore rear end.

Momentarily I disturbed a mother hen and her chicks, who had settled under my bed. But in no time at all, we were all asleep.

6

"Wake up, Theresa! How's your head?" Cloro's laughing face was peering down at me. It was already light outside, and the parrots were screaming their disapproval that I was still asleep.

"*¡Muy bien!* Never felt better," I lied.

Actually my head was all right, but a nice morning shower would certainly have been welcome. However, I reminded myself that these were the best accommodations in town. And the only ones. I vaguely wondered how they all managed to do without plumbing, or even an outhouse. Immediately I was pointed outside, in the direction of some old newspapers. Some of them, I discovered, dated back twenty years. Probably worth a lot of money.

I had as much privacy out there as I needed, since the mists had completely taken over the mountainside and shrouded Chacala in mystery and magic. The aroma of freshly ground coffee, roasted from beans they grew themselves, found its way out to me, and I hurried back to the mayor's little mud hut. As I entered, Esteban handed me a piece of Indian bread, still warm from the griddle, and covered with cinnamon and sugar. What a beautiful beginning to a beautiful day!

The business conference began. Whenever Cloro conducted those artful dealings of his, it was always fascinating to watch, and therefore easier for me to shut up and listen—which was exactly what was required of me, even though I was the one paying. Why had they even bothered to wake me up? When they had settled on the quality, the price, and the delivery date, I was duly informed. I paid a quarter down, which was ten thousand pesos or about $800 in those days, and we were ready to go out and take a look at the merchandise. The men had not been rude or cruel in excluding me from the arrangements. It had simply never occurred to them that I was part of it.

A few of Esteban's young helpers materialized out of the mist, and we started into the jungle. From time to time the tattered patches of fog parted to make way for the bright rays of autumn sunshine, and all the garish jungle birds called out to greet the strange silver light.

When I looked up, I saw that high in the thick, green foliage overhead was a tangle of orchids blooming by the thousands, a riot of fuschia and lavender and bright red forming a canopy over our heads. 'Parasite' is a word that usually has bad connotations. But when the parasites make a forest of orchids, who can object?

We continued into the jungle, the men working with quick and efficient strokes to clear a way with their *machetes*. Every now and then, a deer became startled, froze, and then dashed off into the thick growth. Cloro had warned me that we could also run across a wild boar or a puma, the mountain lion of these parts. I hoped they were all occupied with their own business this morning. We seemed to be making enough noise with our chopping. Would that scare them off or would it attract their curiosity instead?

Every now and then a small stream cut across our path, and I was impressed to see the grey-headed Esteban dart across it, jumping from stone to stone just as easily as the younger men did. When they stopped to confer among themselves, they used a lot of Indian words I did not know. But their discussion must have been about which was the best way to bring us to the place, because soon the undergrowth cleared a bit and we found ourselves in a lush stand of huge red cedar trees, the prize we had come to find.

"OK," said Cloro, "which trees do you want?" He asked it as naturally as if it was just a matter of putting them in our pockets and riding back home with them.

"Which trees—?" I gasped. "Well—I want them all! They're gorgeous!" The air in the forest was heavenly. Later our guests in the hotel would often remark how fresh the rooms always smelled, on account of the beautiful cedar woodwork.

Cloro glanced at me sideways, as if to say, "We're not asking for compliments here. It's time to get to work."

"I don't know how to choose. How big can we take them?" I countered.

The men explained that a diameter of about three feet would be perfect. A log that size would yield a lot of wood planks, but still it would be fairly easy to manage on the way down the mountainside. I began pointing out the trees that took my fancy, and the men marked them one by one with their *machetes*.

And then suddenly, we were shaking hands there, in that wild clearing in the middle of nowhere, a mile high above the sparkling blue waters of the Bahía de Banderas. We could expect delivery in about a month.

I looked at Cloro with an eyebrow arched in question, and he shook his head ever so slightly. "This guy is on the level," his subtle movement seemed to say.

We celebrated the closing of the deal that evening with another meal and more *ricilla*, and the next morning we started back down toward home. Contrary to my expectations, I found going down considerably trickier than going up. I wondered several times how they would be able to manage eight-foot lengths of the cedars I had just bought. But Cloro had done this kind of smuggling before. I just had to trust, and wait and see. I occupied my mind with the kind of machinery I needed to buy for our new carpentry shop. Sure enough, one afternoon about three weeks later, Cloro came over to my place and asked, "Theresa, where's that beautiful American lantern of yours?" I had one of those big, no-nonsense lanterns, with the rubber guard. I was not a hippie camping on the beach, after all. I was a pioneer.

"Well, it's here in the house. Why do you need it?"

"Tonight at midnight, meet me over there on the beach. I got the message at the Rosita this morning. They're coming."

At midnight, there we sat in the sand a short distance down from my house, waiting expectantly in the moonlight. There was a party atmosphere in the clear night. Cloro had brought in several *mozos*, hired hands to help with the work, and the tequila flowed freely amid hushed laughter and jokes while we waited. I hugged the packet with the thirty thousand pesos close to me.

Gradually we became aware of activity far out on the water. Our primitive convoy was approaching. There appeared to be a couple of canoes, with about a dozen huge cedar logs lashed together behind them. Cloro signaled with my lantern. The little tugboats slowly came nearer, the huge shadowy logs in tow. *Put-put-put-put.*

Vaguely in the moonlight, I could make out the figure of the mayor of Chacala, standing up in the first canoe, looking a little like pictures I had seen in America of George Washington crossing the Delaware.

Suddenly he dove into the surf with a dramatic flourish, and swam the final stretch to the beach.

Warm *abrazos* all around, a solemn, but warm handshake for me. We were big buddies by now. Esteban pronounced the gorgeous cedar trunks ready to be floated in on the waves. They had stripped the branches off up in the forest, then rolled the logs to the mountain stream and sent them tumbling down. When one got stuck on a boulder, they jumped in, lifted it over, and then sent them all rushing down again, over and over again until they were at the shore below, next to Yelapa. Now the first installment had arrived at Las Glorias. The next bunch would follow shortly.

Esteban waved his arm to signal the men, and the work began. They separated one giant log from the rest, and waited for the right wave.

I had seen the fishermen do this before, as their ancestors must have waited the same way for ten thousand years. The sea sends its waves in a rhythm, regular and predictable. There are three big swells, followed by six small ones. The men counted, and let the small ones go by, in anticipation of the climax: one, two—up to six, then One, Two, THREE! In they rode toward land, on the crash of the biggest breaker, pushing the log hard in front of them. The men were strong, and the water did most of their work for them. The last wave carried them farthest onto the sand, and because smaller waves followed, the sea hardly pulled them back.

Cloro's *mozos* set to work immediately digging trenches for the logs. Since these were contraband items, they of course couldn't stay on the beach. When they were all were safely ashore, we shook hands all around, and the mountain men slipped away in the moonlight as elusively as they had come.

"If you need more, tell Cloro," was Esteban's parting comment. "I'll get the word. You don't have to make that long trip again."

We waved good-bye to our good friend. Cloro told me that even after buying the shop equipment and putting in the electricity, we had saved thousands of dollars on the wood.

In the next weeks, one by one, as the huge trunks became well seasoned under the sand, our carpenter don Martín started to work on them. He had several young boys around him working as apprentices, sometimes more than a dozen at a time. It was they who slowly lugged all the heavy logs the long distance to his shop, almost three blocks back into the palm trees. There with his big machines, don Martín began to cut *tablas*, the huge rough planks about two inches thick. They were still soaking wet.

Then the *tablas* had to be dried before he could plane them smooth. All day long his little boys made their way back and forth from the shop, rolling the logs in, carrying the planks back out into the sun. They placed them carefully at an angle with rocks behind, so that the air could get to all sides of the wood and hasten the drying. Gradually the whole beach looked like a giant, steaming wooden shutter.

As evening approached, all the *tablas* had to be brought back into the carpentry shop and piled on top of each other, straight and square. On top of the piles, we put twenty-gallon *manteca* drums from the butcher, which we had filled with concrete. We found these lard barrels just the thing, to make highly efficient presses.

Then the next morning early, the boys came to work and began the painful process all over again. They certainly earned their minimum wage.

All this work had to be done in secret of course, because at any time, the inspector from the forestry service might arrive. However, as soon as the man flew into Puerto Vallarta, we all knew it. Cloro was used to dealing with any possibility. The taxicab drivers were his friends, after all—he had probably advanced them the money to buy their cars in the first place. So, a few hurried whispers, a feeling of uneasiness in the air, and quick as a flash, all the boys were on the beach covering up planks.

Since the inspector had to make a stop downtown first to check in at his office, by the time he got back out to Las Glorias, our beautiful beach was again a clear expanse of white. The *tablas* were all buried under a layer of sand.

"¡Hola, amigo!" Cloro was all smiles. "Rough trip? How about a *mezcal* to ease the pain?" They were buddies already. They settled down under the shade of the *palapa*.

"Building? Yes, the rich *gringa* there is making bungalows for a hotel." The inspector looked over suspiciously.

"I don't know where the hell she comes from," Cloro continued and laughed gaily. "How about another *mezcal?*" *Mezcal* is yet another of the little known pleasures offered by the desert maguey plant.

Meanwhile the inspector was drooling over the gyrations of the young professional females wiggling in the sand. And Cloro was making sure he was getting a good view.

With difficulty the man tried to concentrate on me. "You're building a hotel?"

"Sure are," Cloro cut in. "We think Puerto Vallarta is going to be a big tourist center. Don't you?" He grabbed the glass out of his hand. "How about another nice *mezcal?*"

Before long, our inspector was rendered completely harmless. We would be able to work for another few days, because he had to make a trip all down the coast, to check and make sure that nobody was cutting wood from his forests. After that, he came through town again briefly and then headed back to Mexico City. And we were at ease until the next time.

We were never caught. Once the wood started showing up in place, in the doors and windows of our bungalows, Cloro's son had found a friend whose father was a carpenter in Guadalajara, who could sell wood legally. A small piece of paper from him proved that we had bought $12,000 worth of beautiful, lawful cedar.

And beautiful it was. It stood up to all the wear it got, it never cracked.

We got all our professional carving tools from the States. We could do anything in that shop. If you know Puerto Vallarta, you may have seen some of our cedar at the Hotel Playa de Oro, near the airport, because Jack Cawood bought a lot of his woodwork from don Martín, in my carpentry shop. They are solid doors, not veneer, with a beautiful hand-carved design in the middle, just like we had at Las Glorias.

But I'm getting ahead of my story. One sunny morning, right after we had chosen our cedar trees and picked our way carefully back down the mountainside from Chacala, I was out on the beach, squatting in the sand and measuring the foundations for my eighth and last bungalow.

I handed the stake and string to one of Cloro's men who was helping me. "OK, Memo, mark it off," I ordered, and straightened up to take a good stretch.

A well-dressed man was strolling through the palms, investigating pretty thoroughly the floors and walls of each one of the bungalows, in their varying stages of completion. But mostly he was staring at me with great curiosity. He was carrying a fishing pole.

"How's the fishing this morning?" I asked.

"You do speak English!" he said, clearly relieved.

"Of course."

"Well, obviously you're not a Mexican woman, with blonde hair and long legs like that. But you were speaking Spanish to the workers. It seemed so natural."

"Of course," I repeated. "They're my workers." I smoothed my hair a little. It was getting very bleached out from working in the sun and swimming every day.

"Yours?"

"I'm building a hotel. My dream hotel."

He looked around again. "Well, it should be—"

Memo walked over and handed me the string and the stake.

"You do your measuring with that? How?" gasped my American friend. I had to admit it was nothing like the technical instruments of a surveying team, to be sure. In fact, my string wasn't even marked off as a ruler.

"Well, I know already that this string is four meters long—which gives each bungalow a diameter of eight meters," I explained proudly.

"What's that, just under thirty feet?" he calculated. "Don't you use feet and inches here?"

"Twenty-six feet," I said. "No, we use the metric system, same as they do in Europe."

He smiled at me, as if I had a lot to learn. "Are you interested in building?" I asked.

"Young lady, I've helped to expand California. I've built hundreds of houses in the suburbs up there. But I've never seen it done like this."

He looked around. "Is that all you have, that wheelbarrow and some buckets?"

"Oh no. The *burros* will show up later on!" I laughed. I couldn't resist. He looked so concerned for my welfare or my sanity or something. He only smiled weakly at my joke.

"You don't have to have bulldozers and steel beams to put up a building, you know," I continued. "Have you been to those beautiful pyramids over by Mexico City? The Mayan Indians of Mexico built those a couple thousand years ago. They were much more advanced than your American Indians."

I couldn't help myself. This guy was beginning to get on my nerves.

I was grateful for an interruption from Cloro. *"Theresa, por favor,"* he said.

"Sure, Cloro. *¿Qué pasa?* What's the matter?"

"Have you looked at that load of bricks that came in yesterday? About two thousand of them are not good. They were not fired properly and they won't hold up."

"No, I didn't have a chance yet—"

"If you stay here with the men," he continued, "I'm going up the hill and speak to them about it. They will have to come get those bricks and replace them for us."

"By all means, Cloro. I don't want to pay for things we can't use."

Cloro nodded at the sunburned American with the fishing pole, and then turned to walk toward his dusty pickup truck.

"That's my partner," I explained. "He's the one who planted all these palm trees."

He stole a glance at my two boys, running noisily around the patio of my little house back in the corner. One was as blond as I, the other dark as Cloro. "How long have your husband and you—?"

"Wait, man," I said, holding up the palm of my hand. "Partner. Not husband." I smiled. "Haven't you heard? Never marry a Mexican. They're good only for lovers, not husbands."

Again he looked as if he didn't know whether he should laugh or not. For sure I had gotten hold of a nervous type here.

"Let's start over again. Terry Lewis," I offered, extending my hand.

He shook it. "Gene Smith."

"How's fishing?" I repeated, trying to get us off on the right foot this time.

"Well, the brochure said 'great fishing' down here in the Bay of Banderas. So the guys and I brought down our equipment, and we stood in the surf for a couple of days, but nothing. Finally they got bored. And I decided to take a walk."

"You're at the Posada Vallarta?"

He nodded.

"Don't they have some boats there for you to rent? You have to wade way out, up to your shoulders, if you want to fish from the shore. But if you take a boat out into the bay, you can get yourself a marlin or a sailfish."

"Hey, thanks. Nobody told us that at the hotel." He looked down and poked at the sand with an expensive tennis shoe. "What did your partner tell you? I took a little conversational Spanish, but I didn't understand a thing."

I explained to him about the bricks.

"You have your own bricks made?" he asked, startled. I had managed to surprise this guy again. And he had surprised me too. Here was a man who had gotten very rich in the construction business in California, and he didn't know how bricks were made. For all I knew, he thought they grew on trees.

"There certainly is a big difference in the way we build things," he assured me.

"Would you like to see the bricks made?" He was quick to take me up on it. "Maybe I could bring you up there in a couple of days," I offered. "How long are you going to be here?"

"Another week."

I walked him around the property a bit, showing him where we wanted to put the entrance driveway, the office and the restaurant, and eventually the swimming pool.

"This is a great piece of property," he said admiringly. "This would be worth millions in California." I could see from his look that he could smell money. Fine with me. That's exactly what I had in mind for the property myself.

It had never occurred to me to try to find investors for this venture, to ask for money from someone I didn't even know. But here was an opportunity that just walked up to me on the beach and presented itself. Or so I thought. But I needed to go slowly and carefully.

"How much do you think it costs to complete one of these?" he asked, pointing to the earliest bungalow, where the walls were the highest.

Well, there it was. That question was a trap.

"Uh—I couldn't really say," I hesitated. I had heard enough stories from the architects and engineers over breakfast at the Oceano to know that Americans were almost always quarrelsome about building costs. Sometimes the tourists had even tried to get me to take sides against the architects, my friends.

I've mentioned how these misunderstandings arose, like Bill Wulff's trouble with John Huston on the movie set. Americans and Mexicans just didn't operate the same way. Mexicans were giving open-ended estimates, and Americans thought they had iron-bound contracts.

"But you must have some idea how much they cost," pressed Gene Smith.

"I guess you'd have to ask Cloro about that," I said. I was determined not to get into it.

He looked vaguely insulted, as if I had given him a personal snub.

I decided I needed to try to keep the channels of communication open. "Oh, six, seven thousand dollars," I said casually. "Maybe eight."

I could see the wheels of the computer going in his head. "Do you mind if I look around a bit more?" he grinned.

"Help yourself. I have to check on my kids anyhow." I went and got involved in something in the house, I can't remember what. When I came back, he was gone. "Well, it's probably just as well," I shrugged, and went back to work on the foundation.

The next day was payday, a day I hated back in those early years. It was not that I resented giving out money for work well done. I just hated touching the money. It was filthy.

Every Saturday at 2:00, Cloro and I set up a small table on the beach. He sat there with the primitive time sheets and accounts, and I sat next to him with a stack of pesos, which I had covered with a rock so the wind wouldn't take them off. Cloro called out a name, one of his *mozos* approached the table, and I counted out the smelly bills—one by one, otherwise the guys always wanted to try to argue about it. Then each man signed for his amount. If he couldn't write, not even his name, we got his thumb print as a receipt.

When the parade was finished, I ran for the sea water. But that was usually not enough to get rid of the smell. Only alcohol could make me feel really clean. I even put it on a cotton ball and rubbed it under my nose.

Lord knows how long some of those bills had been in circulation! The peso had had the same rate of exchange for decades. Nowadays, when the mint can hardly keep up with inflation, and peso bills of higher and higher denomination are required, there is not the same problem. Most of the money that passes through our hands in Mexico now is relatively new.

In the middle of this show, up walked Gene Smith and his two buddies, fascinated. Probably they thought that pay all over the world was presented in the form of a check in a clean envelope, neatly labeled.

"*¡Hola*, Theresa!" said Gene proudly.

"Hey, you do remember some Spanish! *¡Muy bien!*" I'll do whatever I can to encourage that, I thought. (After all, I'm a Spanish teacher at heart. Not only that. Though I've never used it, I actually have a teaching degree in Spanish.)

"Mind if we look around some more?"

"Sure. Go ahead. I'll be through in a few minutes."

They poked around a bit and then ended up back at the table.

"How about a *coco loco*?" I offered. They exchanged glances. "Actually, a *coco loco* is kind of rough. It might be dangerous for you guys." My lip turned in a sly grin.

"Why, what's in it?"

I gave them a quick overview. "Vacation has finally started!" said the expression on their faces. They looked as if they had just slipped away from their wives for the first time. They trotted eagerly over to the *palapa*, where Cloro had already begun pouring out the liquor.

Their eyes followed each step. Rum. Gin. Vodka. Grenadine. The crazy palm spear, instead of a hibiscus or bougainvillea flower they would have found at the Posada Vallarta."Do you drink these?" Gene asked.

"Sure, every once in a while. But it takes me two hours to finish one," I lied.

Gene's friend Paul let out a guffaw and almost rolled over the back of the palm trunk that served as his bench.

"Careful!" I warned. "Maybe you've had enough already!" Everybody laughed. We were in a warm party mood. Many of the workers had stayed around to drink a *cerveza*, and perhaps have a try at one of the *putas* in the short skirts.

Cloro served up the drinks.

"I've been telling these guys that this is your partner," said Gene. They all looked skeptically at the bright eyes, set far back in his dark skin, almost black from the sun. Amiably, Cloro stretched out a calloused leather hand.

"*Siéntate*," I said to him. "Come sit down and join us."

"No, you go ahead, Theresa. I've got some bookkeeping to do in the office." Since his office was the back room of the tavern, I had a fair idea that the accounts would be finished flat on his back. But I knew that he knew what I was doing with these rich Americans, and I knew he was a bit shy about entering into it. Just as Tiburón the Shark had been shy after he had introduced us that first time on the beach. We had moved again into a different league.

The only ones who underestimated the situation were the Americans. Their looks seemed to say, "Woman, here you've got a big development going, and a great future, and you've got a partner with dirty feet!" But they hadn't seen Cloro in action. I let them think what they liked for the moment. I grabbed a jigger of vodka and washed the smell off my hands.

"Who's your promoter," began Paul.

"What's a promoter?" I asked. I didn't know the word.

They exchanged incredulous glances. "Well, how are you going to work up this whole project?" sputtered Gene, coming to the rescue.

"I don't know, man. I'm just building."

During the next round of *coco locos* and a lot of laughter, I learned that in California, one businessman buys the land, and another one develops it. Somebody else builds the houses or the shops, and still another one sells them. You pay the government for the permits, the water comes in, the electricity lines go up, and six months later, you are all counting your profits.

And they in turn learned that here on my beach, the Playa de Las Glorias, we didn't have electricity yet, but that we would be getting it soon for the new carpentry shop. Since nobody stocked prefabricated doors and windows in Mexico, we had ordered our special cedar from the jungle across the bay, and we were getting ready to make them from our own design. And finally, since the nearest water line stopped at the Hotel Rosita, two miles away, sooner or later we were going to have to dig a trench for it ourselves, by hand. That is, as soon as the one-man water commission of Puerto Vallarta gave us the go-ahead.

When we finished our stories, it was hard to tell what they thought of the business. They looked stunned.

Meanwhile, the whores were in great form, wiggling their little asses and peeling down to brassieres and panties for the Saturday afternoon crowd. I had a feeling the men would be back, if only just to look around again.

Sure enough, the next day they returned, and this time their wives were along. They must have decided that the strange Dutch woman down the beach was more interesting than the swimming pool scene at the Posada Vallarta. They had come to check me out. I invited them all to have a drink on my patio, since even on Sundays, Cloro's tavern was perhaps not the right atmosphere for the ladies. They seemed to be quite nice, but rather conservative, almost school-teacher types.

"I have some beer at the house," I ventured. "It's cold."

Gene's wife Elizabeth spoke right up. "I thought you didn't have any electricity." Apparently they had heard all the stories.

"Well, I brought a gas refrigerator down here from California. You want to see my place?" They did. They almost beat me to my front door. They admired the *equipales*, my leather barrel-shaped chairs, and the Mexican fabric of the curtains.

"So these lamps—" observed Jane, the most stylish of the three, "they're not just for decoration then, are they?"

"Not at all!" I agreed. "If I want to read after dark, they're all I've got." But they were more than just practical, I added, explaining how pretty and cozy they made my rooms at night, when they threw out big moons of light onto the walls and ceiling. I loved to gaze into the deep amethyst flames, shining brightly through the crystal chimneys.

"How are you able to read after working out there in the sun all day?" said Elizabeth, looking exhausted at just the thought of it.

"Well, I guess I am pooped. I usually go to bed early," I smiled. "I have to admit my boys start life around here pretty early in the mornings."

"Aren't you afraid to feed your babies the Mexican food?" they all asked almost at once. They had read in the tourist books that you had to boil everything, even sterilize your fruits and vegetables with Clorox. The prospect of that sounded much worse to me than what came to my mind at that point—my boys tearing into a good juicy *taco de caveza*, dripping fresh from a street vender downtown.

But I resisted describing that scene, and instead I explained how careful we were with the milk.

"A milkman comes on horseback every morning?" They were amazed.

"Yes. But then we have to pasteurize it ourselves. We bring it to a boil and then let it cool. Bring it up again, and then down. Three times." They knew their great grandmothers had done this. But this was 1964. Lupita was busy in the kitchen, starting lunch. *Toooot-t-t-tooo-t*, complained the water pipe, a sure sign that we were almost out of diesel fuel for the pump. It would probably be two days before we had water again. I must have scowled slightly.

"I don't see how you manage with babies down here," said Jane, in a horrified tone of voice, as if she understood about the water. "What about the laundry?"

"Well, you're right, we don't have a washing machine. But your own grandmother didn't have one either," I reminded her gently. "We've got a washboard out back. And when the water pump goes out, then we just go to the creek back there behind the house."

"But what if you want to bathe?"

"The boys love it then! We take the horses and the maids and a big basket of food, and we all go to the river. Make a day of it!" Their faces registered disbelief, almost revulsion. I knew I was shocking them, and I took a kind of secret pleasure in it. At the same time, though, I was not spinning yarns. That was the way we lived.

It's the way I had chosen to live. I had had all the best china and crystal, the handcrafted silver, the finest Irish linens embroidered by the nuns. My paintings, my Oriental carpets in San Francisco, they were better than anything these women had, I was sure. But I didn't care to get into that.

"That's how the Mexican women do it in the town," I continued. "We take everything down to the river in buckets. Then," I added casually, "we can wash the dishes and the kids and the clothes all at once."

The Posada Vallarta and other resort hotels like it are so isolated, that they are almost sealed off from the surrounding countryside. These women were so intrigued by my life, not really disgusted, though it was far from the way they lived in California. Their eyes shone brighter with each new detail about the "real natives."

But they had a problem with that too, of course, since I was so obviously European. They were interested in my speech, which still betrayed a little Oxford English accent from school, and of course a lot of Dutch. I could see them asking themselves, "What is she doing here? She speaks all those languages, she lives in this small house with maids and two small babies—" They couldn't put it together.

When they found out I was born in the Dutch colony of Indonesia, they were brimming over with even more questions.

Lupita and Consuela meanwhile continued to move in and out of the kitchen, making the familiar and homey sounds of preparing a meal. My guests stirred uneasily, as if they thought they might be in the way.

"Would you like to stay for dinner?" I asked. "Lupita can get some more fish just down the beach. It's no trouble."

They were happy to accept. I must have convinced them that even though our life was primitive, it was clean.

"It's too bad I don't have my spices. I could fix you a real Indonesian meal," I said.

"Where is Indonesia, anyway? I think I've heard of it, but—"

I had gotten used to handling that question, though I was never sure how well I did with the answer.

"What do you mean, 'colony'?" they persisted.

"Well, just like America was an English colony once, or Mexico was Spanish," I said. "Except that the Indonesians got their independence only about ten years ago."

"You mean it was something like occupied territory? Like Berlin?"

"*¡Ay!* Yes and no," I hesitated. "See, we had different feelings about it. Because the Dutch who lived there, like me—" This was hard. It was totally a new idea to them. "Most of us were born there. We felt that it was our land too. I still think of going back there some day."

"What's it like?"

"Well, just look around here," I said, sweeping my arms out along the beach and back behind us, up toward the mountains. "This jungle reminds me a lot of my island of Java. I feel so comfortable here! And the people are the same gentle souls. Very soft. Very kind."

I was warming to the subject. I always loved to tell people about my homeland.

"My grandmother. My father's mother. She was a native of Indonesia, almost black. I remember traveling up into the mountains to visit her at her plantation. I have a picture in my head even now," I said, gazing off into the palms. "She was beautiful, a small, dusky woman, my grandmother. I can see her sitting there calmly and peacefully on the veranda in her bamboo rocker. And I remember a dark-skinned houseboy, whose only job was to stir the breezes around her with a beautiful fan of ostrich feathers. And on the other side was a maid, who stood next to her in bare feet, and combed out her long, straight black hair with a tortoise-shell comb."

"A plantation? You mean she owned a plantation?"

"Yes, that was something good that the Dutch did," I said proudly. "My father always told us later, that we should have given the people a better education. But at least we protected their land for them. Even if a native woman married a white man, she still kept the land in her own name."

Just then Bear and Buster came running through the house naked, as if to demonstrate that I do have multi-colored blood flowing through my veins. "You know, the Europeans used to go down to India or Burma or Indonesia, and many of them found women to live with. They're very beautiful, with their dark hair and dark eyes. And the men probably even fell in love, for a while. And some had children. But finally many of them just couldn't stand the tropics, and they went back home. So the law made sure that the Indonesians didn't lose everything."

"That's a good law," said Elizabeth. "I was afraid all those places had apart—" She stumbled. "What do you call it in South Africa?"

"*Apartheid*," I bristled. "Yes, that is a crime. No. It was nothing like that where I grew up."

"But the whites were the masters—"

"Yes, and our servants did live by themselves, in a *kampong*, a little village with a high wall, behind the big house. But they could move in and out wherever they liked."

I laughed at a sudden flash of memory. And we could too. My father was forever coming down there to get my sister and me, just behind the back entrance to our garden, under the big gate. Because we loved the puppet shows. The shadow pictures.

"And we were always trying to join in the native songs and dances. We'd wiggle our little rear ends and move our hands along with everybody else. 'The little white mice,' they used to call us. We loved it when they shared their sweets with us."

"Wasn't it dangerous?"

"Oh, no. But I guess we did stand out! There were only about a thousand white people in that big city of Malang, where I was born. The policemen used to stop all the traffic for us little girls, when we wanted to cross with our bicycles. I suppose we must have gotten a lot of attention!"

"But didn't the white people feel sort of out of place?" asked Amy, who hadn't talked much.

"Yes, it was a lonely life for a lot of Dutch women."

"How could they leave everything they knew, and just go down there?"

"Well, of course a woman, if she had fallen in love with a handsome planter—! And then they all heard about the warm climate and the plantation life, and they had a very romantic idea about it. But after they'd been down there for a while, they got so bored! Eleven months out of the year on the plantation. They hadn't bargained for that."

"Still, it must have been beautiful," said Jane warmly. She was turning out to be a bit more adventurous than the others.

"Beautiful out there in the jungle, yes. But if you're the lonely type anyway—" I tried to think how to explain it. "They only got into town every once in a while, when the company store ran out of supplies. Their husbands had their own work, of course. You know how it is, you have to be there on the land. If you leave for a month, when you come back, it's gone. So the wives just sat there in their plantation houses and thought how beastly hot it was and how bored they were. And they missed the strawberries, and the Dutch potatoes. And they hated the mosquitoes, and the snakes. And the fevers. Some of them were pretty miserable."

"Couldn't they go back home and visit?"

"Sure, but that meant forty-five days on a ship through the Suez. And if they went, sometimes they never came back. Sometimes they met a new man. You know about shipboard romances?"

They all chuckled. The women, at least. Their husbands scowled.

"What about your mother? She was Dutch, wasn't she?" asked Elizabeth.

"Yes, and she loved it in the tropics! She never let any of that get her down. She went down there and never left for seventeen years, until Sukarno kicked us out after the war. To her, Holland was a miserable place—small and foggy."

I smiled, imagining what an independent young flapper my mother must have been. "If she wanted a vacation, she loved to go to Hong Kong or Singapore or Shanghai, to have a ball and to bring back their exquisite silks. She wouldn't have dreamed of sitting on a boat for forty-five days to go back to Europe."

As I talked, I found some shorts and handed them to the maids, so the boys would be dressed at least during luncheon, which was about to begin. I had seen the women's shocked expressions, when the little naked rear ends ran through the room. "Besides, my mother loved my father too much," I continued. "She didn't want to fall in love again."

"But didn't she ever get bored?"

"Nope. She didn't sit still. She learned the language, and she started to work in the pharmacy with my father. And when the depression came, she bought more silks, and she started a designer dress shop in Malang, to help out."

They looked at my basic beach "uniform" and perhaps found that hard to believe. But it was true. "She always loved to joke about that. No matter how bad off the planters were—and the prices of coffee and sugar, and especially rubber, were going up and down all the time! No matter how bad it was, the 'Euro' wives always had to have their latest fashions for the country club!"

I laughed, remembering the way my mother used to joke about it. "She probably could have made a fortune if the war hadn't come along.""Still, the dark people were just servants in their own country, weren't they?"

"Well, many of them, yes. Some were not. But you see, a servant's life was a rich life too. They stayed with us as small children, and up until the day they died. They did live in the *kampong*, but they weren't slaves out there. When they wanted to get married, for instance, it was my father that gave them a big wedding. In the garden of our big house. And when the girl got pregnant, she lived behind the walls there in her own house, and we kept paying her until she was ready to come back and work again."

It was hard for them to comprehend.

"It's like the Indians in Mexico here. They lived together with the Spanish before. They weren't put on reservations, like in America. Even now, they are living on their own land."

I felt like adding, "And unlike your own Indians, the great majority of *them* lived through the Spanish conquest." But I was trying to make friends, not enemies.

The fish frying in the kitchen was beginning to smell better and better. I wasn't sure how we got onto politics, but I was eager to leave it. "Another beer for anyone? Looks like the food is almost ready."

And then out came the beautiful fish, fresh from the clear waters of the bay, and covered with the lightest crispy brown batter.

What a mistake I had made! A whole fish stared mournfully up at them from each plate. Head, tail, fins, everything. Lupita had served up those luscious beauties in just the way we all did in Puerto Vallarta every day. All, I guess, except those who cooked in the resort hotels. I hadn't given it a thought until that moment.

I looked around my table. Dainty, red-polished fingernails tapped around a bit on the beautiful crust. Some glanced from side to side, others picked up their knife and fork, but looked mystified about how to begin.

I inhaled deeply and then quickly took matters into my own hands. I grabbed the fish on the plate next to me and filleted it in a wink, yanking out its backbone by the tail, the head still attached at the other end, and left two shimmering white pieces of meat on the plate. These juicy bits I slid inside a warm tortilla, poured on Consuela's great salsa, rolled it up, and started on the next, handing each one around as I finished.

"American taste buds are so refined," I bawled, while my hands worked at their task. "Perhaps this Mexican food takes some getting used to. Look at that salt, for instance," I said, inadvertently flinging a fish chip into the course grains in the salt dish. "Feel it," I insisted. "It's rough. It's the real salt mine salt."

"Well, it is different from what we're getting at the hotel, that's for sure" admitted Gene. Other heads bobbed around the table. "But it tastes great!" he added.

What was the final score for the afternoon? Another tied game, I suppose.

But I didn't have time to worry much about them.

The next day I received a real jolt when I picked up my mail. Bob Lewis wrote that he missed me and the kids. He was driving down for Christmas.

7

So Bob Lewis chose to enter my life again, if only for a brief time. I'll be damned! I wondered what was behind all of it. How long did he plan to visit?

His letter was short and businesslike. There was no mention of that flame-haired trash, Natalie. She must have moved out on him already—that is, if she had ever even moved in. "Good. Serves him right," I thought. "I guess I'll just have to wonder about the rest of it until he gets here," I shrugged. There was nothing else to be done. I couldn't telephone him. I couldn't even write him and hope to get an answer back before he left San Francisco. International communication was not a big priority item in Mexico.

On the other hand, if I tried to put a nice interpretation on the situation, it was true that Bob had always been proud of his boys. I was the third wife, to be sure, but I was the wife that gave him his children.

Of course, when we got into fights, he liked to moan, "Now I'm saddled with two babies in my old age! A man like me is supposed to be thinking about his retirement. I'll be in a wheelchair when I have to start paying for their college!" That sounded pretty silly coming from a man as fit and athletic as Bob was. And beneath all the big talk, he had a warmth and a tenderness for the babies. He was always good to them. My kids love him to this day.

The letter said he was driving down with the station wagon and a boat. Our twenty-four-foot cruiser. What was on his mind? Whatever it was, the last leg of his journey, since there was no bridge over the block-wide river that formed the boundary between Nayarit and Jalisco, should be interesting.

I went down to the telegraph office and sent him a reply: CABLE ME FROM TEPIC. MEET YOU AT RIO AMECA.

Well, that was still two weeks off. Meanwhile, I had some business to get on with. I had promised my six American friends that I would show them the brick mill.

I had borrowed Cloro's pick-up for the morning. After I sent the telegram, I drove back from town, past Las Glorias and on to the Posada Vallarta, where they were waiting.

I couldn't believe my eyes.

There they were, the men looking as if they were on their way to a match at Wimbledon. The women had on bright shorts, in yellow and white, very short, and little halter tops, still of course with brassieres in those days. Huge straw hats with ribbons, dark glasses, and high-heeled shoes completed the ensemble.

"We're going up into the jungle, girls," I said, biting the inside of my cheek so I wouldn't laugh outloud. Buster and Bear scrambled up the sides of the truck bed to get a good look.

"We know!" they replied. "We're so excited!"

"Haven't you got some tennis shoes and jeans?" I asked. I knew not to expect that anybody would own jodhpurs, like I was wearing.

Crestfallen looks.

"Well, OK. But I'm not taking any responsibility for you girls. On the last part of it, when we have to walk, you'll break your heels. Or else you'll have to go barefoot."

Amy's face puckered up into a scowl. "We don't care if we break a heel." The others were nodding in agreement. "But we can't go barefoot."

"Are you sure you want to go?"

They were undaunted. Somehow they agreed on which two "girls" would ride in the cab of the truck with me; the other woman and the three husbands piled in back with the boys. And we were off.

Our destination was not high in the mountains, but you didn't have to drive far from the sea in those days, before the jungle closed in again.

Huge ropes of orchids hung down from the treetops. Not the teeny Hawaiian kind of orchid, but long, heavy, spectacular blooms. We stopped to admire them. Another time I stopped and explained about the *coquitos*, those palm trees with clusters of very small nuts. We didn't use those for the fruit of the coconuts, but for pressing the coconut oil, to make a rich soap. And later, I suppose, suntan lotion.

We also passed a grove of pineapples, before the road quickly degenerated into something that looked more like a dry creek bed than a highway of the twentieth century. I knew that this was exactly what Bob would be staring at shortly too—for a nineteen-hour drive! This short stretch was a holiday by comparison. When the road gave out, near the "city dump," we started walking. We were all in a gay mood, ducking mosquitoes, watching out for scorpions and snakes, crawling over barbed wire.

One by one, high heels starting snapping off shoes, flying in all directions, the most dramatic time being when a mother armadillo took off after Jane. She must have walked too close to the mother's little armor-plated babies. We were all screaming at that one, first with surprise and fright, then with hysterical laughter.

The trip eventually took us three hours. Even so, when we arrived at the brick mill, the sea, that stretched out in a beautiful vista below us, still seemed near enough to touch.

If they expected to see a factory, they must have been surprised. In front of us was Pablo, Cloro's master brickmaker, who had rented this portion of land for his business. He and his assistants had made up their mixture of clay and sand. They were squatting on the ground, carefully adding to it a little hay, which was expensive, and by hand, they were fashioning each individual brick to the standard four-by-eight size. There were no forms in sight.

As the bricks were finished, the men piled each one neatly onto the square stack in the center, ready to be fired. The earth was workable, but not too wet. In the rainy summer season, Pablo informed us, they made no bricks.

My rich American builders were completely quiet, their mouths hanging open in utter fascination.

When there were about three hundred bricks in the stack, the men stopped.

"Where's the oven?" Gene asked.

"Wait and see," I said, smiling.

The workers began piling up corncobs and small pieces of wood under the rack, and on all sides of the large cube, until we could no longer see the bricks at all. Then with mud, they plastered the whole outside of what was to be their bonfire, leaving an airhole on top of the hollow dome.

When it was set, Pablo reached his arm way in through another airhole at the bottom, and lit the fire. The thing began smoking and steaming like an old furnace, belching out strange and threatening hissing noises.

"*¡Ya está!*" breathed Pablo. "Done!" They all looked as if they were dreaming of tequila.

"What happens now?" said Paul, looking a little bewildered.

"They stay in the fire for two days, at least. After that, they're ready to be used."

"But what happens to the oven? They don't just break it down, do they?"

I nodded my head.

"Well, that's not very efficient."

I introduced Pablo to the men and told him what they had just said. He explained to me, and I relayed it in English, that actually it's cheaper to peel off the dome each time and start over again. Once they had made about ten thousand bricks on a particular plot of land, the earth is gone, exhausted. And they have to move on. So it makes more sense to use an oven that moves with them, than to put money into something permanent.

There would not be anything more to look at for forty-eight hours, so we shook hands amiably all around, and started back down the hillside. The hissing and steaming of the giant beehive faded out slowly as we went.

The ladies were too excited to call it a day. They invited me back to their hotel for cocktails. I had to admit, they'd been a lot gamier than I had expected when I first pulled up to the Posada Vallarta in the pick-up! I accepted.

We barreled back down the mountain, my kids hanging on the sides of the truck, waving to all their friends as we passed by. Soon we were sitting around the beautiful pool at the hotel, our table cluttered with daiquiris and Tom Collinses and something else called "Sundown" Cocktails, although for a Mexican, it was only just toward the end of lunch time.

Once the drinks and some fancy sandwiches had been ordered, and the boys deposited in the pool, the conversation got around to the food in Mexico, as it always did.

"I swear, these people will eat anything!" lamented Elizabeth. "There's no telling what's in some of that stuff they sell on the street."

"You won't get much sympathy from me," I smiled. "I like it."

"Well, maybe you have to get used to it," she sniffed. "I have some friends in California who tell me they like nothing better than snails. What do you call 'em, *escargots*? But I'd never try one."

They all laughed, briefly, until they noticed my silence.

"Don't tell us you like snails too!" said Amy, half hoping to hear a denial.

"You probably don't want to hear this, but it was snails that kept us alive in the concentration camp," I replied calmly.

Consternation.

They thought they had heard everything, and now here was a new chapter in my life, a Japanese prison camp. Questions flew across the table. I filled in a bit of the background quickly, as the drinks came, and then got on with my story about the snails.

"Once the Japs thought my sister Helen was big enough, she had to go into the jungle with the older women to gather wood for the cooking fires. Though she never was more than a skinny little thing. One afternoon during the monsoons, she noticed three or four huge snails, about the size of pears, were attached to her skin like glue. She pulled them off, but instead of throwing them on the ground, she stuffed them in her panties."

It's hard to find a word for the expressions on the faces of these sheltered American women at this point. "She had an idea that my mother could figure out a way to make food out of them," I continued, "and she knew it would be wrong to throw them away."

"But weren't you fed in the camp?"

"Not much."

"But we always heard reports—"

"Oh, sure. All the official reports came out sounding great. Lord Mountbatten told the world that those bastards were following the rules of the Geneva Convention. But I was there." Judging from their cautious reactions, I must have had a mean sneer on my face. "What they were doing was murdering us slowly. In a way that couldn't be detected very easily."

"How do you mean?"

"Well, what they gave us to eat was brown beans. You know, those big lima beans. And they loaded them with salt. Our bread was made from tapioca—"

"But that's—"

"You have tapioca, I know. It's a nice pudding, it's a real treat, with cinnamon and sugar. But this stuff was tough and dry. A kind of a bread, but really more like taffy. We almost pulled out our teeth on it. And they loaded that with salt too." I shuddered at the memories.

"You know how all this salt has got to work in the tropics. We were all desperately thirsty, all day long. And we drank and drank from the dirty water. It got so the kidneys couldn't handle it, for most of the women. The body blows up—belly, feet, ankles, everything. Your veins swell, your heart can't take it, and down you drop, dead."

They sat subdued, some with a hand to their faces, as if to protect, to insulate.

"It was very simple. They didn't have to build execution chambers, and they didn't have to spend any money." I pressed my finger deep into the skin of my arm. "When I used to do this as a child, the hole would stay for hours. It wouldn't bounce back, like it does now. After the war, my father fed all of us careful doses of vitamins, every day, three or four times a day, in small amounts. But I didn't get rid of all that water for good until 1947, when we were in Holland."

"But what about the snails?" asked Jane.

I looked around. Luckily the service in the Posada Vallarta operated according to "Mexican time." There would be plenty of time to tell the story and move on to more pleasant subjects before the sandwiches came. So I plunged ahead.

"Well, she brought the snails back to camp. My mother knew a little bit about nutrition and herbs, and she was really excited. She saw they'd stuck like bloodsuckers on Helen's skin. So she pulled them off, and scooped the slimy things out of their shells. They were really big and dark, like African slugs."

What made these women want to listen to this? I guess it's the same reason we love to go to the movies we know will scare us to death.

"Secretly in the camp," I went on, "she started to wash them off. They had all that green stuff from what they had been eating in the forest, their intestines and their food bag. My mother cut all that off, and kept washing. She washed and washed—you know, she'd never fixed anything like that, so she didn't know. The more she washed, the smaller they got. And when she was finished, the water was all white and blubbery."

The ladies ordered another round of drinks, but this time it was whiskey they asked for.

"You OK?" I asked. They nodded yes.

"Well, she threw out the water, and the next thing she did was try to find some hot coals, so she could cook them a bit, like we did the grasshoppers when we caught them."

"Grasshoppers! Oh, God!" Now the husbands had squeamish looks too.

"Yes. We used to sit in the mud and wait for them for hours, when we were little girls. Grasshoppers and those beautiful black crickets too. We would put them on a string of bamboo, and make a kind of a barbecue. I can still hear the little pop the skin made! We liked the taste of them, as a kind of snack."

Although I knew it made a good story, I can't say that these camp memories were altogether pleasant for me either. I squirmed a bit in my chair. "My mother finally handed us these cooked snails, and they were really tough. We chewed and chewed on those sonsabitches, and never seemed to get anywhere."

I laughed. "But you know, she finally realized that it was the slimy water that was the valuable part. So the next time, she didn't wash them quite so much. And then she cut them up into little bitty pieces to make them easier to chew."

I gulped a bit of my own rum and Coke. "But the part we hated was at the end when she made us drink the water. It was blubbery, like egg whites. She held our noses and we opened our mouths. And we gagged, but down it went. Saved our lives, those snail cocktails!"

"Oof! You mean, you kept doing it?"

"My mother told Helen to bring back any snails she could find, and not tell anybody. We had them as often as we could. The smuggling was getting less and less. And those snails were full of the protein that we needed." I sighed. "Even with that, Helen got hepatitis and I got beriberi."

I stood up. "I think there's just time for a swim before we eat," I said, pulling up my dress. The ladies looked as if they were about to make a dive to try to stop me, when they saw that I had a swimming suit on underneath, as I always did. I strode toward the pool, where Bear and Buster were splashing away like jolly little dolphins.

I needed to wash away the memories. Thank God the childhood of my boys was this one, instead of mine!

When I got back to the table, the six of them were picking at their sandwiches, looking a little grey, but I was determined to get the party back on track.

"Why don't we all meet in town tomorrow?" I asked. "You girls said something about doing some shopping? I can bring you to Nelly Wulff's. It's the most fantastic shop for dresses."

The sunny afternoon and the luxurious tropical garden of the hotel were just too beautiful for the pall to last. Recovery was quick.

"Can we go to breakfast at the Oceano? I think Elizabeth and I would like to talk to your architect," suggested Gene.

"So you do like it down here?"

"We love it. We're thinking we might want to build a little vacation house."

"Well, Luis Alvarez is your man," I said, pleased.

"Can you show us some houses that he's built?"

"Sure. You'll fall in love with them. Just be careful that you understand how the architects operate down here."

I explained how they will never get an answer on exactly how much anything costs, especially a square foot estimate. And I described the scene at the Oceano: the American couple sits there talking, mostly to each other, and the architect doodles on a napkin beside them. He doesn't even seem to be listening. "'A bathroom here, a nice staircase to go up to the second level,' he's saying, scribbling on his scrap of paper, 'and of course, you're going to have all the beautiful Mexican tile?' But you know, somehow it all comes out, if you find an architect you can trust," I assured them.

"Well, I know we'd like to see this Alvarez," said Gene.

"There's no way to call him and make an appointment," I said. "But don't worry. If we show up at the Oceano about ten, we'll find him."

I gathered my kids and tried to clean up the mess of papers and things that they had left. We passed by the table on the way out. "No high heels on those cobblestones!" I warned playfully. And we left the Americans eagerly at work designing a dream house in their heads.

Next morning, we had a good first session with Luis. And that was all they were interested in, for the moment. They were anxious to look for clothes too, and souvenirs and trinkets to bring back home. We made our way toward the central marketplace.

I pointed out the best restaurant in town for "Mexican food" at that time, which was run, oddly enough, by the Romanoff sisters. "That food is delicious," I said. "But you'd better not eat there. You could get sick if you're not used to it."

I didn't have to work hard at all to convince them. To one side was the meat market, with big, bloody carcasses of unidentifiable animals hanging down mostly in a dark cloud of flies. Further down were the ever-present chickens, their startled eyes staring out into ours. And on the other side were the fish, strung up on a tough string of grass, dripping blood. There was no ice in sight. We moved along rather quickly toward the river.

The Rio Cuale, which runs through the center of Puerto Vallarta, was a fascinating sight for the ladies especially. The women of the town were gathered there, washing and gossiping, just as I had described a few days earlier. Some had individual little *palapas* over their heads, and all were hunched over big stones, slapping and scrubbing furiously. Every once in a while, they would straighten up and rub their backs, or laugh and buzz again with the latest juicy story from the neighborhood above their heads. When it was an especially good joke, we could hear their laughter all the way up to where we were standing on the bridge. It was an open-air social club going on down there, and anyone could join.

Some of the women had already finished their wash and were spreading out the little shirts and shorts to dry on the grass or on a rock. Others farther upriver had tumbled into the water themselves and were bathing modestly in their brassieres and panties. They were lathering with large slabs of soap.

"Look at *them*!" said Amy, shocked. Yes, it was hard to picture Amy out there among them.

"The men are doing the same," I said, "but they're farther up, under the waterfalls, because usually they don't wear anything when they bathe. Or just a scrap of underwear. It's part of their recreation, sure. But remember, most of these people don't have running water in their houses."

A man with a little cart was coming toward us on the bridge. He was selling a sorbet on a stick, something like an American popsicle. The women looked at the cart longingly.

"Why don't we get a fruit drink over there instead?" I suggested, pointing across the street. "These things look good, but you can never be sure that his water is clean enough for a tourist stomach. They're all supposed to use a filter, but how do we know if this guy remembered to get one in Guadalajara the last time he was there?" It was hard to get them accustomed to thinking in Mexican terms.

"He wouldn't know how to write a letter to order one, so it could be months before he changes it," I explained. "But in the meantime, a thousand-peso note to the health inspector, and—no problem!"

We strolled over to a juice bar with some tables outside. The locals were not yet bored with tourists in those days, and soon there was a crowd of young boys around us.

Elizabeth looked at them, uncomfortable at first. But in a moment her eyes filled with tenderness. "Why don't they have shoes on?" she asked.

"Well, if a boy's got ten brothers and sisters, and his father makes only a couple of dollars a day, it's impossible for everybody to have shoes. That's the way it is down here."

"Look at their bellies. They're swollen."

"Probably worms," I said, lifting up a raggedy shirt on one of the boys who was crouching too close. "I always advise everybody I see, never to walk downtown with bare feet. The worms are on the sidewalks, in the pig shit, everywhere. They come into your body through your toenails. You've got to wear sandals."

The women were starting to get that same look on their faces as they had yesterday at the poolside.

"It's true in every tropical country," I added, trying to lighten up. "You just have to be careful, and then everything is all right."

It was a funny scene. The women were eyeing the boys, a stream of sympathy pouring out toward them in every look. The boys, meanwhile, were trying to appear as *macho* as possible, strutting by, practicing a worldly leer as they glanced at the long legs of these middle-aged women, and whispering lewdly among themselves about their red-polished toenails. Or as lewd as they knew how to be at the age of seven or eight. What a riot!

"Isn't there a Salvation Army down here?"

"Nope, not even anything like welfare."

"Well, Gene and I are coming back down in February. I'm going to bring some clothes for these kids. I can get a whole bunch of blue jeans and little shoes."

What a wonderful sentiment! I must say that I have always found Americans, especially the women, to be the most generous, the most giving people in the world. I find myself running across truly warm natures like these all the time. "They will really appreciate it," I assured her. "You know, the best thing you can do is to go to the Salvation Army up there and get a big bag full of second-hand clothing. Don't buy one new pair of jeans, if you can get ten for the same price. They won't care a damn down here."

They were struck by my suggestion and agreed to start putting together some clothes as soon as they returned.

The Smiths invited me to be their guest for dinner at the Posada Vallarta that evening. The pitiful glances of these six were beginning to slide over onto me too. "This poor woman. And that little hut she lives in! It looks as if she could use a nice meal too," their expressions seemed to say.

If there was anything I didn't want or need, it was their pity. But I glanced at the clock, decided I still had time to get to the bank and pick up some of my diamonds, and I accepted.

Tonight, I was determined to give them a real show. There was at least one more side to Terry Lewis that they hadn't seen yet. And if I wanted to make them confident enough in me to invest in the hotel, now was the time to reveal it!

I stood in front of my open safety deposit box, and the memories came crowding back. My beautiful stones, each vying with the others in an effort to outshine all the rest, were just about all I had left from my parents, those and some few furnishings that I had left behind in San Francisco.

To my mother and father, it was bad enough that I had married an American instead of a wealthy European in the correct social class. But when I left him, and came to live with my babies on the beach in Mexico, that did it! Hippies were not accepted, nor even mentioned in fact, at the jockey club in Rotterdam.

I had written three glowing letters to my parents by this time, describing my new-found joy, telling them how complete I felt in the mysterious silences of the tropical beach, how fulfilled I was becoming, building my hotel alongside my humble Mexican workers. I even tried to explain how much I thought the place would remind them of their beloved Indonesia, if they would visit. But I had received no reply from them.

I sighed and put those thoughts away. Perhaps they would come around someday. Meanwhile, I had work to do.

I thought of what I was going to wear that evening. I had an elegant silk dress of forest green, with a tiny white-on-ivory print. It had bare shoulders and a luxuriously full skirt. I took the emeralds.

That set was one of my favorites. Designed at Cartier, the emeralds in the ring and the necklace were the size of almonds, but rectangular, of course. There were smaller stones in the matching earrings. And all were done in a kind of butterfly pattern, with lots of diamonds to set off the deep brilliant green of the jewels.

Next, I went to the beauty parlor, to get a few waves and a manicure, something I rarely liked to take time for. And when I got home, I had a long, slow bath. I enjoyed it, though I thanked my stars that this was not my usual life. When my mother tried to interest me in the Dutch version of it, I was quickly bored.

Finally, at eight o'clock, I was dressed "to kill." There was no full-length mirror in my little house, so I had to use the expressions on the faces of my Lupita and Consuela, my precious Bear and Buster, my Carlos and Guilberto as a reflection, which told me with love, that I looked fabulous! "Take a good look," I said to myself. "It might be a while before you see it again!"

I had absolutely refused to wear a girdle—though in those days, it was more required by fashion than by my form. Long days of work on the beach as a "hard hat" had given me a good firm body.

I climbed into the front seat of Cloro's dirty pick-up, all blotched on the outside with specks of cement, and drove over to the Posada Vallarta. The silk skirt got all bunched up in my ass, and my legs started sweating. Naturally, there was no air conditioning in my fairy-tale coach! Luckily it was a short trip. I hiked up my skirt and fanned my legs and promised myself to take a moment to cool off before I made my grand entrance into the restaurant.

My hosts were already seated at a table as I waltzed across the flowered patio toward them. Judging by their wide-open jaws and their inability to complete a sentence, I think I made the impression I was aiming for.

"Sometimes we like to dress up here too," I observed airily and sat down in the empty chair. "It's fun to get out of work clothes every once in a while." That was a lie, but how would they ever know?

"What beautiful jewelry!" said Jane, who recovered first. "Did you get it here in Mexico?"

"No, it's from Cartier."

A gasp. "You mean those stones are real?"

That was enough to keep them going for another five minutes. I must admit I was enjoying myself. I told them the story of all the jewels I carried in my rag doll without knowing it, all those years in the concentration camp.

"To us it's a normal way of life, to have precious stones," I said. "You know, that's how many of the Jews were able to escape from Germany too, those of them that did. The smart Jew had lots of valuable property, to be sure, but he also had gems. See, you can buy the border patrol with gold and diamonds, but you won't get far with a house in Berlin." Their mouths gaped. "With one little diamond of five carats, you can go a long way."

"So this is what you had in the camp?"

"No, these aren't the same jewels. But my mother did have a lot of good stuff sewed in there. When we got to Holland after the war, we didn't have to suffer like everybody else who came in as a refugee. Thanks to the little doll, my mother was able to buy the pharmacy for my father. And with that, they got really rich."

And then a funny thing happened.

The whole dinner conversation turned into rich talk. It was as if they were all trying to impress one another, and me especially, with how much they had and how much they could do. I got so damn bored, I was almost sorry I had come, as much as I had enjoyed the first part of it. Jesus—! I had run away from California to get away from all that! Besides, these people were all in their late fifties; I was just a month shy of being thirty years old. I was ready to ditch this bunch and go out dancing!

As we were finishing the meal, several of my friends came through the patio on the way to the small bar and night club of the hotel.

"*¡Hola, Theresa!*" called out Rafael de la Cruz. I introduced him as the editor of the local newspaper. Next came Bill Wulff and Luis Favela, and then other engineers and architects. Each one in turn stopped at the table for a moment, to invite us inside when we had finished dinner.

The new disco at La Margarita was more what I had in mind for the rest of the evening, but I couldn't do that to my hosts. They were absolutely delighted to be meeting some real Mexicans, especially some educated ones. They had of course seen Luis Alvarez that morning, but otherwise the only "natives" they had talked to so far were their own waiters, and Cloro and Pablo the brickmaker.

We went into the bar, and I completed my Education of the American Tourist in Mexico, part one. Once I made up my mind that I wasn't going to get to the disco that night, it wasn't so bad. And by the end of the evening, as we said our final good-byes, the Smiths hinted very broadly that, when they returned in February, they would be happy to talk to my husband and me about investing in the hotel.

My war paint had been a success.

Finally the day came when Bob Lewis' cable arrived. He was in Mazatlán. From there to Tepic was an easy day's drive. Then his adventure through the jungle would begin. Cloro and I tried to figure when he would arrive at the shores of the Ameca, and we came up with a rough estimate, give or take about six hours.

Cloro gave us all a ride out to the river bank the next morning. Into the pick-up truck piled my two babies and me, my two maids and Guilberto, the stall boy, Kaiser, our German shepherd, and Gene LaPorte, who had recently arrived to spend another few days in Puerto Vallarta. And there were also loads of sandwiches and snacks and drinks. We were determined to make a picnic of it.

Waiting, even six hours, means nothing in Mexico. We were all used to it. I was sure it would go very quickly there with the river for recreation. Cloro waved good-bye, promising to come back later in the day to check on us, and then he drove back into town.

The boys loved Guilberto. We all did. He was a mountain boy, light-skinned and handsome, and he looked as proud and elegant on a horse as any Spanish *conquistador*. He had already taught Bear and Buster to ride like little Indians. Now this morning, he was teaching them the lore of the river. He asked me, very politely, if I would go with the maids and find some brush for a campfire. They were going to go crabbing, to give us a special treat for lunch. Gene and the maids and I laughed over and over again to watch them bouncing and scrambling along the shoreline in search of their prey. They would spot a crab scratching a hole in a pocket of sand beside the water, and immediately Guilberto took out his slingshot. The idea was not to kill the crab, but just to knock him senseless for a moment.

Snap! went the sling, and then one of the little boys ran up to the stunned animal. He put his chubby little foot on the prickly body of the crab, teetering from side to side as he tried to hold it steady and yank off a claw at the same time. If they took only the big right-hand claw, which grew back in time, Guilberto explained, our coast would continue to have an unending supply of these delicacies.

Once they had enough of the choice *pinzas* in their bag, he patiently set about teaching the boys how to use a slingshot.

Our strange, extended family had a beautiful, leisurely morning there at the riverside. Even Gene LaPorte, that elegant old gentleman who was obviously much more at home in the offices of Union Carbide than in this rough jungle landscape, seemed to enjoy himself immensely. Together we raided the cornfields nearby, and also found some mangoes and breadfruit for dessert later.

I had brought a little chest with a few soft drinks. But Cokes were outrageously expensive in those days, so I had also made up some sweet water, as I usually did. Papaya water and pineapple water with lime were the favorites.

And so we sat. I used some of my six hours to study the river. It would not have been possible to cross during the summer rainy season. But this was December. At that time, the river, although it was a block or so in width, was only about three feet deep in most places. In some places maybe four feet. And sometimes a good deal less, where a sand bar had formed.

I had had experience driving Cloro's truck across, and he had taught me that the trick of an easy crossing was to drive from sand bar to sand bar.

Finally, after seven and a half hours, my familiar grey Chevy station wagon came limping up to the other bank, on the Nayarit side of the river.

"There he is!" I shouted, and we all started screaming and waving our arms and jumping up and down like crazies on our side of the river.

Slowly a dark, angry figure, looking every bit like a tired Mexican businessman, climbed out of the car. I could tell from the set of his shoulders that it had not been a good day.

"HALLO!" I bawled cheerfully, deciding that the boys and I could talk him out of any sort of owlish mood, once we got him over to us. "HERE WE ARE! OVER HERE!"

I started wading through the Rio Ameca in my sundress.

The water was murky. A couple of times, of course, I stepped off into a hole in the bottom that was a good deal more than four feet deep. So that by the time I got to the other shore, I was drenched and muddy. Bob, on the other hand, looked as if he had just taken a cool shower. His black hair was neatly combed back, every strand in place. How did he do it?

Here was a man who used to drive me crazy (well, we drove each other crazy, as you can guess). He could drink and party all night, and still come home and hang up his suit, hang up his tie, hang up his shirt on the back of a chair, and place his shoes together neatly beside the suit rack, exactly side by side. His old military school officers would have been proud.

And then there was his wife. You could follow the trail of what I had worn that night from the front door to the bed.

He never sweated. Still, he changed clothes several times a day. If he played tennis, he would say, "Excuse me, I'll be right back," and then he went home, took a shower, shaved, changed totally, and returned in a clean outfit, complete with staring white tennis shoes.

Even now, after driving an American station wagon and pulling a long sports boat through the jungle for nineteen hours, he looked so fresh, he was making me feel like a slob. I could have killed him. It was not a good sign for the beginning of a new attempt at togetherness.

He didn't help any by starting in the way he did. "Are those my boys over there? The ones running around without any clothes on? What's your problem? Do you have to try to prove something by making them look like dirty little natives?"

"What do you mean? We're having a picnic!" I countered, sticking out my jaw.

"Well, it won't happen while I'm in town. I've got a carload of good American diapers back there." He glared.

"Did you have a good trip?" I asked, changing the subject.

"I hit a boulder twice and had two flat tires," he scowled.

"Did you change them in the nude? There's not a stain on your white pants," I felt like saying.

But I bit my tongue.

"What else do you have in there?" I almost shouted, in my super cheery singing voice.

"I've got a case of peanut butter, three cases of Carnation dried milk, and five cases of Gerber's baby food. They told me they don't have Gerber's down here. Damn Mexicans don't know—"

"Bob, they've got 46 million people down here. They must know something about babies."

"Well, my kids are going to eat right."

I wondered how long they were going to continue to be his kids—how long before they returned and became my kids again? I suspected it would be about the first time they spit out the Gerber's baby food. Which they promptly did later on, when the maids tried to feed it to them. The first time, and forever after that. They would much rather have an old chicken bone, or a pile of refried beans, or a hunk of coconut to chew on. They made that very clear.

"I'll bet you've got some great Christmas presents too!" I said with a broad smile, trying to make him friendlier, and prepare him for the proposition I had to make. "We've got some nice surprises for you too!"

He refused to be cajoled, so I just plunged right in:

"I think I should drive across."

He took a deep breath, about to protest, and I keep going. "I've been studying the river for about six hours now, and I know just how we should go."

"Nonsense. Of course I'll drive. I've been driving through the whole damn jungle, haven't I? Seems like forever. I already drove across a couple of streams with this thing too."

"But they weren't rivers like this one. Let me tell you—"

"I'll drive," he said. And it was final.

"Get in on the other side."

"OK. But let me give you some hints. If you stay to the sand bars, you'll do fine. If you look closely, you can see where they are out there, just under the water. And look—You see how the water gets kind of smooth in those places? Just head for those." I smiled brightly. "And you have to go fast."

It was good advice. Did he listen to it? I don't know. I do know, however, that he didn't follow it.

We got about a third of the way out, and the kids were screaming on the other side, and the maids were tugging at them, and Kaiser was running in and out of the shallow water at the bank, and Bob was gripping the wheel very tightly, and muttering under his breath.

Suddenly the car took a dive, and then lurched up onto another sand bank.

"Keep going, keep going," I shouted. "You can't slow down."

The water was going *slap slap slap* as it hit the underside of the car, and Bob was starting to look frantic.

"DON'T SLOW DOWN!" I shouted.

"We're hitting some rocks," he shouted back. "This is a new car. I'm not going to destroy—"

"KEEP GOING!" I interrupted. "THAT'S ONLY THE WATER HITTING—"

Then we spun around in a little half circle and stopped. The water was seeping in under the doors and beginning to fill up the leg space in front. The big boat we were pulling caught a current and started out to sea, spinning us around further, so that by that time, we were almost facing the direction we had come from.

"Shit."

"Well, you've picked up some pretty language in Mexico," said my husband, looking very superior. He continued to stare at me, as if to say, "Now what are you going to do about this mess you've got us into?"

"Shit," I said again, and crawled out of the window of the car. It was clear that Mr. Fashion Plate was not going to go for help.

I slipped again in the mud and shot downstream, with my long, green wraparound skirt all bunched up around my neck. The current wasn't too strong, so I relaxed and let it carry me for a bit. By then I had spotted just the help we needed, hidden in the bushes on our Jalisco side.

There was a *ranchero* waving to me, standing next to his little yellow tractor. I learned later that it was no accident that he was there. He did good business hauling people out of the river when they didn't know how to cross.

We made a deal for 500 pesos, and in another half hour or so, our motley riverside picnic was complete with Daddy.

8

I'm not quite sure if "enjoyment" is the word I want, to describe our day at the Rio Ameca, but I know I enjoyed it a lot more at the time than I did the next morning when Cloro said to me, "But haven't you noticed how the horses never want to go into that river?"

I nodded hesitantly.

"It's because of the crocodiles."

"Crocodiles!"

"*¡Seguro que sí!*" They just lie there in the sun and wait. I've seen a guy take one of those *caimán* crocodiles out of the river, as big as a man. They can grab a cow by the hind legs, and—"

He slapped his leg sharply to make his point, "—devour it in about an hour and a half."

Bob Lewis came up to us, after his first brisk morning walk on the Puerto Vallarta beach. Luckily, he didn't understand Spanish, and I didn't bother to translate what I had just heard. I figured that local river beasts were a part of the charm of Mexico that he didn't need to know about, just yet.

"Hey, Lewis, this is really beautiful," he said, glowing. "I can see what you've been talking about."

"I'm so happy you understand. You should see the boys swim! And the way they can ride horses already—" Tears came to my eyes. I was sharing my paradise with those that meant the most to me. "Have you seen the bungalows?"

"Well, I looked around, but I probably didn't see how everything was going to be. I was waiting for you."

Bob could really be sweet and attentive when he tried. In fact, all my female friends have always adored him. Even when Bob and I were having trouble, they would often take his side.

"Can't you see how sweet he is?" they would ask wistfully.

"Yes, he's sweet to everyone—that's just the problem," my mind would answer. But those days were behind us now. Bob and I were making a new start.

"Let me get us some more coffee, and we can walk around," I said, and I hurried back toward my own little house. Cloro and Bob eyed each other warily. Neither one could talk to the other, so they just stood for a while in uncomfortable silence.

Finally Cloro said *adiós*, which was a word Bob could handle, and even return when he felt like it, and walked off to check on some of his *mozos*, whom he had set to work carving out another canoe.

"Here we are!" I said brightly, returning with two mugs of coffee. "You see what they're doing over there? Cloro draws out the outline on one of those big logs, and then the boys start in with chisels. These huge canoes are all one piece." I pointed out some that were finished, a short distance away in the sand. "And they're all done by hand. It's amazing, isn't it?"

"How well do they work on the sea?" asked Bob. He was skeptical. After all, he had just hauled our big American fiber glass boat through the Mexican jungle.

"Very well. We took one of those all the way across the bay and back," I said, pointing out toward Yelapa, over the calm blue mirror.

"I guess I'll have to try one out," smiled my husband, the sportsman. He loved fishing and riding. He had dozens of golf and tennis trophies at home. And now here was a new opportunity, with a hand-made Mexican canoe. (Perhaps later on, he might even join Cloro for a little bootlegging venture?)

"Sooner than you think!" I replied. "In fact, we bought a small canoe a few weeks ago, and the boys have made me promise that they can take you out crayfishing. They learned it from Guilberto."

"OK, they're on!"

We strolled through the palms, heading toward the foundations of the first bungalow, where it was easiest to explain what everything would look like. I had been hesitant to tell Bob the whole plan, since I was still not sure if he had come to Mexico to stay with us. Perhaps he wasn't sure at that point either. And I certainly didn't know if he'd be interested in Mexican beach life or Mexican hotel life.

I hadn't spent all the money I deposited in the bank in Guadalajara, but I knew that it was not an unlimited resource. And since Las Glorias was my project, I knew that its final success depended on me alone. Still, he seemed open and interested this morning.

We walked into the hole that was the doorway of the first bungalow, and I explained about the Frank Lloyd Wright design with the special ceiling, and all the other features.

"We went up into the jungle for the wood. You should have been there. It was an incredible experience! We'll make all our own windows and doors. I've ordered the tools from Guadalajara. And I have a design for a headboard of the beds, and for a chest of drawers—" The words could not tumble out fast enough.

"You've done a good job," he said warmly.

We walked toward the center of the whole acreage, and I showed him the spot for the office, and the swimming pool, and the long entrance drive. I told him I had asked Luis Alvarez to design us a big bar and restaurant, so that it looked like the prow of a ship pointed out to sea.

"You've got to have a tennis court too," said Bob, catching some of the enthusiasm. "These people need a lot to do when they come down here for a week or two."

"That's a great idea! It'll be the first in Puerto Vallarta," I agreed, making a mental note to get back to the architect immediately with the suggestion. "That'll put us on the map. It'll make us as interesting as the Posada Vallarta."

Yup, I had spilled the beans, even though I had not intended to. My whole future was out on the table. It was just too exciting to contain it.

I realized how far I'd gone when Bob asked the inevitable question.

"How much is all this going to cost?"

"Oh, uh—I don't know. I haven't gotten everything straight with the architect yet."

"Well, how much for, say, one bungalow?"

"Uh—Cloro might know—"

"You're doing business with a beachcomber, and the guy doesn't even know how much per square foot?" Bob's face was starting to get red.

"I could ask him," I offered, "but I think I know what he would say. He'd just shrug and tell you, 'I don't know, but we'll build it and then I'll give you a figure!'"

I laughed a silly laugh, and kissed him on the nose. I thought that since it was such a beautiful sunshiny day, and the aroma coming off the coconut blossoms was so intoxicating, that my husband might appreciate a bit of Mexican humor.

Not a chance.

He scowled. "You know, it would be much more cost effective if you would put up the whole thing as one large unit. That way you could go up, instead of spreading out. And the air conditioning—"

"But we don't have room for that here."

"Well of course, you'd have to take out several of the palm trees—"

"We can't do that. We don't want to do it, but we can't anyway. The permission from the Mexican government—"

"We'd put them back in later. That's the way it's done in America. We clear the land, and put in the buildings, and then we landscape the place later."

"Bob, you don't understand—" I was pleading, as Cloro walked up, all smiles.

"¿Qué tal, señora?"

"Muy bien, gracias." I locked my jaw into a grin.

For the second time that morning, I was glad they didn't understand each other. My future was perhaps going to be more complicated than I thought.

I continued bravely. "A palm tree takes seven years to produce fruit. Cloro planted all these." Cloro smiled again and then moved away, sensing that this was not a good time. "They're important to him. We have the meat of the coconut, and when it dries we have the copra —"

"Nonsense. Nobody's used copra for twenty years. It's all chemical now."

"But think of how it's going to look with the little bungalows. The tourists will love it! It'll be like a native village in Maui or in Tahiti, but even better. You remember, we've seen pictures of what it's really like in Papeete. Well, here in Las Glorias we're going to have a *dream* of Tahiti, not the reality. It's going to be a rich man's fantasy!"

Bob's scowl deepened.

"And with all these trees, we won't even need to think about air conditioning." I knew that from living in this grove already. "A small fan is the most we'll need."

I felt my voice almost starting to whine. "Bob, where are you going?"

He had turned on his heel and was heading toward the sea again. "I've had enough for today," he snarled.

"But can't we finish—"

"Adiós," he said to Cloro as he passed.

I sighed. "Well, that's a start, anyway," I smiled to myself.

And he was gone.

"Cloro, how about a large *coco loco*?" I said, as I slumped onto the sand and leaned my back against one of his rustic benches. My brain was addled from heavy business affairs mixed with heavy domestic affairs, from Spanish mixed with English—especially when my dreams were still in Dutch, after all these years. I needed a break.

When Bob returned, he was calm, and excited again about the hotel. He had met Gene LaPorte on the beach. I found he became more reasonable when he had another man to speak English with. He'd also had a chance to think about how good the Mexicana Airlines connections were with California. As for Las Glorias and the palms, I think it was the point about the money we would save on air conditioning that finally got through.

A couple of nights later the boys took him out in the canoe and showed him the ropes. The little stream behind our house was filled with crayfish, in the rocks among the cattails. The boys had a good flashlight along with them, and when they spied one of the beautiful *langostinitos*, they shone the bright light into its eyes and stunned it. Then, while it was still frozen in shock and couldn't think to grab onto their fingers, they reached out and tossed it into the canoe. Bob was fascinated, and the boys were thrilled.

All in all, it was a memorable Christmas. Bob went back to look after his business in San Francisco, but he promised to return in February, when the Smiths were also coming back. He was already hooked.

He owned an office building on Venice Avenue in Los Angeles that he was going to prepare to sell, and he planned to talk to the international accounting firm of Arthur Young about organizing our whole investment.

When Gene and Elizabeth arrived in February, they were bubbling with excitement, or at least as bubbly as Gene ever got, in the rather cold, calculating way he had. He had found two more investors, one of them a judge friend of his from Chicago. Most Americans were still a bit shy about investing in Mexico in those days. Memories still lingered of Pancho Villa, of the expropriation during the revolution of Mobil and Standard Oil, and the huge salt mines.

It wasn't until they got serious and really checked out the tax advantages, even in the event of a loss, that they became genuinely interested. There was still a bit of intrigue about it—enough to keep it exciting—but at Las Glorias anyhow, there was also an American couple they could trust, a friendly host couple who would take care of them, and entertain them when they came down to look in on their investment, and speak Spanish when necessary. One half of the couple, anyhow. Bob never learned.

We had a lawyer draw up new papers, expanding the Palacios Corporation. There were three investors, who put in about $60,000 each. Bob and I added our own contribution, and credited Cloro for the land. And instead of eight bungalows, there were to be thirty-four. We were going into the hotel business in a big way!

Elizabeth was excited about having one of our bungalows to stay in, any time they wanted to come down. And I even promised to move in my piano, which was being shipped down from San Francisco, so that she'd be able to keep up with her practicing.

Bob returned again to California, to put the house up for sale, and also his insurance business. He continued to fly back and forth that spring, and we got on very well.

By the end of May, I was pregnant.

My days were filled, as design and construction expanded at Las Glorias. The boys were growing like little tropical weeds. I'm afraid I didn't have as much time for them as I had had the first six months. However, ours was a large, but close-knit group, almost like a genuine Mexican family. I never worried a bit when I left the children with Lupe or Consuela, Carlos or Guilberto. They were all filled with warmth and tenderness, and they treated my babies exactly as they had been treated in their own loving families.

Guilberto was their favorite, as I have said. Tall and strong, full of respect, and very shy, he was an astonishingly handsome boy. Later when the hotel opened and he ran the rental of the horses for our customers, he always came back with bigger tips than any of the waiters or bellboys. "Doña Theresa," he would say, "*¡Mire!* just look at what I got!" And his hand was full of bills.

"Keep it, Guilberto. I'm sure you earned it," I used to tell him. His brilliant smile, his dark curly hair and mustache melted the most hardened tourist. But the thing that made him sexiest was that he had no idea whatsoever of the impression he was making on others.

He was totally free and unselfconscious when he played with my boys, almost as if he were the same age as they were. By summertime, he had them diving in and out of the surf with their horses. They practically lived on those animals. They went to the river in town to wash them. They went hunting up in the mountains.

On the beach, they loved to show off for the tourists, and swim with the horses in the waves. Looking almost as if they and the horses were one, they played their circus tricks, sliding back to ride behind, hanging onto the tails, and steadying themselves with their little feet on the large rumps. It's a marvel they were never hurt.

We got our electricity, and the carpentry shop was going full steam. At the beginning of April, we started negotiating for the water. We allowed plenty of time before the rainy season began in mid-June, which would then complicate the digging of a line from the Hotel Rosita.

Once again Cloro the politician proved invaluable. He didn't have a smoke-filled room, but he did have his *palapa* and his *ricilla*, and in Puerto Vallarta that was what was called for. If I was ever tempted to question or resent the large percentage he got from our new corporation for the lease of his land, I had only to remind myself of our dealings with Esteban, the mayor of Chacala, or with Juan, the city *ingeniero*, among many others. Of course, as with practically all official dealings in Mexico, this one was not without its *mordida*, and a rather special one at that.

Juan's title of "engineer" had much more to do with the position of his family in Guadalajara than with the years of schooling he had completed.

We explained that we were under construction for the Hotel Las Glorias, that we planned a restaurant, a swimming pool, and running water in all the bungalows. We had to have the city water line.

"I will have to apply to Mexico City, *señora*."

"Of course. How long will it take?"

"Oh, *señora*, there's no telling," he shrugged. "So much paperwork."

I had already heard how the paperwork was managed in his own office. There were no water meters in the town. Juan made the rounds on horseback with his little notebook. He figured, "OK, there's a family of five, they must be using so and so much water. Next door, a family of twelve, so their bill is a little more than double." He handed out his bills, collected the money, plus any extra required by a "special situation," and the billing procedure was finished—until he or the town needed money the next time. Payment was rarely made by check, but it was sometimes made by pig, or a good fighting cock.

"How long do you think it will take for the paperwork?"

"And then we have to dig the line for the pipes," he continued. Have you noticed that a politician never answers a direct question? "Such a distance, *señora*! It must be over three kilometers."

"Perhaps we could make some sort of special arrangement?" said Cloro, stone-faced. "We are all proud that our little town is growing so fast."

"*Pues—*" he began slyly, "you know I'm going to be married next month?"

"I got your goddam invitation—everybody in town did!" I felt like saying. But I made a sweet smile and waited to hear his price.

"Why don't you give me all my furniture?"

"All your furniture!"

"Yes. All Vallarta is talking about your carpentry shop and the cedar and your beautiful tools from Guadalajara. I think I will need a bed, and a chest of drawers. And the dining room table with all the chairs, of course." He smiled broadly, waiting for our reaction. "And the *sala*. My whole living room."

Now this guy was a typical "Hollywood Mexican." I calculated in my mind how long it would take, if I clasped my hands around his scrawny throat, before I wiped that shitty grin off his face. But what I said was, "Of course. We'll have it for you next month."

"And I'll set my boys to work immediately."

"Any particular design you had in mind?"

"No, you can take care of that," he replied. My sarcasm was lost on him.

About a week later I drove by the Rosita with Cloro in his truck, and there they were, two young kids standing around with shovels, looking at a wheelbarrow as if they were seeing one for the first time. Three kilometers minus a couple of yards to go. I didn't even try to figure out when they would reach us at that rate.

We roared down to the water office and yelled at Juan, whose answer was, predictably, a helpless shrug. What we had paid for was the official permission to extend the line. The work of his boys, it seems, was a kind of bonus. We should be grateful for them.

"Cloro, they'll never get to Las Glorias!" I moaned. "And the rainy season will be on us before we know it."

I made a quick flight to Guadalajara, and bought forty picks and shovels, thirty wheelbarrows, and two miles of four-inch pipe, to be delivered immediately. Cloro hired forty men, and we were in business. We got the trench dug and the pipe buried three feet deep, in one month's time. Bob and I even figured out how to solder it to the underside of the bridge over the little river between us and town, and we did such a good job that it has lasted through all the floods since then. It cost us $28,000.

In return for the work, Mexico City guaranteed us 40% of each fee charged when a new connection was made to our line. I still have all the official papers. We made an exception for the little soccer stadium on the one side of the road, and the *charreada* ring for the horse shows, on the beach side. Those connections, we donated to the city.

We never received a single peso from any of it.

Perhaps we should have heeded that as the first sign of what was to come. If all I had was the money from the connection fees, I would be a rich woman now, since over a third of modern Puerto Vallarta, a city of over 100,000 population and millions of tourists a year, has connected on my line. Even our competition, the big hotel Posada Vallarta out by the airport, connected onto us on the other side without charge: so good, apparently, were the owner's connections in Mexico City.

But we got our water, and the line was completed before the rains came. Of course we did not drink it or cook with it. If the tourists ever had a look at Mexican tap water under a microscope, they would never come back. There was only one small haphazard filtering tank between our kitchen sink and the Rio Cuale. Upriver, women were washing clothes in it, kids were peeing in it, horses were shitting in it—it's frightening to think of all the other possibilities.

All the hotels and restaurants in Puerto Vallarta have their own filtering systems. Bob brought two systems back with him right away from the United States, and we installed them at the same time the water was connected. Still, if we wanted a drink ourselves, we used bottled water, which was delivered daily in twenty-gallon glass jars.

In addition to such special items, Bob continued to bring down the necessities from California also, like peanut butter.

It was hard to say who was happier about that, our own kids or Georgia, an artsy American friend of ours, who always seemed to know when a fresh shipment had arrived. Tall and skinny, with long blonde hair that always looked a little dirty, Georgia used to walk slowly and provocatively along the beaches in those early days, perhaps in search of inspiration, since she was an oil painter. She was always sure to make a stop in our kitchen, to sing the praises of peanut butter.

"God, Terry! I don't know what I'd do without it—or you, Terry. I just crave it," she said, wolfing down another sandwich, sloppy with jelly.

Our workers never minded a visit from her. She was one of the first in our little country village to wear a bikini, long before anyone else dared to. She never seemed to notice or care that her large boobs were always on the verge of slipping out of it. And she always seemed surprised when she found herself in trouble with Ernesto, her jealous Mexican second husband.

One night I was relaxing in the ocean, taking a nice leisurely swim in the nude, which I tried to do as often as I could after a day of riding herd on bricklayers or tangling with authorities over some official question or other. I had the sea to myself.

There was a full moon that night, and the water was filled with tiny luminescent plankton, that gave off an eerie glow when they were disturbed. As I cut smoothly through the surface, I left a long, glowing trail in my wake. It was a magical effect in the moonlight.

When I had had enough, I started up onto the beach toward my little house, past the shadowy big hole in the ground that was soon to be our swimming pool. I was preoccupied with dodging the dozens of little sand crabs that were trying to scurry across my feet. Suddenly behind me I heard a rustling in the huge flat leaves of the banana trees.

"Hell—" I thought, "all these months, and I've never been bothered by anyone on the beach. I guess I should have at least carried my swimming suit along with me."

But that thought just made me angry. It was my beach, after all. I could go skinny-dipping if I wanted to. Often I took the boys with me too.

I hurried quickly into my house and shut the front door and locked it. An obscure white figure was right behind me.

Its harsh banging on the door shattered the night's spell. I thought of grabbing an iron skillet from the kitchen, but it quickly became clear to me that the voice was female, and scared.

"Terry! Are you there, Terry? Let me in!" The banging got louder. "Let me in!"

I opened and saw the pale figure of Georgia, made even more ghostly by the sheet she had wrapped around her. The flesh around her eye was starting to turn blue.

"What happened to you? What are you doing here?"

"Can I come in?"

I felt silly, realizing that I was blocking the door. I stepped aside and she swept inside and fell into one of my barrel chairs.

"Ernesto beat the shit out of me again!" she sobbed. "I didn't do anything! I only stole three of his lousy little plants. Why doesn't he understand how important my art is?" She was drunk.

She had explained to me once, over peanut butter and bourbon, that her *macho* husband controlled all the family funds. If she needed extra money to buy paints or canvas, she had to sneak into the nursery that was his livelihood and steal some of his plants to sell secretly in town.

"Have you got a drink?" she asked. Her sheet fell open a bit and I saw that there were several bruises on her body too. I poured a good stiff whiskey and handed it to her.

"Bastard! In the States I could have him thrown in jail. But there's nothing for a *gringa* to do down here." She tossed down a big gulp of whiskey. "Thanks. That black-eyed *pinche cabrón hijo de la chingada!"*

Her eye was beginning to turn darker blue-black.

"Maybe you ought to try painting something else besides those scrawny Don Quixote figures with the big erections," I suggested. "They're in every one of your paintings. Nobody has penises that size!" I thought maybe she was giving Ernesto a complex.

"That's what I was doing!" She was weeping again. The whiskey probably made her feel even sorrier for herself than before. "I was trying to do a self-portrait," she sniffed. "I was standing in front of the mirror naked, and the son of a bitch just came up from behind and grabbed me. He wanted to fuck, and I wanted to paint, and it started from there." She started inspecting the bruises on her legs. "Bastard doesn't deserve me. He doesn't understand anything about art."

Someone needed to remind her of the fact that nobody in Puerto Vallarta was buying her giant phallus paintings, but it wasn't going to be me. She had had enough for one night.

"I got the sheet from my neighbor, Margarita," she coughed, and the cough sputtered into a giggle. "I think I must have scared her to death."

"Not to mention me," I added.

"Have you got any more peanut butter?" she asked shyly.

I decided she must be starting to feel better. I made two big sloppy sandwiches, and we stayed awake the rest of the night, cussing out the *hijos de la chingada* men we'd known in our life.

Through the long summer months I was once again able to keep my gardener Carlos busy, after our fiasco with the tomatoes and cucumbers. By now there was lots of new planting to be done, around the individual bungalows and near the large patio area by the swimming pool and the restaurant. There were more lemon and avocado trees, and new banana trees to go in. And I had heard from Doctor Calderón about a special hardy grass, the *parra*, which was native to these mountains and therefore grew well there near the beach.

At last I thought I was getting the hang of agriculture in the tropics, when another disaster struck. All two hundred of my special strawberry plants, that I had imported from Oregon, and which were much admired by the local *aficionados*, washed into the sea after the flooding of a sudden summer storm.

The next day Carlos ran up to me while I was sorting through the laundry with the maids. "*Señora, señora*, come see! There are two turtles out there in the water. They are locked together."

My eye went quickly to the beach, and sure enough, there was a crowd of construction workers on the water's edge, cheering on the two huge turtles caught in their mating dance. Carlos was the son of a fishing family from Bucerías, up the coast, and his hunter's instinct had taken over. He was eager to show his *valor* by dragging the giant animals onto the sand and killing them.

"*¡Sopa, sopa!*" he kept shouting, to encourage me to agree to the slaughter. Bear and Buster joined in the chant. They had all had my turtle soup, and were eager for more.

"But you can't kill them while they're mating like that," I urged him. "It would be too cruel."

"It's good food for us, *señora*."

Guilberto wandered up and he too got excited about joining in the hunt.

I was outnumbered. "OK." I nodded my head, sadly, wondering if I should take my boys back into the house with me.

Guilberto ran and got a nylon fishing line, and in no time the two of them were out in the surf, lashing the rope around the hind legs of the turtles. In a frenzy, the reptiles were thrashing around, tapping wildly with their flippers onto the shells of their mates. They were oblivious to the fact that Carlos and Guilberto had slowly hauled them up onto the sand.

Carlos took out a long knife, his eyes bright with excitement. He jumped on the huge shell of the male and drew the knife cleanly across its throat. I looked away. Here were two magnificent beasts, perhaps seventy-five years old, and now one was dead already, or almost dead, just because of a single word from me.

I turned to look again. The tongue of the male was sticking out, blood was pouring out around it, and he was gasping for air. His sad eyes looked straight into mine, and seemed to say, "Let me finish. Please, let me reproduce." He slid away from the female, and I saw that his large organ was still hard, still pumping.

I was stunned, and I felt faint. Hunting was not new to me. I had been shooting before, walking through the mountains in search of quail, or deer. Why had this affected me so strongly? Was I being too sentimental? I glanced down at Bear and Buster, but to them it seemed a natural act, not cruel. The sea had provided us with food, and it was ours to take.

"Can we at least save the female, Carlos?" I begged. "Guilberto?"

"Doña Theresa, she will be very unhappy now. Better to let her die with her man," said Carlos matter-of-factly. I could not argue with the logic of it, but I could not stay and watch either. And later my heart was not in the turtle soup idea either. Instead, I let the boys sell the carcasses in town, where they could get a good price for the meat and the shells.

Bob began spending more and more time down in Puerto Vallarta during the year of construction. And at the *charreada*, the local riding club, he found some good friends who spoke English.

We both had always loved horseback riding, and we were good at it. I had become acquainted with this Mexican-style rodeo several years before, when President Alemán came to Holland in 1958 to visit our queen. He brought the *charros* along with him, as an example of the best in Mexican culture, and they presented a performance at the jockey club in Rotterdam. Afterwards my friends and I met many of them at a big reception on one of the ocean liners of the Holland-America Line, attended also by the queen and the prince and all the princesses. The President of Mexico was presented with a golden spur as a memento of his visit.

Most villages in Jalisco and the neighboring areas had their *charreadas*, and on Sundays, all the men who loved horses and could afford to keep them gathered to perform in the ring. There were also contests between various towns of our region, and the competition was brisk. Sometimes we went out even as far as Manzanillo.

One of the Puerto Vallarta *charros*, Crisanto Mora, was the local distributor of Coca-Cola and mineral water. In the Fifties, he and his wife Ofelia had spent some time as illegal aliens in Chicago, where he sold used cars. Since they loved to swap their America stories endlessly, he and Bob became good friends. Ofelia is still my best friend today.

Miguel Salinas and Crisanto had been chums since elementary school with the monks in Guadalajara. But there the similarity ended. Crisanto, with a big belly and a big mustache, seemed plagued by bad luck, not only in major business affairs, but also in minor irritations, such as his everlasting inability to get his rusty little Peugeot started.

Salinas, on the other hand, was over six-two, which is very tall for a Mexican. He had dark good looks and impeccable manners. He was a rich lawyer, the son of an extremely wealthy senator from Morelos, and his terms of study at Harvard and at Cambridge showed in his speech and in his fondness for reading the classics. He and his wife Lola also became friends of ours.

The men rode and roped cattle and horses, even wild bulls and wild horses, as they do in the United States. But there are also some significant differences from the rodeos in our Old West. The strength and stamina of an American cowboy are not so important as the gracefulness and skill of the Mexican *charro*, and the exquisite training of his horses, when it comes time to award appreciation and points.

In the first contest, the rider must face the judges, then turn his horse quickly around full circle, keeping the horse's back feet together and in place. Points for style are awarded or withheld as carefully as in a gymnastics competition at the Olympics. The last of several events, the *paso de la muerte,* truly lives up to its name. As a rider jumps from his own animal onto the back of a wild horse, a miscalculation could be fatal.

Another difference in Mexico is the appearance of the riders. No *charro* would be mistaken for the rough-and-ready "Marlboro man" of the Western range. He looks exceedingly *macho* in his beautiful dark linen outfit, with a butterfly-style tie at the neck, and a wide-brimmed black sombrero decorated in gold and silver braid. From his slim waist—usually—to his expensive leather boots runs a trim of silver ornaments down the outside seam of each tight brown trouser leg. Among these are embossed buttons and little charms, some representing a hat, for example, or a horse's hoof, or a beautiful fighting cock.

To complete their outfits, all *charros* wore revolvers. That is, until López-Portillo, fearful of assassination (for good reason) and revolution, confiscated all firearms. The resentful Mexican horsemen still wear imitation guns in the ring today.

As I said, those who could afford it, at least two horses, the necessary trailers, the stall boys, and the travel expenses, came together each Sunday for love of the sport, and also "for love of country," as some of them said.

These Sunday gatherings were becoming a happy ritual. The women sat on the sidelines and cooked and gossiped. Our children, many of them the same ages, played together, while the men were at their more serious games. After three or four hours, the men were hot, and the serious drinking began. Usually they dragged in long after we women had taken the children home to bed.

Bob and I bought some horses from both Crisanto and Miguel. We were beginning to feel a sense of belonging.

One Sunday night I had just walked in with the boys, and Lupe was fussing with them, trying to settle them down for bed. Suddenly there was a loud pounding on my door.

"Doña Theresa! Doña Theresa!" It was Elena, the carpenter's wife. They lived in a small shack out behind us, near the shop where Don Martín was making the furniture and the woodwork for the bungalows.

I opened the door. Her wretched face was streaming tears.

"*¡Corra! corra, por favor*! Run! We have to go to the church. She is not baptized yet!"

I could hardly understand her between the sobs. "Doña Elena, what has happened? What do you mean?"

Suddenly I knew, even before she said it.

"Our little Teresita. She is dead . . . *muerta*. Gone to the Lord."

My own unborn child did a flip that nearly sat me down on the floor. "Dead!" I shouted. "How can this be? I just saw her this afternoon, and she was beautiful!"

"*Señora*, please," she sobbed. "Hurry!"

"Run, get my car keys," I shrilled to Lupita, who stood stunned in the middle of the room. "We have to go to the *padre*."

Doña Elena ran to her house to get her children. "Be there in a minute," I called out to her, and made a dive for my station wagon. "My little Teresita," I kept thinking, "my little Teresita!"

Only days earlier my gentle carpenter and his wife had named their newborn for me. "My little godchild to be—" I kept shaking my head. "Maybe she's only very sick. She can't really be dead. I just saw her! We'll go to the hospital."

I screeched to a stop in front of don Martín's shack. Elena appeared at the door with the baby cradled in her arms. She herded six or seven other small children into the back of my station wagon and then sat down heavily in the front seat next to me. I looked at the tiny bundle and then I knew. The child was dead, of no apparent cause.

"Hurry, doña Theresa."

I threw the car into gear and we started toward the church. A Catholic child must be baptized alive. Without saying a word, we knew what we had to do when we met Father Aldana.

"Please, doña Elena, stop your wailing!" I cried. She was only frightening her other children, who sat huddled in the back of the car, great tears running out of their huge dark eyes. They tried to grab onto the back of their mother's neck to get a look at the baby. They groped toward each other, terrified and confused, but still somehow understanding the permanence of death.

I pulled my station wagon up to the church entrance. The mother was out of the car even before the wheels stopped, pounding on the door and praying, "Please, Lord. Give this baby its last breath to receive you, Oh Lord."

"What can I do for you, my child?" asked the *padre*, with a surprised look on his face at finding all this commotion in the darkness outside his door.

"My small daughter," sobbed Elena, "she is almost dead! Please, father, baptize her before she goes." She held the child out in front of her, swaddled in a light blanket and the small, precious gown that was to have served in a happier baptismal ceremony just a few days later.

The *padre* looked down at both of them and started to reach out to touch the baby. "Doña Theresa is her godmother," said Elena, and shoved the bundle into my arms with a sudden movement. Then she pulled back the blanket a bit and touched the child tenderly on the cheek with one finger. "*Mi angelito, mi angelito*, my precious little angel," she cried, "you will go straight to heaven, my angel! *¡Anda, mi hijita, vete con los angelitos!*"

Padre Aldana looked over at me and then started the ceremony. For a moment, it looked as if the baptism would take place there on the porch of the church.

"You, Theresa, godmother of this child, are you clear of bad thoughts?" he said, motioning us all toward the holy water in the narthex, just inside the door. "Are you cleansed of your sins?"

"Yes, father," I said, trying not to think of what might be involved in that question. "Go fast, father! I want to bring this beautiful little girl to the hospital. I think we can save this child."

Doña Elena had fallen to her knees beside me. "Please, God, take this baby with you into Paradise." Some of the older brothers and sisters knelt beside their mother. Others stood frozen in fear, half in, and half out of my car.

"I baptize this child without sin, in your name, my Lord," said the father. "Amen," he said, and we all joined in.

"Thank you, *padre*," I choked, the tears streaming out of my eyes. I had poor Teresita in my arms, but all I saw was the child of my womb, due to be born in just a week or two.

I grabbed a couple of the little girls with my other hand, and Elena scooped up the rest and we all piled into the station wagon, without even leaving any alms in the coffer. In three or four minutes we were at the hospital, where the baby was declared dead.

Only then did the full brunt of it hit us, like a blow to the stomach. We could hardly walk back to the car, where all the kids were crying now in earnest.

Elena stopped at the car door. "Doña Theresa," she said, wringing my hand, "if it was not for you, my baby would not have been baptized. She would have gone into the *purgatorio*. I love you!" she sobbed. "We all love you."

We drove back home very slowly over the cobblestones.

"Martín will make a small casket tonight," she said, calmer now.

The children in the back still sobbed occasionally. She turned around and caressed each one in turn. "Your father will go tomorrow and get a plot in the cemetery," she said to them.

In the Mexican tropics, a body must be buried within twenty-four hours after death. Family members had to travel from place to place, making all the arrangements, for there were no telephones. They went for the priest, who prepared to do a funeral ceremony at home. They had a wooden coffin made, or if they could afford a richer one already made, they bought that. At the cemetery, they even had to dig the hole themselves, or hire it done.

When we entered doña Elena's *sala*, my boys were there with Lupita. They each held a candle, their chubby little fingers wrapped around it in the position of prayer, though their wide eyes told me they understood little of what was happening.

The baby was placed lovingly in a wooden crib in the center of the room, and the novena, the days and nights of mourning, began. Friends and relatives had started to arrive at the little shack. Some of the men carried their own tequila in a paper bag, for this was a reception that was to last nine days: don Martín could not have continued to serve them each night. We all sat there in the small room— Mexican, American, Dutch—none of us able to comprehend the magnitude of death.

While Elena was in the kitchen making coffee and getting out her best cups and saucers, Buster crept up to the crib and looked into it. "What is wrong with her?" he said, looking up into my eyes. "Where is she going?"

"She is going in a cloud to heaven," answered his brother, coming up slowly behind him. They both looked at the beautiful, pale little body of Teresita.

Then, at once they both reached into the crib, one boy trying to move an eyebrow to open her eyes, the other lifting up a leg and then dropping it, perplexed.

"*Está muerta, muchacho*," explained Lupita. "Like the birds you shoot with your slingshot. Sometimes they fall out of the tree. *Muertos*. It's late. Let us go home."

She had explained it as well as I could have done, and with a finality that the boys accepted.

"Doña Theresa," called Elena, coming back from the kitchen, "can you do one more thing for us?"

I nodded.

"Can we go to the cemetery in your big car?"

"Of course. I will wash it, and it will be ready tomorrow."

"And can we put in white flowers," she asked plaintively, "all around the little coffin?"

"I'll get them. You must go to the registry," I reminded her. "It will all be ready when you need it."

Once again we all kissed and hugged the mother and her stricken children and the little angel Teresita in the small wooden crib. One last time, full of tender curiosity, my boys pulled and poked secretly at the baby. Then we went back to our house.

After a priest in Mexico says the last rites at home, the most impressive part of the ceremony for the dead begins. All the friends and relatives walk slowly behind the casket on the way to the cemetery. Not just a dozen or two, but hundreds of mourners, all dressed in black, many of them without shoes. Most of the women wear a *mantilla* over their heads and carry small handfuls of flowers.

Since my grey Chevy station wagon was one of only six or seven cars in town, and probably the biggest, it was logical that it should double as a hearse. I was a hearse driver many times after that in Puerto Vallarta.

Gene Smith's wife Elizabeth, in town with her husband to check on our progress at Las Glorias, was standing on the corner where I turned from the highway, in toward the cemetery. "Hey, Terry, what are you doing?" she called.

"I'm on my way to the cemetery," I said, gesturing to the parade of mourners behind me.

"What—? Where—?"

I couldn't take time to explain. She must have understood as the people filed sadly past her.

9

A few days later I had a bad scare of my own. My three-year-old Buster began to get fussy and show some fever late in the afternoon, about six o'clock. By nine, his fever was up to 104° and I was frantic. I plunged his little body into a cool bath, added the small amount of ice that I could find in the house, and brought his temperature down a bit. But he was still shaking all over, and his eyes were big with fear.

Suddenly, as I sat in the living room holding him in my arms, a juicy worm poked its head out of my son's mouth, and then another.

"Lupita!" I screamed.

Fighting to keep down my supper, I pulled a little bit on the nasty things, but I only succeeded in breaking them both off.

I ran out of the house with him, stuck my finger far back in his mouth, and made him vomit in the sand. Up came the rest of the worms.

We looked down at both parts of them. They were as big around as earthworms, and about a foot long. It was revolting.

"Put him back in the bath," I shouted to Lupita. "I'm going right now for Doctor Calderón!"

I don't remember where Bob was that night, but luckily, he had left me the station wagon. I made the quickest trip I had ever made to town. Calderón was just sitting down to his supper after making several late calls. Immediately he succeeded in calming me down.

"There is nothing to worry about, Theresa. This happens all the time in the tropical countries." He laughed, though I wasn't in much of a mood to join in. "Those worms were uncomfortable. They were just trying to get out—it was too hot for them down there in Buster's stomach!"

"But will he be all right?"

"You did exactly the right thing. Give him some aspirin too, when you get home. And here's a dose of our Mexican herb, *peperesina*. That will take care of the worms." He put it into my hand and gave me a hug.

I drove home somewhat quieter, but still anxious to see my boy. What had happened with the gardener's daughter was still too close in my memory.

But Calderón had been right to treat it all with such an even tone. The next morning, Buster's color was better, and his fever mostly gone. I set him out by the bushes, as the doctor had ordered, and his bowels exploded almost immediately.

"Mama, mama!" he called.

Though I'm not one to dwell much on the bowel movements of others, or even of myself, this one was certainly interesting. My baby boy and I counted thirty-six worms, slithering around in the sand, attempting to get to safely before I could get at them with my trowel.

During those last warm days of winter, our Hotel Las Glorias was shaping up beautifully. We were aiming for an opening on the fifteenth of March. The Ides.

The pool had water in it already, the restaurant and bar were receiving their finishing touches, and most of the planting had been done in the main public areas. We were now organizing a system of brick walkways from bungalow to bungalow, and from the office to all parts of our elegant little jungle village.

Carlos was organizing the planting along the walkways and next to some of the bungalows, and several of Cloro's boys were cleaning all the individual floor tiles by hand, with large pieces of sandstone. Again I found myself in the business of counting bricks.

One afternoon toward the end of *siesta*, Carlos and I were at each end of a large brick pile, checking in the latest order. I squatted down on my haunches to try to find a more comfortable position, and felt a sudden embarrassing gush. My water had broken. Finally, this baby had declared that she was sick of being a week overdue, and that she was ready to come out and meet the world.

"Carlos," I said in a casual voice, "go and tell señor Lewis to get the car ready. I need to go into town."

I decided he didn't need to be in on all the brutal details of my childbirth. I had embarrassed everyone already, simply by appearing in public once the baby started to show. By this time I was enormous.

"And tell him to put the mattress in the back," I added as he ran off.

I had already visited Doctor Calderón at the hospital, when I found out I was pregnant. The sight of the dirty mattresses on the beds, stained brown with blood and the afterbirth of hundreds of deliveries, was revolting. I swore that when my time came, I was bringing my own.

In the sand I disguised my misfortune with the baby's water, dried off my legs as best I could, finished counting the bricks, and then maneuvered calmly toward the house. I knew that my American husband, so squeamish about mosquitoes, roaches, scorpions, not to mention infections and diseases, would be tied in knots at the thought of driving me to a Mexican hospital. One of us had to keep her wits about her.

"I've been talking to Salinas and some of the others," he had confronted me one day. "All the women of our class go to Guadalajara to have their babies."

"That's ridiculous," I countered. "How would I have time to do that? We've got a hotel to build."

"But you've seen what it's like down there. How do you know they can control their doses of anesthesia?"

"How do I know I'll get any anesthesia? Calderón keeps talking about 'pushing.' That seems to be his answer to everything. Maybe I'll get some pain pills. That's probably all."

"Well that settles it—"

"But I trust him, Bob. I want to have it here. They've been having babies in Mexico for years."

Now we drove in silence to the hospital, which in 1966 was at the edge of Puerto Vallarta. (Now it's in the middle of town.)

The nurses made me comfortable in a nice airy room that had a wide veranda overlooking the village cemetery,where I had just recently driven the tiny casket of my little Teresita. What an odd feeling it was now to be there again, lying nearby!

Bob saw me safely deposited on my own mattress, and then he drove off to try to find Doctor Calderón, since of course there were no telephones. My pains were very sporadic.

In a few moments, the cheerful face of my friend Ofelia appeared at the doorway. One of her children had seen us pass by in the car, and she figured out what must have happened. After all, it wasn't too difficult to spot a grey station wagon in those days, especially one driven by a jittery man, with a mattress hanging out the back.

After about a half hour, Bob came running back into the room, frantic. He had driven everywhere. The doctor was not to be found. His wife Alma, who operated the nearby pharmacy, was gone too.

"Why don't you go home and check on the boys?" I suggested. "I'll have Ofelia send word by cab if the pains get regular and closer together," I said smiling, the picture of peacefulness and reassurance. Actually, he was starting to make me nervous too.

Once Bob was disposed of, Ofelia and I got down to the woman's business of waiting. It was really quite pleasant, for she is a lovely woman.

A beautiful *mestiza*—that is, a rather small and dark woman, with mixed blood of Spanish and a little Indian, she could have been one of the best singers in Mexico if it hadn't been for the jealousy of her husband. I had heard her sing on those lazy Sunday afternoons when we sat waiting for our husbands at the *charreada*. And I had heard her talk longingly about the few times she had performed with a band, and how much she had cherished them. But it seemed she was always pregnant. There was no time for a career.

I suggested we walk through the halls of the hospital, to check out the scene. Of course, there were some serious cases there, with people near death. But most of the rooms were stuffed to the brim with large families, laughing and socializing and carrying on as if they were at a picnic. They seemed to be having such a good time that sometimes it was hard to determine which one of them was sick. In fact, in one room, it was the woman holding a fat little baby less than a year old, who was herself in labor with the next one!

I loved looking at Mexican families like that. There is such a closeness among them, so many people, that there always seems to be a friend available for every one of them. And there is always room for one more.

We slowly returned to my room. The sky over the Pacific was starting to shade toward pink and lavender, and there was a heady scent from the rose bushes and ginger plants below the small balcony outside my window.

"I hope this is a little girl, Ofelia," I said wistfully. "I think." There was a part of me that was curious about having a girl after two boys, but there was another part that was not so sure. "I look around me here, and I don't know," I continued. "A girl's life is not so easy in Mexico, is it?"

"Oh, I don't know— What do you mean?" asked Ofelia.

"Well, a girl is not going to be able to run up and down the beach like a little wild Indian, like Bear and Buster do now. Your little girls are so proper. When we're out on the Malecón, they're always so dressed up and pretty in white, or else they're at home with the maid. I wonder if a little American girl will put up with that?"

"My dear Theresa," Ofelia laughed, "you're not having a little American girl, you're having a little Mexican girl! I guess this little *niña* won't know the difference. That is, if the baby is a *niña*, and not another brother to your boys."

I laughed. "You're right about that, I guess— Oooof!" I had to catch my breath. My baby was reminding me that the mystery of its sex was soon to be resolved.

"But what about when you were growing up?" I asked her. I had seen that girls could ride horses or swim or even go dancing when they grew a little older, but always in the company of a maid or a family member. "Did you ever resent it that you had to be chaperoned everywhere?"

"Well, why should I? That's the way it was. My mother or one of my brothers always used to walk me to school in the morning, and somebody was always there to meet me in the afternoon." She shrugged. "If I went outside the house to play, it was always with other little girls, and the maid was there. We all did it that way."

I had seen the maids with young Mexican girls on the streets, always speaking to them very sweetly, always beginning with *"¡Ay, mi hijita!"* or *"¡Ay, mi amorcita!"* "Oh, my little darling, my love." They were friends and second mothers to them.

Still, didn't the girls want to break away sometimes?

"Didn't you ever at least feel like getting those little white dresses and those pretty little white socks all muddy?" I asked devilishly.

"Ay, Theresa!" she laughed. "A Mexican girl is supposed to be a little lady. She has to stay home and learn how to cook and take care of a man. Of course, she can go to church with the others, and she can also go to her little birthday parties."

"Ugh!" I moaned.

"The American girls have so much freedom. I don't know if that's a good thing. For us the virginity of the girl is so important. Every girl must come to her husband as a virgin."

"And that's why your brother or your father walked you to school, so you didn't get attacked?"

"Of course."

"But when you are about fourteen, it all stops. Seems to me that would be a more dangerous age, wouldn't it?"

I decided not to bring up the sore point that, from what I had heard, it was often exactly her brother or her father who was the one a Mexican girl needed to be worried about. So many people in such small houses, with one small bathroom and hardly any privacy. No wonder. Instead I asked, "Why aren't you still protected when you get older?"

"By then we know how to go. We know not to talk to strangers," she explained. "But still, we can't be alone with a man."

"Even the man you really think is the one for you?"

"Oh, never!" she whispered, horrified. "Lola Salinas told me the other day that she had never been alone with Miguel or any man for one minute before her marriage."

My eyes widened in disbelief.

"That was not many years ago," Ofelia continued. "She was 21. The morning she was married, she went to confession before she put on her beautiful wedding dress, and she was chaperoned even then."

"What could she possibly have had to confess?" I taunted her, howling with delight.

"Well, you know, little things. Maybe a bad thought, or—" Ofelia did not see much humor in the subject.

"How did you even get to meet a boy, if it's like that?"

"The boy comes to your house, if he likes you."

"But—"

"Perhaps he has seen you on the Malecón, or in school. Crisanto came to call on me at my parents' house. For three years, we sat in the *sala* and we talked. Sometimes we held hands, if nobody was in the room to see us. And he always looked at me—"

Ofelia mugged a silly look of painful adolescent male desire, and I screamed with laughter and forgot my pains. She looked like Kaiser when he was little, longing for his puppy chow.

"Finally my mother took pity and asked him to stay for dinner. That was a big day!" she sighed. "And then it was official, when Crisanto finally took me to meet his family. I guess that's a kind of engagement for us, especially when both parents meet."

"Everything is so formal. Was it the same for Lola?"

"Even more for her. Her mother was a *marquesa*. Her family had huge holdings from the Spanish land grants, before the Revolution. Afterwards, they still had the *haciendas,* of course, with all their beautiful silver, and their furniture, but no more money. Still, Lola had to be brought up according to her position."

"Whoooa!" I winced and grabbed my belly.

Ofelia went to the door to try to signal a nurse. Perhaps Calderón had left some instructions about pain pills. But, no such luck.

The pain left as fast as it had come. I was happy to have my friend in the room to talk to me and take my mind off what was coming. "Tell me what you meant about Lola," I asked, fascinated. "How was she brought up?"

"Well, they tried to educate her so she would be able to marry well," she continued. "Since one of her brothers was studying to become a priest, all the other children got a free education at the Jesuit school. But still, it was very difficult for them. Her father had no training for a career, of course. He had never needed it. He finally sold shoes in a shoe store, and her mother sold Tupperware. They were proud people."

"How awful," I said. "I never realized—"

"Then along came Miguel, whose father was a senator and a big *bandido*. He was rich, rich."

It happens everywhere, I thought. The nobility needs the money, the *nouveau riche* need the title and the respectability.

"She's very beautiful," I said. "Do you think they're happy?"

"I think so," answered my friend, and looked down at the floor for a while.

It was getting late, and the conversation was suddenly turning sad, so Ofelia said her good-byes, and promised to get word to Bob that he didn't have to come back that night. As for me, it was so much work to wrestle one lousy pain pill from the nurses later on, that I didn't try after that once. I slept very little that night.

Calderón strolled in late the next morning. "Ah, Theresa! So the child is finally going to come now?"

"I think so. My pains are getting harder, but they're still odd. I get one in three minutes, and then the next in twenty minutes, then five minutes and then five again, and I think it's regular, and then fifteen. What do you think, Doctor?" I moaned. I needed some sympathy.

Suddenly I caught the gleam in his eye. "Where the hell have you been, anyhow?" I pouted. I tried to take an angry tone of voice with him, but I couldn't keep it up. He was so jolly, it was impossible not to join in when his huge frame shook with laughter, which was most of the time.

"¡Ay, *Theresa*, you shouldn't ask!" he said, cocking his head to one side with a sly look.

"Well, I do ask. And where's Alma? They couldn't find anyone at the *farmacia*."

"That's just it. My wife is mad at me again. She took a lot of money and she left to go shopping in Guadalajara."

"You mean, she left you?"

"For a little bit. But she'll be back." He shrugged. "She always comes back."

"Calderón, can't you even try to behave yourself?" I shook my head in mock disbelief. "What was it this time?"

"I love to tickle the little pussies, Theresa, you know that!" he laughed. "There were these two sisters who came to me—"

"I don't want to hear about it," I frowned. Though he and I had become very close friends, the *machismo* of any Mexican male was a bit of a sore subject with me. Fun to joke about sometimes, but at other times a bit too close to home. Bob

Lewis, for example. He was not a Mexican male, but he was a male in Mexico. Would it rub off? He had been a model husband recently. But I wonder where he was last night?

"No, that's stupid," I told myself. "Not while his wife is in the hospital giving birth to their third child! That's all in the past now."

My whole frame shuddered, as if trying to shake away the thought.

Still, all I could do was hope he would not catch that plague from his new Mexican buddies. It seems to be in every *Mexicano's* blood that he has to prove to everyone else that he is the best lover, the bravest fighter, the toughest drinker, the most, the most, the most.

I knew Calderón had children all over town by the little secretaries and schoolteachers and hairdressers and waitresses. His wife used to sigh and say, "As long as he comes home and keeps us fed, he can do what he wants."

Was she serious? Who knows? On the other hand, what else could she say? He would do exactly as he wanted to do anyway. At least she got a lot of good shopping out of it, as a result.

Ofelia was not so well off. Crisanto tried his luck with the women too, but she didn't have the guts to throw him out and drive off to Guadalajara to spend his money. For one thing, they weren't so well off. She never had her own car. But she wouldn't have tried it anyway.

In fact, she confessed to me once that she had tried to kill herself.

"Kill yourself! I've never heard of anything so stupid!" I reacted without sympathy.

"But Theresa, you don't understand—"

"Why didn't you try to kill him instead? He's the one with the problem."

I got no farther with her than I had with Cloro earlier, on the subject of vasectomy. They both just shrugged and gave it no more thought. That was just the way it was.

If a young woman is not a virgin, she is a whore, in the eyes of a Mexican male. There's no "in between." If she's not a virgin, she might as well forget about making a good marriage, even with the man she had gone to bed with. The men, on the other hand, claim to need variety. The women suffer, but they accept it.

Sometimes it can be very frustrating to live in Mexico and listen to such stories from the people you love. All I could do finally was make a joke about it, as I did with Gene Smith: take one of these *macho* Mexicans for a lover, but never for a husband!

Ofelia, however, was stuck with her life. Crisanto would stray, and then they would fight. She would become distraught, Crisanto would be repentant, and Ofelia, before she knew it, was pregnant again. As if that were the answer to everything.

And now here was Calderón, leering beside my bed, about to describe some sort of group sex scene. My best buddy in Mexico, but still a man. The enemy.

I wasn't having any of it this morning. And besides, I wanted some pain pills.

"I'll break into the pharmacy," he promised. "Alma would surely send them up if she were here," he said, the corners of his eye beginning to twinkle again.

"Thanks."

He leaned down to give me a peck on the cheek and a little reassuring hug, and I held him by the shoulders. He was a massive man, all muscle, and no flab. If you saw a photograph of him, you probably would never think of him as sexy. But all (or nearly all!) the women around the Bahía de Banderas certainly seemed to respond to that mustache. He was so full of life.

And I trusted him completely with my delivery, even under what could probably best be described as "battlefield surgical conditions." I had been to his hospital before. I had seen him in action. Even if we had been caught in the jungle with only a bamboo knife, I would have felt just as confident.

"Tell that *niño* of yours to poke his head out!" he joked and patted my hand.

"I'm thinking it's going to be a *niña* this time," I said. "But she's taking her sweet time."

He was out the door before I could remind him about the pills.

Of course, he forgot. But Connie Gutiérrez proved to be just the kind of nurse I wanted. Just after lunchtime, she stuck her head in the door, looking like the cat who had swallowed the mouse.

"All the girls are down at El Patio, thinking about you," she said, with a strange smirk on her face. She was holding her hand behind her back. "They're taking bets on whether it's going to be a boy or a girl."

"Well, that makes me feel a lot better," I sulked. "The least you could have done is bring me—"

"I did!" she shouted, and out from behind her back came a big glass, filled to the brim with one of my favorite drinks, an old-fashioned. How did I recognize it from that distance? She'd even thought to put in a cherry and a slice of orange, and a silly little blue paper umbrella.

"God bless you, Florence Nightingale!" I screamed back, and made a lunge for the glass.

"Girl, you must be worse off than I thought!" she teased. "I'd better get you another one of these." She handed it over, and I slurped it down pretty quickly.

For the rest of the afternoon and into the evening, a steady stream of old-fashioneds made their way up to my hospital room—sometimes in the hands of my American girlfriends, who stopped by to check on my progress and the status of the wagers they were making down at the restaurant, at other times delivered by one of El Patio's waiters, who ran all the way up the hill carrying my drink on a spiffy little tray, with a fresh napkin.

I completely forgot about my pains.

Ofelia came back that evening and, shocked when she saw a waiter appear at the doorway with a double, she grabbed it and tried to pour it out into the rose bushes below the balcony.

"Jeeez, Ofelia! That's my medicine. Give it here!" I growled belligerently.

She gave up on me and went home. At least I think she did. I was getting pretty sleepy by that time. I dozed fitfully, but somewhat better that night.

By the next morning, I was very tired and irritated by the whole thing. I did manage to get some pills from Calderón, which was lucky since the gay crowd at El Patio had pretty much forgotten about me, and I spent the day in a kind of daze. Bob came by about noon, but there was not much for him to do. The labor pains still would not settle down into a pattern.

Ofelia didn't visit until late in the day. A Mexican woman has a busy life. She works hard, and much is expected of her. Every day she goes to church, and every day she visits her parents if they are nearby, which is almost always the case. And of course, in those days no woman had even an electric refrigerator, let alone a dishwasher, dryer, or vacuum cleaner in her house, so her daily chores occupied a great deal of time as well.

In the tropics, the tile floors are swept and washed every day with a petroleum solution that smells good to us, but not to ants and cockroaches. In the morning, the housewife must pay a visit to all the separate markets for the day's groceries. By the time everything is brought back home and put away, it is already noon, and time to begin preparing the main meal.

First she feeds the children, and then the husband arrives home to eat. She sits with him, serves him, and gives him all of her attention. When he has finished, he goes to the bedroom for a *siesta*, and she accompanies him. If she is lucky enough to have a maid, at least the food is cleared away in the kitchen and the dishes are done during that time.

When the king of her household wakes up, she has a complete change of clothes laid out on the bed for him—a fresh shirt, clean underwear and socks—to wear back for the second part of his workday. His shoes are neatly polished and ready.

Finally at about four o'clock she has some time for herself. She bathes and gets ready to go out as soon as it cools off for the evening, to take a stroll on the Malecón, or to visit with her friends.

It's not a bad life, I guess, though it would be terribly boring for me. Still, my Mexican girlfriends did not seem to mind it much. Some, mostly those who have been educated in Canada or the States, demanded more from life and got it, but mostly, I think the Mexican women don't know the difference.

Sometimes the American guests in my hotel would ask me, "Terry, how can you stand to see all the poverty down here?" But to me these people are not poor. My childhood in Indonesia taught me that to be poor is to be hungry. Unless her husband drinks, and there is no money then for food either, a Mexican woman has a rich life in a way, within her large and loving family.

Anyhow, Ofelia finally showed up as it was getting dark on the evening of my second full day in the hospital.

I was fit to be tied.

"Please, Ofelia, will you tell these bitches—I mean, these NURSES, that it's OK in America for us to have a bath if we're giving birth? They won't even listen to me." I was practically screaming. "I can't stand this another minute!"

"Oh, no, Theresa, you can't."

"The hell I can't—"

"Don't you know about it? It's dangerous if you take a bath. You could catch a cold and then the milk dries up."

"Catch a cold! OFELIA, IT'S EIGHTY DEGREES OUTSIDE!"

"Theresa, try to be calm. The doctors know best. We don't even have a bath after the child is born. For forty days." She was speaking in a very matter-of-fact tone, as if she were explaining something that ought to be perfectly obvious to any child.

"FORTY DAYS!"

"Of course. It's a *cuarentena*. Forty days. And our husband can't touch us either. We keep our socks on." She laughed. "Serves the bastards right."

My mouth fell open. I was livid, and totally struck dumb at the same time by the stupidity and irony of it all. Did they think their husbands just sat around, or took cold showers during all that time? These *machos* that we all knew and loved? All I could do was sputter. Not a word of coherent reply came to my lips.

In my midnight wanderings last night, I had heard something about the traditional childbirth in Mexico. There was another woman in labor, complaining that her man was probably out with some *chica* while she was there suffering in the hospital.

"But Doctor Calderón told me this baby was dangerous," she said. "I should not have this one at home."

She described how it was with her other babies, a fairly common scene in Mexico, apparently. The woman lay in a corner of her little *palapa* hut, while the whole family walked in and out, going about its business. The female relatives, perhaps a mid-wife sometimes, were there to assist. Meanwhile, the husband was outside, starting the party already, by giving away a lot of tequila in honor of the child he had fathered.

When the babe was born, washed, and wrapped in a blanket, the husband buried the placenta in a hole that he had dug, about a yard deep, and lined with rocks. He covered it with alternating layers of rocks and dirt, and finally at the top, he placed an earthenware pot upside down, so that the dogs and pigs and chickens could not dig it up again later.

And in the normal course of events, that seemed to be the last thing the husband had to do with his child for a good long time.

His wife, meanwhile, did not wash her body or her hair for forty days, in order to ward off the chills and the bad spirits. She never allowed her bare feet to touch the dirt floor of her hut. A bandana covered her ever greasier hair.

I was beginning to sympathize with the husband, in his search of a little "extramural" action.

"I'm already afraid that your baby's going to be drunk," lamented Ofelia, bringing me back sharply from my reverie.

"Yeah, well, I wish I had another one of those old-fashioneds right now."

"Having a baby is something holy."

"I guess that's why you all have so many of them, right?"

It was clear that I wasn't going to be very good company that evening. Ofelia didn't stick around for long, and I launched my attack on the nurses.

"*¡Por favor, señora, agua caliente!*"

"Hot water!" she repeated, horrified, with that same superior expression I had seen in Ofelia's face. I was really getting sick of that look.

"There is no hot water," she declared.

"No hot water? Shit, lady, this is a hospital, isn't it?"

"We do have hot water," she began, taking the elementary school approach that I had also heard from Ofelia. "But not at this hour. The boiler is turned off."

"Well, *enciéndala!*" I snarled, spacing out my syllables, very precisely. "Turn it on!"

"*Señora*, that is not possible."

"Of course it's possible. What are you talking about?"

"The boiler is in the garden, with all the dead people." She gestured vaguely toward the cemetery outside my window. It was now almost totally dark. "We cannot disturb the spirits. They'll get angry with us."

"You lazy—" I stopped. I needed this woman on my side later on. "I'm not afraid of the ghosts," I said. "I'll go. You just tell me where it is."

"*Señora*—"

"I mean it," I said, grappling out of bed and seizing the matches from the table beside me. "Where is it?"

She threw up her hands to indicate that she was not responsible for any craziness perpetrated by the *norteamericana*, and then pointed to a spot below my balcony. I strode out the door, leading with my large belly.

As I rounded the corner underneath my window, I spotted the boiler. I had not noticed it before, but it was not far from one of my favorite gravestones. Certainly I had had plenty of time to study them the last few days. Mexican families go all out for their monuments. This one was a beautiful Madonna, standing serenely amidst several gravesites.

I squatted way down on my knees and elbows. Some tall palm trees were whispering quietly in the distance, and there was the sound of a small mouse scurrying across the gravestones.

Fear of ghosts was not my problem. But I did ask the Virgin standing next to me to help out with the pilot light, and also with the attitude of the nurses when I got back to my room. She must have heard my prayer, because I finally got my bath. It had been over fifty hours since I was counting bricks at Las Glorias.

The next morning at eight, things started to happen very fast. They sent for Calderón, who lived just down the hill, and for Bob. The doctor arrived as I was being brought down the hall to the delivery room.

The nurses slid me onto the operating table, and WHAM! I got such a whack on the head that it ached off and on for the next two months. Or was that from the uncertain amount of gas that they gave me next? At any rate, this *holandesa* was too long for this Mexican delivery table.

Calderón was laughing as he hitched the bottle of intravenous solution back into place.

"Go next door," he told the nurse, "and ask them to bring a couple of planks over here from their construction. And tell them to hurry."

"Planks?" said the nurse, with a blank look.

I was rubbing my head. Any fool could see I wasn't going to fit on the table.

"Yes. Tell them we'll bring them right back. We don't want to buy them, just borrow them."

I screamed out in pain. This kid was on its way.

"Hold on, Theresa," said Calderón. "We'll be ready in a moment."

"It's coming! I can't wait!"

I got some more gas, the rough wooden boards were shoved up under my rear end, and my ten-pound baby daughter arrived, it seemed, all at the same moment.

Bob Lewis was relaxing on the toilet, taking a nice leisure moment with a picture magazine and a cigarette. My favorite nurse barged right in and presented him with his new daughter, enthroned as he was in the little cubicle. Probably she never gave it a second thought. Childbirth and other bodily functions are so natural in this land.

Bob was furious.

"Goddam Mexico!" he muttered. "Stupid bastards don't have the decency to let a man—"

But as soon as he saw his beautiful baby Dido, as we called her, his fury quickly turned to delight.

10

And so my Mexican daughter was born. After two American boys born in San Francisco, and welcomed into a delivery room that looked like the stainless steel drawing room of a U.F.O., this one arrived on top of a splintery wooden plank from the neighboring construction site. No wonder she made us wait three days!

The two doctors associated with my stay in the hospital could not have been more different. Bob and I paid Doctor Calderón in pesos, though it would not have been strange for that time if we had paid him in chickens or cheese, calves or pigs. In fact, soon after the birth of Dido, he found it necessary to buy a ranch in the hills above the village, in order to have a place to keep all the livestock he was receiving as payment for his doctoring.

His favorite, though, was a beautiful fighting cock, for he was a gambler and he loved the cockfights. We heard he lost as much as $50,000 in a single night—and then won it back over the next few fights.

He never sent out bills. If you couldn't pay, well, next month would be fine. What did you owe? Oh, about $300 would probably do it. It used to drive Bob Lewis crazy not to get a written bill or a receipt.

It was not that Calderón didn't care, or didn't keep track of his accounts. In fact, I've seen him meet someone on the street who was able to pay, and yell out to him, "Hey, *cabrón*, you still owe me two thousand pesos! It's been five years, hasn't it?"

In the years between this story and the writing of it, he has flourished. He is well loved in the town and has been extremely successful. Recently he has expanded the ranch to accommodate his Arabian horses.

To Dr. Blanco, then the regional director of the health department, Bob and I gave a gift of five thousand bricks, to be used for an expansion of the hospital. Later I discovered that they looked very nice in the walls of his private home. Later than that, I heard that he was in jail in Guadalajara. His sticky fingers had apparently gone on uncontrolled, at least for a time, after he left us.

He had settled in Ajijic, a beautiful mountain village on Lake Chapala, famous for its gentle breezes and tropical flowers. It's a favorite of Americans who come to retire in Mexico. There he set up a clinic and an old age home.

It seems that he was successful in frightening many of his clients with stories about the crookedness of Mexican lawyers, and in getting himself named the executor of their wills. Naturally, when they died, he managed their estates right into his own pocket—that is, until an irate heir arrived from New York in 1977 to collect her inheritance. Then his little scam died a quick death.

It would have been lovely to play the leisurely mother to a beautiful new baby daughter, but that was not the life I had arranged for myself.

I not only had an infant girl and two baby boys, I now had about a dozen teenagers in my extended family. And they needed an education fast. By March fifteenth, to be exact.

A bit earlier, as we saw the time for our grand opening approaching ever more quickly, Cloro and I had gone back up into the mountains, this time straight above us to El Mosco, to find some more boys to help us prepare the place.

I had grown to love Guilberto and Carlos so much, that I wanted several more of their brothers and sisters and cousins, if their parents were willing to send them down. The hotel maids, some more gardeners and stall boys, who doubled as carpenter's assistants while we were working on last-minute details, and Alejandro—they all came to us from the mountains. It was a wonderful opportunity for those young people to send back good money to their families.

Our bell captain Alejandro is still remembered by the guests who stayed in Hotel Las Glorias in those years, for it was his happy smile and eager handshake that first greeted them when they arrived. With a pleasant, gentle attitude, never pushy, he was always willing to do anything he could to help make people feel at home in our place, no matter how demanding they sometimes were.

Like Guilberto, he was always amazed by the size of his tips. But I wasn't. Service like those boys cheerfully gave is unusual anywhere you travel. Later, when Alejandro felt he had grown up and wanted to stretch his wings, I co-signed a loan to help him buy his first automobile. He now runs the largest taxi business in Puerto Vallarta, and he's got more money than I have.

Our first waiters at the restaurant were supplied by the families of other smuggling connections of my wily partner. In fact, we had just recently imported the boys from Quimixto, a huddle of very small *palapa* houses across the bay not far from Yelapa, where Cloro and I had landed the boat when we first went up into the mountains to get our cedar. The three brothers, Ramón, Jesús, and Luis, were from a large, gregarious family of fifteen. Their father was a fisherman.

When Cloro and I put ashore in Quimixto, we were treated to one of the most memorable meals of my life. There were mounds of fresh oysters and fish. Huge lobsters were lifted right out of the sea next to us, in an abundance I had never seen before, and cooked there on the beach. The aroma was incredible.

Yes, these boys ate well at home, though the menu they were used to was extremely limited. There were always tortillas, of course, and I saw a big hundred-pound bag of beans leaning bloated in the corner of the kitchen area of their little hut. And their father could buy coffee and sugar and salt in town. Otherwise, everything came from the sea, there at their front door. The times when they felt they could slaughter one of their few goats or pigs or chickens were rare occasions, which allowed them to have a special culinary treat.

As with all the country people, everything edible went into a single bowl, to be scooped directly into the mouth with their fingers. The education I gave these boys at Las Glorias was basic and total, and it started with an introduction to the fork and the spoon.

Jesús and his brothers are now middle-aged, and they manage some of the most elegant hotel restaurants in that part of Mexico. Many times my friends have marveled at this, have even felt sorry for me when they heard about the level of learning that we started from. But if they had been there, they would have been delighted, as I was. These boys were intelligent, and they were absolutely burning to learn everything they could.

They had been to school a little, to the government school up in the mountains maybe an hour away, perhaps long enough to be able to write their names and do very simple sums. Their lack of education up until that time was nobody's fault, just a fact of life on the Pacific Coast of Mexico. But my boys were determined to catch up quickly. And once they knew the words, they were most impressive. They had a natural Spanish elegance of body that no amount of my teaching could have given them. I was extremely lucky in that respect.

We gathered together every morning at the big blackboard in the kitchen, where I wrote everything down.

"Fork," I would say, holding the object up in front of three pairs of eager brown eyes.

"*Forrr-keh*," they repeated, rolling their R's in a way that later charmed the women they served.

"That's good enough for a start," I said proudly. I held up the next utensil. "Knife."

"*Na-feh*," they smiled broadly.

"Very good," I shouted with excitement. We hadn't begun with those words, of course. I had started out with *tenedor. . .cuchillo,* since as I said, even the objects themselves were unfamiliar. They needed a Spanish tag to put on them first.

Baby Dido had interrupted our lessons with her dramatic arrival, but now I had to get back to the guys in a hurry, and get them ready for the grand opening party. We also went shopping for outfits. Black slacks, white shirts and shoes for the first time in their lives. In the first few days some of their bright smiles may have been tarnished ever so slightly at the edges with a grimace of pain. But they only had to look around them. The successful people in Puerto Vallarta wore shoes.

We carried on.

"Tablecloth," I said. We were standing in the restaurant, while the plasterers continued working around us.

"Watch now. I shake out the tablecloth like this. Be careful not to hit anything on another table close by. I put the edge down like this, and fold it over carefully so I leave a space. Then the salt and pepper can be placed here on this part—"

Every step had to be taught to perfection. The restaurant at Las Glorias was going to be noted for its elegant dining, to suit our elegant surroundings. I would not stand for anything sloppy in this operation.

Well of course, there was Pepe, but that's another story. One day Cloro approached me shyly while I was showing Carlos how the swimming pool would have to be cleaned every morning. My partner had his arm around a really revolting greaseball friend of his, with skin almost black from the sun.

"Doña Theresa," he smiled.

"Uh-oh," I thought. "This is not encouraging."

"This is *mi amigo* Pepe. We have worked together for years. I told him I was certain that there was a job for him here at the new hotel."

"I can't imagine what it would be, Cloro," I said carefully, trying to signal him with the look of alarm in my eyes. "I've already started training all of our waiters and bellboys."

I looked at the man's dirty shorts, slung as low as the laws of physics would allow, under a huge belly in front, and with his crack showing a little bit in back. It was difficult even to smile pleasantly, when faced with those fat tits hanging down almost to his waist.

"Well, we must have some job—"

"No, I think we have all the help we need, Cloro," I answered in an even tone. "Perhaps you could help him at another place."

Cloro smiled and told Pepe he would get back to him. My jaw dropped.

"Why did you tell him that?" I exploded, when the man had oozed his way out of hearing. "We can't use anybody who looks like that! I've seen him around with you. He never wears a shirt. His feet are filthy in those huaraches."

"Theresa—"

"We want to run a class operation here. You know that. Everything we've tried to do—"

"Theresa, I told him he would have work." He looked at me significantly. I looked back deeply into his eyes. Cloro had never made demands, never even a strong request, like this one. I never did come to understand what was behind it, but I felt the man knew something, and that this job was a way of paying him off. He *would* have work at Las Glorias. The only real question facing us was what kind of work?

"Look at him, Cloro. What can we possibly do with a man who looks like that? The guests—"

"There must be some place where he won't be seen very much."

Then I got a brilliant idea.

And from that day on, El Slimeball came to work at six in the morning to rake the beach. He made sure the sand under the neat rows of individual *palapas* was smooth and free from trash, and ready for our pampered American guests. And I in turn made sure that Pepe's workday was over and that he had disappeared from view before my guests got up in the morning. It was a perfect solution, as long as I kept track of him.

But more of that later.

The training continued. The rest of the staff were good-looking young people with a smart outlook, but without a sly or nasty attitude. We deliberately chose kids who were "clean," who had had no experience at another hotel or restaurant, so that they had not picked up any dirty tricks. And of course it helped immeasurably that Cloro knew their families. If they got into trouble with us, we knew their fathers would back us up. The kids knew that they would be sent back home, for the hotels were organized enough in those days so that nobody else would hire them if any one of us had had trouble.

Luckily, the problem never came up for us, at least until the unions got organized.

In the early days of March, we started to have trial servings in the restaurant. I had kept the menu simple—shrimp, lobster, red snapper, steak—so there was not much reading or writing necessary. I always managed it so that the girl at the cashier's station was good with numbers.

My waiters learned how to prepare the tables, how to arrange all of our new silverware and glassware at each place, and how to fold the napkins stylishly. They caught on quickly how to stand at attention at the doorway, with a blinding white napkin carefully folded over each left forearm, to greet the guests as they entered, if possible by name.

That paid off too. Many of our clients stayed for weeks, and returned year after year. They loved to be remembered, to be made to feel special in this way.

Señor Sánchez, a professional from Mexico City and at that time the *maître d'* at the Posada Vallarta, came in to help us with the flaming desserts, our finishing touch.

Two months before, these boys had never even seen a hotel or a restaurant. By the time he was finished with his brief lessons, they were operating the chafing dishes like pros, turning out *bananas flambés and crêpes suzettes* under the watchful eyes of our guests, with such an elegant flourish that it was hard to remember they hadn't been doing it all their lives.

They started to learn how to tell the difference between an old-fashioned and a whiskey sour, and the other standard American cocktails. For an *aperitivo*, they could recommend the octopus cocktail with a naughty little gleam in their eye that would melt the hardest resistance. They really became a marvelous crew.

And an added benefit was that they all became big brothers and sisters to my own kids.

Once we got a schedule established and they had learned the basics, they didn't want to stop.

"Please teach us English," asked Ramón one day. I was flattered.

So the lessons continued.

"The floor," I said, pointing, "the ceiling." We were still gathered around the familiar blackboard in the kitchen.

Usually the boys reported to work at seven in the morning. There was a pot of beans going for their breakfast. By eleven o'clock, everything had been cleaned up and we were ready for lunch. But since we didn't start serving until one-thirty or two, there was time for a lesson before I went to the bank.

After we had named everything in the place, I started in on the verbs, which are hard in English, because so many of them are irregular. The boys took everything in stride, and their minds absorbed everything easily. It's absolutely thrilling how quickly a student learns if he has the motivation. They loved it! And I loved having the opportunity to teach them, because they really had soul.

As for the others, the bellboys, the maids, and the gardeners, it was not so necessary for them to know how to read or speak much English. They never did sign for their checks with more than a thumbprint, as the bricklayers had done many months before. But those kids I taught more about the American ways, and they learned fast those things they needed to know in order to do a good job of babysitting for the younger guests when they came down to Las Glorias with children.

"Want a babysitter?" I would ask, when I saw a wild or frustrated look in a mother's eye. "Gregorio is available the whole week."

I stepped outside the door of the office and whistled. We had a system: three whistles for one, four for another, five for still another one. Quickly Gregorio came hustling over from where they had their quarters near the stables. He looked sharp in the uniforms that all the gardeners and maids and bellboys wore: white shirts, well-cut beige trousers or skirts, and *huaraches*, since for the kind of work they did, it didn't matter if their toes stuck out.

So an American couple with two or three children, if they wanted to go out dancing or spend a day on a fishing excursion, could be easy in their minds that their kids were safe and also having fun back at the hotel. And the children had a ball riding horses or swimming with our guys, who were sometimes little more than kids themselves. If there were smaller children, who had diapers that needed changing, my maids were good at taking care of them. Our young people made some extra money, the guests could relax more, and everybody was happy.

Las Glorias was a beehive of activity in those first two weeks of March. Everyone pitched in gladly and did all the strange and unforeseen jobs that came up at the last minute. Even Gene Smith and his wife had arrived and were fluttering around, offering suggestions. Our other investors were arriving, to join us for the opening.

The brick walkways were now finished, and they crisscrossed the property to each one of the bungalows. Every few feet of the way, a low mushroom-shaped lamp gave off a cozy glow in the early evening and into the night. I had brought in exotic bougainvilleas and hibiscus plants, to give color to every corner of the gardens. A beautiful new fence hid the stables and the carpentry shop from the view of our future guests.

One morning, when we had about a week to go before the banquet, Cloro and I stood on the airport highway, at the edge of our property.

"Well, you got your angels, *mi amigo*," I said, surveying the finishing touches being put on our elegant entrance driveway.

Cloro was beaming. The one contribution to the decor that he had insisted upon was, that since Las Glorias means "heaven," the grand arch should be flanked by angels. And now, there they were, kneeling in front of us.

"*Muy hermosos—¿no, Theresa?*" he said proudly, as he took in the whole effect.

"Yes, they are beautiful, Cloro," I agreed. A sigh of relief escaped my lips.

At first his suggestion had seemed rather tacky to me. I was excited by the concept of our driveway, winding like a boulevard toward the office, with an island of palm trees dividing the two lanes. The roadways were paved like a checkerboard, alternating black and white blocks of cobblestones about a yard square, in an imitation of the old Dutch tiles that I loved so much in my childhood. The floor tiles of the office and the restaurant continued this theme. But concrete angels brooding at the entrance?

Now, just off the highway, we had a grandiose archway about twenty-five feet wide and at least that high. On a pedestal at each end of it was a concrete statue depicting an angel at prayer, his wings extended impressively behind him. Actually, the whole thing blended together rather nicely now, and I was glad I hadn't resisted Cloro's idea too strongly. He had really had his heart set on those angels.

Perhaps they were blessing the future of our whole operation. Who was I to argue with that?

Or maybe they were there to explain to the Mexican cows about the cattleguard. Animals still roamed freely on the highways in those days, and still do, actually. At least there we tried to prevent them from joining us in the hotel—although sometimes they came onto the property next to the beach, and we always had fun chasing them off with coconuts.

I spotted one of the investor's wives walking toward us. "Hey, Brenda, do you want to come to church with me?" I called.

"Church? Do we have time?"

She came up to us, looking very sporty and neat in one of her small, tailored summer outfits. Her skin was white as porcelain, and her hair was perfect in her little hairnet, fastened into a bun on top of her head. Even so, she couldn't help brushing aside an imaginary strand with a hand that showed off a large diamond, and her nails polished to perfection. She always made me feel like an ox.

But I didn't have time to worry about that. I was a working girl. Besides, though I was often in sweaty workclothes, I was proud of the outfit I had on a hanger back in my bedroom, ready to dazzle everybody at the banquet.

"I've got to go down and talk to the *padre*," I explained. "We want to invite him to the inauguration, so he can—what do you call it?—baptize the whole shootimadoo."

"So he can what?"

"In Mexico the priest is there for the beginning of everything," I continued. "You know, he needs to baptize it."

"I think that's only for babies."

"Well, whatever it is. He has to benedict the place. Sprinkle holy water on the walls—I don't know. Maybe at the door of the restaurant? No, I suppose with the bar in there—"

I wasn't sure how you brought a cluster of buildings into this world. Perhaps next to the entrance to the office?

"That's a new one," laughed Brenda. "But I guess the good Lord should be in on it, all right. This is already paradise!"

"That's right." I nodded, and tried again. "What do you call it when they do it with a ship?" I asked. "And a bottle of champagne?"

"Yeah, OK. That's a—" She had to think a minute. "It's a christening, isn't it?"

Well, isn't that what I said? Sometimes I'm so unsure of my English, but I guess I don't always need to be.

"Let's go find the *padre*," I shouted over my shoulder, already striding toward the station wagon. "He'll be in his sacristy now after mass, having a bit of bourbon or cognac to greet the second part of his day."

I felt her stiffen a little. I had forgotten her attitude about drinking, but it was too late. I plunged on ahead. "We can catch him there if we hurry," I added. Our priest was so jolly that I was sure he would charm her anyway.

Soon we were both sitting in the small sacristy of Father Aldana, one of my favorite characters in Puerto Vallarta. "I'm here to invite you officially to our opening party, *padre*," I told him.

"Yes, I've been hearing all about it! The town is buzzing with the news." He peered out at us over his little metal-rimmed eyeglasses. "You are very socialistic to invite all the workers and their families."

"They have all helped us so much," I agreed. "Will you come and bless the place?"

The father looked pleased. He was clearly a Roman Catholic holy man, but I couldn't get the thought of a Buddha out of my head, seeing him sitting there so placidly with his hands folded across his big belly. The only movement that broke up the serenity was an occasional slow reach for his cognac.

He saw me studying him. "Ladies," he said smiling good-naturedly, "I need my drink, to start working on my sermon for tomorrow. All you sinners—" He shook his head and looked to the corner of the ceiling, as if the subject were too much to contemplate.

"Ask him what he will talk about tomorrow, Terry," whispered Brenda, when I had explained it to her briefly.

I relayed the question.

"I will explain to all my sheep about the wonderful rising of our Christ—" he began. "But does the lady understand Spanish?" he asked suddenly.

"No, but perhaps one of your English Sundays she will come. You'd better be nice to her. She is rich and wants to do something for the church," I warned him.

He made a broad gesture as if to thank the heavens. "Theresa, tell her my liquor cabinet is almost empty. She can fill that up, and it will help everyone!" The *padre* laughed gleefully, smacking his lips. I was at a loss about how to translate.

"*Padre*, she doesn't approve of drinking very much."

He laughed even harder. "How boring that must be…eh, Theresa?" He was patting me on the knee to make his point.

Brenda looked more and more lost. I needed to finish up this business and get back to the hotel.

"Father, we'll be honored to have you there. I'll send my truck to pick you up on the fifteenth."

"No need for that, *mi hija*," he smiled. "One of the taxi drivers is paying for his sins. Many sins!" he emphasized. "He drives me everywhere, to the parties and the funerals."

We got up, and I gave Brenda a look that I hoped meant, "I'll tell you later."

"*Mi querida*, my dear, I wouldn't miss your party," he smiled, his jowls bouncing. "Just tell that old sinner Cloro to have a pouch of money ready for me, and two small pouches for the altar boys too."

He pressed my hand warmly and we started through the door.

"And of course the best bourbon!" he called out after me.

I was right. Brenda was charmed—though it helped that some of the remarks got lost in the translation.

Later on toward evening, I was back in the restaurant with our friend Daniel Lechón, watching him put the finishing touches onto the grand painting behind the bar along one side of the room. This work of art was really going to make our reputation in Puerto Vallarta! Bob had met the painter at the *charreada*, and we had all become friends.

We now had a small, original Lechón on the walls of each one of the bunga-lows, depicting a charming Mexican scene. His style and his subjects could not be called primitive, but yet they were realistic and rural, showing women carrying their water jugs down a mountain trail, for example, or bending over at the river, washing their clothes under a familiar *palapa*.

And now, for the *pièce de resistance*, Bob had commissioned this huge mural of the Mexican gentlemen's sport. It stretched the whole length of the bar, about twenty-five feet, arcing up to a height of six feet in the middle. I was spellbound, and I sat there for hours, as many of our friends also did later on.

There was the round *charreada* ring, exactly as it looked just down the beach toward the village. In the middle of the huge painting, an elegant horseman in his elaborate outfit had just thrown out a rope and cinched the rear legs of a calf, still caught in mid-air. At the one end several men stood or squatted in a group, evaluating the style of the *charro*, and cheering him on. Near them was a horse and rider just leaving the arena, having cleared the sand for the coming event. At the other end of the bar, the next competitor was preparing himself to enter the ring, and his friends gathered around him, their faces full of high enthusiasm for the sport.

But what really drew Puerto Vallarta's "horsy" crowd from that time on was the fascination of seeing themselves immortalized on our wall. For the faces did not come from the imagination of Daniel Lechón. There, astride his horse at the one end and waiting to enter the ring, was my favorite Doctor Calderón with a big hat and a broad smile, surrounded by several of his buddies. At the other end my Bob and Rafael de la Cruz were standing at the fence, talking and pointing at something. Miguel Salinas, the rich son of a Mexican senator, was shown in a last-minute inspection of his exquisite quarter horse. The whole work was filled with tense, but happy movement. Altogether, along the impressive sweep of it were eleven horses, and most of the friends we saw every Sunday.

The gold and brown rodeo colors of the painting blended in beautifully with the rich cedar of the bar and the orange color of the beach chairs outside and the table cloths that we used inside for breakfast and lunch. (At night, we brought out the white linen.)

The restaurant itself rose slightly and came to a point at the beach end, resembling the prow of a ship putting out toward the sea. Through the louvered windows, the diners could see the palms and the lush gardens at their sides, and the waves beckoning in front of them. Of course, if they stood closer to the windows, the illusion was broken by a view of the smaller terraces on the way to the beach, and the larger patio on the other side, surrounding the swimming pool.

Behind the bar in the kitchen I could hear all the busy preparations underway for our grand opening party. The restaurant could seat 160 guests comfortably, but our buffet on March 15 would be attended by many more than that.

The chef Xavier was starting to assume the look and demeanor of an army general, as he attended to all the details.

I grabbed a rum and Coke and drifted out into the deep blue twilight. The place was like a fairyland! —much more beautiful than I could ever have imagined when Luis Alvarez and I looked at his first sketches. The small mushroom lamps gave off an orange-gold glow that was just enough to provide safety on the walkways, but not to interfere with the sunset or the profound mystery of the starlight.

It was this mysterious quality, the fabulous calm of the place that brought our guests back year after year.

If they wanted action and people, they could stay in the busy restaurant, or the bar with its small combo, or the conversation pit around the fireplace. You could spend days there and at the swimming pool without ever being bored. In fact, my friend Penny told me she did just that for weeks, even though she was not registered as a guest, before I even knew she existed. Our place provided a spacious haven of that sort.

But if you wanted the peace that I felt this night, you could also have that. Some of our guests lived at Hotel Las Glorias for months, even years.

At $35 a week in those days, they had a beautiful large room with a kitchenette. The bedroom could be divided from the sitting room by a large drape of hand-woven *manta*, that specially fine Mexican cotton that I had bought by the bale in Guadalajara. I had been keeping my seamstresses busy for months, making the draperies and the upholstery and the bedspreads in all of the luscious Mexican colors that have now become so fashionable.

Of course the guests also had maid service and clean linen every day for that price. Truly a paradise.

I strode across the sand to where the waves shimmered in the moonlight. The thought of my imminent entry into Mexican society kept coming up in my mind. I had never before given a party so big.

For my mother, that was nothing. When I was a little girl in Indonesia, I used to love it when my parents gave the *slametan*, a ceremony of well-wishing to celebrate the marriage of a couple of our servants, or the arrival of the first-born son, or the Islamic New Year.

In a proper *slametan* among the native Indonesians, everything was carefully prepared according to strict rules, and all the details properly carried out. The women spent the whole day cooking the spicy dishes for the feast. At sunset, a special messenger was sent out to invite all the male guests to enter the house and seat themselves in a big circle around large bamboo mats laden with food. Their women were permitted to observe them from an area behind a curtain. Special prayers were said in Malayan, and then the men ate small, ceremonial portions of the food without speaking, before they brought the major portion of the meal home to their families.

Indonesian food reminded me in many ways of some of our Mexican dishes. We too used to wrap our *tamales* in banana leaves, as they do in the Yucatán. And as children, some of our favorite desserts were the sweet plantains or breadfruit, or a mess of sweet *tamales*, stuffed with raisins and nuts.

At our home in Malang, however, the strict Moslem ceremony of the *slametan* gave way to joviality, as our father and mother presided at a long table filled with children and friends and servants, laughing and talking all together for long hours. For unlike many of the colonial wives, my mother loved these people and had learned their soft, exquisite language.

Finally, at the end of the evening, when we were all dreaming only of Bromoseltzer, my mother would send the servants back to the *kampong*, each with a small gift in remembrance of the event.

Then there were the grander parties when other planters came down from the mountains to Malang, to restock their company stores with provisions. Instead of staying at a hotel, they were always welcome at our house. For a while in those years, our life seemed to be one endless party.

Long rows of Model T's were always lined up outside our front door. The women sat in the gardens with their graceful silk dresses and big picture hats, languorously sipping a whiskey julep and watching their men talk of the plantations or their polo ponies.

The only problem my mother had at a time like that was deciding where she wanted to be! She herself had designed some of the women's silk dresses, but she had also won prizes in the jockey club for horseracing. All the conversations, all the groups seemed tempting to her, and she was at the height of our gay society there in Java.

Little by little my father and the other men began to show up in the brilliant white uniforms of the Dutch Indonesian army.

How elegantly my father's fine hands moved to adjust a braid or to fasten his sword!

And then, imperceptibly, the looks became more and more preoccupied, the talk more and more in whispers, as the Japanese moved closer to the islands.

A friend, an Australian pilot, came to my parents and urged them to flee with him to the safety of the British commonwealth. Late into the night, we girls listened to the raised voices of our mother and father in their bedroom.

"I have my jewelry, Freddy. We have as much cash as we need. Please, Freddy!"

I can still hear her voice, pleading but proud, and edged with a certain hint of disappointment, since she already knew what his response would be:

"I must fight for my queen!"

My mother thought of taking us children high up into the mountains to our summer house, with the beautiful rose gardens and the swimming pool and the captivating echoes down into the valleys on all sides. How we loved that place!

But ultimately there was really nowhere safe on Java, where people could escape the Japanese. We stayed in Malang.

We had a fortune, and we lost it.

I kicked an errant pebble into the calm waters of the Pacific and watched the moon rise higher over the dark mountains of the Sierra Madre behind me. My thoughts traveled on to Holland, where quickly my father and mother had made another fortune after the war. That one I chose to throw away, from myself at least.

When the rest of the Dutch were still on strict rations and food coupons, still only dreaming of the days when they would again have enough sugar and eggs, or butter or meat, we were already eating imported oysters from Turkey. Or we were topping off our endless shopping excursions to The Hague with a sherry or two at an elegant tea dance, and probably far too many croquettes and Dutch bitter balls.

"How many evening dresses do you think you'll need?" my mother would say as we entered La Bonneterie, the royal outfitters to the queen.

In a strange way she loved to spend time going shopping, but ironically, her impatience also broke out, at almost the moment we entered a shop.

"You think four will do it? All right. Go ahead and take them. Hurry up!"

It was always, hurry up! The salesgirls received a little gift of bonbons or perfume at the end of the ordeal, and the bill was automatically sent back to the office in Rotterdam.

We would go into Bally, the Swiss importers of fine shoes and boots. "OK, now," she ordered, like a military commander in the line of fire, "find something you like. Take ten pairs, so we don't have to come back for a while." Already in those days, shoes at Bally cost more than most Dutch workers made in a day or two. Yet six months later, we found ourselves there again, and again in a hurry.

"Just find what you want, and let's get the hell out of here."

Once we bought them, our clothes were never safe from my mother, even in the security of our own closets.

"Where's that red sweater I loved so much?" I would call out to her in a frantic teen-age voice. Or I remember panicking, on the first morning back home from school in Rome or Switzerland or Spain: "I can't find my favorite robe!"

She would come into my room singing, "What are you looking for, honey?"

And then came the defiant look that was intended to take all the guilt off herself and put it on me. "Oh that," she would say, tossing off the subject as if it was beneath our concern. "I had to give it to your cousin. You know they don't have any money."

She cut off my adolescent screech of protest: "We'll go buy you another one."

I think she wasn't buying us clothes so much as she was buying our time, providing an occasion when she could be together with her daughters. But Helen and I, on the other hand, would have given anything to have spent an afternoon in the privacy of our own rooms, just reading a good book.

"Damn half-bloods," we sneered, behind our mother's back. She would never stand for such words, even though they were her husband's family, not hers. She always considered us blessed; she was always grateful for the spectacular recovery we had made in Rotterdam after the war, even though both she and my father had also worked very hard to achieve it.

He in his quiet, professorial way, and she flamboyantly, a real go-getter—they made an unbeatable combination in the Dutch pharmaceutical business after the war. Not even her game leg, still painful from the wounds suffered in the concentration camp, prevented her from scrambling up the ship's ladders and confronting the officers above.

"I have a list right here," she would tell the ships' captains as soon as they became regular customers. "It's for about a thousand dollars. Next trip you make, I want these food items. You know, they're impossible to find in Holland."

The captains beamed slyly at the small, gutsy lady whose smuggling instincts had not been stifled just because the war had ended.

"I'll have your drugs waiting in exchange for this list when you return," she promised, sealing the agreement with a conspiratorial grin.

My parents' secret was really no secret at all. Holland, especially Rotterdam, was booming in those post-war years. Every time a ship crossed the line, the equator, by law the drug supply had to be refurbished. We gave excellent service at our pharmacy, and first-rate products.

We mixed our own cough medicines, and our own aspirin pills, we made our own penicillin and sulfa tablets. The directions were printed on our bottles in twenty-seven different languages. In time, big trucks delivered our medicines to 5,000 families all over Rotterdam.

My father had a safe in the pharmacy, but we all knew the combination to it, and we could walk in at any time to get "pin money," as he called it. Five hundred, a thousand dollars at a time. We could never take too much. After all, on a good night he often got ten times that amount in cash from the tankers in the harbor.

He was already paying over eighty percent in taxes, and the Russians were at our doorstep, as he said, already halfway across Germany. Anything could happen. We had our jewelry, and we were ready to leave Holland too, if we had to.

We may have played hard, at the Christmas party at the yacht club in our leopard coats, or riding at the jockey club and showing off our supple boots, but we all worked hard too. In those early years, even Helen and I spent every afternoon after school at the pharmacy, sterilizing thousands of little bottles—and grumbling like typical teenagers.

We dutifully made our appearance at the opera or the symphony in beautiful new gowns, and greeted all the correct old farts of the Dutch society. (That is, if Helen wasn't able to come up with the sneezes, which she often conveniently did.) Even my mother got bored with that after a while, so we knew that she would always accompany my father to the Opéra in Paris, to show off her diamonds, but in Amsterdam, she made him go alone.

Every winter we went to the same hotel in Switzerland for skiing. There was the same orchestra playing some tired old tango, or the same gray old men with their violins and their ancient waltzes. Helen and I used to beg our father to find another place.

Now when I think back on it, I can sympathize more with my father. We probably weren't very likable in those days.

But after all, we girls were made to sit all dressed up at a table with our family. If we danced the predictable dances, we danced with our own predictable half brothers from the same table, themselves all decked out in their stiff tuxedos. And we looked yearningly across the room at the young men who, we told ourselves, were our boyfriends. At their own table, they suffered under the same tyranny.

I do remember enjoying the times we played hostess to the officers of American battleships and submarines, as they came into the harbor at Rotterdam.

For wealthy young girls in a port city in those years, it was considered our social duty to welcome the handsome young officers at a proper formal dance, or to accept dinner invitations with them, in a group, on their ships. We spoke English, we liked showing them around our city, and sometimes we even invited them to our homes. It was great fun. I guess that's where I learned how much I enjoyed being a hostess, and how easy it was for me to make people feel at their ease.

Well, my marriage to Bob Lewis ended forever that chapter of my life as a Dutch socialite. I must say, I had no regrets on that score.

And now, on my own, and in a climate that was a considerable improvement over that of Rotterdam, I was about to blossom again and become *La Holandesa*, the hostess of Puerto Vallarta!

11

We had thought of everything. Absolutely every detail. And it was a good thing too, because it was March fifteenth, and people were already starting to arrive.

I had just squeezed myself into a nifty show-stopper of an outfit—Chinese red silk, tight in the bodice and covered with tiny black tassels, so that the dress was in motion long after I was! Right when I was reaching for my diamonds, Lupita entered with other plans. She handed me my baby for the late afternoon feeding.

I sighed and grabbed for the zipper in back.

"Thank God for that," snarled Bob. "I'd hate to think that we'd have to stop the party later, while you whipped it out and fed the kid. I don't think I'll ever get used to the way these Mexican squaws carry on—"

"It's natural, Bob," I replied in an irritatingly calm voice, and sat down with Dido.

Nothing was going to spoil this day.

However, I couldn't resist adding, "Besides, I'm not a Mexican woman. I'm Dutch. It's this baby of yours here, who has the Indian blood."

I bit my tongue, thankful that at that moment the boys came running into our cramped bedroom. They looked adorable in the long blue and white knee socks and white shorts that Bob had brought down from California. Gene Smith followed close behind them.

"Terry, have you got a safety pin? Elizabeth can't get her dress fastened." He was half-way in the door when he saw me breast-feeding Dido. "Oops!" he gulped, and turned bright red.

"Sure, Gene. Lupita, *el señor necesita un seguro*," I said, motioning for her to look in the mess on top of my dresser. Our proper American investor was looking at the floor, trying to figure out how to back himself out of the doorway without seeming to move or call attention to himself.

"I'm covered, Gene." I grabbed a clean diaper and tossed it onto my shoulder, but I really didn't need to. "It's nothing you don't see on the beach every day," I assured him.

"You ready for the reception line, buddy?" said Bob with a grimace. He hated functions like this where he might be expected to speak Spanish. It wasn't as if he actually tried to speak it on such occasions. He just didn't want to be exposed, I guess.

Gene was not proving to be of any support. "You're crazy, man. I'm what you call a silent partner," he said, laughing and shoving Bob into the wall with his elbow.

"Well, you boys, anyway," Bob continued, looking down at Bear and Buster. "You know how to shake hands like gentlemen, don't you?"

The boys looked up at him with big, questioning eyes. They had become such genuine little Mexican boys that it was hard for them sometimes to understand their father's English.

Of course their blank response did little to improve Bob's mood. "I need another drink," he growled.

I made a mental note to get to Jesús the bartender first thing, and ask him to be careful how much liquor he put in Bob's drinks. It was going to be a long evening.

I handed Dido back to Lupita. Gene proposed a small toast, and the three of us raised our glasses there in the tiny bedroom of Mr. LaPorte's house, where it all began.

Elizabeth came in and joined us just as the glasses touched our lips. "To Hotel Las Glorias!" she joined in. "Terry, can you believe that not much more than a year ago, Gene and I were walking along this beach, and we didn't even know each other? You've done a marvelous job. The whole place looks like it's been in business for months."

I smiled and thanked her. It was important to me that my investors were happy. After all, it would still be some years before the large amounts of their money would be repaid and they could start to realize a profit from our venture.

In the meantime, it didn't seem to matter much to them, I discovered, as long as they were able to continue coming down to paradise to "check on the operation"!

As we entered the restaurant, we found that most of the people who were already there were standing clustered around the bar, admiring Daniel Lechón's magnificent painting of the *charreada*. They were finding their own portraits, and teasing each other.

"*Oye*, Calderón! Your poor horse, *amigo!*" It's true that the doctor's big belly was prominent on the wall in front of us. But we all knew too, that in spite of his build, he was one of the most agile among us. Bob and I even taught him to play tennis later. Their joking didn't bother him a bit. His jovial laugh rang out above all the others.

Across the room I spotted Bill and Nellie Wulff, who had arrived in Puerto Vallarta many years before, when no one had heard of it. They now owned its most fashionable restaurant, the El Dorado, where all the engineers and architects and lawyers hung out every afternoon, sitting for hours discussing business and ogling. The food was good, the atmosphere was warm, but the real attraction of the place seemed to be a good view of the action just outside.

The Playa de los Muertos, in spite of its grim name, was still *the* "social beach" of the village. It was there on my very first day in town that I met Tiburón the Shark.

The Wulffs had become good friends in these months. And although technically we were in competition with each other, our feeling was more that we were all co-developers of the great potential we saw for Puerto Vallarta.

Bill came up to give me a big hug. "*¡Mi güera!*" he always called me—"My little blondie! It's beautiful."

His embrace was overwhelming, half to show me how close to me he felt and how much he admired what we had done with Las Glorias, and half to check out my tits, as he always did with every woman in the room. If there was ever any doubt in my mind on that score, not three minutes later I saw him do the same thing with Georgia, my friend the erotic painter. As he enveloped her in his big arms, he caught the eye of Rafael de la Cruz over her shoulder, and in sign language, the unmistakable message read: "Great fuck, this one!"

He was a tall, good-looking man, and there was no denying his appeal to the ladies, even though his eyes were beginning to droop a bit by then, betraying the fact that he had had perhaps too many drinks, had screwed too much after too many all-night dances.

But over *my* shoulder, the most he could have said was: "Too bad! I don't know about her yet." And I was determined to keep it that way.

"Great-looking dress," said his beautiful wife, as she came up to us. From Nellie Wulff, who ran an exclusive dress shop in the village and sold to all the wealthy and famous who visited us, that was quite a compliment. She tossed back her long blond hair to show off a fabulous diamond earring.

"Thanks," I said. "I love to tell Serena what I want, and then pick up the finished dress later. She's a genius with a needle!"

"You designed that? I'm going to have to hire you to work in the shop in your spare time!"

"Great!" I laughed. "Give me a call in about twenty years!"

Cloro Palacios and his wife Nemecia stood off to one side, trying to blend into the wall.

I just didn't know how to deal with them, so I put it off for the moment. Here he was, an equal partner with me in the whole venture from the beginning. We were standing on his land. We were good friends. Yet many of us in the room had been to the university. My *norteamericano* investors had contributed many thousands of dollars to the project. Now Cloro, former mayor of the village and still majority owner of the place, was feeling his lack of education and wealth. He looked as if he would rather be out on his canoe at that moment.

Luckily I didn't have much time to dwell on it, because just then Father Aldana arrived with a big flourish. He had two darling altar boys in tow, looking too hot already in their little cassocks.

He strode up to the bar, beaming at everyone in turn, and handed over the holy water to the bartender Jesús (which I thought was appropriate) and admonished him to put it in a safe place until it would be needed later. The *padre* himself needed a bit of fortification before beginning the important ceremony.

He surveyed the room quickly and saw to his relief that Cloro was approaching with the bourbon. And my partner, in turn, looked much more comfortable now that he had a particular duty to perform.

They went off to one of the side tables to begin the pre-ceremony. I saw that Cloro didn't joke around with the father like I did; instead he remained somewhat formal, to show his respect for the office. But at least he was on more solid ground now.

Nemecia meanwhile remained pinned against the wall by the doorway.

The marimba band had set up over by the fireplace, where we also had a small dance floor, and they started playing. The altar boys went straight for the food.

We had asked the Chinese owner of La Iguana Restaurant and his Mexican wife to cater for us, and the spread was beautifully arranged. They had put out a huge table of delicate hors d'oeuvres near the bar for the special guests, our wealthy investors and friends from the States, and society ladies like Evelyn Muir, of the San Francisco Muirs, who had built herself a house in Gringo Gulch.

However, half the people there, several hundred by now, were our carpenter's apprentices, our bricklayers and their families, our *burro* suppliers, the guys who had dug the trenches to bring us the very water we were using now. For them in another area, we had great iced tubs full of *cerveza*, and whole barbecued chickens, to be cut up into pieces and served with a huge salad, Mexican style.

I had coached Esteban, Ramón, Alejandro, and all of my bellboys and maids to float around quietly in the background and, without drawing any attention to themselves, to try to steer the rich toward the shrimp and the *langostinitos*, and the others, who probably wouldn't care one way or the other anyway, toward the beer.

And I spent a lot of time fluttering around nervously, overseeing everything, making sure they did their job without hurting anyone's feelings, and worrying about whether there was going to be enough food at either table.

This was the life I had bargained for, right?

Miguel Salinas strode in with his wife Lola, and the room went quiet for a moment. Even the sounds of the marimbas grew softer.

He was wearing pistols as he often did, since his father had been murdered several years back, when it was said he had a chance for the presidency. But it was the charisma of this man, not his weapons or his bodyguards, that brought a hush to the room. He had the power to commandeer all eyes, all attention, wherever he went.

I looked into those proud eyes, little guessing how our lives were linked, that one day the Mafia would offer me four thousand dollars to throw acid into that handsome face, and still less that I would be tempted to do it, if only for a brief, mad moment.

Of course all eyes in the room were also on the perfect figure and face of Lola, who wore an incredible set of emeralds, to show off her deep green eyes and her creamy Spanish complexion.

Behind them was one of my true buddies, tall, jolly Candelario Ramos, who in 1966 was Chief of Immigration. I must say he helped me through a tight spot or two in the years to come.

It's funny how things turn out. Less than ten years later, when he was Chief of Police, and I was in Vancouver on vacation, I saw him there on Canadian television in connection with a big drug scandal in Puerto Vallarta. But he was not the arresting officer in that news story. He himself was the one being led off in handcuffs.

Drugs seemed a long way off from us on that fresh, innocent evening. They didn't actually become very important to our area until the highway opened in 1969, and the invasion of all the young Americans began. Candelario was much more interested that night in hanging on his fascinating date, Sondra Cellini.

"Sondra! How's the grape business?" I asked. She was building a ranch and a vineyard up at Talpa, high up in the all but inaccessible mountains above Las Glorias, near where I had found my Guilberto and Alejandro.

"I drove my truck down. What a mistake! Took me twelve hours," she moaned, "but I had to get supplies." I nodded in sympathy, since the usual trip, by small plane, took only fifteen minutes. She was just starting to tell me about *My Darling Bastards*, the book she had begun writing about her illegitimate children, when the *padre* stood up, indicating that he was finally ready to begin with the official reason for the party.

"OK, everybody," I shouted out, clapping my hands to try to get the complete attention of the people in the room and also those on the patios outside. "Padre Aldana has agreed to bless this place."

The marimbas stopped. The Americans looked stunned and a little nervous. The Mexicans looked only half interested. "I need everyone's attention," I pleaded.

What I really needed was a drink.

I signaled Jesús for another rum and Coke, and threaded my way over to the bar to collect it and the vial of holy water. There it shone, placed carefully atop a little towel, which had been intricately worked by some loving hand.

Bob stood nearby, talking to his friend Gordon, who had come down from San Francisco.

"Why don't we all stand here in a group?" I said, full of nervous expectation. I looked around for Lupita, to see if she could bring the children in, so that we could make it a real family event.

"Cloro, bring Nemecia over here too." He was approaching shyly with the priest. "And the Smiths? Where are they?" I clapped my hands. "We need all the investors up here for the blessing!"

Have you ever had a dream where you are talking, but nobody hears it? You know you are talking because your lips are moving, and the words make sense to you, but everybody looks straight through you as if you are invisible. That was exactly the scene at that moment in the bar.

Bob Lewis turned back to finish the joke he was telling Gordon. Instead of decreasing, the laughter seemed to increase over near the food table. Cloro looked as if he would rather risk a shoot-out with Miguel than suggest to his wife that she should give up the security of her wall.

"OK!" I sang out, raising my cheeriest contralto almost to a screech. "We're nearly ready, everybody!" I handed the holy water to the *padre*, but apparently he didn't want to mess with it quite yet. He needed his hands free for the prayers. I gulped down the whole rum and Coke and slid it over to Jesús for a refill.

Well, it was not a family group, in the sense that everyone was facing forward at the same time, or even in the same direction, but it was perhaps the most I could hope for, under the circumstances. My boys were even on their way through the swaying bodies, to come up and join us. "We'll do this quickly, so we can party!" I promised myself.

"Padre Aldana has some prayers," I announced to everyone—and what do you know? There was a respectful hush.

His prayer went on for a while, a little in Latin and a little in Spanish. But since most of the people in the immediate vicinity were Americans, they started rather soon to get restless.

Then the prayer was over. The father reached for the holy water and told us to follow him.

"Now we're going to bless the other buildings." I bawled. "Come on, everybody!"

Was my cheery voice beginning to wear thin? I saw a couple of guests flinch visibly. Most of them turned away to start a conversation with whoever was nearest.

"Come on, Bob, the father wants us to go with him," I pleaded.

"Shiiit, Lewis, that's not my thing. You go ahead. I'll catch up later," he lied.

The *padre,* already at the archway leading outside, turned back to see where I was.

What could I do? I grabbed the boys and signaled to Cloro and his wife, and we five started toward the swimming pool, with the altar boys in tow. Father Aldana pulled out a sort of brush and dipped it into the holy water. He shook it vigorously, adding a few more drops to the shimmering water of the pool.

Then it was off to the nearest bungalow, as the noise of the gaiety and laughter grew inside the restaurant.

The priest shook some water on the door of number twelve, said an *avemaría,* and then we moved on to the bungalow next door, where he repeated the procedure.

At about number seven, I lost the boys. Cloro and Nemecia and I slogged on through the sand behind the *padre.* Every time I heard the sound of a happy voice coming over the breeze to us from the restaurant, I could feel my hands tightening over my husband's imaginary neck. I could have killed him.

Even Cloro was becoming a little edgy. I heard Nemecia saying *"sí, mi marido"* about something or other, as was her habit, and looking down at the sand.

"Yes, my husband! Yes, my husband! Don't you know my name?" shouted my business partner in an irritated voice.

She used to drive him crazy sometimes. Not only at occasions like this, either. He would sit on his coconut trunk and gaze out to sea, complaining, "She's got running water in her house, and gas for her stove, and still she goes to the river! When will she ever learn?"

The sun was moving toward the horizon, but it seemed to be getting hotter.

Thirty-four *avemarías* we said, not counting the office and the stables. About midway through, I could hear that the *mariachis* had arrived, and were regaling the crowd with an even more raucous sound than we had heard from the marimbas. My feet were killing me.

The last act of the *padre* was to shake some water on the doors of the restaurant itself. We had come full circle. He looked as if he needed his bourbon even more than I needed revenge.

"Ah, here they are, back from their prayers!" shouted Bob, who had obviously not wasted any time at the bar in my absence.

I walked up and got another stiff rum and Coke for myself. Then I went to join my husband.

And as hard as I could, I ground the heel of my shoe into his foot, smiling sweetly all the while.

"Ay! Are you mad at me?" he asked, as if it had never occurred to him that I wouldn't take it as a cute joke.

"Whoa! You are furious, aren't you, Lewis? Well, get yourself a drink, and loosen up," he said, and turned again to Gordon, who had just grabbed Georgia, to ask her about her paintings.

His wife Dorothy angled her way into the circle. "We'd love to see them," she contributed, to remind them both that he had a wife.

"You would?" cooed the painter. "That's wonderful!" Georgia was in good form that evening.

"I never would have guessed that," she continued, giving Dorothy the once-over with her eyes.

How she managed to be slightly nasty with the wife, to flirt with the husband, and to look innocent all at the same time, I'm not sure, but she did it. "I make my paintings for the men—so they'll get jealous and work harder in bed!"

A sultry laugh slipped out, and she looked around to make sure of the impression she was creating on everyone.

"This bitch must be thinking that we're all envious of Ernesto," I thought. Her husband, the one who beat her for selling his plants to buy her canvases, had the reputation of being the best lover in town. How do men get such a reputation? Do they spread the rumors themselves?

Evelyn Muir came up with her compliments. "Theresa, it's marvelous. Marvelous. We'll be sure to come here for bridge!"

I smiled.

"Though I won't promise about the rooms," she continued. "You know our guests always like to stay at the Tropicana when they come down, so they'll be nearer to us." I smiled again. I was not going to add professional jealousy to my list of problems.

From a dark corner came the sharp sound of the palm of someone's hand, connecting with another's cheek. Daniel Lechón passed by me on the way out the door. "Bitch!" he snarled. "I've got to get rid of her. She's destroying my future."

Much as I liked Daniel, my sympathies were with the woman. Still, it was hard for me to understand how an American woman could get involved with a Mexican man, knowing, as she usually did, what she could expect. Their ridiculous, often harmful *machismo* always stood there glowering between the two of them.

"*Señora Laao-is,*" cried Alejandro from the patio, "come out here!" His eyes looked desperate.

I joined him at the archway outside the door of the restaurant. "The women of the bricklayers and the other workers are stealing our food!" he said, shocked.

I looked over. Sure enough, dozens of people were hovering, on all sides of the table. A woman would look first in one direction, then in the other, and then *whisst!* a chicken breast or a pork cutlet would disappear under her blouse. Then she would grab two handfuls of food for her children and move away to feed them, thus giving somebody else a chance at the table.

"I'll go over and try to discourage it," I told Alejandro, trying to reassure him. More than anything, I think he was a little embarrassed for his people.

I made my way through the clusters of families, swollen with all their *bona fide* children and probably a few extra cousins too. I recognized several of the boys, who many a work day had brought hot lunches to their fathers.

Actually, once I got over among them, I discovered that they were having as much fun as the group inside. Maybe even more. I found that I was a welcome addition to their merriment. And I was relieved to see that my presence staved off, for the moment at least, any further lawless raids at the food table.

While I was out there, I looked around everywhere for my boys. "Lupita, have you seen Bear and Buster?" I asked.

She hadn't, but she promised to go looking for them.

Back inside, Bob greeted me with more than usual enthusiasm. But his embrace quickly turned sour. "Can you imagine how stupid we were to put every nickel into this place?" he breathed in my ear. "And you! You were too proud to ask the corporation for a salary. We could have already been making some money."

"Please don't start again, Bob," I smiled and moved toward the bar a bit.

He grabbed my arm. "Come on. Let's go dance. All these sheep will follow."

We had a pleasant dance for a few moments, before he began all over again. "All this was just a bit of fun to you, wasn't it? You never thought of making any money from it."

"We *will* make money. Look around you. There's a lot of enthusiasm here, Bob. We'll make lots of money from this place."

Sondra Cellini floated into view, and my husband started salivating ever so discreetly. For once I was thankful for the presence of a woman to take his mind off me. He moved over to give her a hug, and I was off the hook.

"I've been trying to talk to Mrs. Palacios," whined Elizabeth Smith in my ear, "but I don't get anything but a grunt now and then."

"That's all you'll get," I said. "She's very shy. Nobody can get close to her." But it wasn't that, entirely. I wanted to try to explain further, since Elizabeth seemed to have her feelings hurt a little. "The Mexican people have a strong sense of class, especially these *rancheras*. They want to stay in their place, and they want you to do the same.

"You know the wife of don Martín, our carpenter? Her kids and my kids are friends. I am her *comadre*. . ." I continued, warming to the subject, "I am godmother to her Felipe, and also to little Teresita, who died. But she still will never sit with me in my living room. They only come into the kitchen, if they come in the house at all."

Elizabeth shook her head sadly, as if she would never really understand. I looked out of the windows and saw that the Mexican party had progressed a step further. Now some of the men had tequila and were snorting drinks straight from the bottle. I shook my head too. Maybe Elizabeth was right. Maybe we never will completely understand each other.

Lupita ran in. "I haven't found the boys yet, but I noticed your dress. I brought you the baby."

My hand went to my breast, but I knew before I even touched it that it would be wet with milk. There were two prominent maroon stains on my Chinese red!

"Damn!" I said under my breath, and took Dido off behind the bar and into the kitchen. The chefs and caterers would just have to get an eyeful!

Once I got comfortable, though, I noticed that they could have cared less whether I was there or what I was doing. For the third time in two minutes, the difference in our cultures was brought home to me.

Ofelia came running into the room in tears. When she saw me she looked surprised at first, then came over, her tears running more than ever.

"I was just explaining about our *fiestas* on the church square every Saturday night," she sobbed. I looked puzzled. "To Bob's friend. What's his name, Gordon?"

"What's wrong with that?"

"He seems like a nice man. He wanted to know all about how the money from our carnivals goes to the poor people."

I still looked puzzled.

"Well, Crisanto came up and started hurting my arm. He took me off with him, and he was so nasty! He said all the guy wanted was to look at my breasts!"

"He might be right," I thought to myself. She looked beautiful tonight in a tight black dress, simple but elegant.

"Come on," I said, "let's bring the baby back to Lupita. And I've got to see what happened to my boys."

At that moment, Lupita came running into the kitchen with huge eyes. *"Señora,* I found *los niños,"* she announced. "They are asleep. *Borrachos,* I think."

"WHAT? DRUNK!" Did that word mean something else in Mexican Spanish, besides what I thought it did? "My babies?"

I rushed out the door, following Lupita. She headed for one of their favorite palm trees, near the office.

There they were, sprawled at the foot of it, asleep with some of their local buddies, a son of Ofelia's among them. Lupita said the women at the party told her that the boys had been going around draining all the beer and whiskey glasses. Apparently they had started to climb up to their secret look-out, but hadn't made it to the top.

"Please put them to bed, Lupita," I sighed. It was all Bob's fault. I wasn't sure how, but I was sure it was his fault. Well, at least I took Ofelia's mind off her troubles with Crisanto!

As we started back toward the bar, I noticed that the gala celebration was beginning to wind down. "Thank goodness. I'm ready to call it a night," I yawned, though it wasn't really that late.

As we passed the outside patio tables, Alejandro looked at me with deep question in his eyes. "It's OK. Let them have the rest of it," I told him. "The party's almost over."

I entered the bar, walked up to Jesús and asked for one last drink.

"Give the bottle a good squeeze, to make sure I get the last drop," I said. "That brings good luck."

I slid into bed that night, totally exhausted, but with a sense of contentment. I had accomplished my dream. "Now all we have to do is start counting our money," I mused, as I drifted off to sleep.

The voices that started early the next morning were not angry, exactly, but more confused than anything. But they were also firm, and they grew louder and louder in a hurry.

"Where's the hot water?"

"What's the matter with this place?"

"I'm trying to take a shower here—"

"My wife sent me over to—"

Suddenly Alejandro was pounding on our door. It was far too early for me after last night, but I was fully awake in a flash, with a sick feeling in my stomach.

Diesel fuel! How could we have forgotten it? We had water, of course, from the city line we had dug. But we hadn't given a thought to how we were going to heat it.

I had put in my own little diesel tank for LaPorte's house. Occasionally over the last two years we had run out of fuel, which meant that the water pump was down too, since our system was still tied to the original well, and not to the city. At times like that, we had just done without—not just hot water but all water. For the boys and me that was no problem. We simply loaded the dishes and the clothes in a laundry basket, grabbed the soap, and went to the stream behind the house.

Our elegant guests from Guadalajara did not look as if they would be so accommodating.

"Hitch a ride into town, and get Luis Alvarez out here immediately," I told Alejandro.

As I got dressed, I tried to think what kind of super breakfast would placate our guests enough to make them believe that a morning shower was an unnecessary luxury.

It's warm in Puerto Vallarta in March, of course. And the sea water is warm. But still it was the winter season. The water in the pipes is cool. The nights get chilly, especially as they lengthen into early morning, and a hot shower could not be considered a needless frill. Certainly not among the clientele we wanted to attract to Hotel Las Glorias.

I was seething. How could our architect make such a stupid mistake?

When he arrived he was all embarrassment and apologies, at least until I got pushy and started to carry on a bit too much. Then the apologies turned into recriminations.

"You were the builder. Why didn't you ask for a diesel tank?" he said, glaring.

"An architect is supposed to think of such things. Why wasn't it in your plans?" I screamed back. "Am I supposed to think of everything?"

Meanwhile, our wealthy guests were buzzing around the office, glancing over with the kind of look that you give to spoiled children who are making a fuss in public, and generally looking uncomfortable. The hesitant expression on their faces clearly asked, "How can we break it to this dame that we don't want to stay in her hotel, no matter how pretty it looks on the outside?"

I was way ahead of them. It was not a matter of picking up the telephone and asking the gas company to come right over. There were no suppliers in Puerto Vallarta, and still not even a telephone. It could take all day to try to put over such an order on the radio telephone downtown, and by that time we could be in Tepic ourselves.

"I'm terribly sorry," I announced to the assembled guests, "but I'm afraid we weren't altogether ready to open our hotel." I took a deep breath. "Probably this will all seem very funny one day, but for now, all I can do is apologize to you. I've sent my husband over to the Posada Vallarta, to ask if they can accommodate anyone who wants to stay with them for the rest of the time."

Everyone did.

But I was gratified that later, at least within a year or two, almost every one of them came back to us.

Although in the years to come the electricity went out, sometimes even for a day or two, we had no other major "kinks" to work out in our hotel. Those times when a big storm brought with it an electrical blackout, it was clear to everyone in the hotel that the whole town was affected. Our guests were at least understanding, if not patient. (After all, what choice did they have?) Sometimes it would take a couple of days for the utilities people to find a part they needed in Guadalajara or in Mexico City. That's the charm of Old Mexico! All we could do is sit and worry about the food in our freezers, and organize bridge parties by candlelight.

Thus, on our first morning open, Bob and I found ourselves asking all our sweet waiters and bellboys and maids to help with the arrangements to move the guests down the beach to the Posada Vallarta, our main competitors on that end of town. Then he and I took the first plane to Tepic, Bob grumbling all the way, from anger and profound embarrassment.

When we landed, we lost no time. We scurried all over town, Bob screaming and I translating.

We bought a 5000-gallon drum, a huge thing, and found a truck and a driver who was willing to make the trip through the jungle. We offered to pay for his time, for his trip back to Tepic, of course, and enough extra to make it definitely worth his while. He got all of his buddies to help load the empty tank onto the truck, and then we drove to a gasoline station to fill it full with diesel fuel. We were in business.

Or we were, as soon as I had laid in a very large stock of rum and Cokes for the return trip to paradise. Mostly Cokes for the driver, almost totally rum for Bob, and a mixture for me, over the next nineteen hours.

We had heard that the highway had been improved a bit. What that meant in fact was that the ruts had sometimes been filled in or smoothed over a bit, or just rearranged, and some of the bigger rocks had been removed to the side of the road.

It was still mostly one lane, at least where it counted, on mountain curves or long, slow inclines. If we met a car or another truck, which was rare, there was a stand-off of exaggerated hand signals and generous smiles, until we agreed which one of us was to back up to a wide spot in the road and let the other pass.

Night driving was even trickier. Livestock roamed freely, there were beer bottles scattered about, and of course, no Highway Department had been through to mark the curves or dips on the roadway.

But that was not the worst. Mexican drivers have an irritating habit of littering the road with stones. If their car breaks down or they need to change a tire, they stop in the road, grab several large rocks from nearby ditches and fields, and put them behind and in front of their tires for safety. When the car is fixed and they are ready to drive off, they simply kick away the rock in the direction of their destination, leaving all the others in place. Perhaps this happens less nowadays, but it's still not uncommon on the back roads.

On the other hand, it was also not uncommon that when we stopped to stretch or to take a pee, some friendly folks would run up to see if we needed any help. A vehicle passing by was still a quite a sight to be seen in those days, so that all the *rancheros* and their families used to stand outside their huts and wave to us, having heard our approach for miles. If we actually stopped the truck, even in what we thought was a deserted stretch of road, people suddenly materialized out of nowhere. They would come up to talk, or to invite us home for a cup of hot coffee, or a tortilla, sometimes with a bit of chicken. After several hours of rum and Coke and sulking, we were happy to accept.

"Well, you did it again, Lewis," my husband kept mumbling. Every few hours, he came up with a new variation on the theme. "You really want to keep on going with all this bull? You could be sitting in a beautiful house in San Francisco, like a nice, normal human being. And look at you!"

Bob, of course, was wearing a sporty outfit with white pants that were still white, even in this greasy truck. I felt like a rhinoceros sitting next to him in the cab.

"We can sell it. We can get our money for it, and get out," he ground on. "Come on, Terry. You had the thrill of building it, for Chrissake. How about it? Please, let's go!"

I can forgive Bob Lewis a lot for these years. I really think he hated it much of the time, but he stayed with me, in his fashion, while I was getting my kicks playing "hotel princess." He stayed even after the thing started to turn sour, and dangerous.

As the trip wore on, I only half heard what he was saying. I was thinking about the Rio Ameca, which lay ahead.

Of course there were the snakes and the crocodiles. But since our fiasco that first Christmas, I had seen the river raging and flooded several times, carrying down whole trees from the mountains, furniture and clothing, even *palapas* which had once been someone's home. I had seen cattle sometimes, and I was horrified to spy even the bodies of small children, drowned by a sudden wall of water up above.

We were not then in the rainy season, of course, so it should be safer for us. But I had gained a lot of respect for that river since our first foolish venture.

As we came over the crest of the last of the Nayarit mountains, and the beautiful Bay of Banderas lay beckoning below, I started to explain to the driver about negotiating the sand bars. He was much more willing to listen than my husband had been. Probably he knew it already. But the load was unfortunately too heavy. We got stuck.

I won't repeat the scene. It was much like the other one: Bob irate, Terry trying to look small and helpless, but all the while knowing that it was only a matter of time before she went into the river for the *ranchero* with the tractor.

This time we had the added presence of our hired truck driver, who felt terrible about the whole thing.

"*¡Ay, señora!* We are really stuck! I don't know what to do!" he moaned sheepishly.

I looked at the callouses on my feet and thought how smooth Bob's were, tucked safely inside his expensive shoes.

"What the hell," I thought. This was not a battle I could win. I wasn't going to sit there and continue to carry on a domestic squabble in front of the driver. I climbed out of the window and swam toward the same man in the same cornfield.

All I could think of was the *grande dame* of two or three days ago, shimmering in her diamonds, in her red silk and tassels, officiating at a gala celebration for fifteen hundred of Jalisco's finest.

And here I was now, lying in the goddam river, muddy and soaked, with my dress floating up over my head.

I clambered up onto the shore.

"I saw you!" said the man, in a voice that was altogether too friendly for my mood. "I saw you out there!"

He was almost singing, in a smarmy voice that was growing particularly offensive to me. "I saw you out there the whole time, *señora!*"

"Well, why in hell didn't you make a move to help us?" I started to say, but bit my tongue. Quickly I carried out the necessary negotiations. We decided that one tractor was not enough this time, so he went for a friend.

I sank down onto the rich field of corn and sweet potatoes. "Is Bob right? Should we just go back to California?" I wondered.

We had already had an offer to sell the place at a profit. In the years to come we would have many more. But I loved Las Glorias. And I felt a commitment to my investors. I couldn't just pick up and leave, after sharing so many dreams with them too.

"We will make it!" I resolved, even though I knew that the only people presently staying at Puerto Vallarta's newest luxury hotel were Bear and Buster and the maids.

My man returned with a second tractor and farmer. We hauled the truck across the Rio Ameca and up out of the river. Bob, with his American ingenuity and bad Spanish, and about twenty-five men with ropes and planks, managed to get the big drum buried on our property. I hovered about meanwhile, worrying that the whole place was about to go up in flames. But the thing finally slid easily into the hole, greased by several choice cusswords that I hadn't heard before.

Las Glorias opened again a few days later, with the added luxury of hot water.

12

The early years of our operation tend to become a pleasant blur in my mind now, when I think back to those innocent times. People from outside were beginning to discover Puerto Vallarta at an ever increasing rate, and pour into town to sample its exotic promises. But the highway from the North hadn't opened yet, and the town was still essentially ours.

Sometimes we were still so much like children! In February, we could hardly wait to make a special trip out to Punta de Mita and see the whales ride in on the warm currents from China, and watch their giant bodies clash in their odd mating dance.

One time a baby whale wandered far into the Bahía de Banderas, close to the village. That was a rare sight for us, but not totally unknown. Several of our friends could remember sitting a time or two on a beautiful hotel terrace and enjoying the enormous jets of water play right in front of them, as the whales swam by and shot gushers high out of their spouts.

But this baby was not playing. He must have gotten disoriented, and then suddenly there he was, stranded on the sand over at the Playas Gemelas beaches. The whole town turned out to help push him back into the water.

Later, in '68 I think it was, we saw two large, adult whales in the bay. But these did not fare so well. They got their heads stuck in the big rocks jutting up out of the water at Mismaloya. For days people came out to watch with sad faces, as the gentle animals bled to death from the gashes made by the rocks. There were sharks swimming around, tearing out huge pieces of meat from the carcasses until it was all finally washed away. Generally our dolphins, their natural enemies, kept the sharks away, by poking them in the liver with their snouts. But these two giant corpses, I suppose, were delectable enough to convince them to risk a journey into the bay.

My days settled into somewhat of a routine. Since Bob closed the bar every night, with pleasure, and locked up the money in the safe around one o'clock, it was up to me to do the morning chores. I got up in time to meet the first of our waiters and maids in the village at 6:15, and to pick up several more so that they could all eat breakfast back at the hotel at 6:45, before their morning shift began.

Running a chauffeur service didn't seem unusual at the time. It had to be done. After a while, the heat and the rain and the wind began to wear on me, but they weren't the worst. It took a strong stomach to face Puerto Vallarta's rough cobblestones at that hour of the morning, especially if I'd been partying the night before. Sometimes I had to grab the steering wheel until my knuckles were white. Was it so it wouldn't lurch out of my hand, or only so I wouldn't lose my morning coffee?

And then there were the potholes. Our little town tried to keep up with them, but mostly it seemed to be a losing proposition, especially during the rainy summer season. I would come hurrying around a corner in my loaded station wagon and find a young-old man squatting right in the middle of the road on his hands and knees, mending a hole. No flagman, no flashing light, just a little man beginning his day, as I was. Usually there was no way to drive around him. I just caught forty winks with the rest of the drivers in line, while he finished his job and then motioned us past.

At seven o'clock, I got my own kids up, ate breakfast with them, and then it was back in town again to drop them off at nursery school. If I had dropped off my grocery list at the market on the first trip, I swung by there to get what I had ordered. I also spent many an early morning sitting at the water's edge and waiting while the chef filled huge tubs with the pick of the day's catch. By the time Bob appeared in the restaurant at 9:30 or so, I had had quite a day already.

I soon discovered that being a martyr, or a slave to errands, is not a character I do well. We got a driver for the errands, and I quickly learned how enjoyable it was to have a loving Lupe bring a coffee and a chat to my bedside in the mornings.

"Oooh, my feet hurt this morning, Lupita," I whined luxuriously, and she would treat me to one of her heavenly massages. After all, wasn't I in the office till almost midnight, greeting the guests as they returned from their evenings out on the town? A gal's got to be able to spoil herself a little.

I let my nails grow again, since my bricklaying days were over. I had my hair done and started to become interested in clothes, for in the restaurant every night, I was the lady on view. The Jackie Kennedy shift was seen everywhere, the Beatles were raging even in the jungles of Mexico, and hems rose higher and higher all over the world. I was keeping my body in great tone by dancing at the City Dump till three on many a night, and I looked good.

Thank God for the *siesta*! If it hadn't been for a regular rest from about two to five in the afternoon, I couldn't have kept up a schedule like that. Though there were still no telephones, my house was linked to the office and the restaurant by intercom.

In the hotel business, there's not a moment a manager can call his own. I could hardly put thirty minutes together in a day to do something entirely for myself, like practice the piano. But in Mexico the *siesta*, at least, is taken seriously by everyone. Even so, I often found it was better to sneak off to bungalow number twenty-one for a nap, rather than go back to my house.

How many times my sleep was interrupted by a shrill scream from one of the bungalows! I got so I could pretty much tell what the trouble was from the length and tenor of the sound.

I had instructed my boys to make sure the beach was cleared every morning of the bright little black and yellow sea snakes that washed up dead on the sand after mating. They were harmless, but it was hard to convince a sheltered matron from Chicago of that.

When our guests first arrived, I usually tried to warn them all about the iguanas in the palm trees. I was certainly not about to try to get rid of them.

"They look fierce, but they won't hurt you," I assured the polished ladies as they peered shyly out of the louvered windows in my reception area.

"Oooo! How can you stand them?"

"We like to have them around. They eat the little flies and the mosquitoes," I explained. "You'll appreciate it too, when you can walk out on the beach in the starlight and not be bothered with bugs."

"But look at that one! He must be six feet long! What if one like that drops down on my head?"

"Well, bring him over to the restaurant, and we'll cook him for lunch! They're delicious!"

They peered suspiciously at the prehistoric creature sunning himself on the roof of one of the bungalows. Now and then you could hear the sound, *ch-ch-ch-ch*, that seemed to indicate his total contentment with life. An iguana would sometimes steal one of our eggs, or eat the fruit from one of the trees, but mostly they left us alone, and I liked having them around.

The kids in town used to sell them to some of the braver Americans, but an iguana can't live long in captivity, and anyhow I think that's forbidden now by the health department. But you can still meet some darling boys on the Malecón who, for a price, will lend their huge brown eyes and their little baby pet dragon to your photograph, as the perfect souvenir of Puerto Vallarta.

If the screams mostly sounded startled, and came from several bungalows, that generally meant that the electricity had failed again. All the boys began wandering through the grounds, distributing candles and petroleum lamps. Everyone was invited for free drinks at the bar, while Bob and I hoped the ice held out.

An even shriller scream and a flurry of activity in one place usually meant a mouse. The little fellows mostly lived way up in the palm trees, out of sight, so I didn't even mention them in my introductory nature lectures in the office. But every so often, one of them apparently found something fascinating in a bungalow down below.

It's still incredible to me how a woman can faint at the sight of one of those dear little creatures.

"Look here," I said, holding the thing in my hand after Alejandro had knocked it out with a broom. "Isn't this a cutey little rat?"

Perhaps it was my English that got me in trouble. The lady really got mad at me. She didn't think either I or my pet was the least bit cute. Of course I wasn't holding a big fat rat, like you see in the sewers—I wouldn't have picked up one of those. This one was a sweet little mouse with tiny pink ears and a little tail. But the Americans ladies would have none of it.

I've seen huge crabs on the sands in South Carolina, snakes on California beaches, and I've seen Americans walk right past them, hardly noticing. But once they cross the border into Mexico, something clicks in their minds, and they get really upset at the some of the same things.

They don't want "nature," or even disorder on their vacations. They've paid to have everything perfect, and that's the way they want it. So the boys tended to the cigarette butts and the small creatures. Just the small degree of civilization we had brought to the area had already scared off the rabbits, the possums, and the armadillos from my primitive days, alone at LaPorte's solitary hut.

In the early years, the crabs were still everywhere. They became so much associated with Las Glorias in my mind, that we had a beautiful crab inlaid in tile in the bottom of the swimming pool. They scuttled across the sand at all hours. Or at night when I was reading alone, they would angle sideways under my door, and creep over cautiously to visit me.

When they mated, hundreds of them made a big mound on the beach, and the z-z-z-z-z-z noise that came from that huge pile of claws was almost frightening.

The little beggars were very clever at attacking clotheslines. In the morning sometimes when I went outside to check on my laundry, I found the line down, and my favorite dress torn to pieces. Or worse yet, some items of clothing had simply disappeared. I've watched them eat a pair of panties in five minutes flat.

For all those reasons, we decided that a single crab, a tile one, safely at the bottom of the pool, was enough for our American guests. I spent a lot of money and effort trying to gas them out of the place. *Wh-s-s-s-t* —into one hole went the gas. And out they popped from another hole over to the side. Carlos and Guilberto and I chased them all over the beach for a couple of seasons, until we finally encouraged them to live elsewhere. Those that we didn't gas, we grabbed and boiled. But we had far more than we wanted to eat.

I must have been doing things right at Las Glorias. Even the most squeamish of the ladies would say how welcome and comfortable they felt, how clean and organized the place was.

My beautiful, gentle mountain boys had a lot to do with it. To this day, people still remember being greeted the first thing when they stepped out of the taxi by the bright smile of Alejandro. Some of them still search him out even now when they come down, and bring him gifts.

I used to tell my staff, "These people saved all year long to come down here with us. So make their two or three weeks as happy as you can! They're not millionaires, but if you treat them that way, it'll pay off for all of us."

And it did. By Easter of one year, we were already almost fully booked for next year's high season. I confirmed the reservations by letter in November, and we used the deposits to do our shopping in Mexico City.

Bob started making promotional trips to the States, to encourage travel agents to consider Puerto Vallarta, and us at Hotel Las Glorias in particular. One of those arrangements of his resulted in a strange coincidence.

Many people asked me how I learned how to run a hotel. I don't know. Most of it came naturally, I guess, from seeing what I liked and didn't like in the hotels where I stayed as a girl. But I did have some bit of experience in Spain, in a hostel that I managed for foreign exchange students, and in the travel office in the capital, where I worked for several years.

Then when I was "exiled" to America by my father, after a love affair with a pilot in the Spanish Air Force, I didn't have to work, of course, but I was bored. I tried being an assistant in one of those fat farms in Beverly Hills, with the grotesque machines that shook and paddled the pounds off gross women who paid money for such torture. I had a good figure, so it was my job to lie that I had lost forty pounds on the machines.

But when the overly attentive Jewish manager of the place invited me out for a hamburger and tried to scratch my ass, I sought other employment. Naturally I felt I was more suited to running a travel agency. After all, hadn't I worked in Generalissimo Franco's A.T.E.S.A., the state-owned tourist office in Madrid? I had had dozens of people organizing my tours, setting up the tickets, the hotels and travel accommodations.

Mr. Lapin, of L & M Travel Agency on Oak Street, was impressed by all my experience, and also by the fact that I spoke several languages. I had clearly been wasting my talents on the large ladies of Los Angeles.

"Yes, we can certainly use someone who speaks all those marvelous languages," he beamed. "Go file these papers."

File? Jesus! It took me hours to get through it. A, B, C, D, E, F —they may come naturally to most people, but the years when I should have been learning the alphabet, I was looking for grasshoppers to eat in a prison camp. Goldberg? Goldstein? It took me a quarter of an hour sometimes. The typing was just as excruciating. I found I never got to use any of my precious languages. How would I, in the middle of southern California?

Mr. Lapin held out for about three months, bless him, until the day I sent some prominent doctor client of his to New York City instead of Chicago. I had completely scrambled the ticket.

In Madrid, of course, I never actually had to do any of that. I asked my assistants to take care of such details, and then checked them later if I felt I needed to. I was always a director, not a doer. I couldn't for the life of me find my way through one of those huge schedule books and work out a ticket to Rome, or to Tel Aviv. And obviously not any closer to home either!

Mr. Lapin called me in. "You know, Terry, you're a marvelous girl, but uh—"

"Don't fire me," I interrupted. "I quit. I'm going skiing anyway." I smiled sweetly. "I've never been fired in my life. I've never had a job where I wasn't up at the top."

"You're going skiing?"

"Yes, I am," I said, and I booked a ticket to Squaw Valley. My father had forced me to bring so much money with me to the States, what did I need with his twenty-seven dollars a week?

In 1968 at Puerto Vallarta, we had our largest gathering of agents from all over the United States. They flew down, were met at the airport and shown around the town, and they stayed and ate at all the cooperating hotels. One afternoon, we had luncheon planned for eighty of them at Las Glorias.

And who should walk into my place, but Mr. Lapin from the L & M Travel Agency in Beverly Hills! Same longish hair (trying for a bit of a "hip" touch), same developing paunch, same studied, trustworthy look of a serious California businessman.

The restaurant was specially decorated, because I had decided I was going to be famous in Mexico for Indonesian cuisine. I had gotten all the spices and taught the cooks how to do it, and we had a fabulous rice table laid out, a genuine *rijsttafel* just like many delighted tourists can find in Amsterdam.

I was playing the ultra-sophisticated hostess in an exotic silk print with a high Chinese collar, and I looked as if I had been doing just that all my life. The agents filed in with their little clutch purses and their sunglasses, *ooohing* and *aaahing* at the spread of food and at the mountains of bougainvilleas I had arranged everywhere. The waiters were busy handing around special Bloody Marys to all.

Mr. "Rabbit" (that's *lapin* in French) and I just stood in the middle of the room with our jaws hanging open.

I wish I could say that I recovered first, but I didn't.

He turned to his partner and said, "Here's that Dutch girl that didn't know how to file, remember?" The man nodded. "She told us she worked in A.T.E.S.A. for four years in Spain."

I turned on the charm. I told him I hoped he would have a pleasant stay in Puerto Vallarta, and I showed him to the best seat in the house. The rest of the afternoon, Mr. Lapin just sat at the table and shook his head.

I loved receiving people and making sure they were having a happy vacation. My office became a sort of *'salon'*—especially about five in the afternoon, when the Americans started thinking about food.

From a typical desk clerk in a Mexican hotel, any visitors could learn (if they could understand him), that it would still be two or three hours before the restaurants opened up again. But at Las Glorias in the late afternoons, the lobby began to resemble an informal party of friends. And we whiled away the time until they could go downtown for dinner.

"Terry," a lady would begin, "you know, it just tears my heart out to see the poverty on all sides." Her eyes became moist, and I could see she really felt it. As I have said, I find American women to be the most generous, caring people in the world.

"I know," another would chime in. "So many of them live in houses that are just shells, with all the bricks and sand just lying around outside. How can they do it? They must really hate us."

"No, they don't hate us," I tried to assure them. "But they do think all Americans are millionaires. They know that you all have a comfortable house and a big car."

"But they could have the same—"

"No, they don't have the same system down here. There's no such thing as a building loan in Mexico," I explained. "Your families can get a mortgage for thirty years. That's what makes it so easy. These people don't understand that in America you don't have to have a huge sum of money all at once, to own a nice home."

"How do they do it then?"

"Well, you've seen their little houses half finished? Those are a kind of 'piggy bank' for these people." I was warming to my subject. For the Mexicans are a proud people. And this was now my country too. "When they have a small bit of money tucked away, they buy maybe five thousand bricks, and start building the walls. Now the family doesn't have their savings any more, but they do have a start on their home."

"So they just move in?"

"When they have a door at least. They don't really have to have windows, you know. The women can hang up some cloth, and the house will stay nice and cool. But you have to have a door, they think, otherwise the bad spirits come." The women looked dubious. "In a couple of years, when they have another small sum, they put up some more walls, or some plaster. That way, they can't spend the money on something else."

Usually someone would say at this point, "Well, I have noticed that they all look happy. When we pass by them in the taxi, it seems like everybody in the family is outside together, all the kids and parents and grandparents. They're all busy, and they're all smiling. You don't see that on the streets in America."

It was true. "They're very happy people. And very gracious. How would you like to make a visit some time?"

The women always took me up on an offer like that, with the greatest enthusiasm. And then I found myself leading a small tour again through the center of town, just like years before in Spain.

We would peek into the dark doorways and find a housewife at work in a corner of the room, blackened by the smoke from a small oven. Perhaps the *abuela*, the grandmother, sat picking stones out of a pile of beans before she dumped them into a pot for an irresistible dish of *frijoles*.

"¡La Holandesa!" they would often smile. *"¡Pásele! Pásele!"* And we were invited into the house for a closer look and a chat. Little kids sat on the dirt floor oblivious, completely involved with home-made toys.

"See the concrete washboard with the ripples? And the tank there beside the back door? That's the way your grandmothers or great-grandmothers used to wash clothes too." The women were amazed, and fascinated.

We passed women on the street, just returning from market, and carrying the little plastic buckets that they used for both a purse and a shopping bag. "There's no refrigeration in these houses. They have to get their meat and their vegetables every day," I pointed out. "And that's also why all these guys can make a living with their little soft drink carts. They're the only ones around with ice."

The women looked around, sometimes longingly. "It's a good little business," I said. "They just take their 'store' home with them at night, so they don't have to pay rent for a building."

My pupils had to admit that when the dust and the diesel fumes hung heavy on a long, hot afternoon, the drinks on those carts looked pretty refreshing, even in the absence of the stainless steel furnishings they were used to.

In the hotel, I had a knack for matching up couples that might hit it off and enjoy their vacation together. I've found that Americans, especially the men, as big and handsome and self-assured as they seem, are generally rather shy in new surroundings. Those from Texas and California were perhaps a little more familiar with it all, but tourists from the northern states especially were somewhat uncomfortable in Mexico at first.

As soon as a couple came into the office, I could spot what "type" they were, and consider who else in the hotel might be compatible with them. If I introduced them and got them together, they almost always had a more enjoyable vacation.

Some tourists were in Puerto Vallarta looking for some action, but most of ours at Las Glorias wanted a more quiet time in the sun. Others were more sporty.

I liked to arrange afternoon excursions on horseback for them, to see the spectacular waterfalls up in the mountains. Guilberto went along as their guide. Others were interested in a fishing trip. Bob and Rafael de la Cruz had bought three fishing boats from Mexicana Airlines, and they rented them out with one of our captains for sixty dollars a day. That was an easy expense if three couples went together.

"You'll want a lunch along. You drink beer?" I would ask. "OK, I'll stock it up. And a case of Cokes too."

I sent the *capitán* to get everything ready. "Don't forget fresh water," I reminded him. "And toilet paper." I tried to think of everything.

"Now be sure not to take anything extra," I warned the women. "Leave your jewelry at home!" They didn't always listen. How many times we scrambled for watches and purses and bracelets and hats, and Lord knows what else, as our American tourist ladies in high heels tried to climb into a fishing boat!

If they had some luck and caught a fish, say a thirty-five-pound red snapper, we had it sent to the kitchen and cooked for their dinner at our restaurant, and they were delighted.

Sometimes at our Hotel Las Glorias, there were groups of people that got together in spite of me.

One season, I got a letter saying that sixty Shriners wanted to come down and stay for a week. Fine. We wanted to encourage groups like this, especially when we weren't at our busiest time.

They would be flying their own plane. They gave me their arrival information so I could meet them at our small airport.

When they landed, I could see that the party had already started. They could easily be identified by their funny little Shriners' hats—many of those already askew—and by the smell of their breath. Besides the usual luggage, they had also brought down a hundred pounds of T-bone steaks, and four very slim, very pretty young girls.

They were prepared for any emergency.

I worked with the men to get the steaks through customs, with the help of a little *mordida* for the "uniforms," and then I started to find cabs for the group, as I always did. Back then, we never even considered limousines or buses, because our friends the small taxi drivers would have been upset at losing the business.

This unofficial convention of Shriners moved in, two to a bungalow, and had themselves a blast for the whole week. There was a constant frenzy of activity. And those poor girls worked really hard. I started to feel sorry for them, until I made a quick tally of what they must have made that week.

The last night, the Shriners wanted to have a special party in our restaurant, with a *mariachi* band. I arranged everything in the most elegant style, with a big buffet, an open bar with lots of tequila, as ordered. As the late supper was finishing up, I noticed that the party was drifting toward the pool, and that the musicians were following.

Splash! went one Shriner into the pool, fully dressed, then three, then ten. Suddenly there were sixty pairs of arms and legs flailing around, with everyone laughing and screaming at top volume. Make that sixty-four. But it wasn't hard to hear the *mariachis*, because they had gathered as close to the edge of the pool as it was possible to be.

"Move back!" I screamed, losing my usually cool hostess poise. "Don't stand on my goddam water!" Tequila bottles were beginning to float up onto the surface.

The *mariachis* shifted back slightly on the patio, but they never stopped playing, and they never took their eyes off the girls. They began to drift forward again.

Those overgrown American boys were having too much fun groping around in my pool: it was more than the poor Mexicans could tolerate.

"Back!" I tried again. "Everybody back!"

I was used to organizing things. But it was no use. One of the girls was jumping up and down in the water, twirling her bikini top around her head, and shouting "HEY!" to one of our cute young guitar players. Suddenly all fourteen musicians jumped into the pool, half still dressed, half in their underwear.

They tore the tops off the rest of the girls, and then the bottoms, and then the party took on a new dimension. Remember, this was still in the Sixties, when the Mexican police were used to sending women back to their hotels if they were seen wearing shorts on the streets of our sleepy village. More and more tequila bottles started surfacing.

I retreated to the bar. "Jesús," I groaned, "I think it's time to close up for the night. I'm going to bed." He nodded rather sadly, not knowing whether I meant he was free to go the way of his musician pals, or if he had to clean up as usual.

I didn't want to find out how the party ended. I just went home to make sure Bear and Buster were still safely in bed.

Shriners were not the only tourists who came looking to let loose a bit, even to get laid. As I said, something happens to people when they cross the border.

Not all of them. Most Americans remain as gracious as they always were. We had a dentist who came year after year and became friendly (but not romantic) with one of our young maids. One year, he escorted her to a dentist in the village and sat with her for several days while she had all her teeth fixed. And he paid the bill.

Another woman brought down loads of clothes for our girls every time she came. As I watched her unpack, I saw that some of them were beautiful outfits from I. Magnin, that looked as if they had never been worn.

"Hey, don't give that to the maids," I said. "I would love to have that dress myself!" She thought I must be joking, but I wasn't. After that, there was always a swim suit and cover-up in the latest fashion in her luggage—for me.

"What can we do for the school kids?" they would ask in one of our late-afternoon sessions.

"Well, you can't just send money or supplies," I said, "because the teachers would take them home. If you want to do something, buy a bunch of pencils or notebooks, and we'll take them over ourselves."

And so I arranged another excursion. I told the *maestra*, "There are several schoolteachers all the way from America, who would like to visit your school." They weren't, of course. But the dear Mexican teachers loved to think that these women were schoolteachers, so schoolteachers they were for the day.

"Sure, Terry, whatever you say," they agreed enthusiastically, holding onto the little bundles they had brought to distribute to the kids.

In Mexico in those years, a pencil still cost a lot of money. One child, one pencil, and he had to hang onto it carefully. I was reminded so much of my own schooldays just after the war, as a poor Indonesian refugee in Holland. We invaded the classrooms of Puerto Vallarta, and it became our own version of a Sixties love-in. Everyone was moved: the teachers, the kids, and the women most of all.

We had a bishop from one of the northern cities in the States, who was given the trip every year as a gift from one of his parishioners. He liked to give Mass for our workers, under the palm trees. We had the governor of another northern state, and the president of one of the large TV stations. There were several senators from the Vancouver area.

One lady, a former concert pianist, finally drank herself to death at Las Glorias, but not before she had spent hundreds of hours practicing on my grand piano, which we had moved into a bungalow for her.

By far the great majority of our guests were wonderful, charming people. But there were the exceptions. The "ugly American" is not a totally fictitious character. There were the *nouveau riche*, which I learned to spot easily. The men often drank too much, yelled at their wives too quickly, banged on the tables too loudly.

The women easily became vulgar. Usually they were still in pretty good shape, though middle-aged, and they liked to flaunt their bodies and their diamonds, sitting alone on a bar stool or under a *palapa* with their legs apart, leering at those passing by, or grabbing onto a waiter a little too meaningfully.

Sometimes my job as a hostess involved the painful necessity of announcing, "Hey, lady, this is my worker. He cannot dance. He is a working man." If they grabbed someone else, that was their business. But my boys were my business.

We had very little trouble like that at Las Glorias.

I have called my boys "beautiful," and by that I guess I was referring to their personalities, their loyalty, their eagerness to learn. They were nice, they were clean and neat. But except for Guilberto, they were not really handsome. All were young kids from families of poor *rancheros* or fishermen in the area. They had no experience or desire to deal with that kind of sexual intrigue. Later on as we grew, we had a couple of minor incidents, but a few days of being laid off set those boys straight. They wanted and needed their earnings too much to jeopardize their jobs.

I found that most American women who were looking around were after the handsome ones anyhow. And there were plenty of those all over the resorts, where it was easy to see "special friendships" developing.

The *machismo* of the Mexican male is strong. It certainly does not need any encouragement. When beautiful blonde American girls came down for their hard-earned two weeks' vacation, and especially as the bathing suits got more and more brief, anyone could see trouble coming. The assumption among the beach boys and the self-appointed Latin Lovers was that American girls were easy.

If a girl was simply innocent, or was giving out signals that she didn't intend, I used to try to take her under my wing.

"If you speak to a Mexican man at all, it is a sign of encouragement. You cannot do it," I told them. "It's too bad, but that's the way it is." American girls, being generally friendly and open, did not like to hear it.

"It's true. Any woman is fair game, as far as he is concerned, even his best friend's wife or sister. And a blonde American girl most of all. Any response except 'NO' means 'maybe' to a Mexican male, and you'll never hear the end of it."

Still a look of disbelief. "In fact, it's better not to respond at all," I added.

"Terry, that's so old-fashioned."

"Look at the Mexican women. They've learned to avoid making eye contact with strangers." The sighs of exasperation grew. "You don't have to be mean or unfriendly. But you just can't encourage anything on a personal level. Trust me. They'll never stop."

Some, of course, came down searching for just such an experience. Girls who would never dream of acting that way in Dallas or Santa Barbara would wander on the beach alone at all hours, or would put on an exhibition on the dance floor that left nothing to the imagination.

One sad incident involved Mrs. Noble, a wealthy socialite from Hyannis Port. She and her husband James had been coming down to us for several years, and we all liked seeing them return. He came for a part of the time, but she stayed on much longer, after he had to return for business. They were a very refined couple, clearly used to great wealth, and certainly not the kind of people I have been describing above.

Their bungalow was always on the beachfront, and every day she could be seen sitting cross-legged in front of her door, knitting big, heavy sweaters for her grandchildren, and drinking Bloody Marys. *Clack, clack, clack!* went the needles, really fast. The waiters loved her because she gave such generous tips, and they knew she was especially appreciative if her drink was a bit heavier on the vodka than usual.

Still, there was something rather pitiful about this frail woman in her mid-sixties. When her husband left, she often begged me to sleep there in the bungalow with her, because she was afraid when it got dark and the waves started coming up strong. When I couldn't stay, or didn't want to, I always assured her that I had instructed the watchmen to keep a special lookout for her room.

One January, we got notice that Mrs. Noble was arriving at the airport and wanted to move into her usual bungalow, if possible. She had no reservations.

The taxi pulled up, and out stepped an outrageous figure in a lime green mini-dress, and a large hat piled high with plastic bananas and mangoes. She looked like the centerpiece of a Mexican buffet. The woman had obviously flipped out, and she thought she was thirty again.

There was no word of her husband, but she was ready for a good time. She showed up in the restaurant and ate her dinner alone. The faces of the waiters lit up and they called her by name, but soon their eyes became sad, for they had a genuine affection for her. There was something that had reminded me a bit of Rose Kennedy in this lady—perhaps it was only the Hyannis Port connection. But now her mind was gone.

She spent the whole time trying to get into everyone's pants, but her genteel upbringing had not taught her how to go about it.

She began approaching the young husbands in the dining room, leaning over their tables, and asking them to dance. They sadly complied. It's hard to erase the picture of those gentle but stiff young men maneuvering their way around the dance floor, with Mrs. Noble draped around their necks. Our waiters all got extra kisses, and extra tips if they agreed to accompany her, weaving, back to her room at the end of an evening. Nothing more than that happened, but it touched us all.

The next thing I knew, there was an emergency telegram from her husband. Mrs. Noble had already passed out for the evening, so I went myself in the station wagon, to meet him at the airport.

Though near seventy, he was still a strong man, and he wasted no time. He planted a big kiss on my startled face and said, "Well, I hope she dies as soon as possible. I'm going to marry you, Terry Lewis." I didn't encourage it. A couple of days later, he piled her into a plane, and we never saw them again.

I don't know why I was saving myself for Bob Lewis. He had no such ambitions.

I had started to get involved in several volunteer projects in the village, where we were all trying to bring Puerto Vallarta into the second half of the twentieth century. We organized a campaign to get the school children vaccinated, and then all the dogs injected against rabies. Dr. Calderón and Rafael de la Cruz organized a Red Cross chapter and a local blood bank.

Since I have type 'O' blood, which anybody can use, Calderón often stopped me on the street, saying, "Come on, Terry, I have a baby in the hospital, and it's a real emergency. Can you do it right now?" I would send a taxi back to the hotel with a message that I was in the hospital. They all knew what it meant.

For the next several hours I lay on a cot and watched the blood flow out of my body and into a sick child. It was better for a baby to receive the precious fluid drop by drop, so its little body didn't go into shock.

Bob turned out to be one of the early benefactors of our blood bank, for his ulcer began acting up badly, as it had in San Francisco right before I left him. He claimed it was an old problem, dating back to his military service. When his worst attack came, Ofelia and Crisanto and I lined up over thirty friends who gladly donated blood for him.

By the time Calderón was finished with the black bastard, we were all teasing him that he was more of a goddam Mexican than a *gringo*! Only I could appreciate the sweet irony of that, considering all his previous remarks about life in Puerto Vallarta.

Did it ever occur to me why the ulcer began flaring up again at this time? Not a clue, until one day I visited my friend Beatrix at her house in Gringo Gulch, high above the Rio Cuale. We were sitting on her terrace, enjoying the breeze off the sea while our small children played together.

Totally relaxed, I gazed down toward the river and saw our blue Bronco pulling up slowly next to a low wall that ran alongside the river. Out stepped Bob, fit as usual, looking as if he was ready for a game of tennis.

"Beatrix, have you got any binoculars?" I asked. Americans always did.

I followed my husband's progress as he crept along the muddy bank and then started across the river, teetering from rock to rock so he wouldn't get his shoes wet. I knew where he was going. One of our juiciest little maids, Rodalinda, lived just on the other side. Hadn't I spent several mornings of my life waiting to pick her up for her first shift?

How Bob managed to look stealthy, and hopscotch precariously across the river at the same time, I don't know, but he did.

"I have a couple of errands in town," I said to Beatrix. "Can I leave the kids here with Lupe for a while?"

"Of course."

I flew down the hill, all the old tricks from my days of car stealing coming back to me in a flash.

Down the coast, out of town toward the Camino Real Hotel, there are many dirt roads that trail back up into the mountains and quickly get lost in the dense jungle growth. I parked the Bronco in some bushes, just as I had done at Golden Gate Park years before, and ran back toward town, cursing myself for not having learned a thing in the years between.

Back at the rim of Gringo Gulch, I took a deep breath and strolled out onto the lovely balcony, to wait for the beginning of Act Three. Bear and Buster and Dido hardly noticed that I had been gone. Beatrix and I had another rum and Coke, and then another. We were good friends, and we always had a lot to talk about. She was constantly remodeling her place, so in a way we were both builders.

Seven o'clock came, then eight o'clock, and sunset, as a dark American athlete began to pick his way back again across the Rio Cuale. I grabbed the binoculars. I saw Bob glance up toward the bank and then lurch around, trying to look both ways for his car. The movement caught him off balance, and he went headlong into the river.

Up he came, soaking wet and furious, with mud all over his white shorts and shoes. I could see him yell, scratch his head, and let out another string of sturdy oaths. He never looked up or guessed he was being observed. After poking his head around everywhere along the wall and the low brush for several minutes, he started walking down the dusty road toward home, still raving mad.

I was delighted. For someone as personally fastidious as Bob Lewis was, it was perfect. His clothes were always impeccable, his shoes polished to a spit shine, his office organized with military precision.

In fact, I always wondered about this. He was so correct in everything he did. On the outside. He sure fucked me over often enough.

Nine o'clock, ten o'clock, we had a little supper and then we went back to Las Glorias. I put the children to bed. I saw a stack of wet clothing by the washboard. The bedroom door was shut.

"*Alejandro! ¿Que pasó?*" I asked, when I returned to the office.

"I don't know, *señora*," he said in a whisper. "But don Roberto came back soaking wet and screaming at all of us in English. Nobody understood anything he said."

I suppressed a snort.

"His shoes were full of water," said Alejandro with wide eyes.

Of course they found the car later, and everything returned to what passed for normal with us.

Bob never suspected me, which is hard to believe. Or perhaps he knew very well, and he just didn't want to mention it.

The thought that I had seen him muddy and undignified may have bothered him even more than the fact that I had caught him returning from the luscious Rodalinda, whom I replaced with a heavy girl who had acne.

13

Betrayal in Mexico. The title refers to several incidents in those years. The first one happened the first year we were open.

The road from the PV airport to the middle of town is now one long, busy street. But back then, our Hotel Las Glorias was still two kilometers from town, and there was nothing between us, or close by on the airport side either. We were completely isolated in our tropical paradise.

Although I warned the young female guests not to wander around alone after about seven o'clock, especially in a bikini, I never really worried much about it. After all I had lived at LaPorte's little place, often alone, since 1964 without incident. The fishermen came up to the house sometimes late at night, but only to trade some limes or salt and pepper, and to share their catch.

A handsome young couple in their early twenties arrived from the Midwest to spend their honeymoon. If we knew about it, we usually tried to do something extra for newlyweds, like a bouquet of flowers, a basket of fruit, and champagne waiting for them in their rooms. The Mexican couples in particular seemed grateful for the food, since we usually didn't see them for about three days—so happy they were to get away from their chaperones at last, after all those years of courting.

These two Americans looked as if they had just stepped off a travel poster—blonde, strong, and good looking. All we needed was a lovely sunset in the background to complete the picture. They were shown to a bungalow in the very corner of the property toward town. We didn't see them the rest of that night or all the next day, and we didn't think much about it.

At about eight the second evening, I was sitting with my kids by the big arch in the reception area, enjoying a pleasant breeze from the sea, and getting ready for the arrival of the last plane from America. A stream of happy guests passed through the office on their way to the village for dinner or dancing.

Suddenly we heard faint screams coming in on the wind.

"Did you hear that?" I asked Alejandro. Before he could answer, the sounds got louder. Someone was screaming bloody murder.

"The young couple in twenty-one!" I thought. "Alejandro and Carlos, come along with me. Lupe, you take the children home now. Something's wrong!"

We ran to the bungalow and found the young bride, her hair full of sand, completely drenched with sweat, and sobbing hysterically. Her skimpy bikini was half torn off her body.

"I've been raped!" she kept repeating. "I've been raped!" Her eyes were wild with anguish. Her husband was frozen in shock. It was clear that he was not the offender.

"A douche!" I cried to the young man, "does she have a douche?" He ran to their luggage and started throwing things around, but he didn't seem to know what he was looking for. He shrugged helplessly.

I yelled to Carlos and Alejandro. "Let's get her in the shower. We'll take care of it. We mustn't let her get pregnant."

We half carried the girl inside the bathroom and shut the door, leaving the husband sitting alone on the bed staring in front of him.

"Take off the shower head," I barked to my boys. "Now, grab her legs. We're going to give her a douche."

They quickly took her by the ankles and she screamed louder and struggled. I held her head so that we wouldn't injure her even more when we flipped her upside down.

"DON'T YOU WORRY ABOUT IT! I won't let you fall," I yelled in her ear above the frenzied cries.

Like pros, the boys opened her legs and held her up naked, close under the strong jet of water. It was all I could think of to do at the moment. Young Carlos and Alejandro were magnificent. They didn't have time to become embarrassed.

The bridegroom started pounding on the door of the bathroom, scared.

"Everything is all right," I called. "Just stay outside for a moment."

It was over quickly, and we led the girl back into the room in a daze, and gently slid her into bed. I sent my boys to the bar to get some strong drinks for now, and to order us some dinner for a bit later.

"Do you want to see a doctor?"

The young man began to nod yes, but the girl wouldn't hear of seeing a Mexican doctor. She was shriveled up near the headboard, still sobbing deeply. She didn't want to be touched by anyone, even her husband. He sat on the edge of the bed with his hands over his face.

Gradually we learned some of the details. They had had a little argument, and the girl had disappeared running down the beach with her towel. When she calmed down a bit, as it was growing dark, apparently she had stretched out on the sand, perhaps to compose herself, perhaps to make her new husband suffer a little longer by making him wait.

Suddenly a shadowy man came up from behind and grabbed her. We never knew who it was.

Slowly, with some generous portions of whiskey, they calmed down. The supper came and I ate a little bit with them, and then left them alone, promising that the night watchman would stay right outside their bungalow so they could get some sleep.

The awful thing had not happened on my property, but still, I felt responsible in a way. Carlos and some of the other boys ran down along the shore to see if they could find the guy. They were going to kill him. But of course there was no one.

The next day I saw them off at the airport—my honeymoon couple from the travel poster.

Such violent incidents were rare, and much more typical of a big city than a small fishing village. But Puerto Vallarta was growing fast.

Bob Lewis and I started to feel comfortable in the society swirl of the resort. We organized the first tennis club. For thirteen dollars a month, the doctors and lawyers and businessmen of the town played on our courts. That was a reasonable fee, especially for people like the man who had unearthed a chest of old Spanish gold coins on his corner lot, while digging the foundations for the local Woolworth store! He had just built himself a private palace on the Manzanillo highway, the size of a hotel.

Bob, if he felt secure about his Spanish and felt he could take time off from kissing the secretaries in the office, sometimes acted as the unofficial tennis "pro." Even Calderón learned to enjoy the game, though there were a lot of jokes about his hefty body and his sore balls from making love too much all over the bay area.

Whole families came out to Las Glorias on the weekends. While the men played tennis, the women sat watching their kids swim in the kiddie pool beside the main one, where the crab shimmered up from below. In the evenings the hotel provided a barbecue or a luau on the beach. We had a host bar set up, and for four dollars plus drinks, our guests had all the fish they could eat, with all the trimmings, served on banana leaves in the tropical style.

And we even made a profit!

I'm shaking my head now when I think of those prices. But still today, Mexico is a bargain for Americans. Many retired men and women, who would not be rich in the States, can have the good life and *feel* rich south of the border. They can live outdoors more or less year around, employ a maid and a gardener, perhaps even a chauffeur, and live out their days in style—that is, if they don't have something that is coveted by one of the gangster element.

There were some very rich people. Among them, the owners of prominent factories in Tequila, on the road to Guadalajara, kept houses in Puerto Vallarta. And years before I came, even in the days of Tennessee Williams, some Americans had built beautiful houses on a wooded hillside in the center of town, high up above the Rio Cuale. That area soon took on the name "Gringo Gulch."

In the late Sixties, Elizabeth Taylor bought a house there, with a beautiful balcony overlooking the bay. At the same time Richard Burton bought his house across the narrow street from her, and one day we discovered that a romantic Venetian-style bridge linked them together above the street level.

I'm sure that famous couple loved returning whenever they could, because the villagers left them alone. At a time when she could go almost nowhere in the world without being mobbed, the actress could be seen alone and unmolested in Puerto Vallarta, driving around town in her lilac buggy, just a little bigger than a golf cart. Together they could go shopping, lunch at the El Dorado, attend the gala openings at Gallería Uno, and not be crushed by autograph seekers and souvenir hunters.

Those of us who did recognize them, who grew up admiring Elizabeth Taylor's beautiful velvety eyes, followed the lead of the polite Mexicans, happy that they had found a refuge away from the glare of the world's curious eyes. Little Maria Todd looked like any other village child, when she rode down the hill on her *burro* to get an ice cream near the cathedral, or to play with her friends. She spoke Spanish as well as any of them.

For a while, we thought Burt Reynolds had joined us too, but it turned out to be Juan García-Sánchez, a charismatic self-made millionaire who had started out in his home city of Guadalajara by selling used cars. By the time we knew him, he was breeding Arabian horses and building the fabulous Los Tules, the hotel next to us on the airport side. Soon we all became used to the sight of one of his regular guests, Peter O'Toole, robes flowing straight out behind him, as he rode one of those Arabians along the beach with his host.

García's interest in culture provided a boon to the whole town. He organized, with several of us, a plan to bring in the Guadalajara Philharmonic for a series of concerts. At first they played in the main square downtown, but quickly outgrew their space, and García provided the stately palm gardens of Los Tules as a setting for the starlight symphony performances. Champagne flowed, and imported flowers overflowed from the rustic fishermen's canoes. His sons, all dressed up as English lords, and his handsome wife made everyone feel welcome. Those elegant evenings are some of my favorite memories of the early days.

As a grim footnote to the saga of the rich or famous in our little village, one celebrity we could have done without was James Earl Ray, the murderer of Martin Luther King.

One day in 1968 I found my office swarming with American detectives. They had traced him to town and were checking all the hotels, starting at the airport. Sure enough, though he had kept to himself and we hadn't noticed him much, the man had stayed at Las Glorias for three days, and then slipped away as quietly as he came.

On those long summer nights, when there was still not much action in the early days, the gala openings at the galleries were a favorite way of meeting friends and having a chance to talk, away from the blare of disco music. Puerto Vallarta had its own native son, the gentle Manuel Lepe, whose primitive paintings were already becoming much admired. He showed at the Gallería Uno, next to the Oceano, which provided a cool haven for a casual drink and a chat, when we dropped in on many a lazy afternoon.

One of the most original artists of the period, to say the least, was the Austrian painter George Rauch, who had come to our Pacific resort to make his fortune. I met him at the new tavern that Carlos O'Brian had opened up on the Malecón.

Helen and I swept down on the place one night with our friend Rita Anson, a knockout photographic model from Twiggy's London, who was staying with us at our house. Helen went straight to one of the high barber chairs, as she always did, so she could survey the whole crowd and get a bead on the available men. Rita and I tucked ourselves into a low sofa next to it.

Suddenly there was a Bohemian with wild gray hair, moving in for a closer look at Rita's spectacular bosom. The men always spotted her first. She was about six feet tall, and her smooth English skin was flawless. I just sat back and enjoyed the show.

"You know, I'm a painter. I could make you famous," the man breathed in her ear, moving in even closer.

"What? You mean sit for you?" said Rita in a hushed little voice, her head cocked inquisitively to one side. "I've been a professional model in England." She shook her head politely. "I hate the job."

"But you haven't sat for a painting by me. It will be a new experience!"

"Probably won't be," she replied coolly, "because I'm not interested."

We all laughed. Rauch bought another round of drinks. Others came over to our low table to visit and then moved on. We were holding court, in a way, and enjoying it thoroughly.

However the painter was not to be deterred. The next thing I knew, he was sitting on the floor next to me, holding my foot in his hand. "Marvelous!" he exclaimed. "You have marvelous feet."

I looked down, thinking that was a new one.

"I'm serious," he said. "I'm an expert on feet. I love to paint feet," he emphasized, with an accent much like mine. "Surely you've seen some of my work at the Gallería Uno?"

I shook my head. He had taken off my shoe and was slowly caressing my ankle. "You must sit for me," he said. "You must."

I looked over at Rita. I could see that Rauch was about to tell me he could make me famous, but he was stumped. He had already used that line.

Rita glanced at me and shrugged, meaning, "Sure! Why not?"

"Let me kiss them," George continued, bending over attentively.

I know he must have pictured it as a romantic scene, but I couldn't help breaking into giggles. There we were, the music blasting, people gyrating feverishly to the newest rock music, everyone fighting to get a drink at the bar, and here was this man with my foot, sweating by this time from the alcohol intake and from the corduroy slacks that were too hot for the climate, sitting on the floor and gazing in profound admiration.

I couldn't resist. "When do you want me to come to your studio?" I asked demurely.

"How about tomorrow?"

Smart man. Get me before I changed my mind.

The next afternoon I felt even sillier, as I stretched out uncomfortably on a low Mexican bench. The painter had draped a rough woolen *sarape* in dark brown and white over my bare shoulders.

His manner of working was truly bizarre. This guy, who appeared so casual and moved so slowly and aimlessly in town, was now all business. He had spread out a huge piece of paper on the floor, about six or seven feet long, near the object of his devotion, my foot. He lay squirming on top of the paper, sketching feverishly.

Of course, from that angle, my foot appeared huge, and my tiny body receded far into the background. I dropped one hand gracefully over the *banquito* where I sat, and my chin rested, slightly cocked to the side, on my other fist.

Then out came a new paper and a slightly new position. In the portrait I don't think I am shown smiling, but in life I couldn't help it.

I wish I had kept all those sketches; they would probably be worth a lot of money now. But one afternoon, about ten years later, I was visiting John Huston in the house he had leased temporarily from Elizabeth Taylor. When I walked in, to my surprise I found myself face to face with my own foot. My little eyes, far in the distance, stared down at me from her living room wall!

I never became one of Puerto Vallarta's rich or world-famous, but in a way I guess I became one of its "immortals!"

Bob Lewis continued to find reasons for unavoidable business trips back to the States. There was nothing he liked better than the bustle of an airport or a crowded night club. Even in our small town, he spent hours drinking his martinis in the hotel bars, where he was friendly with all the *maître d's*, and quickly became known as a generous tipper. He hated the *mariachi* music. But a nightclub combo was his style, especially if a slow dance provided him an opportunity to nuzzle up to a great set of brown breasts, barely contained in the top of a skin-tight dress.

He was plainly bored in Puerto Vallarta.

The children were growing like weeds. The boys had brilliant white horses, with long tails that reached to the ground. Bear named his 'Faetón,' for the sun god, and Buster's was 'Cinco Locos,' or "five crazies." Like little demons, they tore all over town, roping any unfortunate calf or pig that happened to stray across their path. In cooler weather, if they got out of the house without my realizing it, they sometimes put on the little *charro* outfits we had made for them.

When Dido could barely walk, she got her own horse, 'Crystal.' The three of them loved to ride up into the mountains with Guilberto and spend an afternoon playing in the jungle waterfalls. On the way, they had to goad the horses mercilessly to convince them to overcome their sixth sense about the crocodiles in the Rio Ameca, but the boys seemed to have no fear.

At home, they rode at breakneck speed through the surf, sometimes sliding back till they were almost sitting on the horses' tails.

"They are devils in the water, your kids, *señora*," whispered Guilberto, half with concern and half with pride.

He taught them how to shoot, and in January, when the Canadian geese and ducks came through, and the farmers begged us to help keep them away from their crops, the tables at Las Glorias featured fresh breast of duck, delivered in person by our tiny suppliers.

The boys also "specialized" in seafood, bringing home crayfish, *langostinitos*, or big fresh scallops in the beautiful shells. Their reach wasn't long enough to throw a fishing net properly from the shore, so they slithered out through the surf like little rats, dropped the net, and then dove down to grab it and bring it back with a fish or two. At night they went out carrying a lantern, to look for abalone among the rocks of the swampy areas. They would come back with their little buckets, grinning triumphantly, their backs covered with mosquito bites.

There was of course no TV in our town; they found all their amusement outdoors—riding, snorkeling, climbing high up into the palm trees. Somehow they survived the tumbles and the scorpions, which loved to build their nests up there.

Well, not all their sport was outdoors. One late spring day, paunchy little Lupita had to admit to us finally that she was pregnant. She had fallen in love with Alejandro, and that method seemed to her a certain road to marriage.

However, she had miscalculated. Alejandro would not consider marrying her, since she was no longer a virgin. He was not a crass boy, just typically Mexican. Lupe surely knew the rules.

Gentle Lupita, so honest and so faithful! She was like an older sister to our kids. When I was busy, all I had to do was nod my head in a certain way, and immediately she did whatever needed to be done around the house. We tried to comfort her, and through the next months, we all made excited preparations to welcome yet another addition to our family.

The baby was born, and Alejandro strutted around with *macho* pride. But he continued to reject the idea of marriage.

But I was talking about my own boys. One afternoon I came to the house after sneaking a *siesta* in one of the bungalows, and I found the house strangely quiet. An occasional muffled giggle emerged from the bedroom.

I opened the door of the room and there was Bear, sucking innocently on Lupe's large tit, and smiling broadly. Buster and Dido eagerly crouched on the bed on either side and observed them closely.

"How does it taste?" piped Dido. "Is it good?"

I forced myself to stay calm. They were having such a good time! Lupe's eyes met mine and her face turned red.

"*¡Mira, Mama!*" said my son. "See! It tastes so sweet!" Two bright eyes proudly showed off his latest discovery.

In Mexico the women enjoy breast-feeding and continue it as long as they can. It wasn't rare in those days to see a young woman in public with two babies hanging off her breasts, a newborn and a two-year-old. But in most cases I hoped the children were at least her own!

I did what I could to distract the boys with a more appropriate game.

The big boys wanted their sports too. Fabulous private yachts, all teak and polished brass, sailed in and anchored at our small marina. Although the wealthy owners hadn't expected to stay longer than they needed to take on fresh water, as they started learning more and more about Puerto Vallarta, they extended their stay sometimes to a couple of weeks.

Other big boats, owned by American corporations, anchored there and were met by businessmen who flew in for a tax-deductible "conference." Years later, President Carter put a stop to that.

Our hotel association decided to announce a sailfishing tournament for November of 1968, in order to encourage business in one of the slow months. It was to become an annual affair, and immediately there was a lot of excitement about it. Local businessmen, like don Antonio from the pharmacy, and don Juan the jeweler, suddenly became big shots, as they put together all the detailed planning of the event. Registrations began pouring in to us from Guadalajara, from Mexico City, and from all the way up the coast to Vancouver. I was elected to stage the first banquet at Las Glorias for the awarding of the prizes.

I surprised myself. The first thing I started to plan was the outfit I was going to wear. I went to the *capitán* of one of our own fishing boats, and asked him to make me a net of fine thread to wear as a shawl over the strapless blue silk dress I had chosen. In Mexico City I found hundreds of Austrian crystal teardrops, and I had my seamstress sew them onto the delicate web one by one. I hoped the effect would be startling!

Next I set about organizing a banquet for two hundred guests. I ordered banks of floral sprays. The table arrangements were tricky for a group that size, and I finally decided that the head table should be set up just outside, under the wide arches of the terrace, and facing the rest of the group seated indoors.

I needed a carpet for the awards presentations in front of the table. An Oriental carpet seemed a natural choice for me, since many a wealthy Dutch home is crowded with fine Oriental rugs of all sizes. Sometimes they even hang on the walls, to contain the heat in winter.

My own carpets at the house were too small for the head table, but I remembered the long red one at the church, which was brought out for wedding celebrations, so the bride could make her grand entrance. I was sure Father Aldana would be thrilled to participate in this way. As is typical in Mexico, of course, he would already be one of the honored *invités*. I made a mental note to check on it.

Naturally the business of the preparations grew out of all proportion, and suddenly it was the morning of the banquet, and no carpet. I grabbed a couple of the bellboys and Cloro's truck, and off we went to town.

At Our Lady of Guadalupe, the housekeeper told us that the *padre* was "out ministering to (read: drinking brandy with) one of the souls who wanted to get into heaven." We stood there disappointed for a moment, and watched her as she disappeared through a side door.

Then I looked at Ramón slyly, moved my head to one side in a silent gesture, and as one, we three made our way toward the door of the sacristy. In silence we rolled up the carpet and in silence we carried it out to the truck and climbed in. Not a word had been said.

Minutes later, the thing was spread out on the shiny tiles at the restaurant. We all stood there admiring the effect. It was perfect! I would ask the father later.

Better yet, I called Jesús over to me. "The moment the *padre* enters," I instructed him, "lead him over to his seat in the corner and give him a glass of cognac. We've got plenty of his favorite Courvoisier, haven't we?" He nodded.

"And keep it coming as fast as he can drink it," I added. "Fill him up the rest of the evening!" Perhaps by the time for the presentation of the awards, he would not even notice that we had stolen his carpet.

At sundown, the boats started coming in from the sea, arriving in front of El Patio Restaurant for the official measuring and weighing of the sailfish. Everyone was in a festive mood, gaily tossing down pitchers of *margaritas*.

When nearly all the boats were in, the guests started gradually moving out of town toward the restaurant at Las Glorias, which looked beautiful under the palm trees with all of the lights twinkling. The sounds of an orchestra greeted them as they arrived. I stood in the receiving line, shaking hands with everyone and keeping a lookout for the priest.

The ladies glittered in their impressive jewelry. Most of the men wore *guayaberas*, those embroidered cotton shirts that are standard evening wear in the tropics. And I must say my own dress was a great success.

The banquet was served without a flaw. Huge trophies, so much loved by the Mexicans, were all gleaming in a line at the front of the room. After dinner, the president of our new international sailfishing tournament made the announcements, and the prizes were awarded. The top prize was a Volkswagen.

Padre Aldana then came up and blessed all the winners. Then he blessed all the losers. And then we all had another cognac with the mayor and his wife. There was never a word said about his carpet.

The next morning the boys and I pulled up in the truck. The *padre* was waiting for us. "*Señora,*" he said, shaking his finger, "I know what you did!"

"Forgive me, father," I said. "We had to steal your carpet." I sank down on my knees and the boys joined me, with huge eyes, the red carpet still rolled up in their arms. I added as an afterthought, "It did look beautiful, didn't it?"

"It was a good party," he smiled grudgingly. "You're forgiven."

"I'll put ten dollars in the basket for the poor. I promise."

"*Está bien, mi hijita,*" said the father, blessing me and the frightened boys. "Better yet," he whispered, "do you have some more bottles of that good Courvoisier?"

I assured him we did.

"Come back next week. I'm going to Spain. I would like to talk to you about all the beautiful places to see."

The following week I played Spanish tour guide once again, and filled him up with all the information he wanted to know.

Meanwhile, I continued as guide to the local area in my own office. When I saw time begin to hang heavy for some of the guests, I arranged an excursion and a picnic to one of my favorite spots, Punta de Mita.

A low, flat spit of land at the north end of the bay, this point appears to have figured in the history of the area for centuries. I loved to regale the wide-eyed Americans with the local pirate stories.

Once we arrived, I settled everyone down comfortably on the luxurious sand, and I went down the beach to look for some friendly fishermen. I knew there was always a supply of fresh lobster and shrimp to be bought at the rag-tag little huts huddled together against the Pacific wind. Then I sent my boys off to look for firewood, so we could have a barbecue on the beach. Sometimes my friend Rebecca came along and made her special *ceviche*, mixing bits of marinated baby shark and spices, and serving it on *tostados*, those crisp corn chips that have become so popular now in America.

When all the preparations were underway, I looked around at my guests. The bright afternoon sun was beginning to make them sleepy. "Look at the rocks out there," I pointed. "A hundred years ago, there were pirates on this coast. They used to change the lighthouse in order to trap their victims."

"Change the lighthouse?" They were hooked. The beautiful blond Americans sat up eagerly at the promise of a good story of clever enterprise and trickery.

"Yup. They covered up the light over there, and then made another huge beacon down at that end," I said, indicating another point on the coast. "The poor ships just ran aground on those rocks."

They chuckled appreciatively. I gestured behind me. "See how flat the sand is for the last two or three miles? They tell me the traditions continue in a new form. Our modern-day pirates use this area as a landing strip for their dope smuggling."

I was warming up. "Looks like a good airstrip for a space ship too," I yawned.

They slid back down onto the sand, not sure how much of this to accept.

I hadn't actually seen any space ships or even pirates, but one day on this point I had met some interesting Americans, Mel and Helen Melton, who were doing work that turned out to be just as intriguing. This devoted couple had made a fortune in real estate in a northern state, but their real interest was in archaeology. For years they had been flying their private plane down to the Bahía de Banderas area, and spending months at a time digging in the sands of Punta de Mita for pre-Columbian artifacts.

"Have you found anything?" I asked one day when my curiosity got the best of me.

"Not today," sighed Helen. "But we already have thousands of pieces that are definitely Chinese."

"How do you know?"

"We've been studying in books for years," she said. "We have lots of broken bits of things, but there are also whole statues, and pieces of jewelry that are exactly like those that others have found in China."

"I've heard something about the Chinese being on this coast before," I said, "especially in Acapulco."

"Yes, hundreds of years ago they were already trading silks and ivory from the Orient," said Mel.

"Isn't there a ballad about a beautiful Chinese princess who came over as a bride to a wealthy Mexican trader down there? She sat on the deck of her beautiful ship in the bay, all dressed in a gorgeous gown of silver and gold..."

"... and afterwards the Mexicans of Acapulco adopted that dress as their national party costume. That's right," the handsome man put in. "I think we can prove that the Chinese were here too."

"I'd love to see what you've found some time," I said, fascinated. "But won't you get in trouble if you take things like that?"

"We don't want to take them," Helen assured me. "We want to collect them here and open a museum so everyone can share them with us!" Her excitement was clearly evident in the way her eyes shone when she looked at her husband.

"We're not doing this in secret, you know. We weren't required to, but we got a license from the government to dig here, and there are two archaeologists in Mexico City who are helping advise us. From the Museum of Anthropology."

I was as excited as they were. In still another way my adopted "home town" was growing culturally.

"We've bought a house down here," added Helen. "You'll have to come visit us some time and see our treasures. Some are really beautiful!"

And so we began a special friendship that lasted until the poor Meltons found themselves on the wrong side of a clash with the official Mexico in which they had put all their trust.

I often saw them at restaurants or gallery openings and continued to follow their progress. I visited them and saw their fabulous collection, which eventually numbered almost fifty thousand items. Unfortunately their story has a sad ending, but more of that later.

If I didn't have time to accompany my guests on an outing, I sometimes convinced them to take a bus trip to Bucerías, a small village half way along the bay toward the point. Big, old wooden buses made the trip up the coast every day, the kind you only see in movies nowadays.

Crowded when they left Puerto Vallarta, they seemed to stop beside the road at every opportunity, to take on even more passengers, loaded with huge bundles and children and pigs and chickens. And just when you thought you couldn't breathe if one more creature of any sort got on the bus, the driver stopped and took on a family of ten! Still, once warned, the Americans seemed to enjoy the trip.

And those who already appreciated delicacies like turtle soup, turtle steak, or turtle omelets could not be dissuaded by a mere lack of comfort for a chance to enjoy the village's claim to fame.

Every so often, the large fertile reptiles struggled up onto the beach at night and laid masses of eggs, which were so flexible and flat at first that they resembled deflated ping-pong balls. When the word spread, the women of Bucerías set up a little kitchen and were in business. There were always a few Americans there, drinking tequila and sampling their delights.

sitting at the pool with Magalie, the wife of our buddy Rafael de la Cruz. Suddenly I was hit by an urge for the famous turtle soup of Bucerías.

"Let's go," said Magalie, and we ran to her car and jumped in.

"Let's take the kids too. They love turtle soup!" I suggested. Bob and Rafael had taken some tourists out on a fishing trip on one of their boats, but our staff could run the office easily during the mid-day hours.

Minutes later we pulled up eagerly onto the wide beach, and treated our children to the sight of their fathers rolling around on the sand with a lot of delectable brown skin, half dressed. Their wealthy American fishing clients were down the beach, totally preoccupied with their tequila bottles, happy and oblivious.

Magalie jammed her car in reverse and drove back to town to find a lawyer. I was not ready for that step yet, but from then on the term "fishing trip" certainly took on a new meaning.

For one thing, Bob Lewis had become more centrally involved in the running of the hotel.

It all began one day at the *charreada*. Bob learned from Crisanto Mora that our elegant friend Miguel Salinas was involved in raising quarter horses. There was a special horse at his ranch in Morelos that he was willing to sell, and Bob's mouth watered at the chance.

"Her name is La Malinche," said Salinas, looking fit and powerful as he stood towering over the heads of the other two men.

"La Malinche is a name well known in Mexico," explained Crisanto. "That was the name of the Indian woman who was translator for Cortés when he landed at Veracruz. She could run as fast as the wind to deliver his messages to Moctezuma."

"So this horse runs fast as the wind, huh?" questioned Bob, intrigued.

"Do you want to see her?" said Salinas. "We can go up at any time in my plane."

When Bob returned from the *hacienda*, he was aglow with stories of Mexican wealth and the famous Miguel Salinas.

"That ranch is beautiful!" he cried. "Miles and miles of sugar cane, a huge old ranch house, must be fifteen bedrooms! Swimming pool, private landing strip, Arabian horses. . .And on the way over there he showed me several other *haciendas* that belong to him too. Plus houses in Guadalajara and Acapulco, land in Sonora. . .The big house and the estate in Cuernavaca has a high rock wall around it that goes for four blocks! Marble staircase. . .antique furniture. . ."

Bob's been around wealth, but I've never known him to be so impressed.

"Did you buy the horse?" I asked, trying to appear casual. Underneath I was as excited as he was. Surely it could bring us nothing but good luck to have such an influential man as a friend.

"Yeah, I did. But Terry, we've got to talk." His tone became serious.

"What do you mean?"

"Sit down." He handed me a martini. It was going to be that kind of a discussion.

"Miguel says that our contracts for the hotel are not legal."

"Not legal! What do you mean? We had a lawyer draw them up. He was recommended by the American Embassy in Mexico City."

"Yeah, I know. It's something about the law. Maybe it changed or something. Anyhow, he says that it's illegal for a foreigner to own property or join a corporation in Mexico."

"But—" I sputtered.

"Let's have him over and see if you can make more out of it. I'm not sure I understood all of it."

Salinas was happy to oblige. He carefully explained to us that a hundred years ago, most of the valuable property in Mexico was owned by outsiders, who took the profits out of the country. The revolutionaries of 1910 made sure that the new constitution would never allow that to happen again. They nationalized all the foreign companies, and made it illegal for any foreigner to own a part of Mexico.

"But I had a lawyer—"

"Yes, your husband told me. Palomo is a very satisfactory young man here in Puerto Vallarta. But he has no experience in real estate or contracts. He is a criminal lawyer."

My mouth dropped open. The obliging young man at the embassy must have just picked his name out of a list without knowing anything about him!

"Doesn't it make a difference that Cloro is still in control?" I asked, referring to his 51 percent of our corporation.

"I'm afraid not. There's still your own 49 percent. And your visa. Technically, you are not allowed any income, except what you bring into the country from outside."

"That's ridiculous!" I exploded. "There are hundreds of American companies operating all over Mexico! How do they do it?"

Salinas remained suave as usual. "There are, of course, loopholes to the law," he smiled. We were speaking in English, for Bob's sake.

"Loophole" was a word I did not know, but I could pretty much guess the meaning of it. I admired Salinas' command of English, his intonation flavored just slightly by the time spent at Harvard and Cambridge. And at the moment I especially envied his degree in law.

"What the big American corporations do now is operate through *prestanombres*," he continued, "Mexican nationals who 'lend their names' to the corporation for a fee, but allow the actual owners to continue operating it."

"Is that legal?"

"Perfectly."

"We'd better have Cloro in on this," I suggested.

When my partner appeared, he nearly groveled at the sight of Salinas. He was delighted and flattered that a man of his reputation had taken an interest in us and was offering us his support. He agreed immediately to have Salinas look into the matter.

His eyes shone with pride, agreeing with our own private estimation—with such a powerful man on our side, how could anything but good come of it?

Still, I worried aloud when Bob and I were alone. "He's got all of our papers now. He could do anything, and we wouldn't know the difference. Are you sure we can trust him?"

"Trust! Who can trust anybody in this world?" Bob smiled sarcastically. "We already trusted the first lawyer!" He paused to let the effect of that sink in. "At least this one has so much money he doesn't need to cheat us."

His logic was unarguable.

"And he knows how Americans think," he continued. "He's full of stories about Jefferson and Washington and—"

"Jefferson and Washington didn't carry pistols when they wore a business suit."

"This is Mexico. His father was assassinated here. You know, there's a little shrine beside the highway, where he got out of his limousine and knelt on the ground and prayed to the Lord for the old man's soul."

There was no arguing with a scene like that.

When Miguel Salinas appeared again, he told us he had fixed everything for us because he found us so *simpatico*, so willing to work hard to make a success in his own country.

A board of five Mexicans was required by law for the new corporation, which was now to be called Bungalows Playa Las Glorias. Salinas himself would be president, and he would represent my interest. Or actually, to make sure of our rights, he told us he had set it up legally so that he represented Dido's interests.

Since she had been born in Puerto Vallarta, she was a Mexican citizen herself. Salinas was to be her guardian until she was eighteen years old. At that time she could own the property in her own right.

The vice president of the corporation was Antonio Juárez, a small-time lawyer friend of Salinas, as were the other three members. They would handle all legal matters, as well as the required *mordidas* for the greedy officials who continued to surface.

For their gift of lending their names to our business, the board members were to be given five hundred dollars a year and unlimited free visits at Las Glorias during the slow season. For President Salinas, that extended to hotel accommodations for all his workers as well, though they would be required to pay in the restaurant.

Salinas represented a Scandinavian firm which sold accounting machines in Mexico. He had Bob's name put on the payroll of that company, so that he could get his working papers immediately. My husband could now legally operate our hotel, though my visa was still about as worthless as a regular tourist visa.

"You and Cloro will need to be at all our board meetings, so you can tell us what you want," he said to Bob brightly. As a woman, I was no longer required, even as a translator for my husband.

Four million pesos' worth of stocks were to be issued "in bearer's name only," since most of us were Americans and could not own them outright. That bothered me, and I said so.

"Yeah," snickered Bob. "If Cloro gets hold of them, he'll hawk them and borrow more money to outdo all the loan sharks in town. He's already getting two percent a month. Can you believe it?"

Salinas as usual smoothed over our objections. "That's not as bad as it sounds in Mexico. Those small farmers don't have any collateral. They don't own their own land. If a new baby comes or another daughter gets married, what can the poor *pendejo* do but get a loan on those terms? Don't worry," he assured us, " that's the way all the big American vegetable growers in Sinaloa operate. You can check to verify this."

"Not necessary," said Bob hastily. "But I'll still want Arthur Young Company to go over all our accounts every six months."

"Of course," smiled our president.

Still, I checked with Gene Smith. He wasn't comfortable holding stocks "in bearer's name only," but he quickly saw that we had little choice. He calmed me down by telling me that they were all aware of the risk when they invested with me, and that I shouldn't worry about it: the American tax situation was in their favor, whichever way the enterprise went. Besides, they looked forward to their tax-deductable trips to check on the operation of Las Glorias.

The deal was signed.

"Your daughter is going to be a rich girl," smiled Salinas. We were giddy with anticipation.

La Malinche. She was the one who started all this. Crisanto had neglected to mention in his story that La Malinche is the supreme symbol of a traitress in the whole bloody history of Mexico. She, an Aztec woman herself, virtually handed her homeland over to Hernán Cortés and his rowdy bunch of Spanish *conquistadores* by betraying the priests and warriors at the slaughter of Cholula, and by preying on the weakness and superstition of the king, Moctezuma.

And Bob and I had just bought not only the horse, but the whole "bill of goods" from Salinas. Funny I did not appreciate the symbolism of it until much later.

I am sad now when I think of my adopted land. Not all foreigners are out to cheat the Mexicans. Many of us in Puerto Vallarta, like Thomas Olds, who built the Tropicana, like Jack Cawood, who built the Playa de Oro, and I, we really loved the town and were proud to see her grow and prosper.

Ultimately the Mexicans stood—and stand—to gain much more, even economically, if they had cooperated with those who wanted to help them build up their country. Bob and I provided jobs and pride for dozens of Mexicans at Las Glorias in those years.

But suspicion and political intrigue are so much a part of the Mexican tradition and nature, that perhaps they can't help defeating themselves. The big bandits, in the highest positions of power, who have stolen billions of pesos from their own countrymen—it's they who have brought Mexico to the brink of disaster where they are now, not the outsiders.

There's a classic joke that I heard time and again from my Mexican friends during the years I spent down there:

God had almost come to the end of his creation of the world. Saint Peter was sitting beside him with the account books, keeping track of everything.

"Let's see," said God, "that about takes care of it! What did we give the Chinese?"

"Slit eyes and silk worms," said Pedro, consulting his books.

"And what did we give the Russians?"

"All those vast grass lands."

"And the Americans? What about them?"

"They got the brains. And all those good Indians." The saint looked out over the world ball and said, "Listen, God, we still have that large piece of land left south of there. What are you going to do with it?"

"I think we'll call it Mexico," he answered thoughtfully. "Let's give them beautiful weather and long coastlines—maybe a hurricane now and then—but give them every kind of fruit imaginable, and thick forests, and coffee and cinnamon and gold and silver…And don't forget oil…"

Peter's eyes grew in disbelief. "My Lord, this is too good to be true! Aren't you afraid you're going to spoil them?"

"Oh, don't worry about that," was the answer. "They'll only screw it up anyway."

14

On the day I die
I will be lying between your arms
With seven bullets in my body . . .

Vera squealed in ecstasy at the music from the tiny tape recorder in my office.

I went to ask the judge:
Is it wrong to kill the man
That tried to steal my love?
On the day I die—

"That's wonderful! How about the next one?" she asked.

I was translating as fast as I could, to keep up with the song from the tape. The music was enticing, and it often happened that one of our guests would buy a cassette, only to find that the Spanish was beyond what she had learned in high school. I considered my translating services as part of the "continuing education" that went on in my office.

Vera was starting to dance around sinuously on my Dutch-style black and white tiles.

The next was entitled *"Sabor a mí."* "The Taste of Me."

"Uhhh—" I said. I wasn't sure how to approach this. But the music was going on ahead.

This morning I awoke
Knowing you will leave me,
My love, my life . . .
I only have time to smell your body,
To feel you, lying next to me . . .
You will never lose the taste of me. . . .

"Oooo—!" came the response. Vera's eyes rose to heaven, and the blush in her face and the writhing movement in her hips left no doubt that her blood was getting hot.

It was eleven o'clock in the morning.

I will never fail to caress your soul—
So lonely this night—
When will you come to my arms again?

"I'm going to get some more tapes in town today. Could we do it again some time? These songs are marvelous!"

The lover only knows how to give until the end—
To suffer is to love—

"I wonder if Sam would take me dancing tonight?" she sighed, and then reconsidered. "No, it's not the same. He stumbles all over his feet—and mine."

Sam appeared in the doorway at that moment and brought with him a quick change in the heady atmosphere.

"Terry, I can't believe how they let all those cows and steers walk all over the highway. Don't they belong to anyone?"

"No, it's a free zone for everyone," I said. "You know, the small *rancheros* don't have very many acres to grow their corn, so they let the cattle wander. If a car hits them, well, too bad."

"But what about the drivers on the highway? That could really wreck a car if you hit one of them. In our country, we'd sue the hell out of any farmer that got away with that."

I laughed. "I hit a cow near Tepic once. I spent three hours trying to find the owner, and then finally I gave up. You know those Chinese monkeys? Can't hear, can't see, can't speak? The Mexicans have that act down cold when they want to."

"Fred, how about a night club tonight?" suggested Vera.

"Are you kidding? The last time I asked a woman to dance, I almost got into a fight!"

"There's the *machismo* again," I said. "You've got to stick to your friends, and the other American women. You know, a Mexican man is out to score with every woman in sight, but he keeps his own woman under lock and key."

"What a country!" he mumbled, as they made their way out to the taxi. Another one was pulling up in the circular driveway.

It was funny to see the tourists coming down from New York and Chicago, all bundled up in expensive fur coats and hats and nylons. One by one the layers quickly came off, along with their inhibitions.

"Remember us from before?" the lady asked, hopping out of the car. "We were here three years ago."

"Of course," I said. Most of the time I did.

"Let me help you pick out a gardenia from one of the bushes in the garden."

"How lovely!" she smiled. "This place has such a friendly, kind of European feeling about it. That's why we like to come back."

On the way to the garden with her, I met my friend Rita Anson, who had a very worried look on her face. Rita had moved in with us after her divorce, and she helped out with the kids and with odd jobs around the hotel whenever we needed her.

She pulled me aside and whispered to me at top speed, "Terry, there are some men poking around the restaurant, asking everybody a lot of questions. I don't like the looks of it."

"Questions?"

"Yes. About who works there and how much we took in last month, and—"

"Well, who's business is that?"

"That's what I thought. You'd better come over."

I excused myself from my guest and started over to the restaurant. Before I got more than a few steps, I found myself face to face with a rather oily looking middle-aged man, accompanied by some police officers.

"Señora Lewis? I am Licenciado Carlos Gonzales." The Mexicans love their titles. This one's eyes told me he was a lawyer on the make. "I am looking for your husband."

"Bob Lewis? He isn't here right now. What can I do for you?"

The policemen started fading back along the path to continue looking around—but not before they had gotten a good eyeful of Rita, whose famous legs were shown to their best advantage that day in a yellow miniskirt.

"Watch it, old girl," said Rita, talking fast in a thick cockney accent, so that even if they spoke a little English, they wouldn't understand her. "I'll be back at the reception area if you need me."

"I represent one of your investors, Gene Smith of California," the lawyer began. "I would like to ask your husband a few questions."

"Perhaps I could help. Come with me to my—uh—to my husband's office. Is there any trouble with the business?"

"I can tell you that when I see your books, *señora*."

I was so surprised that I didn't think to ask if he had a warrant. But then, in Mexico, perhaps such a formality would not have carried much weight anyhow. I got out the books, all properly audited by Arthur Young's accounting firm.

"Hmmm—" the *licenciado* kept repeating.

"What is it you are looking for? Does Gene Smith have any questions about our operation?"

"Do you work here in the hotel?"

"Oh, no sir! I don't have my papers yet. It's my husband's business."

He looked at me sharply. Evidently he had seen me with the woman and the gardenia. "Well, every once in a while I come over to receive the guests and make them feel comfortable. I tell them stories about Mexico. These Americans love Mexico—"

"I will need to talk to your husband, *señora*. When will he be back?"

Out of the corner of my eye, I saw Lupe motioning to me frantically.

"Just a moment. Let me ask one of the bellboys," I said, and strolled calmly out of the office, leaving him to find out what he could from our accounts.

"*Señora*," said Lupe, breathless. "Alejandro heard the officers talking to each other. They said they are going to put don Roberto in jail!"

"Jail! What for?"

"I don't know, *señora*. But you'd better be careful of these men. They look like *bandidos*. They are searching everything. Like they want to steal your silver."

I sauntered back to the office. "Stay close, Rita," I said, as I passed the reception desk and went back to join the lawyer.

"They say that my husband is in Tepic, and they don't know when he will return." I looked the man squarely in the eye.

It was the truth, but also a great stroke of luck. Tepic is the nearest big city to Puerto Vallarta, but it is in Nayarit, the neighboring state. These policemen from Jalisco could not arrest him there.

"He went there to buy a truck. If he can't find one, he may go on to Guadalajara. Perhaps you will have to come back later?"

The lawyer gave me a sour look and went out to confer with his buddies in uniform. I followed, but I couldn't hear what they were saying to each other.

Then Gonzales looked up brightly and said, "*Señora*, I have an injunction here, which forces your husband to stop operating the restaurant. Since he is not here, you will have to accompany me downtown to see the judge. He will tell us what to do."

"Of course. Just let me change my clothes." I smiled the same smooth smile he was using on me. On the way to the house, I motioned for Rita to join me.

"As soon as we leave the hotel, take my station wagon and go over the bridge into Nayarit. It's Bob they want."

"What?"

"They want to put him in jail. Something about the restaurant. But they can't arrest him if he's not in Jalisco. You've got to watch for his blue Bronco on the highway, and don't let him drive onto the bridge!"

"It's a conspiracy. I love it!" she squealed. "But what are you going to be doing?"

"They are taking me to see the judge. Don't worry about it. The judge is a friend of ours. He plays tennis here on the weekends."

I felt very confident about everything. "I'll probably be back in a couple of hours," I assured her.

I put on a pink silk dress with a full skirt so I'd have some breeze around my legs. It was August, and it was hot. I hardly suspected I'd still be wearing that dress three days later.

"Now remember," I repeated to Rita, "don't let Bob cross over from Nayarit. He can stay in Bucerías until we find out what's up."

The lawyer, the officers, and I drove downtown and entered the jail, which at that time was located in an old *hacienda*, just down the street from the cathedral. Guards with rifles stool in the towers that had been added to the four corners.

The men talked with the officers on duty, and then Gonzales turned to me, with the same oily smirk. "*Señora*, the judge has gone home for dinner. You will have to wait."

He turned on his heel, and he and the officers disappeared. I was a "guest" in a Mexican jail.

"Hey, doña Theresa!"

I looked across the court, and recognized one of the men who had helped us with the carpentry. He was hanging from the prison bars in a small scrap of dirty underwear. "What are you in for?"

"I don't know!" I confessed. "But I'm getting out of here in a hurry!"

He laughed. "Not much chance of that! Everybody stays for at least seventy-two hours."

It was true. Until the end of the ordeal, I never saw an official charge, I was never accused of anything. In fact, I wasn't even the one they were after—it was Bob. But that's the Mexican way. Guilty until proven innocent.

I guessed that we were free to move around the large open area. I went to one of the barred windows that looked out onto the street.

It was *siesta*, and there was little traffic, but fortunately a taxi came along, and I signaled to the driver. He had a customer in the back, but he motioned that he would return in a minute. I waited.

Moments later, the taxi screeched to a halt in front of my window. "Señora Theresa!" the driver cried in a shocked tone. It was Cloro's son. "What are you doing in jail?"

"I don't know, Clorío. Go find Ofelia and tell her I'm in here, would you? See if she can get me a lawyer."

I returned to the precinct area to wait. There were two other women in my section of the jail, both whores, both in jail for stealing. They sat bored on the concrete benches, taking in the whole scene.

Out on the patio, several wives of the men prisoners were being frisked as they streamed in and out with hot meals for their husbands. Food is not provided in a Mexican jail. It's up to the families of the prisoners to provide. That meant no dinner for me. The women appeared to have no one either.

"Hey, Theresa!" someone called. I looked toward the window, where Rafael de la Cruz stood, scandalized. "What are you in here for?" he asked. The word was spreading fast in our small village.

I went over and explained as much as I knew, which wasn't much.

"I'll go have a word with the judge," he said, and vanished around the corner.

I went back to rejoin the women, and did what one does in a Mexican jail. I sat.

There was a sort of bunk bed affair out of concrete, built into the wall, a typical construction in Mexico. The whores were sitting on the middle bunk, dangling their legs into the faces of the policemen waiting for their orders below. Apparently if you sit on the bottom, you get legs in your face. And the top bunk was too close to the ceiling to sit on. So I did as they did—and tried to keep the men's wandering hands off my ass. As they did.

I knew these officers. Outside, I was "*Doña* Theresa," treated with great respect. But here I was just some broad who had ended up in jail.

"Hey, *hombre*! " snickered one of fattest ones. "*¡Otra cucaracha!*" He was not talking about the nasty insects crawling up out of the toilet. He was referring to me.

It was going to be a long afternoon.

I leaned back against the wall and took in my new surroundings. The foul odor, both from the place and the people, was almost overpowering. I noticed that there were small grills near the ceiling for air circulation, another typically Mexican construction. Right then I decided to stake out the top bunk for myself, if I was to be detained long enough to need it. The whores were too short to climb up there easily. They wouldn't object.

The men were behind bars across the patio. Whenever their lewd remarks began building up, a guard would yawn and growl at them to back off. If anyone had to go to the toilet, he had to parade past all of us to an open cubicle in the corner behind a partition.

"Toilet" is not quite the word. You were supposed to squat over a sort of slimy platform in the floor with an open drain, trying to keep skirts, pants, billfolds, glasses out of the sewage, while at the same time hurrying in order to avoid being overcome by the stench. To flush, you dipped a bucket of water from a nearby tub and poured it down fast.

In time, I learned that "solitary" was just beyond. That was a bare room, four by four feet, with a concrete bench. No one but a midget or a child could stretch out in there. If you wanted to sleep, you curled up or raised your legs straight up into the air. The "pig's pit," they used to call it in the concentration camp.

On the whole, I was in pretty good spirits. I hadn't been tied up. I hadn't been pushed around, if you don't count the friendly nudges from the officers.

I felt a little hunger, but it was the heat that bothered me the most. Here we were, in the hottest month of the year, and at the height of the rainy season. The center of town was without running water that year, because the floods rushing down from the mountains had knocked out the water lines. And of course, such a luxury as a fan was unthinkable, even for the police.

And so we sat.

At six or seven in the evening, the judge appeared. "*Señora Laao-is,*" he said in a hushed, apologetic tone. "There's nothing we can do at this moment. Of course, I have every confidence—"

"Can't you get me out of here? My husband could arrange to have some money sent for bail."

"I have heard of that," he said, trying for a comforting tone. "I understand you have that in America. But unfortunately there is no bail in Mexico."

"You mean I really have to stay here? I'm not even the one they came for!"

"I know, and I'm sorry," he shrugged. "But it's the law. Just say you did it, whatever it is. I'll give you a small fine, and you'll be home in three days."

My heart sank. The judge was sincerely sorry, I think, but the whole thing appeared to be out of his hands.

He left the precinct, and I stretched back once again against the wall. Then I broke out in uncontrollable laughter. I couldn't help it. At least my husband, Mr. Clean, was not the one sitting in this creepy little place. The poor man would have had a heart attack! The picture of him trying to manipulate that toilet over there was more than enough to cheer me up for the rest of the evening.

Ofelia came to visit, her eyes hollow with sadness. "The children are all right. I don't know about Bob yet," she said. "And I've sent Crisanto to try to locate Miguel Salinas. He should have a lawyer who can help you out of this."

Then she reached down and smiled broadly as she lifted the lid off an exquisite dinner plate from my favorite chef at the Oceano Hotel.

"Great!" I shouted. "We dine in style tonight!"

I looked over at the two women who were to be my bunkmates that night. They were watching me with considerable interest. As far as I knew, they hadn't eaten that day either.

"Here," I said. "There's enough for the three of us."

We all dug in. When we finished, as it was getting dark and the prison day was drawing to an end, I crawled up to my top bunk and stretched out as best I could.

One construction item I hadn't counted on was that the ceiling was only a few inches from my nose. Luckily I don't usually thrash around much at night; otherwise I would be adding bruises to the humiliation I had already suffered. But I was too tired to think about my dignity. I closed my eyes and tried to get some sleep.

This prison was not the most awful one I had been in, nor the least. The memories came flooding back, uncalled for, but inescapable.

The Japanese marched into Java the first week of March, 1942, and sealed off the port of Djakarta from any further attempts to escape.

At first it all seemed harmless enough, even comical. How Helen and I laughed when the strange little men showed up at the club in swimming suits that looked like obscene diapers!

But the conquerors lost no time in spreading the message to the Indonesians that their fellow Asians had finally been freed from the yoke of Dutch slavery. Propaganda posters went up everywhere, proclaiming the Japanese as the new liberators.

I was seven years old.

One day on the way home from school, I ripped down one of the posters and walked on without thinking much about it.

That night after dinner, the *kempetai*, the Japanese secret police, were at the door. We were all hustled downtown to their new headquarters, in the Malang high school, for questioning.

"Are you so stupid that you instruct your daughters to destroy Japanese property?" screeched an officer with narrow black eyes.

My father was calm. It had been such a negligible offense.

A soldier stepped forward and grabbed me. He threw me in front of the room, by the blackboard.

"Down on your knees, brat without brains!" he snarled.

I fought back the tears, hardly understanding his words. I stood up even straighter at attention, hoping to please him.

The soldier laughed with glee and with his proud samurai sword, he sliced an arc over my head.

I flinched and started to cry silently.

He poised his sword again on my neck and drew it back to swing a second time. I could hear my father take a sharp breath, but still he said nothing.

I fell to my knees sobbing.

The sword flew over my head again.

Still my father would not admit that he had told me to tear down the poster.

After hours of questioning, we were all led to a tiny cell for the night. There my mother and father tried to calm us down—four young girls who understood nothing of what all this meant. My poor sister with polio lay helpless in the corner.

"This is not about the poster," I heard my father whisper to my mother. "They must suspect us about the medicines."

All the next day I spent kneeling again in front of the blackboard. After three days, my father relented and confessed that he had given me the instructions about the poster. We girls were allowed to return home, but sure enough, my parents were detained, to face a different line of questioning and torture.

The conquerors knew that much-needed medical supplies were being spirited out to the Dutch Indonesian Army, but they could never catch my mother and father at it. They could prove nothing.

The servants who had always been with our family did not desert us now. They took care of us in our home, and they brought us to the *kempetai* prison to visit our parents.

At first we went during the day, but my hysterical fear of the samurai sword convinced them to try to sneak us in at night, in a horse-drawn cart, after there was a change of guards. We brought along clean clothing, food, and toothpaste.

For three months, my parents were kept in a sort of cage, not big enough to stand up in. But their spirits held strong.

The servants continued to visit and take their instructions, especially the gentle Kudu, our assistant pharmacist, who had been with the firm from my grandfather's time. Every day he padded into the converted high school in his bare feet and humbly greeted my father with a polite bow and a salute, his hands held together in front of him, even though he was now the free man, and technically the "boss" of the operation. Our servants knew they could be risking their life by coming there, if the Japanese decided on a whim that they too were spies.

After three months, the Japs still had no confession and no evidence. In the meantime, my father was able to prove that he had Indonesian blood in his veins. He was not one of the hated Dutch purebreds. They were allowed to return home.

The next few days, the feverish openings and closings of the safe in the pharmacy were multiplied, but with an added caution. My mother and father walked slowly through the rooms, looking around and speaking in low voices.

Then, as suddenly as the reprieve had been given, it was taken away. My father disappeared one day, and we never saw him again until after the war. The huge doors of the safe had been sealed with the stamp of the Japanese Imperial Army.

My mother did not panic. She needed time to disperse the remaining medicine and to organize her valuable documents and jewelry.

With a mixture of alcohol and water, she injected herself in the arm, knowing that the solution would throw her body into a wrenching fever of 104°. When the Japs stormed into the room, Kudu pointed to her shivering frame and claimed she had some mysterious infection, highly contagious.

It worked. During the next nights, still sick with the fever, my mother Dido was able to break the seal and empty out the safe, to entrust our valuables with Kudu, and send along the last of the drugs to our army up in the mountains.

When the *kempetai* finally caught on, she found herself back in prison for two more months.

Then out she came again, and for a couple of days we were again a family, but this time without my father.

One morning as we were sitting down to breakfast, Jap soldiers burst in the door with their bayonets fixed, yelling at us to take away only what we could carry. We were being moved out in five minutes.

My mother screamed to the servants to get a bag together for us girls, while she ran to my paralyzed sister Eleanor. She took whatever medicines she had saved, and grabbed an armload of towels, tablecloths, napkins— anything she could find to make diapers for the four-year-old girl. She wrapped her in a sheet, and we were roughly shoved out of the door.

Our first "camp" was a children's paradise, in a quirky way. The soldiers had taken a small section of the city and put up a high *kadek* fence around it, of tightly woven bamboo. The houses inside remained exactly as their owners had left them at the time they had been arrested or had fled to safety.

We girls wandered through the new prison with wondrous eyes, touching everything—the elegant silver tea service in the dining room, the books, the Oriental carpets, the family photographs on the piano. The closets were full. We played "theater," changing clothes five times a day, and helping ourselves to the hair combs and brushes that were still neatly placed on top of the dresser next to the bed. In the kitchen, a marmalade jar still sat on a sideboard, waiting for someone to put the cap back on.

But a prison, even a palatial one, is still a prison. The women and children began fighting among themselves for what we really needed: amidst all that luxury, there was no food. People started to get sick.

Indonesians came to the *kadek* quietly at night to ask if they could help, but most of the women could not even bargain for fruits or vegetables, since they had not even learned enough of the language to know the names of those simple things.

The Indonesians, on the other hand, were just as lost and hungry as we were. After centuries of being taken care of by the Dutch, they didn't know how to get by without us. My mother snuck out to them what silver she could find.

"Better they have it than the Japs," she said.

Soon our dark friends stopped coming at all, for many were caught and beaten or killed on the spot.

Our games soon turned destructive. We started breaking the china dishes. We rode the bicycles around until even the rims gave out. We shot mangoes out of the trees with slingshots, often taking out a window instead.

Once, when Helen and I suspected there was silver hidden in a mattress, we set fire to it to get it out, little realizing we would melt the silver along with it. We almost burned down the house.

Often I found my mother sitting at an upstairs window, staring out at the Catholic church, which had not been included in our compound. She told me she was praying to Saint Teresa for strength and guidance.

But the real religion in the camp was of a more practical type. Every night, the women came stealthily to our house and gathered in the parlor behind drawn curtains. Out came the board they had fashioned, with the letters of the alphabet arranged in a neat circle around the edge. A cross of wood stood poised on a nail in the center. Endlessly the women asked questions of my mother and then waited, while the cross spun silently around the board, spelling out the answers. Nearly all the questions had to do with the whereabouts and the safety of their husbands.

All, including my mother, began to look more haggard, after weeks without a night's sleep.

And then one day, again without warning, our luxury prison days came to an end. The soldiers were upon us, ordering us into a drab army truck. We were to be transported to the mountains.

My mother seemed desperate, but Helen and I didn't understand. We had always loved our beautiful summer house in the mountains, with the swimming pool and the rose gardens. We pictured the "camp" as something like that.

Barefoot and nearly naked, with only little shirts on, we were herded onto a large van. My mother struggled to get onto the truck with Eleanor in her arms.

When she took too long to climb up, the Japs poked her with their bayonets and pulled her up by the hair.

In panic, women were rushing about through the camp. Some who had hidden in closets were being dragged out and shot. Others, in despair, deliberately stepped in front of the line of fire.

Next, like sheep, like the Jews in Europe, we were pressed into boxcars for the journey to Ambarawa. Many of us had managed to grab a little bundle to take along, but in the confusion of loading onto the train, most of them were lost. I clung fiercely to the little rag doll I have mentioned before.

There were no seats, but a few mattresses were scattered about, swarming with mosquitoes. The car stank of sweat and fear and excrement. We traveled like that for three days.

At night, the large door was rolled aside, revealing the gleam of polished swords and big teeth and small, mean eyes. The Japs were trying to hide our train from the strafing of Allied planes overhead, but it was themselves they were saving. We could get out and go into the jungle, but no one worried that we would run off. Where could we go to escape them? And if one of us died in the jungle, then that was one mouth less to feed later on.

We could tell it was daytime by the sunlight filtering through the cracks in the side of the boxcar. Many of the women no longer tried to cover the dark stains of shit on the seats of their dresses or the slobber of vomit on the fronts. Those who lay dying could be spotted by the flies which crawled calmly over their faces.

The train finally stopped far down the mountainside below the camp. We walked uphill for two hours before arriving at the gate. From far in the distance, we could already make out hundreds of gaunt women, lined up near the entrance to survey the newest arrivals. More mouths to feed, yes. But the new ones could still walk. And they usually had some possessions along, that might be of some value.

I looked up at my mother with hope and anticipation shining in my eyes. "Does this place have a swimming pool?" I asked.

"Yes of course—a swimming pool."

We were content for the moment.

I have described the concentration camp already. But I have not said much about the unspeakable torture that became everyday routine.

The women who offended these small men were used for bayonet exercises. The soldiers tied them tightly to a tree with ropes—straight and tall, so that they would not sag over and spoil their aim. Then the men backed up about twenty feet and charged, screaming a bloody war cry, and sank their bayonets in with a dull thud.

It was then up to the younger, stronger women to cut their friends down and load them onto a cart, to be taken outside camp for the vultures.

At first, some women tried to escape into the jungle. But after three young teen-age girls were caught and crucified on the *kadek*, all further attempts stopped. There they hung naked for days, their breasts and bellies covered with festering cigarette burns. The Japs got a kick out of watching the white skins turn redder and redder in the tropical sun. Finally the birds swooped down and ate them off the fence.

When my mother was caught for some "crime" or other, she had needles shoved up under her fingernails so far that she could not bend the first joints of her fingers.

"The ones that live are worse off," she said.

When poor paralyzed Eleanor died one night in prison, my mother seemed to feel nothing. There were still three girls to keep alive. The rats got to my sister before we did, and chewed off a good portion of her left arm. Dido dug the shallow grave herself.

For any infraction of the rules, the Japs took small bamboo sticks and jabbed them straight through the offender, an arm or a leg sometimes, often her nipple. Then they would laugh and pull them out, leaving the splinters behind to become infected.

As the Allies started to win the war in the Pacific, the guards took pleasure in shooting off their weapons at random through the camp, killing anyone who happened to be walking by. Sometimes they went through and broke a few toes with the butts of their rifles, leaving those women unable to walk.

Food became scarcer.

"No rations today," said the little Jap officer, strutting around with his whip, in imitation of MacArthur.

We lay all day long on our slim cots. The less we moved, the more likely we were to survive.

My mother, being a smart herbalist, continued to find a supply of grass for us to chew on and suck out the meager nourishment. The supply of grasshoppers, dogs, birds, and rats had been quickly exhausted.

Strangely, no one went for the cockroaches, even there.

When one of the women died, their friends repeated a silent ritual. The corpse was stripped of any clothes that might be useful, and the mouth received close inspection to make sure that no gold fillings got by, which could come in handy for night trading.

The strong women, who had been sent out to get firewood for the kitchen, were now forced to cut down trees to rebuild the destroyed bridges. Hungry as they were, they preferred doing that to staying around the stench and the disease, the screaming and the constant bickering of camp.

At first when the monsoon rains came, we danced under the leaky roofs of dried-out palm leaves. But that pleasure soon wore thin. And as the endless weeks of rain wore on, the women became more irritable, and gave the Japs more excuses to punish them.

We discovered we were safest if we just sat quietly and called little attention to ourselves. The women watched each other squeeze the pus out of their sores with dirty fingers.

I still have scars up and down my legs from what we called "camp wounds." Mosquito bites would become infected and fester dangerously in no time, sometimes an inch into the flesh, if one had no resistance to infection. When my mother saw this happening, she took us out and scrubbed the sores hard with rough sand, while we screamed bloody murder all the while.

But she saved our lives.

We learned early on to avoid the clanking sound of a tin cup. A leper was on her way to the kitchen to find some food.

Sometimes, when the coast was clear, Helen and I would sneak into the kitchen to look for scraps. Since she was smaller than I was, she would climb to the top of a big drum and then slip down, while I held her ankles. Inside, she scraped out bits of food that had caked and burned on the side. If a guard surprised us by coming too close, in she went!

To this day, I still hear the midnight howling of the women writhing in their malarial nightmares. Fevers up to 106° carried such hallucinations that they only wanted to sit up and scream themselves free, but they didn't have the strength.

I can still count to ten in Japanese, a souvenir of *Appel* every morning, a roll call we often spent on our knees, to remind us that even though they were short, the sonsofbitches were our masters. And even now, my dreams are still sometimes interrupted by probing searchlights.

One day the planes started flying over the camp. Allied planes. They dropped leaflets everywhere, proclaiming, "Freedom is here!" If only we could hold out!

The women started going crazy, and they dared twice as much as they normally would have. And the Japs seemed even more determined to kill us all, strafing the open compound regularly from their towers. My mother kept us inside, huddling under the bamboo beds, and covering us like a lioness with her cubs.

Suddenly the shooting was over. Dead bodies littered the sandy area.

We crept out after a day of silence and saw that the towers were empty. The gate was hanging open. Still we dared not move. It could be a trick. Or what we found outside might be even worse than what we had experienced in camp. Most women hung back, fearful.

My mother gathered us to her, made sure that I had the only baggage left to us, the small doll, and strode out of the gate with determination.

We found a nearby Indonesian *kampong*, and stayed the night, while she worked feverishly to arrange transport for us. She couldn't have done it if she had not spoken the language, perhaps if she had not had a gold ring to offer, for the Indonesians were ever more fearful.

Stray Japanese were still hiding out, to be sure, but now there were also Sukarno's guerrilla forces, seeking to liberate the country from all foreigners, with orders to kill anybody who helped even the Dutch.

Finally she found a gentle old man who agreed to hide us in a small dogcart and take us down the mountainside.

We walked for three days after that, avoiding every sign of human life until we met the Gurkhas, the crack Indian fighting unit, who had been sent from Nepal with the Sikhs to protect the safety of the Dutch colonials. These tall, magnificent soldiers put us into a truck bound for Malang, and walked beside us as an escort the whole journey.

Indonesian freedom fighters were everywhere, searching out and stealing arms from the fleeing Japanese army, to replace their handmade knives and *machetes*.

It was September, 1945. World War II was supposed to be over. But my mother and sisters and I were once again prisoners in a *kadek*, this time presided over by Sukarno.

The elegant homes in Malang were run down now, the gardens grown tall with weeds. Indonesians who had tried to climb over the fence to steal had been shot by the Japs, and the trees were still littered with expensive clothing and silver.

The word got out that the family of *tuan basar*, "the boss," was back. Our faithful servants began to appear, to bring us food and natural herbs and comfort. They had not fared so badly as we had, but theirs had certainly not been a good life in those years. There was a joyful, if secret, reunion.

"And Eleanor?" asked one of the maids who had taken special care of her.

My mother shook her head.

They clung to each other and wept.

My old *babu*, the woman who slept next to me from the day I was born, broke into tears when she saw me. "Theresa! Your little body! What has happened to you?" she cried.

After that, she appeared daily in the compound to massage my legs and my stomach, swollen from beriberi, to try to bring the water slowly to the kidneys and then out. Patiently she held me in her arms and fed me her special herbal tea, drop by drop.

Kudu came by, and we all wept and hugged him as if he were our father instead of our father's assistant.

"Don't worry. *Tuan basar* is alive. He will come back one of these days."

"I'm sure of it," repeated my mother. Was it blind hope, or did she really know something through her spiritualism?

"When he comes, I have a wonderful surprise for him!" the man hinted.

My mother smiled secretly.

Humilde is the Spanish word I used to describe the Mexican people. Modest, gentle, sincere. They remind me so much of the faithful Indonesian friends and relatives from my childhood. It is why I instantly felt at home in Mexico.

Nevertheless, we spent fifteen more months in the Indonesian *kadek*, without our father, before we were removed to Holland.

I woke up from my reverie of childhood with a start.

I was in a small, dingy jail in Puerto Vallarta, and there was a scratching noise above my head. In the early morning light, I found myself looking right into the little bright eyes of a rat, not a yard away on the rafters. I must have frightened him somehow. His tiny pink feet scurried away for cover.

I made a mental note to thrash around at night a bit more than I was accustomed to doing.

Rita was there first thing that morning, flushed and looking superb in a light green tailored outfit. She made quite a hit in jail, judging from the yells and catcalls on the men's side. They hung on the bars like monkeys, their hard cocks creeping out over the tops of their scanty underwear.

"Bob stayed the night in Bucerías," she whispered. "He doesn't know what to do."

"I'll bet he's found somebody to comfort him," I thought, but pushed the spiteful feeling out of my mind.

"Please check with Ofelia and see what she's found out about a lawyer," I instructed her. "Thanks for everything."

My friend Rita—as much as she drove me crazy sometimes, she really could come through in a pinch!

She could hardly have been more different from me. Her perfect long nails, her sleek reddish hair smoothed back past her ear, her slow, sexy walk, as if she had no idea what effect she had on men, all shouted "high-powered model." Inside she was soft and tender.

She and her husband had first come to Las Glorias from Vancouver, when he wanted to do some deep sea diving. After their divorce, she appeared one day at my door, her eyes swollen and sad. The little bit of alimony she had received would allow her to live in Mexico if she moved in with us.

She started helping out all around the place in her own quiet way. She would say to my boisterous sons in her hushed voice. "Now, don't you think you guys should really try to eat your breakfast?" Four eyes looked up at her with great seriousness. "Because your mother is going to come over here pretty soon, and she'll be very upset." Somehow it worked—sometimes even better than my steamroller approach.

She was a menace on the highway. "Oh, Terry, your whole fender fell off today. The hood is mashed in too." (I don't know how she's doing nowadays on the highways around Vancouver. Perhaps the Canadians have learned to keep a watch out for her!)

But in a crisis? No problem.

The previous hurricane season she had borrowed my station wagon, and still had it as the storm came screaming in. I knew she had not driven into the swollen river, as one of the police cars had, but still I was worried. Suddenly I spotted her slowly dancing her way back from town along the beach, ducking coconuts from the slashing palm trees and jumping high to avoid the waves.

"Terry! Isn't it glorious?" she shouted. "I ran out of gas and couldn't get any farther than that small river. The new highway is washed out."

I shook my head, as I watched my swimming pool fill up with blowing sand and sea water. It had gone from blue to dark green in just an hour's time.

"De la Cruz wants you to lend him your truck for the Red Cross," she continued breathlessly. "People are floating down the river on bits of wood, trying to save themselves, but they have nowhere to go."

For the next three days, Rita and I became unofficial nurses of the Red Cross, transporting hundreds of people, taking in as many as we could at the hotel, feeding them, and guarding the place to make sure the towels and pillows and blankets didn't walk off permanently. I had let my staff go home to their families.

The third night someone yelled "Earthquake!" We all felt the slight tremors. Without comment, Rita and I gathered up the kids and grabbed a couple of Oriental carpets to make a tent. That night we slept out under swaying palms and the turbulent sky.

Four hundred people died in that hurricane.

I've always thought Rita would have made a great Southern belle. With her guts, she probably would have gotten through the Civil War just fine too.

The next one to visit me in jail was Lupita, and then later Consuela, my other maid.

"Oh, doña Theresa!" gasped Lupe. (I hoped the guards heard that.) "What are they doing to you? It's terrible to be in jail!" she sobbed.

"Don't worry, Lupita. You just stay with the kids. Everything will be fine."

By the time Consuela appeared, several more hours had passed—hours of just sitting on the concrete bench. I was bored. Everything hurt, not just my rear end. All we could do was sit and sweat under that asbestos roof and swat flies. I can take only so much of that.

"Consuela, get some money from Rita at the office. Go get me some Ajax and some Lysol and about five buckets. And bring a bunch of brushes. I can't sit around here any longer. This place is a sty!"

She looked at me in shock, but she did as she was told.

A couple of hours later, even the whores were pitching in to help me scrub down the nasty walls of the jailhouse.

"We're not going to have near enough water at this rate. Hey, *muchachos!*" I called to some of the guards. "Would you mind running down to the sea to fill up these buckets?"

They were too surprised to say no.

Soon we had a brigade going, like the firefighters in the Old West.

The three of us women bobbed up and down around the inner courtyard with our little buckets and brushes, much to the delight of the hot monkeys on the one side and the police on the other.

The floors and the toilet were next.

As the heat grew more intense, I showed my companions an old Indonesian trick. When the next bucket arrived, I turned it upside down on my own head, so that I could continue to work in comfort. The salt water streamed down my body. The least hint of a breeze felt delicious, and my pink silk dress stayed cool as it slowly dried off in the stifling humidity.

We had just staged our own 60's version of a wet T-shirt contest! We had no need to complain any longer about the lack of showers in our accommodations.

When we were finished, I stood at the barred window and surveyed the place. Soaking wet and filthy, I looked out onto the plaza in the center of town where only days before, dripping with diamonds, I had swept glamorously to a seat up front, for a concert of the Guadalajara Symphony.

That night Bill and Nellie Wulff showed up with a delicious meal from the El Dorado. "We're with you, Terry," they said. "They can't do this to one of our hotel association. We're a team!"

I smiled gratefully and brought the meal over to my fellow scrubbers. I had really gotten friendly with one of them, who was in for stealing a small amount of cash from one of her "johns."

"Don't you worry, my dear. When you get out, I will help you," I promised. Later she became one of my most faithful maids.

On the third day Antonio Juárez, the small-time lawyer who had become vice president of our new corporation, swept into the jail. He was in a hurry, as he always was. Salinas had made his move to get me out. It cost me $1600. A formal charge had never been made.

After that, Bob and I wanted little to do with Gene Smith. He had been our first investor, and we thought, a friend. He had spent many weeks with us. My own piano was sitting in the bungalow we always had reserved for his wife.

But he hadn't understood that it takes time to get a seasonal business on its feet. The restaurant lost money in the summertime before the highway came in, in 1969. He thought, persuaded by his smooth Guadalajara lawyer, that Bob had been stealing it.

We made official arrangements to take over the restaurant part of the business ourselves.

15

The important local news during that August of 1969 was not that Terry Lewis was in jail, but that the highway to the north had finally been completed. For the first time there was a straight run from the North to Puerto Vallarta! The bridge over the Rio Ameca, where Rita had sat, waiting to see Bob's blue Bronco come into view, was the last link.

The high mountains to the east had effectively cut us off in so many ways before that. Now the new highway made a tremendous difference in all of our lives.

The markets were filled with wares that could be transported cheaply into the bay area for the first time. If we needed to go to Tepic or even Guadalajara to get supplies for the hotel, it was no longer a seventeen-hour trip over rough country roads, as it had been for Bob Lewis the first time.

This prospect of easy access was not lost on middle-class Mexican families. Until that time, our only tourists were those who could afford to arrive by plane or yacht. Now whole families of twelve or fifteen could pile into vehicles and join their luckier *compatriotas* at one of Mexico's most spectacular playgrounds.

Summer became a good season for us at Las Glorias. First, all the government offices closed for a month, and after that school was out. We were running sixty percent occupied, instead of the thirty percent in former years. Gene Smith's problem with the slow season income solved itself, and we were the beneficiaries.

The easy access became immediately clear to Americans too. Hundreds of raggedy vans jammed with hippies started to appear on the beaches. Their long hair and their lifestyle was new to me (a lot had changed since my budding socialite days in San Francisco in 1964!), but I appreciated their quest for freedom, and I never had any trouble with them.

Or only once, and that hardly counts.

One day I came back to the house to check on the boys, and Lupita met me at the door.

"*¡SEÑORA!*" she said, with huge eyes. "A robber has been here!"

I went into the kitchen and looked around. The radio was there, my toaster, my blender, the maids' radio, all gleaming on the counter.

"What do you mean?" I asked her. "What's missing?"

"Your cat food is stolen!" she replied, scandalized.

"The cat food! The boys must have—"

"No, *señora*," she insisted. "I've been with the boys all morning at the little river. The cat food is stolen."

I started to giggle and look around. The peanut butter was also missing. It was starting to make more sense.

"Carlos!" I called. "Come, run with me down the beach. We've got to catch a thief."

Sure enough, about a mile along toward the airport there was a tall, shaggy young man in dirty Levis. He was very busy poking his finger into a jar that looked very much like my peanut butter. We caught up with him and confronted him with the evidence. He blushed and confessed that he had been hungry. His money was gone.

I told him I forgave him. He was so cute, it was hard to be stern. Besides, it was just too silly to think of him lunching in our tropical paradise on cat food, with peanut butter for dessert.

Perhaps I shouldn't have, but I let him enjoy the rest of his stolen goods while we talked.

He and his friends were staying on the beach at Punta de Mita in a caravan of VW campers. They had made it for weeks, frying the daily catch of fish on the beach, and buying tortillas at twelve cents a kilo. Many of them were painting, or making jewelry to be sold in town, but the money had not started to come in yet.

I must admit that gypsy life had a certain appeal for me. I wished them luck and sent him on his way. Carlos didn't know what to make of the whole thing.

Many other Americans were afraid to drive on the Mexican highways. There were so many horror stories circulating up North.

One couple was driving down to Mazatlán and came across a tree in the road. When they stopped, the *bandidos* swooped down on them from the bushes and cleaned them out. Another couple was robbed of everything in the high desert—their car, and even their shoes.

"The poor woman had to take off her shirt, so she could stand on the hot sand!" a friend of mine told me in a shocked tone of voice.

Your hubcaps could be gone when you got back from lunch, your gasoline siphoned off, or even the whole car missing from the spot where you parked it.

Mexicans were so desperate for car parts, they could dismantle a car in two hours, it was said, and leave no way to identify anything. If there was an accident, of course, the rich American was always blamed. Even the cops took sides against him.

It must be true that some of these things happened. When President Echeverría came into office in 1970, he initiated the program of the Green Angels, in an effort to counterbalance the bad publicity.

These highway police, in their now-familiar green trucks, patrol the main roads every hundred miles or so, equipped with telephones, spare parts and mechanical know-how. They have done a lot to calm down the anxiety of American travelers.

But the stories I was hearing from the tourists who drove down to Las Glorias from California and Texas in those days were very different.

"Terry, you won't believe what happened to us!" gasped Susan when she crawled out of her car in front of the office. She and her husband had been down every year since we opened, but previously they had always flown in.

"We had a flat tire outside of Tepic. We were really scared, because of all those stories we had heard. This young man came up and said something to us, I don't know what—but we finally figured out that he wanted to help with the tire. Can you believe it?"

"That's wonderful," I said.

"But that's not all. Suddenly there were several kids around. We thought they were going to start begging. But they just smiled and watched. And then the mama came up and took my arm! She dragged me and Fred back to her house beside the highway and she sat us down in her kitchen and she gave us coffee. And there was clean water in a bowl to wash up, and she ran next door to get a clean towel for us. And then she cut up a papaya and served it to us." Susan was breathless. "What beautiful, friendly people they are!"

"But didn't you always know that?"

"Well, we've heard so many stories about driving down," she said. " —and then she introduced us to all the children," she continued, still out of breath, "and then all of the cousins from next door. And we saw the little saints they had, at a little shrine in the living room, and—"

She paused for a moment. "I didn't dare to ask for a toilet. I didn't see any running water."

I smiled and checked them into their usual bungalow at the hotel. I was happy to hear a story like that about my adopted people. I hoped that kind would spread as fast as the others.

We hadn't heard much about drugs in those days, and I was a real innocent. But I must say, I certainly learned fast.

For the hippies, it was all about marijuana, and to us that seemed more like a game than a crime. But a month before the highway opened, I got myself a good education in the hard stuff.

Lucy was a wealthy American woman who showed up one day in July without reservations. We thought it odd that she would want to be there in the middle of the slow season, when there were very few guests and not much was going on, but she seemed content to relax beside the swimming pool with a book, and sun herself. She was a tall, slender woman with a lot of freckles. Not really pretty, I thought, but her wealth and her bearing made her quite striking.

She sat alone for her meals in the restaurant, she tipped generously, but she never wanted to mix with the guests or the staff. I tried to interest her in a boat trip to Yelapa, which was a favorite of many of our guests, but she politely declined without offering any other comment, and after that I left her alone. Shy, I figured.

Since she had made such a genteel sort of impression, we were very surprised one night late to hear her entangled in a screaming match with the cab driver when she returned from town. She was cussing him out in English, and she knew some very effective words—though they were probably lost on the simple Mexican driver.

"Jaime," I said to our night watchman, "see if you can catch the driver at the cattle guard and find out what's the matter."

The woman slammed the door of the taxi. She avoided coming through the office, which was the natural route to the bungalows, and staggered toward her room past the pool.

"Perhaps she's one of those who can't hold her liquor," I thought. "Too bad."

Jaime came back several minutes later looking perplexed. "The lady asked for drugs."

"Pot too, on top of all that liquor? She should be ashamed of herself."

"Not marijuana," he said, shaking his head. "Heroin."

"Too bad," I thought again.

As far as I knew, heroin was something that gangsters fought over in the movies. I had no idea that we had a serious problem on our hands.

The next morning I asked Chacha the maid, "Did you find anything odd in her room?"

"A lot of needles," she replied. "I don't know what they're for."

I glanced out at the pool to make sure the woman was settled for the day. "Show me," I said.

We took the long way around to bungalow number six, and let ourselves in. Sure enough, the dresser was littered with an odd mixture of syringes and diamond jewelry. The good stuff. Still, it was her business, and I didn't know what I could have done about it anyway, so we left, and I forgot about it.

Until that night. Jaime came running to the office just as I was closing up.

"She wants you," he said in a low voice. I knew who he was talking about. "She's screaming and banging her head on the furniture."

I raced down to her bungalow and opened the door without knocking. She couldn't have heard me by then anyhow, for the screaming and moaning had gotten very loud. I was happy it was July and we were pretty empty in the hotel.

I walked in the door and she grabbed me hysterically. "I need a shot," she cried. "I need a shot!" She fell to her knees and started shaking me furiously. "Do something!"

"I'll go for the doctor."

"No, no no! You can't. I don't need medicine, I need heroin. Do something!"

The lady was accustomed to having her way. But unfortunately she was grasping onto somebody who had no idea how to help her.

"Jaime will stay here with you," I said. "I'll see what I can do." Jaime looked stunned and helpless, but I only shrugged at him and ran out the door.

There were still no telephones at the place. I got in the car and went downtown to find Doctor Calderón.

When we returned, Lucy had bruised her head and arms several times on the cedar headboard of my bed, and on the windows, the doors, anything she could find to punish herself. We found her shriveled up in a corner on the floor, with Jaime bending over her, holding her down. There was a look of terror in his eyes.

"Thanks," said Calderón. "You can go." He left the room as fast as I've ever seen him move.

"I'll give her a tranquilizer," said my friend. "It's all I can do."

"Shouldn't she go to the hospital?" I asked.

"*¡Dios mío, no!*" he said with an emphatic stare that meant 'don't ask.' "This is the most I can do."

I held her down and he gave her the injection. She calmed down within minutes and fell asleep on the floor.

"We should tie her up," said Calderón.

I looked concerned for a moment, but I remembered how bad she had been when we walked into the room. The doctor picked her up and dumped her on the bed. We tied her hands to the bedposts with pillow cases.

"I don't know how long this will last. You'd better call me," he said, and got in his car.

Three hours later, there was a repeat scene. Jaime's supply of sympathy was running short. He was getting just plain angry with her. But there was nothing to be done. Again, he stayed in the bungalow while I drove into town, and again Calderón came out to Las Glorias.

All through the rest of the night and the next day he kept this up, leaving his practice in town every three hours to come out and quiet her down.

About eight o'clock that evening, the military police were there. I don't know how they found out about it, but when I walked into her room, there was a doctor in uniform sitting beside her on the bed. Two soldiers stood at the door.

With deliberate coolness, they said nothing to me. I backed out of the room, and when I came back later, they had gone as mysteriously as they had come.

"I can't take this any longer," I told Calderón when he arrived for the next shot. "I'm putting her on a plane tomorrow morning." Her papers were scattered all over the room. I wired her husband at the Rocky Mountain address I had found, and made the travel arrangements.

The next morning Chacha and I got her packed.

The woman lay on the bed in total shock. "I'm keeping the jewelry and the papers," I said to the maid. "Who knows what could happen to them!" There were rings with big diamonds, a jeweled watch, and one of those diamond heart pendants that were so popular in those days.

Somehow we got her onto her feet.

"Don't leave me, Terry," she groaned, gripping my neck tightly. "Don't leave me."

"Don't worry about a thing. We're taking you to the airport."

"No!"

"You've got to get some help. It's better at home," I said.

"No! I won't."

"I CAN'T HANDLE YOU ANY LONGER!" I shouted, and she sank down on the bed.

The maid and I got her out and lifted her into a cab.

I stuck my head in the door of the car and said, "I'm coming with you."

Her face brightened up so much that I didn't have the heart to tell her I only meant "as far as the airplane."

Quickly I slid into the back seat beside her. "She'll figure it out later," I told myself.

When we got to the airport, I sat her down in one of the chairs and went to confirm her ticket. First class, I had decided, so the flight attendants can look out for her.

When I returned to the seat, I almost didn't recognize the woman. In my absence, she had kept herself busy by putting on make-up, but her aim was way off that morning. She looked like a bag lady or a clown, I couldn't decide.

"Come on," I said, grabbing her and heading toward the rest room. "I'll help you with that."

I held her head over the sink with one hand and lathered up the other. I guess I got soap in her eyes.

"Goddammit, that hurts," she yelled irritably.

"Well, I'd let you do it yourself, but you already tried that," I yelled back. This bitch was really getting on my nerves.

"I'm sorry, Terry." She was whining now. "You're not going to leave me, are you?"

"Let's get on the plane," I said.

We stumbled out onto the runway and climbed up to the front seat of the Mexicana jetliner. Calderón was waiting for us. I sat on one side, while he sat on the arm and jabbed one final needle into her ass. I looked at her bare arms, and for the first time I saw they were punctured with needle marks.

"Here. You might get cold on the plane," I said, and gave her my jacket.

When the last passenger had boarded and the stewardess was moving toward the door, I made a lunge for it. "I've got to get the hell off this airplane. I'm not going," I explained to the startled girl.

I ran down the gangway without looking back.

Lucy's husband flew his own plane down the next week to pay all the bills and get the jewelry back. He stayed a week. Poor man, he probably needed the vacation.

It was difficult for him to tell his story, but he was grateful for our help.

The lieutenant governor of the state where I sent her, he had started out on vacation with his wife in their own plane. When her habit got the best of her, high over the Sierra Madre range, she had gone berserk—apparently not for the first time. She had pulled a gun on him and threatened to kill him, and he had simply had it with her. He dumped her off at Puerto Vallarta and returned home.

Though I found him very charming, I am not sad to say we never saw either one of them again.

We must have all been getting a little jumpy. The next thing I knew, my 'gracious hostess' duties on the night shift at the office were interrupted by the sound of five pistol shots.

We had two watchmen at the hotel. There was not much of a security problem at Las Glorias, but it had been a big deal to get them officially registered and fitted out with guns.

Every night we closed up the louvered windows of the restaurant, we set the tables for breakfast with linens but without the silver, and we locked the beautiful old wooden liquor cabinet we had installed in the bar. After that, there was not much for a watchman to do. Jaime and Nícolas used to fight over who patrolled the grounds and who stayed in the office. Finally I told them to take turns.

The office detail was not the favorite. It consisted of walking the single ladies back to their bungalows when they had had a bit too much tequila. One particular plump lady was beginning her third week with us. Her husband had been with her for two weeks, but he had had to get back to work.

It was Nícolas' night to patrol the grounds. There was no moon, and it was very dark, but somehow, from the pool all the way over to bungalow number nine, he had spotted the figure of a man creeping furtively along the wall and then ducking into the room. Since he knew there was a woman staying there alone, he loped over and peeked eagerly through the window.

By the glow of the orange lamp in the doorway, he could just make out the startled figure of a naked man diving into the bathroom. Without hesitation, he emptied five shots, straight into the pile of luggage in the corner.

Poor woman! If she had come through the office as usual, nobody would have paid any attention. But she had found herself an aging beach boy, and had explained to him how to follow the little stream in back and sneak quietly into her room, without notice.

She was frightened and irate and embarrassed all at the same time. Now she approached Bob Lewis, whom she had been snuggling up to earlier in the evening.

"I must have my luggage replaced," she declared, standing in the middle of the room in a large sheet.

Bob smiled and said nothing.

She hesitated. Then she laughed. "Oh, what the hell!" she said. "At least buy me some new dresses for the rest of the week. I'll tell my husband the airline lost everything."

It wasn't the airline, but I who lost a pile of money on her new wardrobe.

The maids who could sew up bullet holes got a pile of new dresses. And poor Nícolas—I didn't have the heart to fine him for the amount, but he did get a good lecture on the use of firearms.

My own boys continued to grow like weeds. My dream of a life of freedom for them was being realized. They tore along the beach on their horses, like wild Indians. By about the age of six or seven, they had already learned some lessons in *machismo*, however, and a life of teasing took on more interest than a life of danger.

My little babies, who used to join me in innocent games like a spontaneous rain dance on the empty beach when a furious thunderstorm blew in from the Pacific, were now making remarks to each other like, "Hey, man, that's a good-looking ass!" or "Look at those tits, man!"

As the bikinis sprouted along the beach, their favorite game became spotting a girl who was sunning her back with her brassiere undone. They would bound up to her on horseback and screech to a sudden halt so that sand flew in every direction. When the startled girl sat up sharply and looked around, they got the show they had come for.

Sometimes when Lupe had her day off, they would gallop over to visit her house in town. Sparks flew in all directions from their horses' hooves, as they sped over the cobblestones.

"¡He, güerito! ¿Qué tal?" called out the fishermen. "Hey little blondie, how are you doing?" Bear's almost white hair fascinated the dark Mexicans.

Buster blended right in, but Bear could hardly go anywhere without being stroked on the head for good luck.

"¡Su cabello de elote!" the women would marvel, going on about how his hair was like corn silk, how fat and strong he was. Mexicans, male and female alike, are very tender with children. And the boys, although at that age, in any land, they would probably rather do without that kind of attention, took it with good humor.

At Lupita's they learned to grab a chicken from the yard, crack its neck and pluck the feathers off, and drop it into a sizzling pot, almost with a single movement. "We *love* a hard-muscled chick," they would say.

Another favorite delicacy was the sweet veins that run to a cow's udder, when they had been fried crispy in hot oil.

If I took a day off, we would often take the fishing boat out onto the bay. I grabbed some beer and sodas and played *capitán* myself, steering a course for Quimixto.

"Hey, Mom, where are we going?" asked Bear as we swerved to avoid a school of fish feeding on sardines at the water's surface.

"Hey, Mom! Mom!" echoed Buster automatically. As grown up as they sometimes seemed, they were still typical little boys.

"Let's go over and visit the *familia* of Jesús," I suggested.

"Oh, boy!" they both shouted. That meant fresh oysters on the beach. The family was always glad to see *la patrona* of the hotel, where by this time three of their sons were earning good money. We were treated like royalty.

There was nothing formal about our surfside picnic, however. Bear and Buster loved to show off, grabbing the rough shells and opening them up as fast as the fishermen did. Then they would slurp down the tender oyster in one gulp, without even waiting for a squeeze of lime or some hot sauce.

I used to stretch out on the sand while they played, and listen to the regular scrubbing noise of the waves, grinding over the sand. A frigate bird would fly over, looking for some action. This was the life! How pleasant it was to get completely away from my twenty-four hour responsibility at the hotel.

I was happy to be able to give my boys this kind of life, though I wondered sometimes whether they were becoming as spoiled rotten as Helen and I were in the old plantation days. Probably not. Life in colonial Indonesia was more like life in old Mississippi than in old Mexico.

There as girls, we each had our own personal *babu*, who slept on the floor next to us every night. In the morning she set aside the mosquito netting and announced to us in her musical language that there was oatmeal or a plate of eggs for us on the veranda. We never had to lift a finger for anything.

When we went horseback riding or bike riding, a *sjonhos* ran alongside us. It was this little boy's job to see to it that we didn't fall, or at least hurt ourselves.

When I look back on it now, our treatment of him seems thoughtless, but at the time it was quite natural to us.

Once we were swimming while he sat watching over us from the bank. I got the bright idea to make a sailboat out of one of my little white patent leather shoes. Of course, in no time it went floating out of reach. When we returned home, it was the *sjonhos* who got the beating.

Another time I made a bargain with a new little friend on the street to trade one hour of riding on my bike for his bird, a splendid macaw with bright plumage. The boy rode off and we never saw the bike again.

My servant didn't get a mere slap. My mother beat the hell out of him, and took payment for the bike out of his wages over the next year. Perhaps in the back of her mind was always the possibility that the boys had secretly made a deal with each other. It did happen.

But after all, there were wages. These people were not slaves. We took care of them and loved them, and they stayed with us. In her loneliness, a plantation lady's *babu* was often her best friend. All the kids played together, at least at an early age.

If that *sjonhos* had quit and run off after his beating, for example, there would have been hundreds wanting his job, for they ate well, they had clean clothing and a good home to live in, and the payment was regular. Unfortunately that is no longer true of my Indonesians now, in their independence.

When they became too old to work, they still stayed on with us, keeping their families intact. Their children, perhaps their grandchildren, had already taken over their jobs. We had many servants in our home, softly padding around barefooted in their exquisite sarongs. We needed a good number of them—they generally moved pretty slowly.

It certainly was the good life here in Mexico. But there were times, I had to admit, when the boys' love of freedom got out of hand. Like yesterday, for example, when I pulled up to the Catholic nursery on my afternoon rounds.

"Your son left," said the sister.

"Left! What do you meant 'left'?" I sputtered, indignant. She could offer no further explanation.

I flew through town, looking everywhere, asking everyone. Bear was famous in town, as I have said, because of his blond hair. No one knew. But the word spread fast in the village, and within the hour Alejandro had found him in the main plaza, astride one of the *burros*. He had a tight grip around its neck, and he was fast asleep. Apparently he had gotten bored at school and had decided to pad over to the Oceano and charge a Coke on 'his' account. In those days, my bar tab was filled with big dirty crosses made with determined little fingers.

Two things happened about that time which brought about a big change in my life externally. Cloro had begun feeling useless around the place and was getting restless, and then Gene LaPorte came to me and said he finally wanted to have his own house back.

Gene had been like a Big Daddy to us through all those years. Whenever he came down, I sent one of the maids over to clean up his little guest house and fill the refrigerator with a few supplies. When we met him at the airport, he was always loaded down with presents for everybody. The bellboys loved him because whenever he passed through the office on the way to his place, they got a couple of dollars to help carry a parcel or two. He and his guests always ate in our restaurant. Our relationship was perfect. But the main cottage in the corner was his, after all, and he wanted to start coming down more often.

Meanwhile, Cloro had said to me, joking, "Well, Theresa, you sure closed up my business!" Naturally the *palapa* on the beach had gone the way of all shacks when our beautiful new bungalows went in.

"I've still got a little corner of property on the other side of the highway. I'll tell you what I'm going to do," he continued, his eyes gleaming. "I'm going to make a new *palapa* for the coconuts. You've got your 'heaven,' Las Glorias, over on this side with the angels. I'm going to open up 'hell' over there. We'll have the whole universe!"

I laughed and asked him what he meant.

"I'm calling it *'El Infierno,'*" he said, loudly appreciating his own joke.

And so Cloro was in the coconut business again.

There was a new shack across from our entrance, right on the highway, with the same little ratty chairs, and the same colorful characters sitting around enjoying the afternoon sun. He had a new ice box, and a new little *oficina*, where he took his naps and entertained the same old girls. In no time, his business was making a lot of money.

A couple of his early customers were two *norteamericanos* who were looking for a place to open up an American-style meat market.

No problem. Cloro built them a place next door, really fast, with a walk-in cooler with big hooks for their sides of beef. They started buying beef in Guadalajara and making T-bone steaks out of it, and all the other familiar cuts which became a welcome novelty to the villagers and a joy to the visiting Americans. They found some investors, and in another part they were planning to have fresh fish too.

Their enterprise pleased me no end. Until then, we had had to ship our beef in from Mexico City. And I've already described how it was my job to bring Xavier down to the beach every morning with his huge tubs, and wait for him while he picked through the day's catch. What a convenience to have all this across the road!

When LaPorte wanted his little house back, I said to Cloro, "Jeez, man, you did that meat market so fast—Why don't you put up a second story on it, so I can move in while we get a house built for ourselves?" Bob and I already had our eye on a corner of the property at the far southern end toward town, and we planned to set ourselves up in comfort.

In no time we had a temporary apartment over the butcher shop in 'hell.'

Next came Hans, the German doctor. "I met this *hombre* today," said Cloro, the machines turning in his head. "He's like a priest. But a *médico*."

"What?"

"Yes, he wants to help the poor people. He asked me if I could make him a little hospital. His wife is a doctor too."

In a month, a new doctor had set up his office in hell. Two doctors. Then along came Oscar, the dentist, and an American-style clinic was born. He got himself a dentist's chair in Guadalajara and began the business pulling teeth for all the poor people—at least during the times when our fickle electrical power cooperated with him.

In another year we had Eduardo, a handsome Argentine who had studied medicine in Guadalajara. He was facing his two years of social service, required by law before he got his degree. He and his wife and children were extremely poor, and I was able to help them out by letting them have one of our bungalows sometimes on the weekends, so that they could spend a special time together in Puerto Vallarta.

At El Infierno, we all had a blast living together, those young doctors and my family and I. We saw each other every day, and often ate together. I did their errands in town when I could, since they had no automobiles of their own. They treated me and my kids free.

The hurricane I described came through when I was living in this apartment. Buster was sitting by the window when the first big blustery winds hit. He got bitten on the rear by a scorpion, and he was screaming bloody murder. I picked him up in my arms and started out the door—when we both just missed being clipped by the asbestos tiles of my own roof, which flew through the living room at that moment. All my expensive carpets were sliced in two. But I never looked back. I had to get my baby to Hans, the German doctor, for an injection against the poison.

Freak accident, right?

Then it started to happen in earnest.

One bright autumn day, Nacho, one of Cloro's coconut cutters, was killed on the property. He had scurried up the tree barefoot like a cat, as he had done hundreds of times before, his *machete* tucked into his shorts. As he tied a cluster of coconuts onto the long rope to be lowered to the ground, he was stung by bees. He fell straight out of the tree in front of us. The *machete* poked clean through his stomach.

Two months later, one of Cloro's taxi drivers was killed in town.

A month after that Oscar, the dentist, died in a highway accident on the Guadalajara road.

A year later, after Hans and his wife had moved to Peru to continue their missionary work, she died in childbirth.

"Jeez, Cloro," I said when we got word of that last sad news, "change the name! This *infierno* is a jinx!"

I was glad we had finished the new house and moved out of his place by then.

A year after Hans' wife died, Eduardo was killed on a visit home to see his family in Argentina.

"You've got to take this seriously, Cloro," I pleaded. "You told me yourself about Halloween—how strange you thought it was that Americans joke around on one of Mexico's holiest days. Don't joke around with this!"

El Día de los Muertos is the important religious festival of November first. The day of the dead.

The Mexicans celebrate it not with costumes and silly games the night before, but by making a visit to the cemeteries to honor their dead loved ones. They bring garlands of flowers to deck out the gravesites, and pray for the ghosts who sometimes, if their souls are not yet at rest, still hover around.

Of course, with their earthy approach, they also turn it into a festival for the living, by taking a picnic along, and plenty of tequila. The children have little sugar figures in the shape of skeletons, to munch on. Still 'hallow' is central to the spirit of Halloween in Mexico.

But Cloro refused to give up the name.

Soon after our talk, he himself was dead. Of a full life, I guess is the best way to describe it—though the official cause was a cancer which went through his body like lightning.

And on the first anniversary of his death, his son Clorío, who had gone for help when I was in jail, and the only child of his with any promise of amounting to something, died of a gunshot wound in the head.

El Infierno. I still shiver when I think of it.

Poor Clorío. All my partner's children were alcoholics, but this one, 'Little Cloro,' seemed to have the best control over it. When the boy was in his teens, my buddy Cloro hoped that we could teach him the business at Las Glorias. Then eventually, the favorite son could take over his father's share.

I sat in the office endless hours with this tall, shy young man, going over the figures, explaining the operation, but it was too much for him. He didn't have his father's 'savvy.'

However, he had taken over the taxi business, and when Cloro died in the spring of 1970, El Infierno became his too.

On the anniversary of his father's death, he had sunk very low. His wife Rose had just given birth to a mongoloid child.

The typical Mexican male's reaction: "How could she do this to me?"

In the early afternoon, he was already drunk on tequila. At sundown, he was still sitting on the dead stump of a palm tree with his coconut cutter, don Andrés. The man had a little shack on our side of the highway, near the entrance to the hotel, under the angels.

There sat Clorío, singing and drinking, feeling sad but powerful under the tall coconut palms his father had planted years before. A pistol gleamed darkly on his hip. The little children of don Andrés rushed back and forth to get ice for the drinks of the son of don Cloro.

He had hired the *mariachis* to cheer him up. A whole orchestra of *rancheros* stood around the littered courtyard playing their sad songs. Get drunk, spend money. The sadness will go away.

Ah, find a woman! That was the next step. His wife was sitting at home with the newborn and two other little babies, wrapped in a turban and waiting out the required forty days after childbirth. At eleven or so, Clorío got behind the wheel of his truck and all the *mariachis* piled in back with their instruments, off to serenade the lady love.

I saw them drive off, laughing and singing. All the musicians stood on the bed of the truck and hung onto the sides.

"He's drunk again," I said, feeling a vague premonition. "Every time he does this, it lasts a week. He spends a couple of thousand dollars, and the business takes a dive."

Many times when he was alive, Cloro used to come to me and say, "Can you and some of the boys accompany me to pick up my son? He is drunk again." Sometimes it was Clorío, at other times he was talking about one of the brothers. I would call Guilberto and Carlos, and off we would all go, to bring the boy back home to his mother.

The *macho* Latin lover found his girlfriend, and they spent maybe half an hour together at her little house, while the band played in a shabby pick-up on the street. They drove around some more, perhaps four or five hours.

But Clorío had not had enough. He drove home with the *mariachis*, to stage an early morning fight with his wife. She was to blame. The mongoloid had brought him bad luck. The brat was crying when he walked in the door. Rose could not make him stop.

He grabbed his wife's hair and pulled her roughly over to him. He took out the pistol to scare her into submission. In the scuffle, the gun went off and splattered his brains all over the wall of the bedroom.

The neighbors came, and then the police. Confused babies were crying everywhere. And soon Rose was huddled against the wall, on the hard concrete bench of the Puerto Vallarta jail.

Cloro's family took the young man's side against her, violently accusing her of the crime. She was in jail for seventy-two hours, until her family in Tepic found a lawyer, who got her out because she had the other two babies to take care of.

Cloro's family still hates her. She has moved to Mexico City to study nursing.

El Infierno. At first we had looked at it as a pleasant joke.

16

One sunny morning I was in the restaurant, making final arrangements for another one of those big luncheons that we staged for American travel agents. I was sitting at a table by the fireplace with Xavier, going over every detail of the menu.

A taxi screeched to a halt on the cobblestones in front of the office. The driver got out, hurried through the office, and then into the restaurant to find me. In silence, but with a significant look in his eye, he handed over a small slip of paper.

Scrawled in bright red lipstick were written the words: *"¡Theresa, a tu casa!"* I thanked him and he left. I knew what it meant.

"Xavier, immigration is in town again. You'll have to take over," I said.

Our chef was a pretty temperamental homosexual sometimes, but he had complete command of the kitchen, and I knew he could handle the party coming up. He had good taste and good instincts—though he wasn't quite so elegant as he thought he was. But at this point I had no choice.

The note was from Candelario Ramos, our local immigration officer. It tickled me that he had written it in lipstick. Quite a ladies' man, that guy.

He stood almost six-foot-two, and he had his uniforms made specially to show off his good shape. The handsome square face, and the dark green, almost black eyes turned women into jelly. He probably just happened to have the lipstick on him instead of a pencil!

"Theresa, go home!" That's all I needed.

Every year, about ten days before Christmas, the top immigration authorities arrived from Mexico City for their *mordidas*. A guy's got to have some extra money to buy presents for his children, after all. Again ten days before Easter, the same thing. Their wives must have pressed upon them the importance of new dresses for the whole female brood at home.

And Theresa Lewis was still without her legal working papers.

I went home as I was told, and prepared to play the busy housewife. We had moved into the new house, some distance removed from the hotel. I enjoyed the place, and I had too little time to spend in it anyway. This afternoon should be a pleasure.

We had chosen a spot on the south end, nearer to the highway, but not on it. After several years of sea noises and extreme humidity almost at the water's edge, I was anxious for a change. I had all my new avocado trees planted, and lemons and papayas, and the whole lot was surrounded by a six-foot fence.

A wrought-iron gate at the end of a beautiful driveway announced the name, "Robert W. Lewis."

As the little government Jeep cruised onto the property, I was casualness itself, sitting at the piano and working out a little Chopin etude. I had finally shipped all my beautiful things down from San Francisco, and I had taken back my piano from Elizabeth Smith's bungalow.

The kids were romping in the new pool, and I had set Lupita and Consuela at work polishing the silver grape clusters which hung over the edges of a huge serving bowl I had bought long ago in Denmark.

The officers started in the restaurant.

"Where's the *señora*?" they demanded.

"*Señora Laao-is?*" said Alejandro. "Oh, she doesn't work in the restaurant."

"What about the hotel? Is she in her office?"

"*No, señor*. That is the office of don Roberto."

Same scene in the kitchen:

"You mean the lady never cooks here, never does anything?"

"Oh, she might come over once in a while with the kids to play in the pool," said Xavier, who was much too busy putting the finishing touches on sixty desserts to be bothered.

Candelario was with them when they stood at my fence, spying on our cozy domestic scene. He waved a stiff, formal wave, and they all stalked off.

Until the next holiday.

A few days afterwards, a sadder message. Jesús slipped quietly into my office, his beautiful eyes moist with tears. "Doña Theresa, *mi madre está muerta*," he said bravely.

I came around the desk and gave him a hug. "I'll come with you," I said.

My days of hearse driving were over. When the grey Chevy station wagon got too banged up for me, I had presented it to the local police. Since it was their very first car, they were very impressed with themselves as they flew over the cobblestones of Puerto Vallarta, hanging out the window and calling, "OOooooOOOOooooo," to hurry the cars out of their path. They ruined the thing in eight months. And it was a relatively new car.

Yes, the family of Jesús would have to make other arrangements to get a hearse to carry the body of his mother. But I still wanted to pay my respects. I got my children dressed, and we set out for the wake, which in Mexico is held at home. There is no money for funeral parlors, and little need anyhow, since in a tropical climate, the body must be in the ground within twenty-four hours.

All the friends and relatives of the deceased gather outside in a circle in the yard, all around the body. Everyone prays and says the rosary, and they all drink a lot of coffee and tequila.

"Doña María had a beautiful life," they repeated. "And such beautiful children." Jesús looked proud.

The women were kissing doña María's hands and feet. My own children were fidgeting. I pulled up my little black veil and whispered sharply to Lupita and Consuela to keep them in line.

As I turned my attention back to the scene of mourning, *zzzupp*! A blue Bronco sped by on the street beside us. This was a small neighborhood, with small streets. I could have almost touched the car, almost grabbed my husband's scrawny neck as he went by, oblivious.

"Lupe!" I whispered. I was furious. "You and Consuela take care of the kids."

I called to Alejandro to come with me. We had driven the truck Bob had bought in Tepic. By the time I had spit out all my instructions and jumped into the front seat, the Bronco was out of sight. I told Alejandro to drive around the area. Bob's car would be easy to spot.

But after half an hour on the bumpy dirt back streets with no luck, I had cooled down. Or perhaps my sore rear end made the decision for me. "Let's turn back," I said. I suspected that all of our staff knew which one of the maids was Bob's current little chosen pussy, and even where she lived. But poor Alejandro was acting innocent, and I didn't push it.

We pulled up again at Jesús' house. The air was filled with *avemarías*." Lots of tequila, lots of coffee.

All night long this scene went on, the candles dripping slowly into the hot night air.

Then all of a sudden, *zzzupp*! The blue Bronco again. One little dark head sank down low on the passenger side.

"So he didn't get enough! Now he's going to take her out somewhere!" I fumed. I motioned to Alejandro again, and off we went.

The Bronco headed out of town, and we were right behind. Bob must have seen us, because he turned up into the mountains on a rough dirt road toward the brick factory. We followed.

"Faster, Alejandro, faster!" I screamed. I was going to ram that sonofabitch in the back with our big two-ton truck. Maybe knock him off the road, I didn't care.

"*Señora*, it won't go any faster," he pleaded. Poor guy, he was only nineteen or twenty. Too young to be caught in the middle of this.

Or was he? I thought of the little kid of his, that Lupita's mother was stuck caring for, and I got even madder.

The road started winding steeper up the mountain, and the rocks got sharper. We heard a sudden pop! and the big truck swerved to a stop.

Flat tire.

The blue Bronco sped on ahead and out of sight.

"SHIT," I yelled, "FIVE MILES OUT OF TOWN, AND NO JACK!" Alejandro was terrified.

Help was there for us before we knew it. Before I could strangle my chauffeur.

A long Buick station wagon came careening around the corner, loaded with hippies singing at the top of their lungs. Clouds of marijuana smoke poured out the windows. There were several surfboards tied to the roof.

They stopped, and I looked into the car. A dozen of them peered out, jammed in between all their little canvas bags. But I was not to be deterred.

"I've got to have a ride back to the village. My truck has a flat," I announced.

"Sure, ma'am," said the driver. "But where you gonna sit?"

"Come on," I said to Alejandro. "Follow me."

I climbed up onto the hood and lay down on my stomach, grabbing onto the windshield through the vent window in the corner. My main bellman looked as if he would rather die, but he climbed up on the other side, and we started down the mountainside.

He squeaked out a few good cuss words (which I had never heard from him) on some sharp corners, but we made the five-mile trip to Las Glorias. It seemed like a hundred and five. The road was steep, and we were rolling around on the hood like rag dolls.

A couple of times I worried that we might take the more direct route down the mountain.

Back home, I had almost forgotten why I was so angry. But we were far from through. We had to get the tire and take a taxi back up to the stranded truck.

We changed the tire and drove back down.

Then I picked up the kids and the maids, who were still in mourning, and brought them home.

It was four or five in the morning when I staggered in the front door, and I was raging mad.

I shut the door and locked it. I grabbed the bottle of rum and left the Cokes behind in the cupboard.

I went upstairs to the bedroom and sat on the bed, the events of the night still whirling around in my head.

At about six o'clock, I heard Bob Lewis fiddling with the iron gate. I grabbed the shotgun that he used for duck hunting and crept out onto the balcony.

He was leaning against a palm tree in the courtyard, taking off his shoes.

I let him have it, furiously pumping out three shots with the shotgun. Bob screamed out in terror.

I wasn't going to kill him, of course. I just wanted to make it a night he'd remember.

He stood shrunk behind the palm tree, with his shoes in front of his face. He looked so funny that I started to laugh, and that made me even angrier. I pumped the gun again, but he was already gone in a flash. I had only burned him a little on the stomach, but he wasn't taking any more chances. He spent the rest of the night in one of the bungalows.

I calmed down the maids and the kids, who were all standing at the door of my bedroom in shock, and then I finally sank into my bed. I had hardly dozed off, when there was another noise.

Candelario Ramos was crawling over my balcony!

He rushed over to my side and half got into bed with me.

"Do you want me to kill him?" he asked dramatically. "Don Roberto is no good for you. You are a good woman, a hard-working woman. So good for Puerto Vallarta. I'll take care of him."

An hour earlier it might have been tempting, but by then I just thanked him and said good night.

But I didn't sleep much. My stupid situation kept repeating itself in my head in grotesque variations.

What was I going to do about all this? How was I going to keep from really aiming at a vital part next time?

"I've got to get out of here," I vowed. "Talpa! I'll go see Sondra Cellini. Nobody can reach me all the way up there."

I hadn't visited Sondra for quite a while.

About a year and a half before, we had had a particularly unbearable summer, and we had wanted to get our horses away from the extreme heat at sea level. At that time, I piled the kids and the maids into the little DC-3 that makes the trip in only twelve minutes, and then I made preparations for my own trail ride up through the mountains.

In a tropical summer, the horses really suffer. They get ticks, and their hair doesn't shine as much, even though we kept them bathed and groomed every day.

It's rather deceptive from the coast, but the land behind Puerto Vallarta rises to about nine thousand feet very quickly. In the mountains, the climate is about ten degrees cooler than it is below.

I had decided to take Alejandro and Guilberto along, to give them a chance to visit their families. It would be a good vacation for all of us. We eagerly set out, astride three of the horses, with four more tethered alongside us.

Once we got going, I realized I had forgotten just how invigorating it is to go back into the wilderness. I hadn't spent much time in the beautiful Sierra Madre since Cloro and I went to Chacala to pick out the cedar for the bungalows.

The way up to Talpa was the same scene. We rode straight up the sides of steep ravines, following the small paths that were still slippery from heavy rains, and choked with vegetation. Often Guilberto and Alejandro had to jump down to clear the way with their *machetes*.

Every so often we passed a little adobe hut, with a small plot of corn nearby. Sometimes the *ranchero* had dug a rude ditch to give him irrigation from his own private waterfall farther up the mountain. But for the most part, it was total Tarzan country. Not a sign of human habitation. It took us three and a half days.

The boys were impressed at how easily I could ride through rough country. But after all, I explained to them, I had been on a horse since I was three years old, tearing through the spectacular volcanic countryside of Indonesia.

We had brought hammocks along, and a supply of tortillas and Spam, so we could camp out at night.

Guilberto pointed out the poisonous snakes and spiders to avoid. But I was thinking more about the luxurious ferns and bamboo, and the elephant ears that rose to a spectacular height, clinging to the huge old cottonwood trees. I made a mental note to come back and pick up some little slips to plant around my house.

Now once again I was heading for Talpa. "Maybe this time I'll bring back some of those plants," I resolved, as I climbed into the creaky DC-3. It had been only a couple of hours since I shot my husband.

At the front of the tiny plane was a row of seats, as if for parachuters or skydivers. But this plane was filled with the noise of happy *rancheros*, with their chickens and prized fighting cocks. That took the glamour off considerably.

My stomach made a flip when the plane took its first dive. "Too much rum last night, you dummy," I said to myself.

When we were again on the ground, in Talpa, I approached the town's taxi driver. "I want to see Sondra Cellini. Can you take me to her house?"

He looked mystified.

"La Gringa," I clarified. His eyes brightened. Her name was perhaps too difficult for these simple people, but she was well known in the small village. The ten-minute ride through town and up the mountain on the other side cost me a dollar. Soon the columns of her porch came into view.

Sondra was one of my favorite people. She had come from a rich American family in the Midwest, by way of the early feminist movement in Berkeley. Divorced at a young age because she couldn't have children, she fell in love with a married United Airlines pilot and had two boys and a girl with him, the "darling bastards" of the book she was working on.

Mr. Parker had been a real ace in the Second World War, and he and Sondra loved flying into the little grass airstrips of Mexico in the Fifties. They fell in love with Talpa. Parker was dead now, but Sondra had built a large house herself on their favorite spot.

She made some money painting landscapes and selling them in Puerto Vallarta. With Parker's small social security payments for the kids, she had brought in Chenin Blanc and Cabernet Sauvignon vines from the Napa Valley in California, and surrounded herself by her vineyards and her own livestock. She was completely self-sufficient, living out her dream in the wilderness. Exactly the tonic I needed.

"Terry Lewis!" she yelled from the rows of grapevines as we approached. She dropped her hoe and ran to the cab.

"Fantastic! My back is killing me anyhow. Come on up to the house!"

In no time I had sunk down on the floor in her elegant living room with a stiff rum and Coke in my hand. My stomach, which hadn't yet completed the journey with me, was slowly coming back down to earth.

"I need a rest," I said.

"I'll bet you do," she sympathized. "You can stay as long as you like. You know this is your place too."

"It's beautiful! I can't believe how much you've done since I was here." I looked around at the pale lavender decor, the old colonial fireplace, and the antique-style cedar furniture she had made. Along with the chairs, she had also carved a dramatic sculpture of four horses' heads. It was covered with a thick glass slab, to make the dining room table at the end of the room.

I sighed and took it all in, thinking of all the loving work that went into that house. She and her workers had even made their own adobe bricks and patted the stucco over the top of them by hand, in true Mexican style.

"I'm putting in a swimming pool next," she announced in an excited voice. "And a sauna. That seems to be the only way I can get people to come up and visit me!"

"Man, could I go for a sauna right now," I yawned.

"OK, Lewis, out with it. What's going on in your life?"

I told her the latest escapade, and we both had a good laugh. My perspective began to brighten in the clear mountain air.

"You should have shot the bastard in the knee!" she joked. "What I can't believe is that you had that Candelario Ramos right there in your bedroom and you didn't grab him. Those shoulders!"

She was squirming around on the rug in mock sexiness, demonstrating how the scene should have been played. "You're a fool, Theresa."

By then we were sampling her wine, and she poured me another generous glass. "How is my lover Candelario?" she asked.

"Well, he sure helped me out the other day." I told her about the note written in lipstick.

"And Rafael? There's another one you could have in a minute."

I laughed.

"I mean it, Terry. It'd be good for you."

"Sondra, I can't sleep around. You know, I never have been able to do that."

She shrugged and looked at me sympathetically, as if I were a child who still had a lot to learn.

"Every week Rafael counts up the women he has laid," I explained. "Bob told me. He wants to check to make sure he's on schedule, I guess." Sondra snorted, but I continued firmly, "I don't want to be on somebody's list."

"Well, I'm on it. And Bill Wulff's, and Calderón's, and about a dozen others," she said. "And look at me. I'm smiling!"

She didn't say "look at you." She didn't have to.

"Bill Wulff too? But you used to model dresses for Nelly—"

"All in the family!" she laughed.

She stretched out her body and mussed her brown hair, which didn't need it. She had a small, but firm athletic shape.

"I don't believe all that," I said. "You don't have time for so many lovers, with this big ranch and your three little kids. What do you do when you're stuck up here on this mountain for weeks at a time?"

A handsome *ranchero*, about twenty years old, was tending the lush bougainvilleas outside in the garden. She glanced over and then rolled her eyes suggestively.

"No! With your kids around?"

"I just explained to them that their father died several years ago, but I didn't. They take it in stride. If they find us in bed together, they just back out the door quietly and leave us alone."

"Sondra!"

I couldn't help it. My proper Dutch upbringing left me scandalized. I sipped on the wine and tried to consider all the possibilities. "But do the men respect you?"

"How the hell should I know?" Her green eyes formed a suggestive leer. "Respect is not what I had in mind!"

She looked out into the garden again and stretched. "The wives don't. Alvarez tells me the women see me coming and grab their husbands and sons and pull them back inside the house." She laughed at the picture of it in her mind.

"Alvarez too?"

I thought of Bob Lewis. What was he doing right this moment? Why should he have all the fun?

"I'm still a young girl," I told myself. "I need some fun too."

But still, I didn't know if I could manage my life like Sondra did.

"How about a snack?" she offered, breaking in on my thoughts. "I made a great cheese the other day."

"Sounds good. You don't have to go into town for anything, do you?"

"Coffee and sugar. I could grow it up here, but that's more of a job than I want to take on." She gazed proudly over the veranda at the fabulous view. "And the mail of course."

"Yeah," I laughed. "Once every other week. I've tried to get messages to you before—"

"Well, I never mind drop-in guests." She spun around. "What are we going to do tonight?"

Before I could reply, she continued, "There's a little party in town. The real ranch music! You're getting too spoiled down in Puerto Vallarta with all those modern discos opening up."

"Great," I agreed.

That night about nine we piled into her big two-ton truck with her kids in back, and sped down to the village. Sondra drove it around the curves like a sports car.

We danced, and her three kids danced with all the girlfriends and boyfriends from school, and we had ourselves a ball. Bob Lewis was in another world, far down the mountainside.

About three o'clock in the morning, I was really dragging. After all, I hadn't had any sleep the night before. I looked around the place. No Sondra.

Much earlier I had seen her headed toward the river with some young man, José, I think she said, but she should have been back by that time. I waited an hour or so, and gathered up her kids.

"Come on," I said, "let's go to the truck. Your mother can get a ride back later."

We all walked out to the road where the truck was parked. It was locked. Sondra had the keys. We sat down beside the road and waited. Five o'clock. Six o'clock. About seven, the village started to come alive. The church bells were ringing, and an *abuela* made an appearance here and there with the broom she had probably used for decades. I stifled a choice comment about Sondra as the *padre* passed by.

"*¿Los hijos de la Gringa?*" he asked.

I nodded, still cross-legged on the ground. The kids didn't seem to be bothered. They had made up some game to occupy themselves.

"Surely the taxi driver will wake up soon," I told myself.

Who came passing by at that moment, but young José, returning from the big house of *La Gringa* on the mountain! We all yelled at him, probably embarrassing him by exposing his recent activities. We didn't care, we wanted to go home.

On second thought, he was probably proud of the publicity. He went back for the truck key.

"You had the keys the whole time!" I accused my friend when we finally walked into her house.

"Sorry, I forgot all about you!" she laughed. She had a big pile of breakfast tacos, with beans and rice, ready and steaming at the table to placate us. We forgave her immediately.

I slept through that day and night. I had no idea how tired I was. As it started to get light the next morning, I was at first only dimly aware that the birds had suddenly stopped the raucous noise they were making to announce the dawn. I heard the low, reverberating growl of a mountain lion.

"Aha," I thought lazily. "That cat must be on his way to the river, to stir up some mischief."

I rolled over in the bed and found myself face to face with two big red eyes. The menacing sound was like a loud purr, but the eyes were not friendly. I dared not move, even though there were bars on the window. He was only three feet away. He sniffed around the bars some more, and then continued his rounds of the house.

I bounded into the kitchen. Sondra was already up, making coffee. "You'll never believe it!" I started.

"The puma?" she said calmly. "Yeah, we've got to do something about that."

"What about your dogs? Doesn't he attack your chickens and your ducks?"

"Oh, I lost two dogs last year. And the ducks—don't you see me pushing the damn ducks into the pen every night? Why do you think I take the trouble?"

"But—"

"I've got my .22 in case something happens."

"A .22! What are you going to do with a little .22? That cat was three feet tall! His claws were huge!"

"Well, we'll just have to shoot him. If we can catch him. Maybe we'll put him over the fireplace afterwards."

No, I definitely did not want to exchange Sondra's life with mine. Though there were still parts of it that were certainly appealing.

At the end of a week, I was thoroughly relaxed. As I was packing up my things, she came into the bedroom. "How about that young Guilberto? He's a doll!" She was still on the same subject.

"I could never do that. How could I treat him as an employee after that?"

"You'd be amazed how things like that just take care of themselves," she shrugged.

"Not me, I couldn't handle it. Not with somebody who didn't have an education."

She laughed. "Take 'em all! The boys are really fun! Take my word for it. Like a bunch of puppies!"

I just shook my head. I still needed time to think this thing out.

"Remember, Theresa, this is always your place," she said as I was leaving. "When we're eighty years old and nobody wants us any more, we'll still be up here working the land. I'll make sure you're buried over there under that big tree where you like to sit."

I hugged her and then dived down the mountain again in the DC-3.

The telegram was waiting when I reached Las Glorias. It had come that morning. "YOUR FATHER DIED DECEMBER 31. FUNERAL ON SATURDAY."

It was Monday. It had taken that long for the message to reach me. I made plans to fly to Rotterdam.

As I strapped myself into the seat belt for the transatlantic flight, my heart was full. Poor father! My life hadn't turned out at all as he had hoped. I wondered if he had been unhappy with his.

When we had docked in Holland right after the World War II, my parents, my two sisters and I, times were excruciatingly hard. My father was fifty-six years old.

Generally life in the tropics was considered so difficult, so wearing, that the Dutch military were allowed regular vacations back home, and full retirement after only twenty years.

Well, my father had been working in Indonesia for thirty years without a rest. Then he had spent the war years in one prison camp after another, and now as he stepped off the boat in Rotterdam, he had to begin life all over again, with small children.

A new life, and with no opportunities. Rotterdam had been leveled by the war. Eighty thousand had died in the Nazi bombing. The harbor was filled with the rotten hulls of sunken ships. Food was rationed, there was no housing, and there were no jobs. And it was bitterly cold in January of 1947.

Coming through the Suez, we immigrants from the tropics had received some clothing from the Red Cross, and Care packages with chocolates and little toys for the children.

Immediately the scene turned into a huge, confused bazaar. You got a size 10 and you needed a 14. Someone else was trying to trade a 16 for an 8. My first brassiere came flying through the air at me, and I hung onto it, though there was room for about ten pounds of breasts inside, and I had none. I was twelve years old.

A man's woolen coat came sliding past.

"Hold onto that coat!" shouted my mother. "It's good quality." I put it on, and I couldn't find my arms. I had never seen a woolen coat, but it had big buttons and pockets and a beautiful belt. I loved that coat. I wore it for four years and finally grew into it.

My mother tried to buy more for us in Cairo, but she discovered that the Nippon guilders she carried were not much more than pieces of paper, highly inflated during the war, and all but worthless once the Japs lost.

We grabbed everything we could on the boat and held it close. After three concentration camps, one after another, we had become selfish. And we didn't yet know how bad it was in Holland.

It was worse than we could have imagined.

My mother arranged for us to be taken immediately to The Hague, to the house where her father still lived. Her two sisters had not been put in Sukarno's camps after the war. They had already arrived from Indonesia with three children each, but with no word yet about their husbands.

Though not small by ordinary Dutch standards, the narrow house became cramped in a hurry under the strain of the newly enlarged family. It did not help that my seventy-year-old grandfather had married the housekeeper, his constant companion during the war, and she stood to inherit his estate after his death.

My own parents' family quickly swelled with the arrival of three more grown children from their former marriages, who had spent the war years in Europe. We all looked at our new brothers and sisters with suspicion.

The bickering began almost immediately. My mother became a tiger. "Can Freddy take care of our registration papers for us?" our aunts whined.

"No, he cannot. Freddy needs his rest so he can go out and look for a job," she replied firmly.

We did not even have documents. My father stood in line for days to get our own registration papers, just so that we would be eligible for the meager ration coupons that were available.

There was no coal for heating that winter, the coldest ever, we were told. When the fighting got unbearable, my mother moved us all up into the attic. Eight of us crowded into one room. We were less comfortable, but at least we had a little place to ourselves.

For two years, my father went out every day into the bitter Dutch streets in his shabby suit to look for work, along with a quarter million other Indonesian émigrés. For a smoke, he and Helen picked up stray cigarette butts out of the street gutters. (She had the habit from her days of running to the kitchen for Nel from Delden.) But mostly he sat in a corner of the attic and died slowly.

"Tell us some stories about the war, Daddy," we would say. Tears began to roll down his face. With difficulty, he told about being confined in solitary, his only companion a young girl about our age, who was being tortured in the next cell for suspicion of spying. The two were able to communicate by tapping quietly on the pipes that ran along the length of the walls.

He never saw her until the day her body was taken away. But every night he had heard her singing a sweet Indonesian song, to comfort herself and ease her pain. It was a song of the rice patties, of sea and sunshine, that haunted him for years after the war.

The men who escaped the cholera epidemic and the vultures were sent on a forced march to Thailand to build the bridges, and then on to Burma for the railroad. Mostly he couldn't talk about those years at all.

The only time he ever brightened up was when he told us his story about the lice. All prisoners were required to present a hundred lice each day to the Japanese. To escape the beatings, my father outwitted his captors by picking through bird shit and saving the tiny seeds they hadn't digested, to pass them off as lice. The Japs never knew the difference.

Overall, the camps were probably harder on the men than on the women. They were taller, which infuriated the Japanese even more, and they didn't have their families with them. They could only worry that they were alive somewhere, and that they would see them again.

And my father must have also been preoccupied about his eventual reunion. Years of being beaten in the groin and having bamboo spears stuck through his testicles had made him impotent.

In The Hague, my mother made short work of the closets in the narrow house. Though her mother had weighed close to three hundred pounds when she died, Dido was still able to find much that was useful. She could not actually sew all that well, but she was able to design and fashion a frock out of almost any piece of fabric.

In three months, we all had new dresses—though the inside seams would not have stood up to close inspection. She herself looked like quite a dame when she stepped out every day in her high heels, her little hats with the veils, and her long red fingernails, to board a tram and look for another apartment or a situation for her husband.

When the family's fighting became too much to handle, we moved out of my grandfather's house. We moved from room to room, from school to school, and finally ended up in a hell hole of a government pension. There were still no jobs.

Of course, my mother knew she had the jewelry from my precious rag doll, but she was saving that for a big investment. It paid off. Finally she was able to buy a pharmacy in an old bombed-out building in Rotterdam, and we began to rebuild our lives.

But we were the lucky ones. Thousands of dark Indonesian half-bloods sat for months, years, at the narrow Dutch windows among the dying plants, and stared out at the freezing rain without hope. Their soft eyes dreamed of a land of palm trees and bananas, that they could never go back to. They could not even immigrate further to the United States, for the United States was not receiving dark-skinned people. They were stuck. Many of them had left magnificent plantations and houses full of servants.

My father began to oversee our education. We were behind in everything, since the Japanese had forbidden any kind of lessons in the camp. And anyway, there had been no time for them. Food was a much bigger priority in those days.

So there I sat, a tall, scrawny girl entering her teens, squeezed into a small desk among sixty or seventy eight-year-olds.

I couldn't read or write. I had never held a pencil in my hand. I didn't even know the days of the week.

Thank God I didn't have puberty to contend with in those unfriendly surroundings. I didn't begin my periods until I was seventeen, so under-nourished we had been at the camps.

For years, my father engaged special tutors for our lessons. Every day after school, and only after we had scrubbed out thousands of little bottles and corks at the pharmacy and made the deliveries on our bicycles, we had two or three hours of lessons in geography and mathematics, history and reading. We had only a couple of years to learn the whole curriculum of elementary school. Our day started at five o'clock in the morning, and continued long after supper.

Every evening my father also massaged my skinny legs and my swollen belly, to help bring the water to the kidneys. After two years, when all signs of beriberi had finally disappeared, Helen and I started ballet lessons to strengthen our weak legs.

Then it was time to work on our teeth, which were all rotten. When the pharmacy began to make good money, we started our visits to the dentist, twice a week, to have them capped.

The kids in school called us the *cucarachas*, because of the strange musical accent we brought over from Indonesia. We called them the "cheese heads," and got into fistfights on the playground. We hated their pale pink skin and their pushy ways.

My father sent us for speech lessons, to learn correct Dutch.

At last we caught up.

I remember the day exactly. I had just passed an exam over three thousand different herbs. I had had to learn the difference in the leaves, their colors, and their scents, as well as the Dutch and Latin names.

My father came into the pharmacy where I was up to my elbows in tiny bottles. "I'm so proud of you!" he exclaimed. "Your grades are so good that I've enrolled you in the *gymnasium*! " That was the pre-university school, which meant years more of learning Greek and Latin.

I broke down and cried.

That evening, they found me on the window ledge of our new fourth-story apartment. "I WON'T GO TO THAT SCHOOL!" I screamed. "If you don't take me out of that school, I'm going to dive down from here!"

My poor father had no idea. His dream was that we would become pharmacists, and he thought it was ours too. "She doesn't have to go to the school," he said to my mother sadly.

After that we began a series of finishing schools. Or rather, we were enrolled, and my father paid the tuition. Then Helen and I would sneak off to the movies, which were forbidden. Or if we had been sent to Switzerland, we took long skiing weekends. Or we escaped to the French Riviera for some sun. By then money wasn't a problem. My father must have known what we were doing, but he never mentioned it. Perhaps he felt guilty for robbing us of our childhood by not escaping to Australia when he had his chance.

Somehow I did get an education. During my year in Rome, studying the Italians mostly, I met a fascinating young prince who was a sometime geology student in Madrid. Through his stories, I fell in love with Spain, if not with the prince. I convinced my father to let me go there.

And after five years I had passed the exams in Holland and gotten a teaching degree in Spanish.

My father was proud. "Learn all you can," he always told us. "Any day the Russians could roll over the Low Countries, and you'd have nothing." He pointed to our heads significantly. "But they can't take away what's inside your brain."

The Russians were a real fear in those days. When Hungary was invaded in 1956, we were each given a large amount of gold coins, and told how to get a ticket on the Holland-American Line, to make our escape to America.

It was becoming clear to him that none of us was going to become a pharmacist, but still he did not give up on us. At least, we might marry one. From the early years, he hauled us all over Europe to the hoity-toity pharmaceutical conferences to show us off.

But the dull sons of pharmacists, with their thick glasses, were not our style. We liked the handsome, sporty guys.

Covered with the required diamonds, we slept through marvelous dinners at Versailles, and long nights at the opera.

He brought young men home to meet us, and then ended up having to pay for the entertainment. "You take her out for a nice dinner," he would say, stuffing some bills in the pale boy's pocket.

We felt like cattle.

With my escape to Spain, I finally achieved some amount of independence—or so I thought.

17

I have a happy picture of myself in those days, tall and blonde and slender, charging down a street in Sevilla or Barcelona or Madrid, with a pack of middle-aged tourists in tow. *"¡Miren la holandesa!"* yelled the good-looking young men. I was known everywhere, and I had a "boy in every port."

I still saw my suave *príncipe* in Madrid, who gave fabulous parties in his home and at all the right resorts, and who had seats in the second row at the bull ring, where we brushed elbows with Hemingway, with Frank Sinatra and Sophia Loren.

At five in the morning the prince and I closed down the bars, and I reported to work at A.T.E.S.A. at seven. I now had my own savings account and my own car. Money was no problem.

At the travel office, I learned quickly about the black market. The exchange rate in those days was 46 pesetas to the dollar. At my own desk, I did my clients a favor by giving them 50. They were thrilled.

Then every so often I would stuff my bag full of their hundred-dollar bills and fly off to Tangier to exchange the money again for 69 or 70 pesetas. I stayed at the Ritz, I visited the Casbah or lay on the beach at Casablanca, and then after a week I was ready for work again.

"You have enough cash, honey?" my father would ask.

"No, I'm stone broke!" I answered, and more came flowing in from home. Several times during the winter season, I needed long breaks to go skiing at St. Moritz or Chamonix. I started to dress well, and my mother loved me for it. For the dark Dutch winters, when I visited home, I even submitted to luxurious furs of leopard and mink and Russian bear.

The tourists adored me. I was filled with hundreds of little stories for every occasion. "Did you notice that you had to get off the train and walk a few hundred yards at the Spanish border?" They all nodded their heads. "We have the English-gauge railroads here in Spain. That's several inches wider than on the rest of the Continent. One of the princesses of Kent married royalty here, and she got the contract for all the railroads in this country. And that's why it's different today!" I would say in an excited voice.

They also loved my dark tales of the unfortunate strains of hemophilia in the royal houses.

"Who's ready for some shopping?" I would call out. All the hands went up in anticipation. I got off the bus in my serious little dress, and led the thick-ankled group into one of my favorite shops in Toledo. They got real bargains there, and I got ten percent commission. If I didn't, we didn't visit that shop any more. At the end of it all, I usually got a five- or ten-dollar tip from the tourists on top of it. I was living high.

My prince was too elegant to press the question of sex, and I was much too Puritanical to respond completely. Nice girls didn't do such things in the Fifties. At that time I saw no need of it. We were having a ball anyway.

The Dutch men I found much too slow, too boring. But I loved those dark Southern types!

After Prince Carlos left, I met Antonio.

He was not rich or titled, but he was a pilot in the Spanish air force. That made him wonderfully glamorous. He would take me off on his motorcycle for weekends of camping in the woods, which was deliciously naughty for me. He recited poetry, and I learned all the romantic flamenco songs of gypsy lovers.

In 1959, when Morocco was fighting for its independence from Spain, Antonio was shot down over Marrakesh and his left leg was crushed. That misfortune added considerably to his mystique. I fell hopelessly in love with him, as I nursed him back to health in the military hospital in Madrid.

My parents were horrified. We were raised Catholic, so in theory that was no problem. But the Dutch have never forgotten the cruel wars of the sixteenth century. The Spanish Duke of Alba is still a symbol of everything we hate. Besides, the Pope had not yet made it possible for marriages to end in divorce or annulment. The thought of even my involvement was more than they could take. I had not yet mentioned marriage.

When they visited Spain, they refused to meet my Antonio. I was crushed.

When his leg was healed, and he was due to visit his home at Santander in the north of Spain, he suggested that we stop seeing each other. It was hurting me too much. Sadly, I agreed.

For a day.

I hopped the first train with no luggage, desperate to see my lover. There were no seats available. I had no ticket, so I hid in the toilet. The conductor came by, discovered me, and threw me off the train at the next station. When the train started moving again, I jumped back on and the whole drama continued, for four hundred kilometers. We were reunited in a desperate scene of love and remorse. Antonio let me drive his Mercedes back to Madrid.

When I arrived, my father was waiting for me. "Let's go have lunch," he said soberly. Innocently, I jumped in the car, and he drove me straight to the border, and home to Rotterdam. He had already arranged with my landlady to have my bags packed and in the trunk of his car.

People find it hard to believe that I allowed myself to be kidnapped and kept prisoner by my father at the age of twenty-five. What they don't know, is that it was against the law in Holland to get married without parental consent until the age of thirty! Incredible. That one's been off the books only about ten years.

In Holland, I sulked. I was not allowed to go anywhere. I didn't speak to anyone, including my parents. I cried for Antonio. His letters were intercepted by my father, translated by a neighbor whose husband was Argentine, and then burned.

My passport was confiscated. My father locked it in the big safe in the pharmacy and had the combination changed.

My mother tried her usual solution on me: shopping. For two long months I visited all the right shops, and stood still for the seamstresses, under the close supervision of my "warden."

I was being outfitted for America. A year in the United States with my sister Helen, who had recently been married, would get Spain out of my system.

"I'm sleeping with him! We're already married!" I screamed out, to hurt them.

I was a real mess. My social, emotional, and physical development had been thrown so completely out of whack by my irregular childhood, that I didn't have the real independence I needed, to get out from under such tyranny.

And so I was shipped out. On the Holland-America line, which did so much business with my father. Antonio arrived for me in Rotterdam shortly afterwards, but I didn't hear about that until years later.

Father's send-off was, "if you ever go to Spain to see this young man, then you are no daughter of mine."

After several days of lunches and dinners with the old fart captain who was a friend of my father's, I was ready to let loose in New York.

Going through customs was a cold experience. I wanted to turn around and take the first plane home. The man asked to see my letter of credit and my return ticket.

Proudly, I said in my best Oxford English, "I am a visitor, not an immigrant." I was not to be confused with those sad, lonely Indonesians on the streets of Holland. I was wearing my diamonds, on my father's advice, and in my pocket I had $6,000 in cash, more than that little guy made in a year.

The New York experience did not improve once I got to the YWCA (after a small detour to the YMCA—my English was not as good as I thought!). All the girls were too busy for me. I sat in the lobby, looking for the friendly face of a Deanna Durbin or an Esther Williams, as I had come to know American girls from the movies, but all I saw were bodies with their hair in curlers, flying up and down the staircase, or rushing off to work or to school. I felt even lonelier.

I was used to the graciousness of Europe, where the director of the school or the manager of the hotel received me and introduced me to everyone. All I got here was a grudging 'hello,' or sometimes a shove if I was standing in the way.

The only person who was nice to me in New York was a black policeman, who stopped traffic once to help me cross the street to the drug store, to get a cup of coffee.

Coffee in a drug store? I was amazed. There was nothing like that in my father's pharmacy. I was fascinated, and a little depressed, by the plastic packets of butter and marmalade on the lunch counter. I longed to fly back to my beloved Madrid.

My father had booked a Greyhound trip for me to California, not having any idea of the size of the United States. But after I had made the short, required excursions to Boston and Washington, I wouldn't hear of it. I found a travel agent who exchanged my ticket for a flight on TWA.

I was met at the Los Angeles airport by Helen and her new American husband, Bruce Dexter.

She had met him in Torremolinos, while she was visiting me in Spain. He was a good-looking, serious-minded young man who had degrees in both political science and English. What he wanted to do was write. Helen fell for him, and wanted to help him.

I saw huge signs in the airport that proclaimed the name of 'Bruins.' That's my maiden name, and so my name at the time. I was so flattered.

"Aren't you nice?" I said to Dexter. "You even put my name up there!" He had me believing that for weeks afterwards. Funny how one can be completely thrown by a new place. I don't think I would have been so naive in Europe.

The Dexters welcomed us at their home in Westwood. Very Beverly Hills. White carpets, black servants. I thought it odd that we were never allowed to walk on the carpets, except at parties. The furniture was all covered, and the paintings were cordoned off with little ropes so we wouldn't get too close to them. "The Americans are strange," I thought.

They took me to see Liberace at the Beverly Wilshire, and he and I got acquainted at the piano, gabbing about our favorite songs.

The Dexters expected me to be absolutely numb with wonder at it all, but they had a girl on their hands who knew her way around the Lido in Paris and the Via Veneto. I felt right at home in those luxurious surroundings. They didn't know what to make of me.

They had already made too many assumptions about us. When my father wrote them a gracious letter saying that his daughter Helen had received a proposal of marriage from their son, they were horrified. They wrote back some formal reply to my parents, but to Bruce they vented their true feelings. "Are you out of your mind?" they wrote. "You know goddam well that Indonesians are black!"

The elder Dexter didn't have his papers, since he was a Russian Jew who had escaped as a child. Under Dutch law, Helen and Bruce couldn't get married without them, so my father sent them off to London to become residents there so they could be legally married. From that moment he supported them both.

The doctor and his wife were greatly relieved to discover, when Helen arrived, that she was white and blonde.

When I came to town, they took the covers off the furniture, threw a big party, and officially presented the bride to about a hundred of their friends. Helen and I were dripping with diamonds (which my father cautioned us that we could always pawn if we needed to get out of a difficult situation).

We were a success.

When living with the folks proved too much for them, Helen and Bruce Dexter found a small place of their own. "Could you get me my diamonds from the safe?" Helen asked her father-in-law. "We've found an apartment of our own."

"Uhhh—" said Dr. Dexter. "You'll have to come back tomorrow."

He had sneaked into the safe, taken out the jewels himself, and brought them to a jeweler for appraisal. Apparently he hadn't seen enough good stones to be able to determine their value himself.

The next day, he treated their little drudge from Indonesia with more respect. But the jewels only confirmed his opinion that my father should continue to support the newlyweds.

I moved in with them in their new house, and stayed for nine months. But Bruce longed to write his book, and finally they sold the Mercedes which my father had given them as a wedding present, and flew off to Málaga to get started on it.

I was stranded in California.

I enrolled in the English language school at U.C.L.A. I had already studied English for eight years, but my father expected it. The only thing I remember from those months was a huge boring hall with lots of tape decks.

One of my boyfriends was the son of the Tunisian ambassador, which meant that he had an unlimited supply of the best champagne. Together we laughed at the little cookie parties arranged by the Los Angeles matrons to entertain us, and at the excursions organized for us by the student council.

Once you've been to the Folies Bergères, a California square dancing demonstration seems dull by comparison.

I moved into a new studio apartment, my first on my own.

I didn't have any one particular boyfriend, but after Helen left, I started depending more and more on Bob Lewis, a friend of Bruce Dexter's. We played tennis, went dancing and horseback riding and hunting together. He was a bit older than I was, but he drove a sporty Jaguar and seemed young and fit, and I didn't mind.

He wanted me to move in with him, but I didn't know how to explain that to my father, so I said no. I liked my freedom. He understood, and even helped me paint the walls of my apartment to brighten things up. And I started driving the Jaguar.

My tourist visa ran out about the same time my electricity and phones were cut off. Bob came in one day and found me sitting in the dark.

"What are you doing that for?" he asked.

"I don't know what happened. They just went off."

"Well, when was the last time you paid the bill?"

Now that was a new question for me. I had never opened the envelopes, never paid a bill in my life. Those things were arranged at the bank, as far as I knew.

"Where's your checkbook?" pursued Bob. He stumped me again. I had a savings account, and when I needed cash, I withdrew it. Simple as that. He helped me get everything back in order.

Bob Lewis was separated from his wife when I met him. In November, his divorce became final. He had been married to a beautiful model, and I found it extremely flattering that he seemed to prefer me. We became closer and closer, taking several weekends off to ski in Squaw Valley. I, of course, had "given up" both jobs I had attempted in southern California, so my time was my own.

As Christmas approached, my father and I were fighting over the phone about coming home to Rotterdam. Just before the holidays, Bob and I took off to Lake Tahoe again to ski.

We got drunk on the way back, and as we drove into Carmel, we said (I can't even remember which one of us), "Why not get married?"

We pulled into the Highlands Inn, where they have a little chapel just for lovers like us. I had only my ski clothing with me, so I went out and bought a cute little dress.

At the hotel Bob said, "You can't get married like that. You have to have some stockings." So he went back and bought me a girdle and some panty hose. My first. You can imagine my trying to get into them in my condition. He also presented me with a beautiful orchid corsage.

We were married right before Christmas in 1960. Our witness was the lady who dusted the chapel and collected the donations. Since I had sobered up a bit during the ceremony, we went back to the room and got drunk again.

I was the legal Mrs. Lewis, an American wife. Actually the third Mrs. Lewis, but that didn't matter to me. Bob had been so nice. I was on top of the world.

Still, I didn't gather up enough courage to call my father and tell him until my birthday, January 17. He simply cried his eyes out over the telephone.

After I moved to Puerto Vallarta, I never saw him again. It had been almost six years. My biggest regret was that he would not answer my letters or come over to visit me.

He still had such great affection for Indonesia in his heart, I know. I was certain he would have loved Mexico, as I did.

And now he was dead and I was landing in Rotterdam. I had missed his funeral.

I stayed with my mother for two months. At that end of that time, I had accomplished one of the major *coups* of my life. I had talked her into returning with me. "Where the wild Indians live," as she said.

She should have said 'gangsters.'

Adolfo Rey was one of several brothers in a very influential political family in Mexico. They were cousins of a former governor of Jalisco, and "had connections" in Mexico City. Adolfo was the immigration officer in Guadalajara. When my five-year permission ran out and I was eligible to apply for working papers, everyone in Puerto Vallarta recommended going to him, to get the fastest and best of the lawyers. All he had to do was ask in the capital, it was said, and the papers came right through.

Unfortunately, he had gotten in some kind of trouble with the law himself during the fall of 1969, and had fled the country. My papers were still locked in his office.

When my father died, I asked Candelario, "What am I going to do? I can't get back to Holland!"

He patted me on the back and said, "Don't worry about anything, Theresa. Give them fifty dollars at immigration in Mexico City, and they won't give you any trouble."

It was true. The old Mexican *mordida*. I should have known.

"When you come back through, *salúdalo*, greet the guy with a smile and another fifty dollars," he assured me.

But since I had had to give up my tourist visa when I left the country, I took the extra precaution of visiting the Mexican consul in Rotterdam, who was a client of my father's pharmacy, and arranging a proper visa for the return trip.

We landed in Mexico City with all my mother's baggage.

Two immigration officers with guns were there to greet me, flashing some sort of document past my eyes. "Would you step in here?" they said, pointing to a little private room in the airport where they detain criminals.

"Nice friends you have," observed my mother. "So high in the government. They must really appreciate you."

My papers were not in order. The officials did not seem to know what could be done about it. It would have to be straightened out at the main office downtown.

"How did you know I would be on that plane?" I asked. I did not get an answer.

"Look, I've got my mother with me," I said. "I have five hundred dollars that I can put on deposit as a guarantee, if you'll let me arrange for her to continue to Puerto Vallarta without me."

I wrote a note to Bob, explaining what had happened, and another in Spanish for the taxi driver, so that my mother would be brought straight to Las Glorias. I saw her onto the plane. And then I was put in a car and escorted to the main immigration office in Mexico City.

I sat there, a prisoner more or less, in that anteroom a day and a half.

My case was apparently very complicated. I mentioned the name of Adolfo Rey. They smiled. I reminded them that I had gotten a new visa in Holland. There was no response. Things were moving very slowly, even for Mexico.

"What beautiful secretaries you all have!" I commented, trying to get on the good side of my officer. He smiled.

There were about thirty girls jammed in the office, very stylish and beautifully made up. I couldn't help staring at them. After a while, one of the girls stuck her tongue out at me.

"*Señora,*" said Señor Velasquez who was "working" on my case, "*son cariñas.*" They're whores.

"*¿Cariñas?*" I whispered, fascinated.

"*Sí, son internacionales—gringas, brasileñas, inglesas—*" Apparently I had gotten in on a raid at one of Mexico City's poshest houses of prostitution. There were girls from all over the world sitting there, like me, waiting to be deported.

That night I lay on the hard sofa in the office and listened to their stories. It passed the time.

The girl next to me told me that the beautiful dusky one in the corner had had an affair with one of the immigration officers. When she'd dumped him, he'd turned in the whole bunch. All their possessions had been confiscated.

The next morning, my new friends were all shoved into a black truck like cattle, and shipped off to their home countries.

My fate was not so bad, though I never saw my five hundred dollars again.

I was released without comment. I never saw the accusing document. I never got any papers. I didn't know if I was legal in Mexico or not, but I was there.

I flew back to Puerto Vallarta with a vague feeling that this wasn't the last time I would be hearing from the Rey family.

My mother took an instant dislike to Bob Lewis, and I guess I must have begun asking myself all those questions I hadn't wanted to think about.

I started breaking loose. At first innocently enough, by spending afternoons out "with the girls."

My mother didn't stay long the first time, but she was hooked on Mexico. She returned to her home in Holland, and for the next several years, she flew over to see us, often without warning, whenever she longed for the tropics.

Actually, my friend Dorothy Sparks was more like a mother to me in those years, and she and I got on fabulously. I could really talk to her.

Back in the days of Cloro's *palapa* tavern on the beach, I had seen her every day, her chubby body jammed into a one-piece bathing suit, standing knee-deep in the surf and casting out her fishing line. We got acquainted.

One day she came to me and confessed that her boyfriend had died without leaving her anything. All the money had gone to his children back in the States. "Is there any way I can rent one of your bungalows by the month or by the year?" she asked sadly.

"Of course."

And so she became one of our first customers at Las Glorias.

She was a really swinging, sexy broad for a 65-year-old woman. It wasn't long before she had a Mexican boyfriend, Ernesto Sánchez, the new immigration officer in town, who took over when the handsome Candelario became our chief of police. He was dark-skinned, big-bellied, and he walked like a duck. They made a great pair, and we loved them both. Dorothy was like a grandmother to my kids, long before my mother became acquainted with them.

Ernesto lost no time in office, piling up bigger and bigger *mordidas*. A lot of foreigners in Puerto Vallarta needed their tourist cards renewed, and didn't have the energy or the time to go back to the border and re-enter the country legally. No problem. For about $200, Señor Sánchez could fix us up.

He was well on his way to getting rich, when he made an unfortunate mistake. He asked for a bribe from the wife of one of the top officials of the American embassy in Mexico City. She turned him in, and he was exiled to Chiapas, the rough jungle state on the border with Guatemala, the closest thing Mexico has to Siberia. In town they laughed at the thought of him hefting his little round body up onto a *burro*, and taking the six-hour trip through the jungles, just to get to the nearest telegraph line.

But my friend Dorothy Sparks was not laughing. She had really loved the man. We both had something to commiserate about, during our long afternoons out.

"You've got to live your own life," she would tell me. She was not an enemy of Bob Lewis. She loved him too, like all the women did. But she also saw my self-respect taking a nose dive.

It was not that we were whoring around. We would just walk over the beach to the Posada Vallarta and spend long afternoons eating lobster (what luxury, if you are eating someone else's lobster, and you are not responsible for quality control!), and drinking tequila.

The afternoons sometimes stretched out into the evenings. We would meet some friendly Americans at the pool and have a few more drinks and laughs. If I was too tired from all the alcohol and sun to go back to work, I hid out at Dorothy's place, to sleep it off.

"Have you seen Terry?" Bob would ask, snarling at the door of her bungalow.

"Oh, no. I left her at the Posada Vallarta." She flapped her eyelashes innocently and hoped that the sounds of my snoring behind the *manta* curtain were not too loud. Luckily the waves pounding on the beach were covering for me too.

Bob hated being left alone for long periods of time. Unless, of course, he had something going with one of the maids. He was still unsure of his Spanish. And we had already been harassed twice now by government officials.

Recently we had bought a little ranch up in the hills, where we had fruit trees and a little pineapple grove. At times, I would load up the truck with some choice garbage from Las Glorias, to feed our livestock. Not as many times as I told Bob I was doing it, however. It became easy to find some "business that had to be tended to at the ranch," when I needed to.

Little innocent things like that. They were my first attempts at striking out for myself. It's a common story, I suppose. I was Daddy's girl, and then immediately I was Bob's girl.

There were a few months at the beginning of my Mexican story when I was my own girl, and I found out that I liked it. Bob, after all, was not ten years older, like he told me when we got married, but twenty. With the cares of the operation of a hotel, and without a government to back him up and allow him to feel legally secure, the age difference began to show. On the other hand, I was just beginning to discover my own energies.

Cloro died less than four months after my father. One day he got a nose bleed, and the next day he was in the hospital. It was too serious for Puerto Vallarta, so we had him flown to specialists in Guadalajara. He was riddled with cancer. We sat with him in the hospital as he got worse, day by day. In four weeks he was dead.

I loved that man as much as any parent, and I was profoundly sick at heart to have to say good-bye to him. We arranged for the company to give a monthly pension to his wife.

Almost immediately afterwards, those new youthful energies I was talking about were required once again.

Perhaps my remark above about the Rey family sounded like paranoia, or idle accusation. What evidence was there, to make us think that they were tied to our troubles? None whatsoever. We never suspected it at the time. After all, we didn't have "connections in Mexico City" like they did. That made the dark threats to our position as foreigners all the more effective, perhaps, because we couldn't figure out where they were coming from. But a pattern was starting to emerge.

The next trouble came from Pepe. That greaseball—the smuggling buddy of Cloro's, with his tits hanging down nearly to his shorts, which in turn hung down nearly to his knees—was still with us. Every morning early, he still raked the beach, ever so slowly. After Cloro's death he became even more obnoxious. Twice I had complaints from women in the beachside bungalows that he had been peeking in at them through the louvered windows.

I was furious. I confronted him with it, and when he gave me his usual smart answer, I fired him in a rage.

He turned me in to immigration, and I ended up back in jail. The replacement officer for Sánchez was new to the town, knew nothing about any of us.

Officially Terry Lewis could not cuss anybody out. Officially, she couldn't even work. Her papers were still locked in Adolfo Rey's office in Guadalajara.

That was number three. Twice in Puerto Vallarta, and once overnight in the main immigration office in Mexico City.

I sat down on the middle concrete bench and hung my feet over the edge, telling my rear end to prepare for the worst.

Luis Favela came into the precinct area. He was an engineer and architect, who had married a rich American wife. We had become good friends, because they liked to come and play tennis and swim at Las Glorias. He was now the mayor of Puerto Vallarta.

He looked over the horn rims of his glasses. "Theresa! What are you doing here?"

"Well, I don't know," I said. "I don't have a lawyer."

He went into his office, which was in the same building, and called Miguel Salinas. Our village was becoming sophisticated. The mayor had a telephone.

Next came my friend Rafael de la Cruz, who had been appointed the mayor's secretary.

"What's the matter, Theresa?"

"Well, I don't know. That black bastard Pepe turned me in. Do you think it's serious?"

"I'll check on it."

Toward evening he was back. I was finishing up a choice dinner, brought in from El Patio by Ofelia.

He stepped toward the door of the mayor's office. *"¡Andale!"* he said to the officer in charge. "Come on, open it!" He looked over to me and said in English, "Follow me."

"Now, where's he taking me?" I thought. I followed him.

"It's the best we can do for now," he said, gesturing toward a cot that he and Favela had set up in the office.

I broke into laughter. They couldn't get me out, but at least I was to be provided with whatever first-class accommodations they were able to muster in the shabby jail. I thanked him. I saw that they had even set out a little stack of magazines next to the bed, to keep my mind occupied.

"Stay put, Terry," he said. "Tomorrow when the judge is in his office, everything will be OK."

At seven the next morning, Rafael came over from his house, which was nearby, and led me back into jail for the day. He said in English, "I'll see you a bit later. I'll make sure you get a lawyer."

After a long afternoon's *siesta*, Favela returned and called me in. "I can do nothing, Theresa," he apologized. "Please excuse me. You mean a lot to all of us. But there is nothing to be done. Please excuse my *pueblo*," he said, also apologizing for Mexico.

What he could do was open up his office again, and let me sleep on the camp cot, which he did that night. It sure beat the hell out of my concrete bunk!

The next day was Thursday. On Thursdays, the priests from all over Mexico take the money from their *limosnas*, the alms, and oversee the women of the parish as they prepare a big meal for the local prisoners. Once a week at least, we all eat well. The priest buys a suckling pig, and the women make up a huge, steaming pot of beans and a stack of tortillas.

So Thursday afternoon about two, I was dozing on the bunk of my choice, when in walked my buddy, Father Aldana. He was dressed in his black habit, which officially had been forbidden to him outside the church since the Mexican revolution. But his church was only a block away, up the hill.

Several women carried in large woven baskets, piled high with deep-fried pork rinds, and the aroma was delicious. My *compañeros* started going crazy, yelling to be served first and joking around with one another. It was a party.

The priest began making the rounds, ladling out beans and salad and huge slabs of pork for each one of us.

He rounded the corner of the bunks and looked up. His double chins quivered. "THERESA! What are you doing here?"

"Well, I don't know," I answered. I grabbed onto the rope that was used to give a boost to the lucky person who got the top bunk, and swung down beside him. *"¡Hola, padre!"* I said, laughing. *"¿Cómo estás?"*

All the prisoners looked on in amazement, not accustomed to addressing a man of the cloth in such a familiar way. The priest dropped his glasses into the beans. I could see this simple, amiable soul trying to take it all in. "Here's this Dutch broad, who sits with me in church and tells me about Spain—"

He scratched his head. "She steals my carpets—And now she's in jail, swinging from a rope like Tarzan!" All at once he started shaking with laughter.

When he had finished the serving, he told the officer to open up the mayor's office, and we sat on my little cot among all the official papers, and had a talk.

"I guess it was my mistake, *padre*," I said, and I told him the story of Pepe.

"Oh, mi hija—" he said, sadly.

I was still his child, and it felt good.

"I think it's wonderful what you do for the prisoners every week," I said, patting him on the knee. "Don't worry about me. I'll be out in no time."Of course, it was true. Luis Favela came in the next day and said, "Come on, Theresa. Your seventy-two hours are up. I'll take you home in my car."

And so the ex-con was on the streets again. No papers, no formal accusation, no hearing, no explanations.

What was my legal status? I didn't know. But I did know that exciting things were about to happen around Las Glorias, and I needed to find out.

Bob and I had a new partner. He was a rich rancher and oil man with a thick Oklahoma accent and big plans, Doug Walker. In 1969, when the highway first opened up, he had come down to Las Glorias for a couple of months with his wife and three kids. He and Bob struck up a friendship, and I was always glad when my husband found someone who spoke English and shared his interest in business.

Gradually we learned that Walker also had hotels and motels back home, not to mention race horses, and that he was looking to expand even more.

I stayed out of it at first. Between my Dutch and his Oklahoma speech, we were always having to ask each other to repeat that last phrase. I made sure I never called him by his first name. It always came out 'dog' or 'dough' or 'duck.'

Besides, I was busy with my mother flying in and out, and keeping track of my three kids, all the maids, and the operation of the restaurant. I didn't have time to sit for hours drinking and smoking and talking business.

But this business started to intrigue me. Walker had connections with Ramada and Holiday Inn in the States. He envisioned moving our office and the tennis courts, and putting up a four-story building with fifty more rooms on that spot. It would rise above the coconut trees, overlooking the sea on one side and the mountains on the other. With eighty-four rooms, we wouldn't need to add much to our staff, and we could make a lot more money.

Walker was thinking of giving us the total sum needed to buy out our original investors, then selling it all in turn to a major chain for a huge profit. He would stay on with me to operate the franchise.

Bob was thinking of getting out. He had had it. Several times already we had had offers to buy Las Glorias, for two or three times the price. *"Please*, Terry," he begged, "let's go! Let's just sell it and get the hell out of here!" But I had always refused.

I can forgive him a lot for staying with me those years, against all intelligent advice.

It seemed also that our legal situation, that is, who actually owned the place, and who could sell it, was going to be cleared up too. There were rumors flying everywhere throughout Mexico that the new president was about to appoint a commission to oversee the selling of beach land to private individuals. The *Fideicomiso*.

Ironically, the *'fidei'* part of that word means 'trust.' I would ponder that one bitterly over the next years, as I sat waiting in one anteroom after another. But all looked bright to us at the time.

We agreed to go into business with Doug Walker. He was going to pay off Gene Smith and the others, with 16 or 17 percent on their money.

We consulted a new architect, who talked about continuing our motif with huge arched windows and a large entrance. (Alvarez had long since moved to Mexico City.) We had a topographical engineer come in to check on the underground water level, since it was a big building we were talking about. The man was a brother-in-law of Ignacio Rey, Adolfo's older brother. We played right into their hands.

My mother had decided she liked Mexico so much that she wanted to build a house right beside ours. She had hardly moved into it, when one morning she looked out of her bedroom window on the second story and screeched. She came running over to us.

"There are hundreds of people out there!" she yelled. "They're putting up a barbed-wire fence all around the property!"

Sure enough, we ran out, and saw seven or eight hundred gypsies milling about, setting up camp in our front yard. Big military trucks were parked at the entrance, along with dozens of rusty pick-ups everywhere. Several soldiers stood idly by and watched, as a few of the men set up a triple-layered fence of barbed wire around our two houses. We were blocked off from our car, and the rest of the world.

"What's going on?" I screamed to the officer in charge.

He shrugged. "You will be notified," he said.

I looked around at my filthy new neighbors. They were not really gypsies in the true sense, but poor *rancheros*, paid to move around and squat on the land. They were setting up their little raggedy tents, and feeding the chickens and pigs they had brought with them. Some of the women were preparing breakfast.

"*¿Aqua, señora, aqua?*" Some nerve.

But it wasn't their fault. They were under orders to do as they were told. I hooked up the garden hose and let them use my water.

Bob Lewis was livid. "Kick them off!" he shouted at me.

"We can't. We'll be shot," I told him. "We just have to wait and see what's going on."

Toward evening we received a visit from a lawyer representing Ignacio Rey. The paper he had brought assured us that the powerful man could do us the favor of giving us "protection," for a mere $40,000. If we paid, the squatters would be removed, and it would never happen again.

"How can they do this?" raged Bob.

"They're doing it. We're foreigners. What choice do we have?" I said.

"But I don't understand how they think they can get away with it! They've done some pretty shabby things in the past, but at least they always tried to make it look legal. Now this—"

The lawyer sat on my sofa and smiled. He didn't let on whether he understood us or not.

Bob went to the mayor. Nothing.

He took off for the American consulate in Guadalajara. They were sorry, but they did not get involved in business in Mexico, as long as no American citizen had been hurt.

"The authorities—" began the consul.

"There are no authorities!" yelled Bob. "We haven't seen any police. Just this piece of paper from Ignacio Rey."

He called Doug Walker, who flew down immediately.

It was beginning to smell really rank around our place. The utilities had been cut off.

"Listen, you all," our new investor said confidentially. "This forty thousand is so little compared to the money we're talking about. Let's just pay them off, and then we won't hear any more about it."

Bob sputtered. "This guy Rey," Doug continued, "he knows the *fideicomiso* is coming in soon. He's just trying to take an extra bit out while he still can."

He had talked to Antonio Juárez, Miguel's lawyer friend who had gotten me out of jail the first time. One of our *prestanombres*, he was also the vice president of our corporation. "If we pay the man, will he do anything more?" he had asked.

Juárez assured him that it was guaranteed: the squatters wouldn't be back. But if we didn't pay, they might extend their little tent city to the hotel, or burn down the houses, or—? It was impossible to say.

Doug made out a check for $40,000.

The barbed wire was cut away, the utilities were turned back on, the trucks pulled out, and the squatters moved on to another spot.

To some other poor bastard who had gotten in the way of Ignacio Rey.

18

I really got to know my mother for the first time during those years. She was a tough old bird. But she had always been like that.

My father was the scholarly professor type—quiet, calm, with slim, elegant hands. I remember once when the whole family was out for a drive, the front tire blew out. He handled the car beautifully and brought it to a stop, and then he said helplessly, "Now look what happened, honey!"

Dido sputtered for a while and got out of the car. "Goddam sonofabitch! Can't do anything in this world outside of your laboratory!" she mumbled, as she got down on her knees to change the tire herself.

We girls sat in the car, spoiled, and fussing because we had to go to the bathroom.

My father got out and encouraged my mother, and when it was finished, he gently complimented her. Freddy wasn't being stubborn. He was a good sportsman in many ways, at polo for instance, but he simply did not know how to change a tire. And he knew she did.

'Sonofabitch' she meant quite literally sometimes. As much as she loved the Dutch tropics and the soft people, she believed strongly in the rightness of the old colonial system. She disliked my dark Indonesian grandmother, and she must have been an impossible daughter-in-law.

"Stupid, ugly, black bitch!" she would snort when we walked in the door after one of our required visits to the old plantation.

We girls were all decked out in new dresses, gifts from our grandmother.

"Damn half-blood, she can't even go out and buy the dresses herself—" she continued. "And at the Chinese store, where all the *cachos* shop!" A *cacho* is literally a 'peanut,' but it is not a nice word.

Our grandmother generally couldn't be bothered with a brood of young blonde granddaughters. She would send the maid out to buy us presents. Partly, no doubt, because she knew it would infuriate my mother, just as it did.

My father merely sighed. He had learned to weather out the explosions.

In spite of appearances, they loved each other deeply.

And furthermore, Freddy was master of his house. When he was working again in Holland after the war, we no sooner heard the key in the door every night, than we girls were all standing up to greet him, impeccably groomed and dressed in the latest fashion. My mother had a martini ready for him, and his Christian Dior smoking jacket and slippers standing by. The maid was right behind her with elegant platters of smoked salmon and eel and assorted cheeses.

Several times, driving back from a late shopping trip, she nearly killed us all on the highway, in her haste to perform this evening ritual.

They were happy, especially in Indonesia before the war. My father was dashing in his crisp white military uniform and saber, the heir to rich lands of coffee and tea, sugar and rubber, and we heard he was quite a ladies' man with the dark beauties of his native land. But when my stylish mother swept in, she dazzled him from the start.

Small and svelte, she took over the household with a couple dozen servants, learned their language, worked alongside my father in the pharmacy, and reigned at the polo club. Their life was a colonial dream. Her first Swiss husband always wanted to remarry her, but she never considered it.

When the Japs came in, she had all of our hair died black, so that we would appear to be native Indonesians. "At least the girls might be saved," she said. It didn't work. We were taken away.

During the ordeal of the concentration camps, she never doubted that Freddy was alive and would return to us. She had a sixth sense about those things. She simply knew it. She may have been forced to show us mostly her tough side in those years, but her spiritual side continued to be just as strong.

"Your husband is alive," she told one of the distraught wives during a séance. "He is on a submarine in the fjords of Norway. Saint Teresa will take care of him. Don't worry. He'll come back to you."

After the war, many women came to our apartment in Holland to visit her and thank her. They assured her that everything she had seen and predicted had come true. The submarine officer's wife even wrote her story for a Dutch magazine years later.

And just as she promised, my father came back too. Most of the women were desperate in the captivity of Sukarno's camp, but my mother never wavered.

We had been there several months, when one day, a shrunken old man with a long gray beard slowly made his way up to the gate of the *kadek*. He was nearly wasted away from tropical malaria, his ribs pierced tightly through his skin, but he was alive. They were in each other's arms immediately.

As soon as he was able to prove to Sukarno's troops that he was born in Indonesia, we were free.

Our faithful Kudu could hardly wait to make his presentation to my father. Although the pharmacy had been legally turned over to him when my father was arrested, he had saved back half the earnings from all those years, to present to him after the war. My father wept when they saw each other again, and gratefully took the money.

But there was no future in his native land. We all started making preparations to move to Holland.

My mother had broken her leg two years before, while smuggling in the Ambarawa camp, and even then it was still an open, pussy sore. Through it we could see the steel rods and wires, which had been inserted by the camp doctor to hold it together.

The British officers in charge of emigration made arrangements to transfer her by military plane to Djakarta, while they sent the rest of us along on the train to meet her.

She refused. She lay beside the landing strip on a stretcher, surrounded by grim and tired soldiers. "I will not be separated from my family!" she declared. "I will not get on that plane. It is not ready for take-off."

The commander looked as if he wanted to gather her up and toss her onto the aircraft himself, just to silence her. But she remained adamant. "We have survived this far. You are not going to get me on that plane!"

She thought her instinct was telling her that separation might lead to danger, even still another camp for some of us. But that evening we found out the "real" reason. The plane she should have flown in had engine trouble over the mountains and crashed. All sixty-three people were killed.

When we finally got to Djakarta, which we had always known as Batavia, we had another long wait for the boat which was to take us to Europe. The Holland-America line had lent its passenger ships for the huge operation, but there weren't enough for the quarter of a million refugees who all wanted to leave all at once.

Besides, the waters all through the Indian Ocean had to be cleared first of Japanese mines.

Our time in Djakarta became a gala celebration. We stayed at the most elegant Hotel des Indes, in huge old rooms with wicker furnishings and ceiling fans. Every night my parents dressed up in exquisite silks and tuxedos, for champagne dinners and dancing. They laughed and partied into the morning, despite her stiff leg and his weakness from tropical disease.

After all, who knew if we would live through the pending trip? Who knew what the Nippon guilders from Kudu would be worth, outside of Indonesia?

By day Dido went out to exchange the money and some of her diamonds, and to buy real Dutch guilders for the journey. She carried everything in a small black alligator bag.

One afternoon when she returned to the hotel, she was shaking. Some dark, surly characters had kidnapped her at knife point and were on the verge of murdering her, in order to sell her flesh for steak meat—so desperate was the situation in Djakarta in those days.

She had screamed loudly enough to attract attention and beat them off with her cane. She barely escaped. And with the bag.

Then finally we were on our ship. "A toast to the beginning of our new adventure!" she cried, ever an optimist. None of us knew how badly devastated Holland had been by the war.

My father offered his services on board as a pharmacist. That way, he was also able to get us extra vitamins. He started massaging my legs and overseeing all of our recovery.

We were jammed way down in the hold, in hammocks. Several nuns were down there too, with dozens of orphaned children under their care. The cabins above had been given to women accompanied by their own babies.

Very quickly Dido observed that most of those small children had slanted eyes. She stormed up to the captain's cabin and burst in on him. "So, you've reserved your cabins for the Japanese whores! We won't stand for it!" she screamed. She was almost breathing fire. "There will be no Dutch women who remained faithful to their husbands stuck in that hole, while the whores of the Nips are in cabins!"

My father just shook his head.

But the same day, we went up, along with the nuns and the orphans, and the "whores" went down.

I remember the trip as blazing hot, especially standing at the *embarcadero* in Calcutta to take on fresh water. But for a child who had been hemmed in by high fences for years, it was kind of fun. It was a huge adventure.

People on the boat continued to die from beriberi and dysentery and cholera at an alarming rate. They were simply thrown overboard. "Oh God, there goes one!" Helen would cry. "Who was it? Can you tell?" We would scurry along the deck to the stern, to see if we could make it out.

Being confined for over a month, even on a large ship, began to wear on us. When we pulled into Suez, Helen stood up on the railing and then dived three stories into the canal. I went in after her, and then my little sister. My father, unable to hold us back, had to dive in with his white uniform to take care of us. Not to save us, really. We had all learned to swim almost as soon as we could walk.

I've described my father's desperation those first two terrible years in Holland. In some ways it was worse than the prisons, for there was no hope of an end to it.

It was my mother who held us together. She had her rough times too. She was having to learn how to be a pretty young wife, living with a husband she loved and finally feeling good, and yet unable to have sex with him.

Helen and I used to listen to them late at night in the bedroom. We cried when we heard their fights. My mother got so frustrated and angry, that she would pick a fight over any subject that came up. Freddy remained calm.

Helen and I vowed that we were going to kill our mother. We were never going to kill him. Not until we were married ourselves did we understand what their feelings must have been.

It was Dido too, who finally got us back on course in business. She always had a keen business sense, and my father always admired her for it.

One day she went to a seer in The Hague, where we were living. She took along a bit of his fingernail and some of his hair.

The exotic woman spread out her cards on the table, one by one. "You are going to find a business," she said. "But it is not here. You have to go by train. Yes! It's in Rotterdam. There will be a building for you in Rotterdam to make a new beginning."

Dido came home delirious with excitement.

"I've found out about the first organized bus tour to Paris!" she told my father. "It's for two weeks. I want you to go with them. I sold a small diamond today," she smiled.

When he protested, she wore him down.

"For years, you've been dreaming of your student days in Paris! I've gotten you all new suits and shoes. Just go ahead and have a good time. When you come back, life will look better."

Reluctantly my father agreed. We all saw him off at the bus.

She deposited us at home and then got on the first train for Rotterdam. She followed the old woman's instructions exactly. She started through the city on the tramways, systematically scrutinizing each building. And then there it was—a big pharmacy, formerly prosperous, but with a bomb crater right in the center. It was owned by a Mr. Johnson.

She called on him, elegant in her little fox wrap from her mother's closet, with the crystal eyes staring out.

"I have this much money," she declared, spreading out on his desk the jewels she had hidden in my doll. "We need the pharmacy. You must sell it to us."

Her nerve must have appealed to him. He was a very wealthy man. "You have enough money already," she told him. "Just take my diamonds." She had saved out enough to make the repairs on the building and buy chemicals and equipment.

"But don't sell the jewels," she added when an agreement had been reached. "I'll be back next year to buy them back from you."

When my father returned from his vacation in Paris, he was stunned. They stood in front of the destroyed building in Rotterdam.

"Well, here's your building," she said. "I bought the lease. Now we all have to work hard to get my diamonds back." Within a year, she did. We were once again on our way up.

Helen and I went crazy sterilizing the little bottles and folding thousands of packets of medicine and making deliveries. My mother worked alongside my father in the store, mixing medicines and labeling the bottles. With her bad leg (the sore didn't heal until 1949, when she had an operation), she would swing up the rope ladders onto the huge ships in the harbor and negotiate with the captains.

"I'm glad I broke my damn leg," she would say fiercely. "That way the Japs would have had to chop it off before they ever got me on my knees again!"

In camp she used to scrub the sore out harshly with sand, to avoid gangrene. When it bled too much, she put a bit of spider web over it to stop the bleeding, a trick she learned from the natives. In Holland, her medical care was much more sophisticated, but still it pained her for years.

Soon the phone in the pharmacy was ringing constantly, with calls from Egypt, from Greece, from Gibraltar, from everywhere, informing my father of the ship's arrival and of the order they wanted filled.

Dido was wonderful with the employees, and many of them stayed with us for twenty or thirty years. She was always sweeping into the place with presents, or with sandwiches on fresh bread, or cookies for afternoon tea. She got to know all their families and all their problems.

And she found a way to control them.

"You need money to buy a car? Here! How much do you need?" she would say, darting toward the big door of the safe. She became their banker. They had luxuries that no pharmacist's assistants would ever have, and she in turn had their loyalty. She had effectively tightened them down with bank notes.

But she was not mean-spirited about it. If payments were late or they were in trouble for some reason, it didn't matter. They paid when they could.

Dozens of the "zebras," our Indonesian cousins, streamed through our apartment. They came with their hollow eyes and their shabby clothing, and sat in the beautiful parlor overlooking the harbor. They had every color of skin, and every combination of eye and hair color imaginable. Helen and I hated them. We did not understand.

"Go cut up the cake," my mother would order us. "And bring cookies for the children."

We carried in tea and beautiful mocha cakes and bonbons, barely repressing a sneer. My mother would take us aside and scold us. "You must be good to other people," she said. "If you are good, then good will come to you. Just see how fortunate we have been!"

We had thousands, millions, but there was nothing to buy in post-war Holland. Even the apartment, the best we could find, was small and cramped. My mother redecorated it extensively, but she couldn't get around the fact that there was no elevator in the building.

My father no longer wanted Indonesian art in our house. "We are European now," he said sadly. But I knew his soul remained in his sunny homeland in the tropics.

Cash flowed around us extensively. Everyone was paying dearly under the terms of the Marshall Plan, so that the queen could retrieve her jewels and the priceless paintings from our museums, which had been put up as collateral. Our taxes were crippling.

My father had already lost everything once in Indonesia. He resented having to bail Holland out too. So he saw to it that there was plenty of cash for all of us as well.

My mother thought nothing of buying a $50,000 necklace that caught her eye, or of giving as much to the church, when the bishop came to call. When they built a seaman's club in Rotterdam, the Estella Maris, she donated a thirty-foot window of leaded glass, depicting her beloved Saint Teresa, whom she believed had gotten us through the war. She didn't look on such gifts as charity, but as an exchange for the good luck that had befallen us.

And now she was in Puerto Vallarta with my family.

We would return from an outing at Punta de Mita, and there she would be on her balcony, looking out to sea, or sitting in the restaurant entertaining everyone with drinks and stories.

"HALLO! Where've you guys been?" she called out when we walked in. It never occurred to her to give us any warning.

The moment she arrived, the quarrels started.

Helen moved into her new house with her. Her son Robby looked like a young blond Dutch kid, so naturally he was my mother's favorite grandchild. Mine were all dark, almost black from the sun, even Bear.

And besides they were not really mine, they belonged to that bastard Bob Lewis.

She liked to give Helen's Robby thousand-peso notes as spending money. That was a lot of money in those days, more than a maid could make in three months.

Robby would then run out onto the balcony and show off his new booty to my three kids, dangling the bills in front of them and taunting them. The kids, to get back at grandma, set up a baseball game in her yard—a good American game, which their father had taught them. They played at it exuberantly—until they succeeded in knocking out a couple of windows.

"Get out of here, you little brats," she yelled in Dutch. "Look what you've done!"

"You get out of here!" they answered in Spanish. Somehow they understood each other, at least at this volume and intensity.

"This is not your land! You built your house on our father's land! You go back where you belong!"

Then in a couple of weeks, like clockwork, Helen and my mother had had a fight, usually about how badly she was bringing up Robby, and Helen would scoop him up and move back to one of our bungalows in a huff.

It was a real circus at my house.

My mother wanted me all to herself. She had a habit of popping in on us at any time of the day or night. Bob Lewis was no dummy. He knew how she felt about him, but in her presence, he tried to continue being a gentleman about it.

However, to me he said, "I don't want to see that old bitch. Get her out of here." When I would make up some excuse and she had left, he locked the gate. Within the hour, she had found some other reason to return.

She climbed the wall. Bob left to play dominoes in town. He had suddenly acquired a great love of dominoes.

"That black sonofabitch!" she fumed.

"Who is it you mean, mother?" I asked, thinking I could laugh her out of her mood.

"That—what's his name? Your husband."

"You want to be sarcastic, mother—I think it is time for you to go back."

She couldn't go back. She had friends coming from Holland to visit her. Constantly. They all stayed in her house, and she entertained them royally in the restaurant, at company expense. Sooner or later she fought with them too, and they returned.

Then she took on my spoiled kids again.

I can't claim that my three children were angels during this time. One day I walked into the house, and all three of them were busy on the living room floor. My Russian bear coat was spread out all over the black and white tiles, in pieces.

"What are you doing?" I yelled.

"We're making _un sombrero cómo él del gringo Davy Crockett!_" piped little Bob. "_¡Mira!_"

Proudly he put on his new coonskin cap. The tail stretched out behind him about nine feet.

"That's my coat! Who gave you permission?"

"Dad did."

In fact, he had. Odd how fastidious he could be about his things, and care nothing for mine.

"These kids have got to learn to think American," he said.

I spun on my heel and walked out, unable to find the words.

When I returned, my mother had found a response. When he came looking for me at her house, she stood on her balcony and accidentally dropped a full bottle of rum on his head.

If that had been me, I would have been tempted to kill the woman, but he just drove into town again.

Even the maids were fighting among themselves. The kids would come into grandma's house after an afternoon of hunting for mussels, loaded down with sandy buckets and pails. Dido's maid went off like a rocket, screaming about the mess on her white marble floors. Then Lupe came over and screamed at that maid in defense of my children.

One day the boys came in after playing tennis at Los Tules, next door.

"Mom, there's a strange *gringo* over there, always listening to the same music. He must be crazy. He talks to the mirror, and makes all kinds of funny movements."

"What do you mean, he talks to the mirror?"

"We climbed a palm tree and saw him. He's real tall and skinny, and he has a long cigarette holder."

They were breathless with the excitement of this new curiosity. "And he talks funny. He doesn't move his lips! It's not English, like you talk."

Well, a lot of people have told me I talk funny too. But I knew what they meant. They had been spying on Peter O'Toole, who was leasing a beautiful apartment on the grounds next door, with a towering *palapa* roof of woven palm leaves, and beautifully decorated with mirrors and inlaid Italian tiles.

"That's the way the British talk," I said, and I tried to explain. "Stay out of the palm trees, boys," I added, suppressing a giggle. "It's not nice to peek in people's windows."

And the circus continued.

It wasn't long before we heard from the Reys again. This time it was Norma.

Although I didn't know it at the time she appeared, she had been a girlfriend of one of the Rey in-laws, the man who made the topographical charts at Las Glorias for Doug Walker's new hotel project. She was tall and sleek and sensual. It's hard to believe that the man could have become bored with her, as the story went.

But the family had other plans. Bob's hot pants were an open secret in Puerto Vallarta. If she came to work as our secretary in the office, they felt it was only a matter of time.

They were right.

Norma was ambitious, and she learned fast. I have to give her credit for that. I was impressed at how good her English became within a short six months. But then I didn't know what an intimate relationship she had with her teacher. She sat in the office for hours, her large breasts falling over the books.

I was still so stupid in those days. Maybe my head was addled from translating from Dutch to English to Spanish all day long. I should say, from finding ways to "interpret" the statements, to try to contain the ongoing fights in my family.

"You're doing such a good job!" I said to Norma one day. "I know you don't have much money. Why don't you move in with us? My mother has an extra bedroom upstairs. Half the time she's in Holland, and you'll have complete privacy."

Rita Anson and Dorothy Sparks shared the floor downstairs. It was a big house. We all loved to gather in my living room next door, one big happy family.

Norma became especially friendly, and took a lot of time with me. We were like cozy girlfriends. One day she even walked over and pinched a hair out of my nose.

"Ouch!" I yelled.

"That's been bothering me," she cooed in a soft voice.

So I laughed, along with everybody else.

"Terry, you're so beautiful," she said, "—if only you'd fix yourself up. You know, you really should start plucking your eyebrows."

"I don't have time for that, with the kids and the restaurant—"

"I'd love to help you with it."

Before I knew it, I was pinned to the sofa, with Rita and Dorothy standing around, enjoying the show. Norma was at work on my new look.

"Now for some make-up!" she said.

I looked in the mirror afterwards. I had to admit that it made a difference. But I drew the line at all that blue and purple stuff that was in fashion down there in the early Seventies.

I started spending serious money on clothes. They were making me into a real Mexican go-go.

In turn, I began to show my new protégée how to set a beautiful table, and how to organize an elegant buffet.

"Have you noticed how Norma is starting to wear her hair just like yours?" Rita asked one day with a strange look that I couldn't interpret.

I was flattered.

One afternoon, while Bob was up in Los Angeles doing promotion for the hotel, Norma came to me in the restaurant. She was distraught.

"My grandmother is dying," she said. "Can you lend me three thousand pesos? I have to fly to Guadalajara."

Three thousand pesos represented two months' wages, but I agreed readily. After all, her grandmother was dying.

I even drove her to the airport.

"You what!" said Ofelia. "Why couldn't she take the bus, like any other secretary?"

"I don't know. I guess the grandmother was really seriously ill," I explained.

We were sitting at the pool that weekend, relaxing with the brilliant sunshine and some luscious Frank Sinatra records, munching on *nachos* and pouring down the tequila. All eight of our little kids were having a ball. We usually got together when Bob was out of town, since he couldn't take all the noise.

A call came over the intercom from Alejandro. *"Don Roberto ya regresó,"* he said.

"Kids!" I yelled. "You father is back from California."

"Oh boy!" They jumped out of the pool and tore through the tall palms toward our house in their little swimming suits. They knew there would be lots of presents.

Ofelia and I strolled leisurely behind, the proud little mamas.

The kids were already at the suitcases when we walked into the house. So was Norma.

"Hey!" Bob called out cheerfully. "Look who I met on the airplane! Isn't that a coincidence?"

Ofelia gave me a look that I didn't understand.

Bob reached down into the suitcase and brought up something slinky and expensive. "This is for you," he said to me, beaming. It was a matching bra and panties and slip set from Gucci.

I never bought that stuff. I didn't even wear a bra. But I smiled, happy that he had thought of me while he was away.

I held them up. They were a size eight. Two sizes too small for me.

"Were you gone so long you forgot my size?" I asked, trying to make a little joke about it. Bob was embarrassed.

Curiously, they were exactly right for Norma. But I didn't like her that much, after all.

Ofelia was a much better friend, and I had spotted a sad, envious look in her eye. She had never had anything that fine. So I tossed them down on the sofa, deciding to give them to her later.

"Yup, I walked down the aisle of the plane and there she was! Small world," said my husband.

The kids jumped into his lap with their new trucks and T-shirts and were hugging and kissing him. It was a sweet domestic scene.

"Let's go to the office and see what Terry has messed up while we were gone," he said to Norma. It was probably true. Most likely they could find something. I hated the paperwork.

"Nice new boots," said Ofelia to Norma. "And isn't that a new outfit too? Your grandmother must have died."

"Oh no," she said breezily. "We just brought her to the hospital for a couple of shots and she was better right away."

By the middle of the next week, Ofelia could not contain herself any longer. "Have you noticed that Norma has the same kind of underwear I have?" she began.

"No. What do you mean?"

"Gucci. Same color and everything. I saw the labels."

I refused to believe it. Then I started making excuses. "Well, I guess he has the right to buy a present for his secretary now and then."

That's how this whole story started in San Francisco, right?

Stupid.

"A pencil sharpener, maybe," said Ofelia, shaking her head. "Terry, wake up! There's something going on with this Norma. Don't you think it's strange that they arrived on the same plane?"

"Well, I explained all that. Her grandmother was dying and—"

"Then why didn't she get her little third-class ass on a third-class bus for ten hours, like the rest of us?"

I didn't have an answer.

"No, Bob Lewis' girlfriend moves her ass in comfort!" she said. "First class."

I was starting to get mad. I remembered all the times I had been out searching for Bob in recent months. He was never there.

"Oh, *señora*, I think it's something with the horses," Alejandro would explain.

That was my trick. Still I hadn't understood.

Actually, I had been happy to have Norma take some of the load off. She was so efficient, that it gave me more time to go to the El Dorado beach with Rita for a long afternoon, or stay out until three in the morning, dancing at the City Dump, the latest disco in Puerto Vallarta.

Norma had become quite the little hostess of Hotel Las Glorias.

"I'll bet if we go over to her room right now, we'll find a lot more," said Ofelia.

"You're on!" I shouted, loping through the sand ahead of her.

I was shaking. I didn't know what we were looking for exactly, but what we found was a whole new wardrobe in the closet. Lots of those slinky little mini-dresses that she loved to wear to show off her long, sexy legs. And there was another pair of new boots in the corner.

We walked into the bathroom. Lots of good-quality stockings strewn about the place. Crowded among the new toilet articles was a framed photograph of her.

"Look at this!" said Ofelia, picking something up out of the trash. It was the other half of the picture.

There was Bob Lewis, the owner of the arm that was tightly around Norma in the first half. He had a stupid, blissful smile on his face. I didn't recognize the night club in the background, but the soap she had stolen was from El Tapatío, the most luxurious hotel in Guadalajara, where the famous tropical gardens sprawled all the way down the hillside on the way to the airport. They must have stayed there for three days.

Something snapped.

In a frenzy I scooped up an armful of the new stuff and tossed it off the balcony, onto the huge guava tree in the garden right beside the house. Ofelia let out a whoop, and joined in. Dresses, stockings, brassieres, boots, luggage, perfume—everything went into the tree.

Then we stood back on the balcony and admired our work, exhausted. It looked like a giant Mexican Christmas tree. We buckled over into loud guffaws of laughter.

It was the best thing we could have done: those bitches love their new clothes.

Then I wanted to set fire to everything, but we couldn't reach the stuff. It was too high off the ground.

I spent that night with Ofelia.

Bob Lewis never mentioned it. Subdued, he sent the bellboys over to climb up and untrim the Christmas tree.

After an appropriate amount of time, my husband was nuzzling up to me again. He was full of good will and apologies.

"I know it wasn't right, Terry," he claimed. "I won't do it again. It's over between me and Norma."

We made up. We were still sleeping together, but rarely.

I was relieved. I didn't know how to explain the situation to the kids, or to my mother. We were already trying to keep our slipping political predicament from her. Now at least, if she brought up the subject of Norma, I could say we had worked everything out.

My husband was so nice to me for a while.

"Terry, you need to get away from here. Why don't you go on a shopping trip to Mexico City?" There were some things we needed for the hotel, so I took him up on it. Norma was still around, so she could easily take over my duties. Bob swore there was nothing between them.

I was not accustomed to screwing around in marriage. I'm sure my mother, as frustrated as she was after the war, never once ran out on my father. Or perhaps I should say I was not accustomed to considering it for myself. I certainly should have been accustomed to it.

Next I was encouraged to go to Guadalajara. And then to see Sondra in Talpa "for a break. You've been under so much strain."

One evening I flew back in from Talpa and found the office empty. Nobody managing the restaurant either. "Some business in town, I think," said the faithful Alejandro.

I went over to my house, and saw Bob's car. "He *walked* into town?" I pondered.

I heard happy giggles from upstairs.

In my bed!

I went berserk. I crawled up onto the balcony and through the tiny bathroom window. I could see two nude bodies rolling around on the bed.

As I squeezed through the small opening, I got a big sliver in my rear end. I must have cried out.

I fell into the room head first, and charged at them. Norma was on her feet in the middle of the room, wrapped in my sheet.

"You nympho slut!" I screeched. "How dare you roll around like this with that—that—"

I yanked her by one of those juicy tits, and grabbed back my sheet. She went running naked out of the house.

Then I started after Bob, swinging. "In my bed, you sonofabitch!"

"Terry, I can explain—"

"Right!" I screamed. "You get that *puta* out of my mother's house. I don't want any whores around here with *my* children!"

"OK, OK!" he agreed. "Just stay calm. She will have to leave. It's a good idea."

Bob was kind enough to help her find a new apartment in town.

She stayed on at the office. After all, she had become indispensable to the operation.

Funny that when we finally agreed to go our separate ways, Bob and I never had a big scene. I guess that had been the one.

We never came to any specific agreements. We just drifted from then on.

My mother returned from Holland with some friends. We were at the restaurant entertaining them one afternoon. Norma was at the cashier's desk. Our waiter Ramón came over embarrassed, and suggested that I talk to Norma.

"Your mother's bill is eight hundred dollars. I'm not putting through any more orders," she said haughtily.

I hit her on the temple with the telephone from the intercom.

"You get that asshole of a husband of mine over here this minute," I said, nearly stuffing the telephone in her nose. "Who do you think you are?"

She was screaming and crying hysterically into the intercom. All the guests were watching the drama with great interest.

Bob came running in, and I started yelling at him.

"The bill is more than we can handle, Terry. I suggested to Norma—"

"Since when do you 'suggest' to that cunt?" I yelled.

My mother strolled up to the cashier's desk with a cigarette in her hand. She never smoked.

"Who's running this place anyhow?" I shouted.

Norma started to make a smart reply, but before she could get the words out, Dido put the cigarette out on the back of her hand.

Very slowly, she turned it around and around.

All hell broke loose.

"Look what you did to her!" said Bob, his eyes huge. He took poor Norma in his arms to comfort her. "You have no right—"

The waiters came running up. Norma was passing her hand around, getting sympathy. All the bellboys appeared out of nowhere and stood around.

"You're going to regret this, Terry," Bob was threatening. "She didn't do anything, she was just—"

"Out! Out!" I was screaming.

I apologized to the guests and closed down the restaurant for the afternoon. The staff all saw murder in my eyes, and they fled fast.

And I closed down Norma for good. Her position as young budding hostess of Las Glorias was no longer required.

I grabbed a bottle of rum and jumped into my new yellow Falcon station wagon. Soon I found myself on the Manzanillo highway. Anywhere. It didn't matter. I just had to drive.

The roads were graded, but they had only a thin layer of gravel and asphalt. I went higher and higher up into the mountains for an hour, then two. The road started back down the mountain toward the sea.

I came to one sharp hairpin curve, and defiantly, I pushed the accelerator instead of the brake.

The car flew over the underbrush and down into the ditch beside the road at the next level, and stalled.

I sat in the front seat panting. I had another snort of rum and calmed down a bit.

"Now what are you doing, Lewis?" I asked myself.

It was so peaceful there beside the highway. A little *burro* stood drinking calmly in a stream nearby. The profusion of ferns and orchids was stunning.

"You let a little whore like that make a fool out of you?" I kept scolding myself. "Where's your pride?"

I heard voices, speaking German. Somehow the sound of that put everything in perspective, I don't know why.

Far in the distance, a *piqueur* was leading a trail ride. I had "landed" at the Club Med at Playa Blanca. The tourists looked so calm and happy, following in a single line through the prescribed path in the mountains. A perfect, orderly vacation in tropical paradise.

I had left my own far behind.

I got out of the car and stretched. I had another drink, sitting on the hood of the car, while I took in the beauty of the bay and the white beaches below.

I got in the car and headed back.

In a couple of weeks the immigration authorities were at my door again.

Apparently Norma had decided that if she could get rid of me, she had a good shot at an American passport.

19

I was sitting in my living room, polishing my nails a bright, Chinese red in preparation for a nice dinner and an evening out on the town with Rita, when some very serious-faced men drove up in a cab and started through my garden toward the front door. I greeted them at the entrance.

With a dark glow of appreciation, their eyes went straight to the big cut-outs in my mini-dress. I had learned some things from Norma and Rita, but I was also determined to do it my own way.

Sometimes, when friends offered to bring something down for me from the States, I said, "If you see some stylish-looking cotton material, why don't you bring me about three yards of it? I'll have my seamstress make up a dress for me." I made the designs, and she sewed them up in no time.

I had a deep tan, and was really starting to look sharp. This particular dress was from the special Mexican *manta*. It was white, with black tubing around the cut-outs. I felt pretty spiffy. I didn't realize I was dressed for three more days in jail.

"*Señora,*" they said, "we are from the immigration office in Mexico City."

I thought, "Well, here it goes again. It's Easter time, and they've come for their *mordidas.*" They stood to make three or four times their monthly salaries every time they put in an appearance. I could have almost marked out the dates on my calendar in advance.

"Come on in," I said cheerily. I refused to let them spoil my evening. This shouldn't take long.

"Don't you usually deal with the lawyers of Miguel Salinas?" I asked them sarcastically.

They did not smile. "*Señora*, we have had a report in Mexico City that you have injured one of our citizens. Is it true that you are the owner of this hotel?"

I went through the whole thing about how it was really my husband's project, and that we were legally organized in a Mexican corporation with *prestanombres*, and so forth. I couldn't say more. I still didn't have my official papers.

"We would like to take down a deposition from you in regard to this poor, unfortunate young girl," said López, who appeared to be in charge. "We have engaged the services of a local secretary to take it down."

"Fine," I said.

Who should walk into my house but Norma! She was carrying an old beat-up typewriter case, and she looked rather ill at ease. I showed her to the most uncomfortable little stool I could find.

Then I sat down on my plush white sofa, and held my hands out in front of me like broken wings, so my nails would dry. We got started with the deposition.

I knew there was not much I could say in my defense about mistreating Norma. I declared officially that I was wrong, and then I immediately started in on a long speech about how much Las Glorias had done for the Mexican people, how many jobs we had provided in the building of the hotel, how we had thirty-two happy employees who had been with us, most of them, from the beginning, and how I myself had taught many of them to read and write. I urged the officials to take statements from them also.

Norma was looking more uncomfortable. Then I launched into a long statement about the Rey family. I described the filthy squatters huddled around their camp fires in my front yard. I reminded the men that I should have had my own legal documents by this time, but that they were all tied up in Adolfo Rey's office in Guadalajara, and that he had had to leave the country for mysterious reasons.

Norma kept sinking lower on her stool, although at that time, I still wasn't aware of her own connection with the Reys.

The men looked quite interested and impressed—that is, until I got on the subject of that family.

Apparently they had expected to find a monster, a greedy American who exploited everyone and grabbed up all the profits in expectation of fleeing the country as soon as possible. Instead they found someone who spoke to them in good Spanish, who genuinely loved Mexico and Puerto Vallarta. They saw I was surrounded by a normal household of kids, maids, husband, boarders, and a hotel operation that ran smoothly and fairly.

López smiled, and quietly instructed Norma to delete the portion about the Reys. She spent several minutes going through the papers, erasing bits here and there, and tearing out other whole portions.

Her long legs tried to balance the typewriter in her lap on the tiny stool, and her tits were bouncing all over. It was quite a show. Since the men seemed unable to concentrate while this was going on, I offered them a drink.

It was strange. I didn't have to say much about the actual incident with Norma. Ramón had already told them how it all started, but they really didn't seem very interested in it.

At the end of it all, López simply stood up and said, "*Señora*, I must ask you to pack a small bag. They will need to talk to you in Mexico City."

My heart sank. I expected them to start hinting about a bribe, to get the hell out of there, and go on to the next place. But this was trouble.

If they couldn't be bribed, then I knew that somebody very high up was involved in it. No wonder they hadn't really investigated the specific charges against Norma.

I started giving orders to Lupe about the suitcase, about the kids and how to manage the household in my absence, and about what to tell don Roberto if he returned from his trip to America.

Alejandro appeared at the doorway and said quietly, "Doña Theresa, don't worry about the children. I'll take them to *mi casa* in Mascota. They will be safe there." Bless him!

"OK! ¡*Estoy lista!*" I smiled when the bag came down. "I'm ready." I was determined to be in a cheerful mood.

"Shall I have them send out a taxi to take us to the airport?"

"We will not be going by plane," scowled López. "That is, *señora,* unless you would agree to pay for the transportation.

I thought that was a pretty crusty request, but I was still cheerful. I replied, "Well, I guess I can manage a plane ticket to Mexico City."

"No, *señora.* You misunderstand," said López patiently. "There will be four tickets. For you, for my assistants, and for myself."

The petty immigration officers looked delighted at the prospect, since the alternative was sitting on a second-class bus for twenty-eight hours. But enough was enough.

"We'll take the bus," I said, resigned.

"It is the best our government can do for us, señora. Perhaps it is better to work for the American government, where everything is first class."

"Bastards," I said under my breath. I gave him a fierce look that made it clear I was not interested in that subject.

I was led out of my house in handcuffs. All the staff lined up in the driveway and silently watched us drive off.

We provided quite a spectacle at the bus station downtown.

There I stood, chained to señor López, my blonde head towering above the swarm of little dark heads waiting in the street for the grubby bus to Mexico City. The smell was incredible, and it got only worse inside.

We didn't get one of those little country buses that took the tourists to Bucerías, but this one was hardly better. The floor was littered with pieces of glass from broken bottles, dried fruit bits and mildewed taco shells, piss, and globs of spit. It was clear that cleaning out the bus had not been not a high priority item. A good archaeologist could probably have traced its history back ten years.

In addition to that, any fool who drives a lot on Mexican highways knows that he can make the best time if he follows a long-distance bus at eighty or ninety miles an hour. Mexican bus drivers have no fear. Not of oncoming traffic in the passing lane, not of missing a mountain curve, nor of having a blow-out.

Memories of battered buses, crippled by a broken axle and turned over on their sides in a mountain ditch, flooded into my mind. It was going to be a long night.

At about eleven o'clock, the scene on our bus started to get pretty lively. Once the children and the livestock had quieted down, the radios started up, screaming out from every seat.

Señor López had decided he liked me. I could tell from the way he began rubbing my leg.

I did the best I could to discourage him, but I could hardly get up and find another seat. He was handcuffed to my arm.

Besides, I had other worries. For instance, that the suspicious-looking taco I had bought from a *ranchero* when the bus stopped beside the road was going to give me the *chorros*. Montezuma's revenge, I think it is called in America.

We arrived at the main immigration office in Mexico City about midnight the next night. I expected to be put into some kind of cell, but they apparently had no provisions for cases like mine. I was escorted back up to the same office complex where I had been detained when I came back to Mexico with my mother.

Licenciado Gutiérrez came in the next morning, and the depositions started all over again, with exactly the same results.

I was there three days.

I made seven long statements. Each time, they ended up in the trash. On the third day, I asked if I could please take a bath. I offered to pay for a room in the hotel across the street, and I promised not to run away. Surprisingly, they agreed.

At the doorway, a man I hadn't seen before took me aside and said to me quietly, "See here, *señora*, if you leave out one name, one *name in particular*," he repeated, with deliberate emphasis, "you will be free to go."

Well, there it was. It couldn't be clearer than that.

"But I'm telling the truth, *señor*," I pleaded.

"Please, doña Theresa, don't make our job more difficult. You are right, perhaps. You are honest. But this is dangerous talk."

He moved away quickly.

From the hotel I telephoned the Dutch ambassador. He could not, or would not, help me.

I took a long, cold shower. I resigned myself to the inevitable.

At the elevator of the twelve-story immigration building, on my way back up to the office, I suddenly turned and found Ignacio Rey standing next to me, with a broad smile on his face. The man himself.

He looked very powerful, and brimming with good health. Even handsome, perhaps. It was said he spent an hour a day in the Turkish baths, to steam out all the tequila on his brain.

He was wearing a big pistol in his back pocket, but I didn't see the usual bodyguards.

"Hola, Theresa," he said, patting me on the shoulder. He had been a guest at Las Glorias already in our second year of operation. Even earlier than that, while I was seven months pregnant with Dido, he had asked me out, though I didn't know who he was at the time.

I looked him coldly in the eye. *"Je ne suis pas Theresa,"* I said. Then I turned quickly and got on another elevator.

I entered the office above, made a short, not very informative statement about Norma, and within a couple of hours I was back on a plane for Puerto Vallarta.

That was number four.

When I returned to Las Glorias, I found that a colleague of Calderón's, Doctor Soto, had rented a room in my mother's house.

A heavy, bald man with a red face, he had droopy eyes and an irritating habit of running his tongue suggestively over his thick lips. He was continually squeezing me on the knee or patting me on the ass. He wore white cotton pants, held together with a drawstring, as if he was always ready to go. Our distinguished new boarder had a reputation in Puerto Vallarta as a good "battlefield" doctor, and an enthusiastic lover, though I couldn't imagine it. I did not trouble to find out.

What I didn't know right away was that he was a good friend of the same engineer who had given us Norma.

Life continued pretty much as usual.

For a time, I stayed away from the office, just in case, but I continued to conduct my "seminars in Mexican culture," from my living room. By this time, many of our guests had been back with us for several years. They knew Bob and me, and they liked to seek us out.

If we particularly liked them, we even threw a little party for them sometimes. They loved to visit an actual home in Mexico, instead of being limited to the atmosphere of a hotel.

I spieled out my stories about Cortés and Moctezuma, about Pancho Villa and Emiliano Zapata, and they were captivated. And I bristled with the same advice that I gave out year after year. "The trip to Yelapa is beautiful. You'll love it! But be sure to watch your purses in the crowds, as you get on the boat! Hold them right under your arms," I would say. "And remember, there's a safe in the office for your valuables."

Or: "Drugs are dangerous! Your American consul can't help you if you get caught."

During those years, most of the beach boys in Puerto Vallarta were as harmless as my old "shark," Tiburón. They wouldn't try anything shady, like pushing drugs, on the beautiful young American girls, though they would never stop trying to maneuver them into bed. Then gradually the crew from Acapulco moved into town, and sadly, I couldn't say that any longer.

I loved teaching our guests about local customs.

"What's that yellow flower that I see sometimes in the little carts? They have them frying in a hot skillet," one lady observed. "I've never seen a flower like it."

"You mean the squash blossoms? I'm sure you've seen the vines crawling along the ground at home," I said. "When the squash starts to grow, that huge flower provides a shade for it, till it's big enough to stand the hot sun. Like a mother for its young child. Then, when its job is done, the Mexicans pick it before it begins to shrivel up. They're very good to eat."

"How do you know all these things?" she asked.

"I don't know—" I said. "I know there's a lot about herbs and 'country' medicines in the Bible. Here in Mexico we have the same simple life they did.

"Perhaps in Indonesia too—" I added, thinking about how my mother brought us through three war prisons alive, with her knowledge of the protein value to be found in the humble grasses around the camps, and in the little animals that we would never consider eating ordinarily.

Sometimes I learned from our guests too.

One day, a girl came running into my living room, convulsed with laughter. "Terry! Terry!" she cried, barely able to talk. "Do you know that's a marijuana plant growing in your garden?"

It was news to me. We went out and looked near the entrance. There was a weed that had gotten away from me, already grown up as tall as I am. Obviously, I hadn't had a lot of time for gardening recently.

"Marijuana?" I asked. Strange that with all the odd lore I had picked up along the way, I didn't know what a marijuana plant looked like. I must have been nodding during that part of my pharmacy exams.

"Marijuana!" she announced with glee. "Can I have it?"

I agreed to it, and she quickly pulled it up by the roots and took it back to her bungalow. It hung there to dry for five days, upside down, and then she and her friends had a ball.

I took my own advice, and stayed out of it.

I've always had a passion for chickens! Sometimes we would be having an elegant afternoon tea in the living room, when one of my beautiful roosters would zip through the house, chasing one of his favorite hens. Sometimes he even nailed her right there on the checkered floor in front of us.

"TERRY, WHAT'S GOING ON?" cried all the well-dressed ladies at one time.

I shrugged. "Oh, it's just a cock who wants to get a little ass for a minute. He'll be finished soon. Don't let it bother you."

I have always felt that travel was broadening.

Then I would launch into a discussion of chickens, though I don't know if I had their complete attention.

"We have several chickens in the yard. They're good because they eat the little worms on the hibiscus leaves. And every day, we have about eight fertilized eggs—that is, if the iguanas don't get them. They're very good for you," I said.

"Fertilized eggs?" one asked, trying to concentrate.

"Sure. If you open up that chicken right now, you'd find one and a half eggs, almost done. She's ready to give one, and the next one will come tomorrow."

They looked mystified. "She's got a whole bunch of little buds in there. You know, the old-fashioned chickens—"

"Oooh. Really?"

"Yeah. It's been like that for thousands of years."

The cock strutted out the door, and back to his nest, his tail feathers proudly flying behind him.

Another woman changed the subject. "Where did you get this?" she cooed, picking up one of the heavy antique irons I had found long ago in Chacala.

I explained about going up into the mountains for the cedar wood to build the hotel, and what a primitive life the people led up there.

"It's like your great-grandmother probably used to iron her clothes. Would you like to have it? I have some others."

She was overjoyed. I liked giving things away. It's a charming Mexican custom that I wanted to imitate.

Some of the more adventurous would come to the door and ask, "Do you think it's OK to walk into town from here? Is it too far?"

I encouraged them, especially as more hotels began filling in the space between. "Wear a swimming suit under your dress, and then if you get hot, you can just jump in the pool and take a dip to cool off. They won't mind."

"It looks pretty far," they would say, hesitating.

"Don't worry about it. You can always get a cab back," I assured them.

"One time when I lived here by myself, before the hotel," I continued, "my little Buster was really sick, and there wasn't anyone around to help me get to town for some clean water. So I walked down to the Hotel Rosita. Look, you can see it way down there in the distance," I said, pointing to a speck on the water's edge. "I got one of those big ten-gallon bottles of water and carried it back here so I'd have pure water for my son."

They couldn't believe it. I could hardly believe it myself then, seven or eight years later.

"You carried it? How?"

"Well, I couldn't carry it on my shoulders all the way. It was too heavy. So when it got bad and started to slide off, I put it in the sand and rolled it for a while, and then I picked it up again and—"

"What was the matter with him?"

"Well, you know, stomach ache. Dysentery, something like that."

"Didn't you have water?"

"Well, there was a truck that made deliveries, but if I ran out, I was out of luck until the next time. They didn't want to come way out here for just one bottle."

"I guess that answers our question," one of them sighed. "It sounds like an easy walk without a ten-gallon bottle!"

I laughed and recommended Connie's El Patio Restaurant on the Malecón, for some good people-watching when they got to town.

The men loved to go out on the fishing trips, or, if the shrimp boats were in, to have a look at the genuine Mexican fishing scene.

I had a good pair of binoculars, and I was always on the lookout. If I saw some shrimp boats heading toward Bucerías or the beaches out toward Punta de Mita, I made a beeline for the kitchen to ask Xavier, "How many kilos of fresh shrimp do we need?"

"Let's see," he said, scratching his black curls with the point of a butcher knife, "I've got room for around sixty."

"All right!" I shouted. "Make some space in your deep freezes. I'll be coming in with them later."

Once on the way to my car, I met Ken and Pat Harley, who had been guests at Las Glorias four or five times. They looked a little lost. "Want to go with me to meet the shrimp boats?" I asked.

"Sure!"

We loaded up the station wagon with large steel drums and baskets and plastic bags, and the kids scampered in the back, as always.

"Have you got the magazines, Mom?" Bear reminded me.

"Sure do."

"What magazines?" Pat asked, without much curiosity.

"We gather up all the old *Playboys* and *Penthouses* from the maids and the bellboys," I explained. "They're not allowed in Mexico, so you can imagine we get a pretty good deal on shrimp if we have some of them along!"

"But how—?"

"They get left in the rooms," I said, guessing his question. "I don't even want to ask what the maids and the bellboys do with them."

Ken came alive. He joined my boys for a last quick look before we used the magazines as currency.

We drove up onto the beach on the other side of Bucerías. In this part of the bay, the water is calmer than it is in Puerto Vallarta, and better for bringing in the boats.

The government hadn't organized the *sindicatos* yet, those fishermen's unions, so there were tons of shrimp on the big boats, and no rules about how it had to be sold. Down the beach there were a couple of trucks with ice, all the way from Guadalajara, waiting to start loading up.

"Let's go!" I yelled.

The boys were out of the car already, negotiating with one of the guys to take us out in his canoe. Pat spread out her towel on the beach.

The rest of us piled into the canoe, and in no time we were approaching the gritty side of one of the big shrimp boats. Huge nets hung out over the rail to dry. They smelled strongly of deep sea salt water. My mouth started watering for the taste of a good *bouillabaisse*!

"*¡Hola!*" I called.

A sailer stuck his head over the edge. "Come on up!" he said.

We climbed up the rope ladder, and the smell was at once overpowering. Huge nets lay about the deck, crowded with dead fish and big conch shells. There were a couple of rows of tiny seahorses on one side, drying out to be sold as earrings in Puerto Vallarta.

Over in the corner there were a couple of small manta rays, with their long hooked tails broken and drying between their fins. Mexicans bought these because they looked like devils. They used them to cast evil spells on their enemies.

"Jeez," said Ken, standing on the deck cautiously in his white slacks and new tennis shoes, "when I think about the health department in the States—"

"Don't think about it," I said.

There was a dirty young woman with greasy hair, hanging out of the steering cabin. She had on only a brassiere and slip.

"Terry, what's this woman doing on board?" asked my tourist friend.

"Well, you've got to understand," I explained. "They're out on the high seas for two months. That woman is their cook and whore."

"Two months!" he gasped. "Whore!"

"Yup."

"But I thought shrimp lived close to the coast."

"Well, they don't have any of the mechanical equipment you have in America. They've got to follow the shrimp, wherever they go. See over there—" I pointed. "They dry a lot of them out in the sun, and then we take them and use them for soups and omelets."

"Two months! Then why do they need the *Playboys*, if they've got their own whore along with them?" He looked around and saw seven sailors working on the deck. He was doing the math quickly in his head.

"I see," he said, stroking his chin. "I guess she keeps pretty busy!"

"*¡Pase usted!*" called out the woman, who saw Ken's obvious interest. "*¿Le gustaría una sopa de pescado?*" she asked, in her politest manner.

"She wants to know if you want some of her fish soup," I said.

"Sure!"

She handed him a bowl, brimming with shells and chunks of all sorts of fish meat. The eyes from a couple of heads stared up at him from the middle of the bowl. He looked stunned.

But the aroma was heavenly.

My kids even looked up from their game of grabbing shells on the deck, and tossing dead fish back into the ocean to see if they could be revived. In moments, we all dug in with relish—Ken not so fast at first, but it didn't take him long.

Then we got down to business.

"I want about a hundred thirty pounds, sixty kilos, of your biggest shrimp," I said to the captain, knowing that they wanted to reserve the very biggest ones for export to the States. I slid the tops of the magazines out from where I had buried them in one of the baskets.

"A hundred and thirty!" he said. "We've got the best!"

"These *Playboys* and *Penthouses* are a present," I said. "I'm here to pay you." I wanted to continue good business relations, after all.

I handed over the magazines.

Seven sailors made a quick circle. After a few moments of critical evaluation of the centerfolds, we got back to business, and the transaction was happily concluded.

They loaded us up in a jolly mood, their brown, almost naked bodies swaying to the beat of a song from a radio blaring in the cabin: *"El sol y la flor para ti, para ti –"*

"The sun and a flower for you, for you—"

Perhaps they were thinking of a long-awaited reunion on the beach that night with the girls waiting for them back home.

On the way back to Las Glorias, Ken leaned way back in his seat and stretched. "Ah, what a life!" he said. "Good food, fishing on the high seas, a woman along for the ride. Give me the simple life!"

Then a funny look came over his face. Perhaps he was thinking of the girl's greasy hair—or of his wife in the back seat.

It wasn't long afterwards, speaking of the *sindicatos*, that I had my first union trouble.

Every six years, when a new *presidente* is elected in Mexico, the revolution begins stirring up all over again. There is great frustration about the social conditions in the country and about corruption in high offices.

Sometimes it might seem to us that they don't even appear to notice it, but they do. And there is frustration about voting. The people want to vote, but the next president, usually the man who has been serving as their equivalent of secretary of state, has already been chosen by the party. And only one party has held power in Mexico for decades. Voting seems a futile exercise.

So around an election year, one can expect to feel the military presence everywhere in the country. Then begin the strikes.

Mexicana Airlines always goes on strike. In the early Seventies, many labor unions were being born and flexing their muscles, and they all went on strike. Millions of dollars poured into union treasuries from hotel owners under siege.

Ben Benito, a short, stocky waiter with a boxer's build, began stirring up the rest of our help at Las Glorias. He, like the others, had been with us for years. One morning I discovered that there was a flag on our restaurant. Literally. A red *bandera* flew brightly in front of the big arched entrance.

We were closed down.

It was the job of the workers to stay with that flag and protect it, twenty-four hours a day. If there are a few dozen workers in the company to divide up the hours equally, that's not a big deal. But our seven waiters had quite a job.

I couldn't stay closed. We had promised to provide meals, as part of the hotel package. We were losing a lot of business. I began negotiations, which dragged on for four or five weeks. In the end, it cost me $12,000 (not to mention the business I lost while we were closed).

Fined. For what? Nobody knows.

Within four months, the local union leader was driving around town in the latest Mustang.

The waiters all came back, looking sheepish.

"We're sorry, doña Theresa," apologized Jesús. "We couldn't help it. We were pushed."

I'm sure they were. If they hadn't complied, they would have been out of a job.

Only union members could be hired from that time on. In Puerto Vallarta, that meant only members of the 'democratic' union. That, in fact, had started it. Half the help had wanted to go with the 'republican' union instead.

The one who bore the brunt of it, of course, was the owner, *La Holandesa*.

Ben Benito came back, all smiles, expecting to resume his favorite job of running drinks out to poolside, so he could ogle all the bikinis. I managed to curb his pleasurable activities, while staying strictly within the rules.

He didn't make any mistakes, and neither did I. It was easy simply to ignore the little fart, with an attitude of serene indifference, which I can be very good at. He was only five-two, after all. I could look right over his head.

Under the new rules, we had to get a time clock in the restaurant. All the help were allowed a fifteen-minute leeway in reporting for work. You can imagine, from that time on, whether the early shift was ready at 7:00 or 7:15. With seven waiters, I figured I lost two hours and fifteen minutes of work every day after that.

It wasn't only hotel owners who were affected. My Dutch girlfriend Nilche was fined almost $5,000 for trying to fire the maid who worked in her own house.

Under the new rules, you could only fire a maid if she made three serious mistakes. Like burning your blouse, or ruining the potatoes. You had to write up an account of each offense. Then you had to get witnesses. After that, you had to face her in court.

Nilche lost, and paid sixty thousand pesos.

"I'd rather pay the bitch and get rid of her than have to keep that face around my house!" she told me fiercely.

At last the long-awaited day came, when the presidential *fideicomiso* was announced, the commission appointed to regularize Mexico's *ejido* lands. This property had been held in "trust" by the government since the revolution. It could never be owned outright, but only leased, as with Cloro's land.

Echeverría's plan was a good one. He saw the possibility that in the long run, tourism could bring even more income to Mexico than oil. But he looked around the country and he also saw that much of the coastal property was in a state of decay.

Before the revolution of the nineteenth century, only a few hundred people owned property in all of Mexico. The *peons* were held in check, as tenant farmers on huge land holdings next to the exquisite *haciendas* which dotted the land.

With Pancho Villa and Zapata, the land reform began. Each tenant farmer could now lease and work seven *hectáreas*, or a little over seventeen acres, of his own. The topsoil, that is—never the subsoil, so there was no incentive to look for minerals.

Zapata started inland, in the high Mexican deserts of Chihuahua and Coahuila, where the land was rocky and the situation was most desperate.

But several circumstances in Mexico worked against them. First of all, of course, the mayors, the lawyers, the doctors of each village grabbed off the choicest land, right next to the town. The little *rancheros*, who probably couldn't even read the documents, got what was left, sometimes as much as four hours' walk from home.

The women refused to move out there with him. They had to stay close to the markets. They had no electricity, no ice boxes. Besides, the need for keeping the family together, the extended family, was strong.

As large as they are, Mexican families are a tight, affectionate unit. Every night, the sons receive a blessing from their fathers before they go to bed.

If the daughters have gotten themselves into trouble, there might be a lot of yelling at first, but the new baby is always taken in and brought up with the rest. If a brother or sister dies, there is no question. Their children move in too. Orphanages are almost non-existent in Mexico. As the kids grow up and marry, they move into houses right next door to the parents.

So every little farmer, who wanted desperately to succeed, went out to work his land, often spending hours just to get to it.

To plant a crop, he had to borrow money from the bank. If it was a good year, he paid it back. If not, he couldn't.

Furthermore, even if he had a stand of *coquitos* or banana trees already growing, the highway system and the railroad system were so undeveloped in Mexico that there was no way for him to transport his produce to market. Gradually he sank deeper and deeper in debt. Gradually, small independent farmers were forced to yield up their land for pittance, and allow the large ranchers to graze their cattle on it. The *rancheros* stayed on and worked for them. In very few years, the situation had again reverted to its pre-revolutionary state.

It sometimes appears to us in America that Mexicans are lazy. They are not. But they are trapped.

Cloro was shrewd. He planted his acreage in coconut palms. But when Echeverría looked around in the Seventies, then, he found that most coastal lands had deteriorated. His plan was to terminate the lease agreements and expropriate all the property along the coastline.

Rancheros could now buy their land and develop it themselves. If, as with Cloro, they had already done that, they could pay the money and have legal ownership. Others would be given seven *hectáreas* somewhere else, in return for the property—up in the mountains, for instance, in the case of Puerto Vallarta.

Many farmers were happy about this. But most of them were more conservative, and very uneasy. Their family had been on the land for generations. What could a fisherman do on mountain land?

There was a lot of talk, a lot of fights. A lot of soldiers were sent in to keep the peace.

In America, we read about the glorious success of the tourist program in Mexico, about how the government has created fabulous resorts out of nothing—in Cancún or in Ixtapa, for instance—and how the legal climate has changed for new investors. It's true.

But there is a dark side to it as well.

For Las Glorias, it looked like a wonderful stroke of luck. Cloro had always made money from his land. But now we, and his wife and the children that were left, were on the verge of being able to buy the property, and make profits that few could have imagined. Of course, there was a dark side to that too.

One day a lawyer friend of mine met me at the post office, and said, "Theresa! *Cariño*, there are some important men coming in from Mexico City this morning. Could you drive me to the airport and meet them with your station wagon?"

"Sure!" I said. We jumped in the car, and shortly I found myself looking into the shrewd eyes of the top commissioners from the *fideicomiso*. They had come to study the problems in Puerto Vallarta.

"A million-dollar operation, and they can't afford a jeep in Puerto Vallarta?" I thought. But I soon discovered that they were trying to keep a low profile at first.

I drove them to a nice hotel downtown. In a few days, they moved out to the more sumptuous Camino Real, on the Manzanillo highway. But that proved to be too far out for them to do business.

So one day, señor Espinoza came to me and asked if they could move into my mother's house (where Doctor Soto already had a room for $250 a month). My mother was away in Holland for a while, so I agreed. "Jeez," I thought. "I'm going to have my land settled in a couple of months! How lucky can you get?"

The commissioners proceeded very carefully, talking to all the *rancheros* who had the use of beachfront property, not just the land extending out from the center of Puerto Vallarta on both sides, but all up and down the coast. It was a huge undertaking.

There was a constant stream of big shots coming in and out of my mother's house, to consult with Espinoza. I was impressed.

But it made me vaguely anxious when I saw that Ignacio Rey was among them.

Espinoza was a big black Indian from Tepic. He carried a pistol like many of them. And he also had three or four bodyguards, like many of them. Right away, he spotted Rita. When she did not show any interest, he didn't start on me, perhaps because Soto was still running up and reaching out toward my breasts, saying coy things like "let me love your little *chiches!*" Charming.

Espinoza had found himself another Dutch broad, the famous Xaviera Hollander, who, we heard, began receiving two dozen roses from him at the Hotel Delfín, near the "social beach." I wasn't interested enough to follow the progress of that affair.

The men appointed a local commissioner and opened an office in town, with lawyers and papers, so that everyone could appear and make a claim for his land. I gathered all my documents together and made my own preparations.

We started seeing Miguel Salinas around Las Glorias much more that summer of 1972. We had always had the agreement that as president of our corporation, he and his men could have free accommodation during the slow season. But suddenly he seemed to be taking an unusual interest.

It was not lost on any of these men that Las Glorias had the best beach on the bay. It was the broadest and also the cleanest, because of the palms. Many properties around Puerto Vallarta consisted of decaying mango groves, a messy setting for a hotel.

What was lost on me at first was that the Salinas family and the Rey family were bitter enemies.

They had been carrying on a political and personal feud for decades. Once that became clear, I realized how much we needed dear old Cloro's savvy, to get us through all this. Little six-year-old Dido was our only Mexican link to the land.

That was a busy summer. The American FBI were also coming in and out with their helicopters, spending some of the hundreds of millions of dollars that Washington had invested in fighting the drug problem.

Three agents spent a month with me at Las Glorias, while they tried to locate the marijuana source in the mountains above town.

These Mexican-Americans were big. I was used to small Mexicans. Because of their knowledge of Spanish and their Hispanic background, they were perfect for this particular duty. They hated it. They had left air-conditioned offices in Washington and New York.

They didn't have much to say, though I have to admit I tried to probe as much as I could, since my curiosity was getting the best of me. They would sit in the bar for hours and drink *cuba libres* and snarl about the "God-forsaken hills, with all those damn mosquitoes and snakes!"

"Goddam *burros*," one of them kept repeating. "Every time I sit on one of those damn wooden saddles on one of those goddam mules, and drag my fuckin' feet through the mountains, I think of my white Cadillac back in New York."

For my pains, I heard a lot of cussing, but not much information.

At the end of a month, they had achieved some success. A huge eighteen-wheel flatbed truck came rolling into town, loaded to the sky with marijuana. Tons of it.

They dumped the entire load on the playing field of the stadium in the center of town, and set fire to it. Puerto Vallarta was high for days! The soldiers guarding the fire had the choicest spot. They wouldn't let anybody approach as close as they were standing.

I managed to get some for one of our guests, in fact.

Her husband had been a British attaché in Singapore during the war. Her arthritis had started back then, and by the time she was staying with us at Las Glorias, it had become very painful. I went to Calderón, and he gave me permission to fill up a bottle of alcohol with the stuff. The other guests were amazed, but I knew that the Indians in Mexico had used marijuana for centuries as a medicine for arthritis.

One day I met Helen Melton downtown. She looked years older than she did the last time I saw her, only a few months before. I asked her how their archaeological work was coming at Punta de Mita.

"Oh, Terry, we had some wonderful things!" she said. "Mel found one piece, buried about six feet down, that was priceless. There were twelve men sitting around a table. A fine sculpture! And they were wearing coolie hats! Priceless!" she repeated.

There were tears in her eyes. "We knew we had our proof that the Chinese had been here on this coast."

"What happened?"

"Well, Mel called the two archaeologists in Mexico City. You know, the museum directors who had been helping us? They told him to take pictures of the piece immediately, but to take the original to Boston."

"Can you do that?" I asked.

"He got full authority from them to take it out of the country for examination." She swallowed silently, as if something was stuck in her throat. "We were sitting in our plane at the airport, waiting for take-off. Some *federales* came running out onto the runway. They grabbed Mel and took him off, with all of our things. They rode him across the state line and threw him in jail in Tepic."

This gentle woman, who had been filled with such profound feelings of love for the Mexicans, broke down and cried. She couldn't talk for a while. She just kept shaking her head.

"He was in there seven months. He just got out," she said. "Oh, Terry, he couldn't take that! It just broke him!"

I put my arm around her.

"We've lost everything. All the artifacts, even our beautiful house in town."

"Couldn't you find anyone to help you?"

"We had lawyers. Those men at the Museum of Anthropology were our friends! But they didn't dare to say anything against it."

She dried her eyes and tried to regain her composure. "I'll be saying good-bye now. We're going home tomorrow, to the States."

We hugged a sad farewell, and she turned to leave. "You know, Terry," she said, turning back, "it wasn't our treasures they wanted, at first anyway. Somebody just wanted our plane! So they confiscated everything."

I felt like apologizing for my adopted people, but there was really nothing I could say.

20

It wasn't long before Ignacio Rey's squatters moved in on the luxurious Los Tules, next door. Their beach was almost as good as ours at Las Glorias, and it seemed an easy target.

Juan García-Sánchez, the cultivated man who had brought the Guadalajara Symphony to Puerto Vallarta, had overextended himself with his wealthy Mexican investors. The *fideicomiso* was putting so much pressure on him, that his backers refused to lend him any more support.

One day the beautiful gardens of his place were filled with tanks and soldiers carrying machine guns.

Soon after that, a good-looking young man walked over the beach toward our hotel, slowly, contemplatively, as if deep in thought. He introduced himself as Armando Quirarte.

Though my defenses went up almost at once, since I knew he was somehow involved with the Reys, we took an immediate liking to each other.

His story, though I only heard it gradually, was an interesting one. He had grown up in Ameca, a dirt-poor village in the mountains between Guadalajara and the Bay of Banderas. He was one of sixteen children. To go to school every day, he had to walk a couple of miles each way, sometimes without shoes. It reminded me of what I had heard about the American pioneers two centuries ago.

When he finished public school, he had aspirations to continue on to law school, but no money. Guadalupe Zuno, the founder of the university at Guadalajara and a former governor of Jalisco, took an interest in him, and finally set him up in his own household as a law tutor to his son.

The name 'Zuno' sent up more warning flags in my head. But this man was so *simpatico*, and his smile so genuine, that I wanted to give him the benefit of the doubt.

When Armando graduated, *cum laude*, he was set up in the government forestry office in Guadalajara, in a job that involved settling land disputes. Typically, there were a lot of "perks," and a minimum of work. The office space, the secretaries, the airplanes were free. The work hours were short—from late morning till lunch with the big shots. But Armando had a lot of energy, and he worked hard. He was not one to slide through his life.

In that way, he was able to provide for the education of his brothers and sisters, as is necessary in Mexico. There is no student loan program; the whole family must pitch in, if one of the children wants to get an education.

Now his sisters are teachers. Some of the brothers are engineers and accountants. But also typically, they have been too fearful to try to advance themselves in the competitive world. They stay near their family in Ameca.

I was impressed with Armando's spirit.

He told me much later that he had heard a lot about this *Theresa, la Terrible* (I can only guess where), and that this was not an official investigation—he was only curious. But I didn't know that at the time. He was just a friendly, attractive man, a few years younger than I was.

I invited him to lunch in the restaurant, and the conversation was slow and easy, though he did manage to ask a lot of questions about our operation. His keen eyes twinkled mischievously above a huge mustache.

Bored at Los Tules, he started coming over every day. Sometimes he talked a little about what he had been reading, usually something in the classics or in philosophy, which seemed rather out of character to me for a man in the forestry service. Sometimes we just laughed a lot and drank too much.

"Well!" I thought. "A lawyer working for the *fideicomiso*! Can't hurt to be friends." I suspected he was starting to fall in love with me a little.

The Armando story has a happy ending. We are still great friends. He did try briefly to help me with the president's commission, but early on he found there was not much he could do for me.

By then he was totally smitten, and was calling constantly at my house. I instructed Lupe to tell him I was not at home.

Not one to be put off, he looked around to make sure. I hid under the bed to escape him. That didn't deter him in the least. He just scooped up my three children, and took them out on the town for a treat.

I spent so much time hiding under my bed that I finally started to feel pretty silly. "What the heck!" I told myself. "This is a sexy man, who could be a good friend."

He could never be a lover. Too short.

But after that I relaxed, and we had great fun together. Those dark Spanish eyes must have been starting to get to me. Anyhow, I'm a sucker for anyone who likes my kids.

The story of Juan García-Sánchez does not end so happily. Here was a Mexican, not a foreigner. Except for that, our stories were the same. He loved Puerto Vallarta and wanted to create a paradise there, as we all did. Now he too was trying to fight the system.

Every day we saw him drooping more and more. The amount he needed to save himself and his hotel was three million pesos, or about $250,000.

One day the papers screamed out the news that he had jumped to his death from the seventh floor of a Guadalajara office building.

He left behind a beautiful wife and his five adored sons.

Not all of the government's official projects, and the ways they were managed, were malicious. Some, though still corrupt, were just plain inept.

In his own homeland, Echeverría began to take on the nickname *el parlanchín,* "the chatterbox."

There was the Third World College, for example, which he had set up in San Francisco, a small village up the coast a bit from us.

Again, the plan was a good one. He wanted the sons and daughters of the local *rancheros* to learn about small industries, to acquire some skills that would allow them to become more independent in the modern world.

On a hill overlooking the sea—a couple hundreds yards off in the distance—a huge *palapa* was built as an open-air reception hall for the new school.

Baking equipment and knitting machines were brought in for the young women. Some of the men were to be taught brickmaking, and others commercial fishing. The grove of *coquito* palms on the property was cut down, and acres of tobacco were planted.

A cafeteria was built right on the beach. Brick dormitories were built for the future students. We were all following the progress of this project from a few miles down the coast in PV.

To give an idea of the thought that went into this place, there were ten urinals in the men's dormitories, each decorated with an exquisite bronze dolphin. An art object in itself. To flush, these sons of *rancheros*, who had probably never even seen a urinal before, were asked to grab onto the tail of this piece, and send the water rushing out of its mouth, and down the hill into the Pacific.

The bronzes were easily worth millions of pesos.

The machines for making the bricks, on the other hand, were a different matter. The order for new machines was lost somehow in the bureaucratic shuffle. Used ones showed up at the college. After all, there was a good chance that these simple guys would forget to oil them, and that the salt air would ruin them in a short time anyway, right?

Someone up the line undoubtedly made a huge profit.

At the inauguration of the new school, hundreds of people came for a gala celebration in the giant *palapa*, spilling out over all the beautiful terraces that surrounded it.

We drank richly and sampled elegant seafood canapés. As we drove into the grounds and up the hill, a splendid sign welcomed us, and announced to the world in twelve languages that Mexico was to become the teacher of the third world in science, agriculture, and economics.

Perhaps some students came to the college, I don't know. I do know that no one ever finished a course.

The giant *palapa* roof still stands forlorn on the hill, a leaky haven for the area rats.

The bronze dolphins have long since been stolen, as have any salvageable parts from the machines. What is left lies rusting in the classroom buildings.

Someone should take down that sign.

Another project was initiated by the government to take care of the country's terrible litter problem.

Americans will readily admit that Mexico has some of the most spectacular scenery in the world. But at the same time, they are always horrified to see how trash is dumped everywhere, utterly ruining the beautiful landscapes. After the five days of Easter holidays, for example, it looks as if a hurricane has come through the coastal areas. The beaches are one giant pig sty, five thousand miles long. Apparently no one ever mentioned that it was a good idea to throw away trash.

At some point in the early Seventies, we started hearing a catchy little song on the radio: "*¡Ponga su basura en su lugar!*" Put your trash in its place.

"Its place," we noticed, were big decorative oil drums labeled BASURA. They were popping up everywhere in Puerto Vallarta—along the beach, in the plaza, by the bridge downtown, next to the church, everywhere. Each of these blue barrels had a lid featuring a cute little duck with a bright orange bill, a yellow bow tie, and a jaunty white hat. Apparently someone in high places had a friend who was an artist.

To throw away the trash *en su lugar*, you had to open the duck's big mouth and toss it inside. The cost to the Mexican people? Millions of pesos. Who knows?

Those Mexican people, as one might have predicted, walked right past the nifty barrels. They, who had never stowed trash before, were now expected to put it into the mouths of ducks?

Within a year, they were all gone—not just the ducks, but the barrels too.

Even if anyone had actually used them, filled them up, the government had provided no trucks to haul the trash away. The same government employee shuffled along in his *huaraches*, loaded the heavy barrels one at a time onto his *burro*, and tossed it all onto a flat wooden cart.

Then he would hope that no wind came up, to take it all away. Usually he was not so lucky. The *basura* got a wider distribution than ever before.

And so our cute trash barrels disappeared. But not the jingle.

My maids would walk through the house for months afterwards, sweeping or dusting or polishing, and singing, *"¡Ponga su basura en su lugar!"* until we all wanted to commit bloody murder. It was worse than *Feliz Navidad*, once it gets lodged in your brain.

We all just shook our heads, calculating how many trucks could have been bought for the millions of pesos that went to someone in exchange for those damn ducks.

For Jarretaderas, a small village just over the bridge in Nayarit, the *fideicomiso* had big plans.

It was a peaceful little settlement, one of our favorite places to go for the turtle eggs. Thirty or forty fishermen and their families made a small living on the beach. Some of the women had set up shop in seedy little *palapas* here and there, where they served their special omelets with fabulous *picante* sauce. No licenses required, no taxes to be paid. They cleaned the plates with a quick pass in sea water. The simple life.

A government *licenciado* appeared one day and announced plans for an opulent new planned community for the wealthy, to be built right there on that beach. It was to be called Nuevo Vallarta. Though we in Old Vallarta were quite put off by the name, some of us attended the meeting—I, for one, to see whether a local nursery could be included in the plans, to provide green plants and trees for our gardens.

The fishermen gathered around and learned that they would be given new land in the mountains. They were to have their own new paradise, with new houses, running water, sewage lines, a new school, and trained nurses to assist in the child delivery. Many of the young men could start a good job right away, in fact, by making bricks and learning how to lay them.

The broad avenues of Nuevo Vallarta were already charted and ready to be built. Hotels and apartments would follow in no time. There would also be a great need for maids, waiters, and gardeners soon enough.

Still, some of the conservative fishermen balked. Heads were shaking left and right.

. What did they know about farming the land? They had been fishermen for generations, perhaps centuries. And now they would no longer hear the comforting roar of the sea. What was to become of the nets they had made, or the wooden canoes? Their children started getting restless. Then the tequila bottles came out, and soon nobody was listening to the city lawyer from the *fideicomiso*.

But the project went on without them.

The fishermen were uprooted, and relocated inland. The dredging began on an expensive canal system. A beautiful building went up in the center of the area, to handle the sale of lots. Some lots were sold.

That was fifteen years ago.

Some houses have been built. The grounds of Nuevo Vallarta are beautiful, but nearly deserted.

The fishermen in the hills are still waiting for their water, their sewage, perhaps even for compensation for their land. The nurse has stopped visiting.

Now, if they want to put their boats out to sea beside the stagnant canals, they have to pay a fee at the new pier.

"Why don't you fight it?"

"Oh, *señora*, I would be killed. There is nothing we can do."

Screwed in Mexico.

And not just we foreigners who settled there because we loved the place.

In Puerto Vallarta itself, it was discovered to be shocking, that in such a paradise, raw sewage poured directly into the bay.

Millions of *fideicomiso* dollars were spent to study the problem in Egypt and throughout the third world, and to design a new system. Huge pipes then came rumbling into town. They were laid for a third of a mile and then the project mysteriously stopped.

Raw sewage now poured into the bay a few hundred yards farther out. But more of that story later.

In the meantime, my social life was heating up. First there was Armando, and then suddenly there was Malcolm MacNeill.

After the final Norma incident, I wasn't exactly looking around, but I wasn't exactly pushing men away either. I became something of a flirt. It's amazing how life changes if you show a little interest! I should have taken the cue from Sondra Cellini—or from my husband, for that matter—years ago.

A couple of my girlfriends and I were sitting in the bar one night, celebrating someone's birthday. Jesús had kept the drinks coming, and we were all singing our favorite Mexican love songs, to the accompaniment of the little combo over by the fireplace.

Gradually we began to notice the obvious interest of three guys over in the corner. The one I spotted was a big guy, about ten years older than I was, with an open, honest face and a hearty laugh. Soon they all came over and joined us.

Malcolm and his friends were lawyers in Vancouver. The rain had gotten to them, and they had come down to paradise for a little sun. We had a few laughs, and then the evening was over.

But by the time we parted, he had told me about the dream of a boat he was having built for himself in Taiwan. He described glowingly how he planned to sail the world for about three years, and live onboard. At the stern, he was even going to bring in special soil and grow a small vegetable garden, so that he wouldn't have to depend on what he found in port. We had a fun evening, and I didn't think much more about it.

Then I started getting long love letters from him. It was a little embarrassing at first, and I didn't know how to handle it. I liked him, certainly. He admired me for my guts. And here I had found another one who was nice to my children.

We began "dating," in the casual way people do in a resort.

He started sending me presents. Hardly anything romantic, like Gucci underwear—no matter what the size.

From Malcolm I got binoculars, and a fishing rod.

Bob even liked him. I must say that put me off a bit! But lately he had been acting rather strangely anyhow. We didn't see each other much, but we passed each other occasionally, on the way to somewhere else.

Like the time I came charging out of the bedroom, dressed to kill.

"Where you going, Lewis?" Bob asked me in a jovial tone.

"Out."

"I wanted to talk to you. Could you—?"

"I'm really in a hurry. Can't it wait? You can see that I'm all dressed up."

"Oh, the hell with it," he said, and slapped me hard on the rear end.

I think he meant it as a playful slap, but it caught me off balance, and I went sailing across the floor on my knees. I hit the back of my head on the bedpost.

"You bastard! What'd you do that for?" I yelled.

Bob got such a foolish look of apology on his face that I burst out laughing. He slumped to the floor and laughed even louder.

"Shit. I guess I'll change my plans," I said. "My knees are killing me."

"Where were you going, anyway?"

"Dancing. At the City Dump."

"You'd better take care of your knees first!" He laughed again.

Then he said, "Boys," to the four wide eyes that were peering in the door by that time, "go get some alcohol for *your mother*."

"You did it again, you sonofabitch," I moaned, rubbing my legs. "No dancing for me tonight."

It was as if we had suddenly become jolly acquaintances, buddies, instead of husband and wife.

Malcolm MacNeill caught me at a very vulnerable time in my life, probably the worst ever.

Usually I didn't hear them, but this time I couldn't ignore the rumors around town. Bob was once more about to become a father. And, as if to prove it, his ulcer had begun acting up again.

I was furious. I knew I wasn't the mother of this brat, but I certainly did not want to listen to any more details.

For years I had noticed that my already finicky husband was unduly careful of an attaché case that he carried around. Recently that had really started to bother me. I don't know why actually, after twelve or thirteen years of more or less married life, but it did.

He always carried the thing with him on his business trips. When he came home, he always checked to make sure that it was locked, and then he put it in a special drawer in his office desk.

"Nobody outside of the foreign office cares that much for an attaché case," I thought. "Your purse, maybe. Your billfold, but—"

I don't know what I expected to find there, but suddenly I had to find out what was so important in that damned briefcase.

Ofelia became an eager accomplice, and we sneaked off to Bob's office to find out.

I broke into the drawer, and we stole the thing. Secretly, we brought it over to her house.

I quickly picked the locks. The thing was filled with several business papers that I recognized. Nothing very exciting. I was disappointed.

Then, at the bottom of the pile I found a big fat brown envelope.

I took out the papers, and read over and over a lot of words like "plaintiff," and "defendant." I didn't know those words. Again and again, the plaintiff and the defendant kept coming up.

Ofelia was no help.

I went for her dictionary. Still standing at the bookcase, I started to read the papers over more carefully. Then it dawned on me. They were divorce papers.

I was not wife number three, as Bob had told me when we got married. I was not even number four or number five.

I was wife number six! And he had a child in California who was older than I was.

I sank down on the sofa and wept. Perhaps the only time I have ever really done it.

Not in the concentration camps during the war, not during the deprivation in Holland. Not even when I lost Antonio. I had been proud of how tough I was.

But now the tears just poured out, and I couldn't stop them. It hadn't mattered (though it was beginning to), that he was twenty years older than me instead of ten, as he told me up in Carmel. But wife number six!

I saw all my self-respect dissolve. All the years, the kids, the hotel that we had worked on together.

Ofelia, who had thought she was joining in on another one of our crazy adventures, was unable to do a thing for me. She just held me in her arms, for an hour or more.

"He followed me to Mexico!" I said between sobs. "I didn't ask him to come down here. Why did he do it?"

She could only shrug and make me a strong drink. I could see on her face that she was reliving in her own mind all the rough times she had had with Crisanto's unfaithfulness.

"I never needed him! He followed me!" I sobbed over and over again.

Someone observing us here could probably have seen that the tone was gradually changing.

"I *never* needed him!" I announced suddenly. "I don't need that sonofabitch now either!"

I stood up, resolved. Malcolm had invited me to sail with him to Mazatlán, and I was going.

And I was also going to start what I called my "divorce file."

The first thing that was going into it was that photo of Bob and Norma at the night club. When I got back from Mazatlán, I was going straight to Guadalajara to find the place, and get a whole picture as evidence.

No black bastard could do that to me!

During my escape to Mazatlán, I discovered that I was going to need a little more practice before I became a real *bona fide* gay divorcée. The trip was pleasant enough, but it wasn't the great romantic adventure of my life. I don't know why, maybe my heart wasn't really in it. But I loved Malcolm for being willing to take me away, and to put up with me.

He spent much of the time looking a little confused. Perhaps it hadn't turned out the way he had hoped, either. But we promised each other passionately that we would continue meeting, and I flew off to Guadalajara to start my detective work.

That attempt failed on the first try too, and soon I was back home at Las Glorias. Bob asked where I had been, but he didn't seem much interested in the answer. His ulcer was getting worse.

Puerto Vallarta was no longer a sleepy fishing village. There was no end of sexual escapades in those days. I could have found a lot of good teachers to help me find a new life, if I had cared to put some study into it.

My friend Judith, for example, was sitting with me at the pool one afternoon.

"You won't believe the party I went to last night," she said.

"Where?"

"That big house up on the hill," she answered.

I knew where she meant. A wealthy American family was selling their house and going back to the States for good. Last night the hostess threw a farewell party for herself that had become the talk of the El Dorado set several days before the event. Very upper crust.

"You were invited to that?" I asked, envious.

"Through Carlos," she said, naming a business client of hers. "So I asked Ruben, and we made a sort of double date of it. Why not?" she added. "We knew it was going to be some party!"

"Was it good?"

"Very expensive. Very posh." She snorted suddenly with laughter. "My Ruben didn't have a very good time."

"What do you mean?"

"Well, we were all mingling, having drinks on the terrace over the bay, and sampling the goodies. Sally's husband was very gracious, going around and making everybody feel at home. And her kids were all dressed up too. They were sitting at a low table in front of the fireplace, playing chess. Very domestic scene."

"And—?" She was leading up to something, but what?

"And, this guy comes up to Ruben and says, 'You too, huh?'" She giggled again.

I was totally lost.

"Well, Ruben didn't know what the guy was talking about. And he kept pressing it. He said something like 'how was she for you?' And then he started to say, 'Did she—?' But I didn't hear the rest. He was whispering in Ruben's ear."

"What?"

"I don't know, but he looked at me like he wanted to kill me. He said, 'My God, how could you get me into this? Let's get out of here!' Well, I didn't want to leave yet, but we went. Then!"

"'Into' what? What were they doing?"

"Oh, they weren't doing anything. It was all just as suave as can be. I mean, the room was filled with doctors and lawyers and architects and—"

"JUDITH!" I yelled. Would she never get to the point?

"They were all Sally's lovers. Every man in that room—there must have been forty of them—had slept with her. That's what the party was for. She was saying good-bye to all her boyfriends! And her husband, the poor bastard, was the host!"

We both dissolved in laughter. That woman had figured it out. No beach bums for her. She had the best.

She must have had a very complicated social calendar too.

Though I thought it was a funny story, I couldn't see myself in that role. I was delighted to be the latest 'hostess of Puerto Vallarta,' but I didn't think that I was ready to become its madam.

For one thing, I could see every day that the more typical story of an American woman with a Mexican man ends up quite differently. Like Patty.

She had started coming down here with her husband years before. He was a pilot for Pan Am, and they had a lot of money. When he asked her for a divorce after thirty years of marriage, she got a good settlement, and she lived high in Puerto Vallarta.

She met a local veterinarian, ten years younger than she was, and went off the deep end. She got crazy for the man. For her too, it was very important that he was a professional. She could take him to parties and not have to confess to her friends that he made his living on the beach.

But we all called him the 'glorified gigolo,' since she had bought him the truck he drove around in, and had set him up in veterinary practice. He was married, with six kids, but he kept promising he was going to get a divorce.

You can almost fill in the rest of the story.

She was still very feminine and sporty, and she had a lot of energy. They decided to go into business together. He said he was tired of fighting the bulls and the horses. He wanted to have a quail farm up in the mountains by Chico's Paradise. They would live together, and set up a successful business together by selling the baby quail to all the hotels and restaurants in town.

So she built them a fabulous home up in the mountains.

Pretty soon it dawned on her that she was spending a lot of time alone up there in the beautiful mountain house, while he was out making calls, or so he said, in her truck.

The calls involved lots of vodka gimlets at the Playa de los Muertos, which we still called the 'social beach,' and lots of flirting with all the other horny American women. And she was stuck up there with no telephone, no bus service.

She sat for two years on that quail farm. It cost tens of thousands of dollars to haul all those expensive materials up the mountainside, but after two years, she wanted to sell it and get out.

"Listen, man, I don't want to live in the bushes any more. I'm going to build us an apartment house in Puerto Vallarta," she told him. And she did. She set him up in a new office on the ground floor of this place, and continued as his veterinary assistant. They had a sort of penthouse apartment on top, where they got the cool breezes and a view of the sea.

The guy specialized in small animals, so to speak.

Then he met a Canadian woman who was younger, and had even more money. He moved Patty out of his office, and fixed it up as an apartment, so that this woman could live there.

There was a scene, but he refused to listen or to leave. He had his practice to think about, after all.

For another year Patty lived alone on the top floor, and the happy couple enjoyed the downstairs apartment.

I saw her one day, coming toward me downtown. She looked heavily sedated, and we all knew it was from the quantities of vodka that poured into her every day. I was standing in the plaza, using the town's one public telephone. I confess I turned the other way and crouched down to avoid her.

She spent thousands of dollars more in legal fees to get her veterinarian out of there. She had no life, no future. There was nothing I could say to her.

I was too busy to get involved in something like that. My own days, it seemed, were spent on that telephone with lawyers in Mexico City and Guadalajara, and in the *fideicomiso* office, trying to get my documents verified. Nobody seemed to know how to deal with Las Glorias.

I had been standing there in the plaza for an hour, making one phone call after another. My kids were running around, pestering me about leaving, and then scampering off to invent new games, as they were always able to do.

I noticed a man across the square, who had been having his boots shined for at least half an hour. Expensive boots.

"Half an hour on a pair of boots," I thought. "Interesting."

He stared at me in an intimate, almost cocky way, obviously enjoying the scene of the tall Dutch broad conducting her business in the open air, dealing affectionately with the multi-colored kids that darted around her.

He smiled, and I smiled back. There was nothing more to it.

I was not going to end up like Patty.

A couple of days later I was having dinner with some American friends on the balcony at the Méditerranée, overlooking the Malecón. We were laughing and having a good time together. The waiter came up with another round of drinks.

"From the gentleman at that table," he said, with a slight bow.

The man with the very well-polished boots!

"How nice," I thought.

I read the note he sent, which wished us a nice evening. "I want to meet you," it said in English. He was definitely not talking about the others at the table.

I raised my glass to him, and he returned the gesture. A flash of electricity across a crowded room? No, it wasn't that at all. But something had definitely passed between us. Most of all, I felt the power he transmitted through his dark eyes.

I had no idea who he was, but he must have been important. Everything about him showed that he was used to wealth and command. He got up to leave, without coming over to the table, and my heart sank a little.

He was short.

I turned back to my friends.

A month must have gone by. The bureaucratic activity at Las Glorias was stepping up.

Espinoza continued to hold court at my mother's house, with a stream of officials in and out constantly.

One particular evening, there was a top-level conference being held in my living room. All the commissioners were gathered there, with several others that I hadn't seen before, about thirty-five or forty men. Armando was there, and Doctor Soto. Ignacio Rey had flown in late with his henchmen, in a fleet of military helicopters.

There were so many of them that only my large living room would accommodate them. The best champagne, smoked salmon, all kinds of meats and cheeses started appearing from everywhere, as the meeting began to wind down.

It was impossible for the men not to notice Rita and me coming in and out of the house, conducting our own business. They had decided to invite us to join them later for dinner—for decoration, I suppose, since I was sure that my input was not required on *fideicomiso* questions.

She and I had gone off to her bedroom downstairs to dress up, so that we would dazzle them. We were laughing and bathing and experimenting with hair styles and make-up.

She had gone shopping with me in town recently, and helped me pick out a special number with a long skirt and a bare back that scooped so low that you could almost see cleavage. There was no question about cleavage showing over the draped, Grecian front. It was a knock-out.

Well, there was a bit of a question. Neither Rita nor I had much in front, so we were giggling about how to press our breasts in from the sides, so there would be more. The kids were running in and out, and Lupe was trying to settle them down to feed them supper.

Since we had on some rather modest but slinky robes, we left the door open, and the men were enjoying the show as they helped themselves to the hors d'oeuvres.

I heard Espinoza say to his driver, "Go pick up Ingeniero León at the Camino Real." The driveway was crowded with cars. But I figured it was up to the chauffeur to get his car out. It was not my party.

Later on, I was standing in front of the mirror in the bedroom, taking out my curlers, when the engineer walked in and put his arms around me and spun me around.

"Here's the woman I've been after for two months now!" he shouted to the house at large.

A few of the guys looked up and smiled and went back to their business. Rita raised an eyebrow which said, "Not bad!"

"Where have you been?" he said. "I've been looking for you."

"Well, I've been right here," I said.

With a move of the head, he motioned Rita out the door and then kicked it shut with the back of his foot.

He kissed me long and hard on the neck, and my knees gave out underneath me.

I tried to continue talking, but I found that my voice trembled. "This is my place, actually," I said.

What was that tremor all about? I was in charge here.

"I didn't know who you were!" the man said, pinning me with his eyes.

I discovered he was only a couple of inches shorter than I was. And even more important, that it didn't matter.

"I'll see you later," he promised. And he turned on his heel and strode out to join the meeting.

And so my affair began with Enrique León.

That night, we had an exquisite dinner at the Camino Real, with all the big shots.

"Come," said Enrique, before the dessert came. He led me out to a car he had borrowed, and we started to drive down the coast.

He stopped the car at a point overlooking a small cove. There was no one below on the sand. "Let's swim," he said.

He took my hand and led me down to the water. Slowly he slid my dress down over my hips, the glow in his eyes expressing profound admiration.

"You make my blood run fast," he said in a rough voice.

Then we were naked in the water. I didn't need to see the man in the soft moonlight to feel his power. His body was tight, athletic.

The men had all addressed him as *engineer* because of his degree from Rice, but he devoted most of his time to the cattle business, which he conducted all through the center of Mexico from the Texas border to south of Mexico City.

His muscles were hard and smooth from riding eight hours a day.

"My beautiful, tender young colt!" he said to me as he stroked my body next to him in the sand.

It sounds a little silly now, but what greater compliment, I guess, from a cattleman? It wasn't the least bit silly at the time. I was completely his. He could call me anything, do anything he wanted.

I had never been adored. *"¡Mujer!"* he kept saying. Woman! And he was a real lover. He made me a woman.

For the first time in my life in Mexico, I was not this broad who worked hard to support herself and her husband and children, and acted as arbiter in all the fights that broke out in the family and in the hotel. I was a woman. I had someone who wanted to take care of me.

My joy was total. I made love to him all night long on the beach, with an abandon I didn't know I possessed.

At dawn we returned to his rooms at the Camino Real. On the way into the hotel, I sent a message back to Rita, telling her not to expect me home. We stayed there for three days. He made love to every inch of me, and I shocked myself by doing the same with him. *"¡Mi amor!"* he called me. *"¡Mi cielo!"*

I had a lover! I was a lover! It was an incomparable revelation to me.

It was not all heavy breathing. We chased each other around the rooms. We got caught in the shower together by room service. We laughed constantly for three days.

How long had it been since I had laughed so freely?

There came a time, of course, when we were forced to face reality.

He was married to one of the richest women in Mexico. They had seven children. She had been raised in a plantation house that her father had copied from Tara, in *Gone with the Wind*. There were several Lear jets on their private landing field, and a 747 at the family's disposal.

But by the time I met Enrique, his wife was an alcoholic, in and out of mental institutions, and it was he who cared for the children.

He had his own wealth, from several generations of successful gun-runners over the northern border, from the Civil War to Pancho Villa. They owned real estate, apartment buildings, and hotels in El Paso, in addition to their ranching. With all that wealth on both sides, there was no question of divorce.

When he took me home after three days, I was a changed woman. I was no longer *Theresa de Las Glorias*, or Bob Lewis' wife from Holland or Indonesia or somewhere.

I was the lover of Enrique León.

We made plans to meet in Mexico City.

At first, we met in his own apartment there. But then someone stole his jeep, and the traffic was all the time becoming more and more unbearable. It seemed easier to meet at the airport and go by taxi to a downtown hotel. Enrique kept a suite overlooking the Bellas Artes in one of Mexico City's oldest, most elegant hotels, the Del Prado.

We rolled up to the entrance and were greeted by a huge Russian doorman, six foot three, who instantly cleared the way for us.

We swept into the huge lobby, filled with paintings by famous Mexican artists like Diego Rivera, and took over the place. The atmosphere was all cashmere suits and starched white damask in the dining room. I tugged on the back of my miniskirt, which barely covered my ass.

"Suite 601, *señor*?" the bell captain would ask Enrique, but there was no need. It was his favorite.

"There are these messages for you, *señor*," he said politely, handing him a stack of notes.

Then we would run up to the suite and behave like little furry animals.

Later, in the real world, back at Puerto Vallarta, it was just before Christmas. I got a message to telephone Armando in Guadalajara. I went downtown to call him back at the forestry office.

"Theresa!" he said. "We need three bungalows next week."

"You're crazy, man, don't you know this is December? All our bungalows are full," I said.

"Can't help it. We've got to have them."

"Who's we?"

He didn't answer my question. "We're sending a very important judge down there. And he wants to bring his family."

"Oh yeah? Who's that?"

"Judge José María Macias. He's the federal judge for Guadalajara. Listen, Terry, I don't care what you do with those Americans, but get me those bungalows! No, wait a minute," he paused, "I need four."

"Four!"

"Four. He has seven children, and he'll be bringing along some maids too."

"OK. Four you got. But this had better turn out to be something important," I said, and hung up.

I decided that the more important people I knew, the quicker I could get my papers straightened out.

21

That Saturday evening I was in the office, monitoring the heavy traffic of guests returning from the day's excursions or shopping, and others leaving for supper and dancing. About seven o'clock, a fleet of taxis squealed into the entrance of Las Glorias.

Out stepped Judge José María Macias, seven children, three maids, with thirty pieces of luggage.

"Looks like the first leg of a world tour," I laughed to myself. "This man is out to impress us. I wonder why."

There was no denying that the man was impressive. Tall and slender, with olive skin and thick grey hair, he was dressed in an exquisitely tailored suit. We could have been filming a television commercial for Madison Avenue.

Children piled out of the cars, ranging in age from twenty-five to about seven. I saw that he was very attentive with them. There was no wife to be seen.

"I believe you have rooms reserved for us?" said the *juez*, in good English.

"Yes, *Señor Juez*," I smiled. I was polite, but I was determined not to dissolve in a little puddle of submissiveness, the way most Mexicans do in the presence of a judge. And I was still a little irritated that I had had to bump good customers from four of my bungalows, and send them to other hotels.

"Now, who's going to pay for all this?" I asked myself. Sure enough, I never got back one lousy dime for the week. But I did receive a lot of valuable insight in return for the favor.

Unfortunately, I proved too stubborn to act on it.

Judge José María registered, then got his entourage situated, and made arrangements at the restaurant for dinner for his kids. They all went straight to the pool for a swim.

Then he came back into the office. As he spoke, he looked me over very carefully, the way Armando had done. "Here's another one who has heard all about *Theresa, la Terrible* ," I thought. "I wonder whose side he's on?"

"Are you dressed for dinner, *señora*?" he asked politely. "I would like to escort you to dinner."

"Thank you, *Señor Juez*," I said, "but it's impossible for me to leave the office right now."

"I would like to talk to you," he insisted, never taking his eyes off me.

"Perhaps I can make some arrangements," I said.

Bob was in Mexico City with the station wagon, buying a load of supplies for the beginning of the high season. But by that time, Las Glorias ran smoothly, for a short time at any rate, without either one of us in the office. My curiosity had gotten the better of me.

"Let's see what this guy has on his mind," I thought.

"Where is your husband?" he asked. I explained.

I saw that he would happily have taken out both of us. It was not a romantic evening that he had in mind, whether he had left his wife behind in Guadalajara or not.

"I will go to the bar and have a drink, *señora*," he said. "In half an hour, I will be back for you."

He was a very imposing figure. I felt like saying, "Yes, my general!" with a salute, but he seemed a bit too sober to appreciate the joke.

I went home and put on a flowered silk dress, with a skirt somewhat longer than I liked to wear for Enrique, and some modest jewels. Then I jumped in the truck, which was my only transportation, and wheeled around in front of the restaurant.

"Esteban, please go and tell the *juez* I am ready," I said.

I was busy clearing out some mess in the front seat, when I glanced in the rear view mirror and saw him approaching. He had changed clothes.

He was wearing an English blazer with brass buttons, grey slacks, and a very elegant red, white, and blue tie. Perfect for Newport, perhaps, but the most Puerto Vallarta would generally consent to was the *guayabera*, that popular embroidered sport shirt, even for its most expensive restaurants.

"Whoooa, Terry," I said under my breath. "We're in for quite an evening."

I loved the contrast, so I decided to play it to the hilt.

"COME ON! LET'S GO!" I shouted from the driver's seat of my pick-up.

"There is no need for you to drive," he said. His face betrayed a flicker of an expression that I had often seen, much more boldly, on my husband's. "We can take a taxi."

"Oh, I drive this road a thousand times a month. It's no bother. Jump in!" He did.

"Where do you want to have dinner?"

"El Camino Real."

"Great!" I said, thinking how interested all the waiters and bellboys would be to follow this latest chapter in my life. Especially the one who had caught Enrique and me in the shower.

But they had a wonderful chef, and this meal was on him. "I love the big hotels!" I said.

We started off, *bumpity-bump*, over the cobblestones, our teeth rattling in our heads. I was sliding all over the place, trying to keep my hands on the wheel, but the judge remained perfectly composed. How did he manage that?

He glanced over occasionally, studying me.

At the hotel we had an exquisite meal, interrupted here and there by the introduction of a rich friend from Guadalajara. During the evening, I knew he was questioning me about Las Glorias, but he was so smooth, that someone else at the table might not even have picked up on it.

I told him all about building the place, from the foundations up. I even included the stories about my giant vegetables and my chicken fiasco, trying to loosen him up a bit.

But I left out any mention of the Reys. After being hosted twice by the immigration office in Mexico City, I was starting to get wise.

We finished eating, and he led me out onto the dance floor of the hotel. He had lived all over Mexico, in America, and in Europe too. But as elegant as he was, he couldn't control the typical *macho* smirk that came over his face as we danced.

"Look what I've got!" it said to all the bankers and lawyers from Guadalajara, who were sitting on the side lines with their fat wives.

I was enjoying all the interaction, but the dancing was boring me stiff. I longed to break out in a good disco beat.

How they ever found "Fever" at the Camino Real, I don't know, but when I heard the first few bars, I grabbed him.

"COME ON!" I brayed. "Let's really dance!" He declined sadly, so we sat that one out.

Or rather, I bounced along with the beat, and finished my champagne. He watched me, rather enviously, I thought.

Very politely, he escorted me home. That is, I drove him back in my truck. He might have made one small attempt to put his arm around me on the way back, but I couldn't tell for sure, since we were being jolted around so much by the road.

"Gotta keep both hands on the wheel!" I yelled and made a joke about it.

We said good night.

Though he was only in his mid-fifties, I felt as if I had just had a date with Cary Grant.

The next day, about mid-day, he appeared in the office in white shorts. "I understand you are a good tennis player," he said.

"Shit, man. Now I've got to go play tennis with this guy," I thought. But what I said was, "Yes, *Señor Juez.*"

"Good," he said. "Could you give me an hour of your time?"

"Sure. Let's make it about five this afternoon, when the sun isn't so hot."

"No, I think now would be better."

My face must have showed a bit of impatience, because he continued, "This evening I hope you will join me at a small cocktail party."

I accepted, and told my secretaries that I would be back in an hour. As we left for the courts, I could see them in the back of my head, all making a dive for the louvered windows, to watch the match. The whole staff was following the *juez* affair with great interest.

It was a good match. He was a good tennis player.

Then he left for town to spend an afternoon with his children, and promised to be back for me at five o'clock.

I was happy I had chosen some more expensive jewelry for the evening, because the small cocktail party was at a huge mansion owned by an heir of one of the tequila fortunes. It clung to the hillside overlooking the Camino Real.

It was a splendid party, but stiff. I started wondering how I could escape. I didn't have time for this, after all. We were very busy back at the hotel, and I didn't feel that I could be away so often from my paying guests. However, I also began to realize from the way these big shots were speaking to him, that I had a very important man on my hands. My respect for him was growing.

Later, we had dinner at the restaurant in Las Glorias, beside the fireplace, and I began asking the questions. They were difficult ones for him to talk about, but I could see that he wanted to confide in me. His slender, perfectly manicured hands shook a little as he spoke.

His father and grandfather had been lawyers and judges in Guadalajara. His wife was a well-known concert pianist. Recently, she had left him for another man. At first he had wanted to go out and shoot the guy, but thought better of it, and settled instead for divorcing her in disgrace. He got the children, and she didn't get a dime. He was very lonesome.

By then, the gossips had gotten to me too, with the information that he was looking for a new wife. But for now, as far as I knew from him, he was simply combining a business trip with a pleasure trip for his kids.

"This has been a very special time for me," he said, in a way that made me realize he was not talking about the fun he was having with his children. "These days in Las Glorias have lifted my spirits."

I gave him my hostess smile, but I also felt a tingle of pleasure at hearing that.

"I would like for you to accompany me to Yelapa tomorrow," he continued.

His manner clearly showed that people never declined one of his invitations. And by then I had decided to devote the week to him. Who could help me more with the *fideicomiso* than a top judge in Guadalajara?

"There is the case of a sailing vessel which has run aground in Yelapa. Perhaps you have heard of it?"

In Puerto Vallarta, we had heard of nothing else the last few days. Some young Americans had had an accident on the beach near the south point of the bay. A kilo of marijuana was found onboard, and they were being detained.

"I would like for you to go along and translate for me, with the young people," he said.

There was really no need of that. His English was excellent. But I agreed.

Next morning we took a private speedboat across the bay, and during the trip he became much more relaxed. He told me how much he admired Bob and me for what we had done at Las Glorias.

"I used to fly into Puerto Vallarta as a young man," he said. "There was nothing here. It was a real dump. You have done a good job."

'Dump' from the man who took me out to dinner in an English blazer two nights before! I noticed that he was humming "Fever," and that he had started calling me 'Theresa.'

When we arrived in Yelapa, we were met with a flourish by the mayor and his men. (That may sound official, but of course Yelapa was still only a tiny fishing village. The mayor lived in a *palapa* hut and wore dirty *huaraches*, just like everyone else.)

Judge José began questioning him. A beautiful sixty-foot sailboat stood alongside, ground into the beach, and working itself in still deeper, with the shifting sand. The young kids would need a couple of boats to pull it free.

The whole village was eager to help us, everyone falling all over himself to play host to the judge. José also talked to two or three fishermen after he had finished with the mayor, and then we went down the beach to seek out the small colony of American hippies who lived there and made jewelry.

Their story couldn't have been different from the mayor's. "He planted the pot," they said. "We've seen how that works. The day after those guys ran aground, there were military helicopters circling over Yelapa. Over and over again."

Warning signals went off in my head. Everyone in the bay area knew who traveled with an escort of military helicopters.

"Somebody wants the boat," they complained. "Those guys swore that they had no marijuana aboard when they had their accident."

Two young American couples were involved. Unfortunately, they had gone off to Puerto Vallarta for the day, so we were unable to talk to them about it.

On the way back home, I mentioned the Reys for the first time.

The judge looked sick. "Don't speak in haste, *mujer!*"

"And don't call me 'woman' like that," I snapped back. "I'm not one of your Mexican *pollas.*" ('Chicks': the word was becoming international.)

"Excuse me, Theresita. I think I am falling in love with you."

I was totally caught off guard. There was an uneasy silence.

Luckily, he changed the subject. "I wish I could help these young people, but I'm afraid there is nothing I can do."

"You believe the marijuana was planted, don't you? Why does a big federal judge take an interest in such a case? Why are you trying to help some young American kids?" I asked.

He was still guarded. I didn't get straight answers, but I did gradually discover that he had received a call from a friend he had made when he was Mexican consul in New York. The Justice Department in Washington was showing an interest. Judge José had been caught in the middle.

But not even he was powerful enough to fight the Reys. Nor Washington either, it seemed.

"When I came to Las Glorias, I expected to find someone completely different," he said.

The transition of his thought was not lost on me.

Again he changed the subject. "I will have to contact the insurance agency. The boat was lost at sea."

He looked almost overcome by nausea. He was a fair man, and a good judge. His conscience pained him deeply.

"Lost at sea" was heard more often by the insurance companies than they cared to admit. People used to sail down to Acapulco and then become bored. They didn't want to take the trouble to return by sea, so they simply sank the boat. Teams of claims adjusters came through regularly to investigate such cases, even to send divers to the bottom to verify their stories. The boat owners who were clever enough collected their forty thousand dollars and bought a bigger boat.

This man had been a respected judge for twenty-five years. I was hurt too, by his pain.

"Te quiero," he said, looking over with his sad brown eyes.

"José," I said, "I am not free to be loved."

I had to admit to myself that I was thinking more about my rancher than my husband. But that didn't need to enter into our discussion. "I have a husband and three children," I said.

He was shaking. It was a funny trait I had seen in others, when they became intimate with me. I couldn't believe I affected men so strongly, but I liked the feeling!

"I want to be friends," I assured him.

I did. I had started the week thinking he could help me with my divorce, or he could help me with Las Glorias, but he had completely won me over by his sense of justice—a trait I hadn't expected to find in a Mexican judge.

"You are welcome at Las Glorias any time," I said. "You and your children. The whole summer, there is always a lot of room."

We said good-bye at the end of the week.

The next morning, thirty-seven red roses arrived, specially flown in by Mexicana Airlines. The next day again, thirty-seven roses. One for each year of my age.

This continued every day for a month, along with boxes of bonbons, which my kids enjoyed. One day the record "Fever" was also hidden in the tissue paper.

Bob was amused, but not worried. He knew I liked the more sporty type instead. But he listened to the whole story with interest, still thinking that this man could possibly help us.

Those delusions were dispelled about six weeks later, in early February.

Gwen and Bill Piersante were good friends of ours, who had been coming down to Las Glorias every year for the last five years. They had fallen so much in love with Puerto Vallarta, that they had begun building a big house on the Gold Coast, over in the same area as the tequila mansion. Bill had made his fortune by importing Mexican marble and tile, and as a friend, he had generously provided all the tile for my own house.

The legal status of property owned by Americans on the coast was still unsure at that time—somewhere between the *prestanombre* situation, where a Mexican corporation was required as a "front," and the new rules coming down from the *fideicomiso*, where for a fee, a bank could hold property in trust for an individual. But Gwen and Bill had lots of money, and they didn't seem concerned about the problem.

By this time their home was nearing completion, and they flew in often from Chicago and stayed with us while they checked the progress.

They had designed a very large place, with five bedrooms, a swimming pool, and a large guest house off to the side. It was all done in Mexican style, with handmade bricks, and lots of marble and tile, naturally.

Gwen was eager to begin buying furniture and decorating the interior herself. One day she asked if I would be willing to go along with them to Guadalajara for a week, to offer suggestions and to translate for them.

Usually they were able to muddle through pretty well with Bill's Italian, but this time apparently they wanted to be more precise in their dealings. When they mentioned providing my room at the Hilton, I was happy to accept.

So while I was in the capital of Jalisco having a ball, spending thousands of dollars of their money, Bob Lewis was having his own drama at Las Glorias.

About eleven o'clock one morning, he was at work on the books in his office. Although it was February, it was usually warm enough during the day to wear tennis shorts and a T-shirt, and that was his customary attire.

Three men walked into the office and told him the judge wanted to see him downtown.

Without much hesitation, Bob said, "OK. I'll follow you guys."

"No, no, no," they replied. "You go in our car. We will bring you back."

Bob told the secretaries he would be back in an hour, and got into the back seat. Two of the men sat on either side of him, while the third one drove. The dumpy little car pulled out of the driveway and turned left, exactly the opposite direction from the village, and started heading out of town toward the border.

Bob objected, but the men wouldn't talk to him.

"Who are you? Where are you taking me?"

"Guadalajara," they answered. No more.

"Are you *federales?*" he asked. There were bulges in the pockets of the men on either side of him. He felt the unmistakable impression of steel on his bare legs.

They only smiled, which Bob took to mean 'yes.'

"What's the charge?" he persisted. I guess he hadn't learned anything about formal charges from my prison career in Mexico.

The road to Guadalajara passes through a portion of Nayarit, so technically Bob was being kidnapped across state lines, which was illegal. But these men did not seem interested in technicalities.

"Have you got any identification?"

Silence.

Bob started worrying more and more. His ulcer began acting up. He knew the *federales* had sleek, fast cars. So who were these creeps?

For the rest of the trip, no more was said except, "Where is your wife, *la señora Laao-is?*"

Bob explained that I was helping some of our guests with their shopping in Guadalajara, and that I was staying at the Hilton.

Nowadays, if you drive like hell on those mountain roads, and are lucky enough not to come upon several long lines of cars stuck behind the huge trucks, you can make the trip in about four hours. But it took much longer then. An hour outside of Guadalajara, near Tequila, Bob's bladder was making serious demands.

"Guys, I gotta take a piss," he pleaded.

They stopped the car and told him he could do what he needed to do in the bushes some distance off. By this time it was dark.

"Uh-oh," he thought. "I start over there away from the car, and they could shoot me in the back, and claim I tried to escape." He stood right at the door in full view, and relieved himself.

When they reached Guadalajara, they drove straight to the Hilton. The Piersantes and I were not there. It was about seven in the evening. The shops did not close until eight, and then of course, we had planned to go out to dinner.

The men shrugged in disgust and drove to the place where one of them lived. Bob still hadn't seen any charges or any identification. But he had seen their weapons. They carried good-caliber revolvers.

He persuaded the men to give him a glass of milk for his stomach.

"Can I use the phone?" he asked.

Silence.

At eleven o'clock, Bill and Gwen and I were getting ready for bed. They had taken a suite for us in the Hilton with adjoining bedrooms. Gwen and I were in our robes already, walking back and forth, talking about what we still needed to shop for, and eagerly looking at the goodies laid out on the bed in my bedroom. We had had a good meal with a moderate amount of wine, which was generally all they were interested in drinking.

I was enjoying my view from the seventh floor, when we heard a knock on the door. My door.

"Now who even knows I'm here?" I thought.

The knock became more insistent.

Bill, who was still dressed, went to answer it.

He let out a little screech of surprise, and Gwen and I saw that one of these shady characters had pulled him out into the hallway.

He was protesting loudly, and Gwen had started to yell too, when another one yanked her out, in her satin robe.

I ran to the door and saw Bob at the elevator with the third guy. He held up his arms to show me the handcuffs. I shut the door fast and double-locked it. Then I ran to the other room of the suite and did the same.

Gwen was outside, screaming bloody murder, and probably going for their eyes. Three people I loved, out in the hallway of the Hilton with some gangsters! But mine was an automatic reaction. Those days, the first thing I thought of was to call my lawyer, which I did.

"Stay where you are," he said. "I'll be right over." It was Juárez, the vice president of our corporation.

After that I called downstairs to the management of the Hilton, and started yelling at them about the way Americans were being treated in their hotel. I described the whole scene, shaking with fury.

I couldn't hear anyone in the hallway any longer, so I presumed that they were on their way down in the elevator.

"*Señora*, we are dreadfully sorry," said the man, oozing concern. "We will send somebody up right away to check this out."

"But—" I sputtered.

"Start with the elevator," I intended to say, but he had hung up. Nobody ever showed up at the room. Nobody checked on anything. I just paced back and forth between the two rooms.

The scene in the elevator must have been delightful. Of course I heard about all of this, from start to finish, only later on. But I can picture it: three thugs with no expression on their faces, Bill snarling at everybody, my husband in handcuffs, trying to explain as much as he knew of what was going on, above Gwen's shrieking.

I could see her polished nails and her diamonds flashing in all directions. She was still in her little satin robe.

Bill tried to knee one of the guys in the groin and got the same for his troubles.

The doors of the elevator opened, and they were all led out into the sumptuous lobby. The men on duty at the night desk looked up at them, but showed no surprise. Across the room, Bob saw Luis Racán, another greedy, small-time lawyer friend of Miguel's, who had also been appointed as one of our *prestanombres* at Las Glorias.

"What's he doing here?" Bob wondered briefly.

He didn't have time to pursue the thought because at that moment, Antonio Juárez burst through the doors, accompanied by his three-hundred-pound wife, Teresa. She had become a good friend of mine through the years, and she had insisted on coming along.

Without blinking, Juárez pulled out his pistol and started shooting. The three hostages hit the floor.

Then Racán started shooting.

The shady types (we never did know who they were, or what authority they had) started shooting back.

There, in the foyer of one of the most glamorous hotels in Mexico, bullets were bouncing off the marble walls in all directions. The chandeliers were buzzing.

The hotel staff had long since disappeared.

Except for one.

Apparently the night watchman had not been included in the plans. He grabbed one of the thugs. But another one grabbed Bob and hustled him toward the door.

Bill started after them, but Bob yelled, "No! Take care of Gwen. Get her out of here!" Then the first one wrestled free from the night watchman, and shoved past Bill before anyone could stop him.

For a moment, all they could do was stand there in the lobby and stare at each other. Then, shaken and subdued, they crammed into the elevator and came up to my room. Gwen and Bill, Racán and Juárez, and the three-hundred-pound Teresa. Gwen was nearly fainting from fear.

"They took Bob!" she sobbed, when she saw me. We all quickly compared notes, and then the two lawyers ran out to find the police, to see what they could discover.

My friend Teresa came through. She managed to calm down all of us while we waited.

Sure enough, Racán and Juárez found Bob Lewis in the Guadalajara jail. He was still dressed in tennis shorts, shaking from the cold night air of the mountains. He had not been accused of anything. He had just been thrown into the large cell with all the drunks.

Since our legal representatives were local, they were able to get him out finally about four o'clock, with the promise that he would appear before the judge later that morning.

Back at the hotel, I was helping Gwen and Bill pack. The joy had been taken out of our shopping trip. They flew back to Puerto Vallarta immediately. They never stayed with us in Las Glorias after that.

Bob was released by the judge about eleven that morning, about twenty-four hours after it started. He never saw a charge of any kind.

"How come I was thrown into jail so easily?" he demanded. "I'm an American! You can't do this! Somebody paid off that little shit who locked me in here!"

His lawyers simply shrugged.

Sadly, the Piersantes never got to enjoy their dream and their beautiful house together for very long. From then on, they became anxious. And Gwen died shortly afterwards of bone cancer. Bob and I were genuinely grieved.

It was our habit to be gracious to all the hundreds of customers, even the regular guests, who came through our hotel. But with only a few did we feel that they had become our friends. The Piersantes were two we really liked.

There's another postscript to this story that's not exactly sad, and not exactly funny either. It difficult to say how to characterize it. It happened later, actually past the time I'm dealing with in this book, but it belongs here with this episode.

Antonio Juárez came back to the hotel to tell us that Racán was following in a moment with Bob.

"Thank you, thank you!" I said. "I don't know how I can pay you right now, but—"

Then an easy solution occurred to me. I still had on the jewelry I had worn to dinner the previous evening. It was one of my favorites, a set of emeralds that my father had bought for me in Paris when I was young.

I took off the dinner ring, and handed it to him. There was an exquisite stone in the center, about the size of an almond, with diamonds all around it.

"You keep this for now," I told him. "I'll send you the money as soon as I can get to the bank in Puerto Vallarta, and then you can return it to me."

His eyes lit up.

When Bob got back, he was really upset to find out what I had done. I figured he was upset about being in the filthy jail all night, but he kept harping on the emerald.

I couldn't understand why it bothered him so much. It had seemed natural enough. The man was the vice president of Las Glorias, after all. If we couldn't trust him—

Then he confessed. "I already did that once," he said. "I gave him your diamond heart as a promise of payment a few months ago. I paid him back, but I never got the heart."

"That's terrible!" I said. Actually, I didn't mind the heart so much. It was a tacky little thing, though much in fashion in those days, with tiny diamonds. I like them big! Bob had given it to me as an anniversary present or something. It looked a bit silly alongside the rest of my things. I never let my mother see it.

Bob, of course, felt the opposite. I remembered my fur coat that became *sombreros del 'gringo Davy Crockett.'* And there were also my china and crystal, which disappeared later. But since the emerald had nothing to do with him, it was the little heart that became his preoccupation.

And of course for both of us, it was really the principle of the thing more than the money—and what another underhanded maneuver would bode for our future at Las Glorias.

Juárez had the money from me in two days. And he also still had the emerald. The next time I saw him, I asked him about it.

"You never gave me a ring," he said, poker-faced.

"Of course I gave you the ring. I was wearing an emerald that night. You remember—"

He didn't remember.

"Don't pretend—"

"Where's your receipt?" he asked.

There didn't seem to be any answer to that one. He was my own lawyer, after all. Why would anyone think to ask for a receipt?

He was spending a week at Las Glorias at the time, free, with Teresa's sister. Those two had been carrying on an affair for years. Miguel also, our president, often breezed in with his secretary. Both, it was said, had children with those little *putas* as well as with their wives. They would come in one week with one family, and another week with the other.

If they could cheat so easily in that way, why did I think they would be honorable with my business transactions?

Years later, in 1979 after we had lost everything, I was visiting Ofelia in Guadalajara, where she had moved. That emerald still pissed me off. I couldn't stand the picture in my mind of *my* ring on Teresa's fat little finger.

In the years between, Antonio had done well. He had gotten himself a high government position and milked it for all it was worth. He and his wife had just finished building a $5 million house.

"They've got more money now than they can spend," I told Ofelia. "Surely the bastard will give me my ring back this time. Let's go."

In the meanwhile, my kids had heard from their father that he was unable to forget that piece of shit, the diamond heart. In fact, he had become so bothered that he had finally traced it to Teresa's sister, Antonio's mistress. He followed her to Kansas City, where she had become a proper American wife and mother, and screwed her to get it back. There must be some sort of rough justice in that.

Where is the thing now? Probably with Norma. That's appropriate. My kids also told me that one time Bob brought her home to Baltimore to meet his parents.

I have never met his parents. His whole family thinks Norma is his wife Terry.

At any rate, Ofelia and I jumped in her car and pulled up in front of the huge, gaudy mansion.

Little Teresa, who used to play with our kids in the pool at Las Glorias, answered the door. We checked to see that her father was not at home. Lord knows what he would have done if he had found us there.

Big Teresa was even bigger than ever, if possible. She was thrilled to see us. We sat in her living room and had a drink, while I told her about the emerald. She was shocked.

"Do you think you could return it to me?" I asked humbly.

"Come with me," she said immediately.

She led us into her bedroom and opened up the safe. Drawer after drawer came out, filled with expensive jewelry. But no emerald.

"Here. Take this," she offered, holding out a set of rubies in her little piggy hand with its beautifully manicured nails. The rubies had about a third of the value of my single stone.

"I don't want your jewelry, I want mine," I demanded. "Your husband took it from me. Now, where do you think it is?"

"Oh, Theresa, I'm sure Antonio wouldn't do that. He's—"

For good reason, it was difficult for her to finish the sentence. "Take something here. Take anything!"

She was starting to beg, and it was getting on my nerves. "We had so many good years, Theresa! Our friendship is too important—"

"Our friendship!" I blew up. "You're talking about that crook of a husband of yours too, I guess! Can you still say that, after everything he and Miguel did to us at Las Glorias?"

"Theresa, he didn't mean to—"

"Oh, didn't he!" I screamed. "I don't want any of your damned jewelry. Your husband worked very hard—" I corrected myself. "He *stole* very hard, to give these stones to you! I wouldn't touch them. *¡Es un regalo de un peurco!* It's like accepting a gift from a pig!"

Ofelia stood up and tried to hustle me out of there. I was out of control. Suddenly poor fat Teresa seemed to be to blame for everything that had happened to me in Mexico.

"You think you're so holy—" I yelled. Ofelia was afraid I was going to punch the woman. "You go to church every day, you go to communion every day!" I was panting with fury. "Don't you even know what your goddam husband does? How he makes his money?"

Ofelia was easing me toward the door. She and I were almost wrestling with each other. "Who do you think *really* paid for this house?"

Teresa was trying to appear invisible. Which she found difficult.

"I'm ashamed to have the same name as you!" I shrieked, kicking the door.

"Holy Teresa, forgive her!" I murmured, raising my hands dramatically in prayer. "She's a disgrace to your name!"

Ofelia shoved me out the door, down the stairs, and out onto the street, before I started breaking up the million-dollar furniture. When I had calmed down, I think I was glad I hadn't told the stupid woman about her sister. I don't think her piety could have handled that news.

But of course, I'm getting way ahead of myself. That episode is far in the future.

Bright-eyed and optimistic in the early Seventies, I continued making my telephone calls and appearing at the office of the *fideicomiso* in Puerto Vallarta.

And I continued with my sleuthing in Guadalajara, for my "divorce file."

I found the night club, and got a print of that picture of Norma cuddling with my husband. Some African-sounding name—I forget. I went to the luxurious Tapatío and demanded a copy of the receipt for Bob's week-end there.

Then, to make myself feel better, I bought an expensive dress and checked in at the Hilton. I paid ten times more than I should have to get my hair done. And I called José María.

He was attentive, as always, and especially famous in Guadalajara. I loved sweeping into a restaurant, and having the way parted for us by the pompous *maître d'*. We went out several times on these trips—as friends. It was a wife he wanted, and he knew I would not be the one.

At Eastertime, he showed up again at Las Glorias with his all of his children and maids. It was my busiest time with the Mexican trade, but I was happy to provide the bungalows he required. He had a new girlfriend, a young lawyer from Guadalajara, about thirty-five years old. She was slim and pretty, and she had long, dark hair.

That afternoon, my secretary ran into the office, howling with laughter. "Doña Theresa! Look!"

She ran to the louvered windows and pointed toward the tennis court.

There was José María, soaking wet but handsome as ever, teaching the new girl to play tennis. She was wearing a cute little skirt and top, and she had on a blonde wig, fixed in the same style as my hair. She was having trouble keeping it on.

All the bellboys were soon clustered at the windows with us, enjoying the show.

Then the lovers finished and came toward the office. We all got serious immediately. He greeted us in a friendly way, and introduced the girl. She had added a long pony tail attachment to the wig, to make her look like a teenager.

My heart went out to him, but Enrique had totally come to dominate my life and my joy. I could not also be there for José.

22

1973 was the year I became a rancher's lady.

Enrique would circle over Las Glorias three times in his twin-engine Beechcraft, and everybody knew the signal. At the sound of it, my blood ran hot. I tossed a dress and a pair of jeans into a small bag and hurried to the airport. Enrique was waiting for me on the runway, I jumped in, and we were off!

We flew to Guanajuato and Zacatecas, those beautiful old colonial towns in the center of Mexico, or to Vera Cruz on the Gulf Coast, or every once in a while we buzzed up to El Paso to see about his business.

Some of my favorite memories are of negotiating for cattle with the Indians high up in the mountains of Chihuahua, or visiting the small *ranchos* all over Mexico. Enrique would spot a field down below, circle over it three times, and make a dive, scattering cattle and chickens in all directions. Sometimes the highway was the clearest place to land.

We drank, we made love, we danced all night, we made love, we hired *mariachi* bands, and we made love. In the mornings we grabbed a good supply of oxygen to clear the alcohol out of our heads, and off we went again.

I was initiated into the "Club 20,000." Translation: we reached that altitude quickly, he grabbed me passionately, and we rolled around naked in the rear of the plane all the way to Texas—or at least until it was time to take the plane off automatic pilot, and resume the controls.

He was vital and enthusiastic. We were totally absorbed in each other.

I used to disappear for three and four weeks at a time. I knew the kids were safe with Lupe—though Ofelia didn't appreciate having to cover for me with Bob. He must have guessed, anyhow.

Once again I found the Mexico that had attracted me in the first place. I got to know again the fresh, damp, heady aroma of the growing jungle, or the smell of the sea, and broiled fish in the mornings. We sat peacefully outside together in the evenings, far up in the mountains and away from everyone, just watching the fireflies or listening to the frogs.

It was fascinating to watch Enrique with the Tarahumara Indians in Chihuahua.

Normally an exuberant and outgoing man, he could turn a normal business call on the phone into an agitated yelling match, if his orders were not carried out with dispatch. But with the Indians, he could not deal that way. He had to become someone else. He took on their reserved demeanor and waited them out.

We would land in one of the pale green Alpine meadows. Even the log houses in the area looked like Swiss chalets, except that they were not painted.

We met the Indians and placed ourselves in a little circle, squatting on our haunches. Around came a bottle of vodka, which they had distilled from their own potatoes. In no time, my head was spinning the way it did long ago in Chacala, and I started to have all sorts of silly thoughts.

But my rancher remained stoic.

"I think it will take three weeks to get the cattle together," said the chief of the small settlement, in his limited Spanish.

Minutes went by.

"I don't have three weeks. The cattle are due at the King Ranch before that."

Long pause.

Then: "Why don't you hire three men and do it in one week?" Enrique suggested delicately.

The bottle went around again, during some heavy thinking.

"I don't have the money to hire three men," answered the solemn Indian.

After several more minutes, Enrique would say, "I know! I'll give you an advance so you can hire the men" —as if it were a new idea, and he didn't have to suggest it every time he dealt with these guys.

I just sat there and shut up.

"No, I don't like to take advances," was his answer. "I like to get the whole amount at the end."

Not by argument, but by the sheer power of Enrique's determination was the deal finally concluded. He already had the routes planned out in his head, and he had to move according to schedule. He couldn't make a special trip back for a hundred head of scrawny cattle.

Once the business was done, the women came out, in heavy ponchos just like the women wear in Peru, and served their goat cheese and their handmade flour tortillas. We ate them with gusto, and then made love all night in the cool mountain air.

I earned some good money during those trips too, as his assistant.

I was working on commission. Three or four hundred head of cattle were delivered by small trucks to various central spots, and then we transported them north by rail or highway. We had to stop every night and bring them out for their water and alfalfa. At the border we weighed them and dipped them for hoof-and-mouth disease.

I was the one who managed and counted and poked them with the electric cattle prod, while Enrique rode around, high in the saddle with his pistols and cowboy hat and boots, and gave his men the orders.

The pistols were never very far away. There were also guns on the plane.

In public, he walked tensely, as if he was always expecting someone to take a shot at him. Yet the people loved him, and they knew he loved them. He paid them well, and treated them with respect. They would cheer when we landed, and he gave them the Churchill V-sign.

The first time we went into El Paso, he was already on the radio before I knew it. "KILO ECHO 675. Captain León here. Request permission to land."

I could see the brown Rio Grande snaking through the dusty fields ahead.

"Rick, I can't land here. I don't have my papers!" I said, squirming into my blouse.

"Don't you worry. We won't tell them," he replied, laughing and grabbing me by the waist to pull me toward him.

I hesitated.

"I'm American enough," he said. "I studied at Rice. We don't need papers." And sure enough, nobody ever asked us for them.

We partied with the rich cattlemen and the politicians in El Paso, I picked up a new pair of boots from Tony Lama, and together we discovered the first motel in the area that featured a water bed. Rick brought me breakfast in bed the next morning, and we were off again.

It was during this period that I disposed of the Norma episode in my mind, once and for all.

There was a Canadian couple in Puerto Vallarta that we really liked. Like the Piersantes, they had stayed at Las Glorias several times, and then decided to build their own house down there. While waiting for it to be finished, they had taken a small, dumpy apartment over near the El Dorado.

One night we were invited to a party at their place. Bob and Rick were both out of town, so I went alone. There were about a dozen people there, all friends. We were drinking and having a good time.

"Now for the entertainment portion of the evening!" cried Greg, our host. Everybody started to gather round.

"Terry! Hey, Terry! Come along back here. We've got a treat for you."

A treat? Now, what the hell were they up to?

I followed Greg and Anita, and the rest of the party followed me. We all crammed into their spare bedroom. Against the wall there were bunk beds out of concrete, just like in the jail, and also in many little Mexican houses. They're very popular, since you don't have to move them, you don't have to dust them, just slap a couple of mattresses down, and you have bunk beds.

"Lie down there, on the bottom one," said Greg, hardly able to contain his excitement.

I gave him a funny look, having no idea what was coming, and I lay down. What I saw, on the underside of the top bunk completely broke me up. It was a big heart out of red spray paint, with the words, 'BOB LEWIS.'

In fact, 'I love you, Bob Lewis.' 'I love you, I love you,' covered the whole area.

I laughed till I cried. Then so did everybody else, as they each took their turn lying down on the bottom bunk, to get the total effect. We had discovered the dingy little love nest where Bob had set Norma up, after my mother burned her hand.

Bob's life was an open secret in Puerto Vallarta, as I have said already, so we all enjoyed the joke. None more than I.

The joke was on him. I had Enrique.

When I was not flying around Mexico being a cowgirl, I continued to haunt the offices of the *fideicomiso*. Once a month at least, I appeared at their door with all my papers, to make another declaration or to carry in some more documents. I could almost see them all roll their eyes in exasperation as I entered.

And yet, as well known as I came to be, they could never seem to find my file.

The office was always in chaos. There was a steady stream of good-looking young architects and engineers and builders coming through the doors. All the handsome lawyers from Guadalajara milled about and joined the others, flirting with the secretaries.

These girls were the pretty daughters of local fishermen, who had now moved up into the powerful world of government commissions. Yet, they could hardly spell *mañana*. I sat with them for hours, practically leaning on their shoulders as I corrected their mistakes.

Besides, it took a long time for them to type my documents with fingernails an inch long.

A gorgeous young lawyer would walk by, and the girl would roll the gum around her mouth seductively, hoping to be invited to the El Dorado for lunch. If she was successful, it usually meant that work was over for the day.

Those were long lunches, with lots of *margaritas*, courtesy of Mexico City. For dessert, if the girl was interested in advancement, she fucked the boss.

For years I too sat there at the El Dorado during the long *siestas*, when all the offices were closed, and followed their progress.

The day came when I finally had all my papers in order. It had taken months.

Bill Wulff had already finished. The El Dorado was his. Maximo Cornejo now owned the Tropicana officially. They had paid the government at the rate of 500 pesos per square meter.

And everyone agreed now that I was entitled to buy Las Glorias outright, because my daughter Dido was a Mexican national. What a relief!

I began dreaming again about our plans for the place.

Besides Doug Walker's fifty-room hotel building, I wanted to build a kind of fishing village in the back, like I had seen once in the Carolinas.

There were lots of guests at Las Glorias who had told me they would love to have a house next to the hotel, where they could use the beach, the swimming pool, the tennis courts, the restaurant, and all the rest. When the time came, I would put them in touch with an architect. They could use our utility lines.

For a small maintenance fee, they would also have the services of our watchmen when they were away in the States, of our maids when they got ready to come down for a vacation, and of me as manager to rent out their houses when they were gone, if they chose to do so.

It was perfect. We could have made a very good living from that project alone.

The next time I called at the commission office, the news was bad.

"*Señora*, I am sorry to tell you that your daughter cannot own property."

"I'm sure there's been some mistake," I said, my stomach sinking. "We've been through all of this. My daughter Dido was born here in Puerto Vallarta and—"

"*Señora,*" the lawyer said patiently. "You don't understand. The law has changed."

"Changed!"

"Yes. A Mexican national born of two foreign parents cannot own land in her name until she is eighteen. And only if she chooses to become Mexican at that time."

He smiled proudly. "It's a new law."

Eighteen! Dido was only seven. She had just had her first communion, with the little white dress and the white shoes, and all the candles.

"You mean, we got together all these papers, and had everything notarized, and then you sent everything off to Mexico City, and—" I began to sputter with frustration. "—and now that's all just down the drain? Months and months of work down the drain?"

"Yes, *señora* ," he shrugged.

At the same time, however, Miguel Salinas was telling Bob and me that he knew exactly what he was doing, and that there was nothing to worry about. He was the president of our corporation. He was our protector.

He himself had recently surrendered a parcel of land in the area, expropriated in trade for a small piece up in the mountains, as the local *rancheros* were being forced to do.

The news was in all the papers, praising the work of the commission and its fairness. Even such a prominent person as Miguel Salinas had had to comply! What they didn't mention, of course, was that the land in question amounted to about a millionth part of his property in Mexico.

Miguel was constantly in and out of our place, bringing in his lawyers and bankers, especially once he saw that Ignacio Rey was constantly in and out, also showing the property.

Our guests would be sitting calmly on the beach, and suddenly a fleet of military helicopters roared in, blowing sand everywhere. Into all the bungalows it went, into all the food in the kitchen, and when they left, there was a layer of sand on the bottom of the swimming pool.

The fights between Bob and me grew worse and worse.

"Terry, you should have left this goddam country years ago. You can't win. Don't you know that?" His voice would get strident, and that would make me even madder, and more determined to fight.

"I know we can win. Miguel says—"

"How do we know what Miguel is doing here with all those bankers? How do we know he's even working for us? Let's just get out of here before—"

"Never! I built this place, and I'm going to own it!"

And on and on.

At the same time, almost every time I finished my monthly visit at the *fideicomiso* office, one guy would take me aside and whisper, "Listen, Terry, just give me a million pesos, and I'll fix everything up for you. You can have the whole thing. A million pesos. No more worries. Trust me."

'Trust me'? A million pesos was $80,000 in those days. I could have gotten it from Doug in a minute. But if we decided to go that way, how could we ever prove that we had given the guy anything? Or would that turn into another emerald story?

Others on the coast were waiting too, but for their own reasons. They were not ready yet to make their claims at the office. If the land was legally in their name, the commission paid them for it, ever so slowly, and moved them to another place. But when they looked around and saw their neighbors getting offers of thousands of dollars from the big hotel chains up north, they decided to stall.

In the end, they got nothing at all.

One day, after a particularly trying session with the commission, I walked into the restaurant at Las Glorias, totally preoccupied. The restaurant was filled. I had completely forgotten about the banquet we had planned for another group of American travel agents.

As I entered, all eyes looked over at me expectantly. I saw that my guests were all nibbling on salads or hors d'oeuvres, but that not one person in the room was being served a main course! What had happened in the kitchen? The place was obviously falling apart without my attention!

I ran into the back to see what I could find out from Xavier. There he was at the stove, completely engulfed in smoke. Steam and flames shot almost to the ceiling. The oil had caught fire.

I panicked.

Without a moment's hesitation, I ran outside, just around the corner by the swimming pool.

I grabbed a bucket and scooped up a big load of sand. I rushed back into the kitchen, took aim, and threw the whole bucketful of sand onto the stove.

Xavier was covered from head to foot.

He turned around in a blinding rage, his butcher knife pointed straight at me. He was absolutely speechless.

Then without saying a word, he turned on his heel, walked straight out of the kitchen to Bob at the office, and quit.

All the waiters stood around the edges, their big brown eyes almost out of their heads.

"*¡Señora Theresa!*" said Ramón in a hushed voice. "What have you done?"

I was sputtering. "The whole building could have burned down!"

I was screaming. "Why didn't somebody do something?"

I looked out the window at the tense back of Xavier, receding in the distance. "Now where's he gone off to?"

"But *señora*, the fire was already out before you came in," said Ramón. "He was only chafing the red snapper and the shrimps." He gulped and continued bravely, "There was no danger."

I had ruined his whole dinner. Forty travel agents had seen me rush out of the kitchen, and then back in a split second later with a bucket.

But they hadn't guessed yet that I had actually garnished their seafood with sand.

"Jesús," I called, "I've got a headache. Get me a double vodka. I have to think." I sank down at the table where long ago I had taught them the restaurant business, and their first English words.

When I calmed down I realized that I had often seen Xavier chafe three or four pans of food at once. He was a real artist.

And I was turning into a real nut case.

There was nothing to do for it. I went out to the dining room and confessed. We all had a good laugh, and free drinks went around for everybody.

Luckily, there was enough shrimp salad in the walk-in cooler to feed forty people, though I explained they would have to wait for it a bit. I went back to the kitchen and had another double vodka.

I sat slumped over the table while the feverish preparation went on.

Then I thought of Xavier. He was a good chef. We had stolen him from one of the hotels downtown. He was a bit too temperamental sometimes, perhaps. Perhaps he gave the good-looking boys too much food for their meals, or too many special treats, but overall he was a valuable asset to us.

It took Bob all afternoon to persuade him to stay.

He didn't speak to me for six months.

The fighting with Bob heated up even more. One day I broke into the safe, took out all the official papers, and got on a plane for Guadalajara. Perhaps Judge José María could help us.

I had borrowed a short black wig from somebody, and I had on lots of purple eye shadow and a frumpy little print dress. I don't even remember why I thought it was important to be in disguise. Perhaps so I wouldn't involve him unnecessarily if he couldn't do anything? I don't know.

Getting off the plane, I felt like one of those cartoon figures at Disneyland. I was really going off the deep end.

Clutching onto my attaché case, I went straight to the federal building, where Bob had been held prisoner. I strode into a large room. A dozen secretaries were all busy punching away at their typewriters.

"I'm sorry, *señora*, the *señor juez* is in a very important conference," declared his personal secretary.

I hardly heard her. I went straight for the door and shoved it open. Several important-looking men sat around a large table. I had startled them. From the head of the table, José looked up at me, completely mystified. He didn't recognize me. I ripped off my black wig with a dramatic flourish, and stood there holding it in my hand, almost in tears.

"Theresa! Theresa!" was all he could say at first. He came over to me, explaining all the while to his colleagues, "Excuse me! This is a dear friend of mine." He put his arm around my shoulder.

"She's Dutch," he added, as if that would explain everything.

"Perhaps we should convene at another time," he said to the men, and the meeting was adjourned. José led me back through the long line of secretaries, my wig still in my hand, my own hair dripping wet from the humidity, while he tried to understand what I was doing there.

We went out to lunch, with all my papers. But he didn't need to look at them. "Listen, Teresita. Your husband is right. Just listen to him."

He looked at me sadly. "You can't fight those two people," he said, without naming names.

"Jesus," I thought. "Maybe I'd better listen. I've got the Reys on the one side and Salinas on the other. I've got Espinoza staying in my mother's house. But if he can't help me, and Armando can't help me—. And Enrique tried, and now José—"

Pick a sentence. Anyone with any sense would have concluded any one of them with "so why not get the hell out?" But my Dutch blood rose in my veins, and I simply could not do it.

Sadly I returned to Puerto Vallarta, determined to fight it out.

The town was really exploding in those days, with new people coming in every day both to visit and to stay permanently. I was starting to be looked on as one of the old timers!

The local judge often called me downtown to translate, if he needed to question somebody who spoke only English.

One morning I met him on the plaza, while I was on my way to the bank.

"Theresa, would you please come to my office? There are three American girls in trouble there, and I need to hear their testimony."

"Sure," I said.

I walked into the office. The official recorder was already there beside the desk with her little machine. The judge took his place, and then the girls were shown in by a couple of dirty policemen.

They were beautiful girls, tall, blonde, Nordic types, about nineteen or twenty years old. Right away I could see that they were from good families in the States. They were terrified as they walked in, and their eyes were red with crying.

"Try not to be upset," I assured them in English.

Three heads snapped up at the same time. You could almost reach out and touch the feeling of relief in the room. "I'm going to help you tell the judge your story," I said.

As they began to talk, it all began to sound familiar. The girls were traveling together, staying in youth hostels. The afternoon before, they had met a whole group of American hippies on the beach, who had already made several Mexican friends. They had gotten some food and some liquor, and the girls brought out their guitars and a flute, and they had a party on the beach. They built a bonfire and kept going into the night.

Gradually the joints were passed around. Nobody knew where they came from, or who started smoking.

Suddenly, the beach was filled with *federales*, who must have been hiding in the dunes. They were armed with machine guns.

All the young people were made to lie down on the sand, and surrender their property. Everything was put in a big pile, purses, watches, wallets, guitars, towels, food, everything. Then they were taken into custody immediately, about fifteen in all.

I looked up at the judge, waiting for a reaction. We had heard several of these stories in Puerto Vallarta. It had almost gotten to be a joke, when we saw a nice-looking van on the highway with a license plate from California or Colorado or Texas, that the *federales* had made another raid. Most of the time, we heard, it was the cops themselves who had sold the kids the marijuana beforehand. They had simply admired their car or their truck.

I had been through it already with José María and the sailboat at Yelapa.

But these girls were so young and so scared, that my heart went out to them. There was no insurance company to cover their loss, nor the loss of their friends' vans either, if marijuana was involved. The guys simply returned home and continued their car payments, with no car.

The judge's face was unmoved. Of course. Guilty until proven innocent.

However, I knew that Mexican judges were often more lenient, and less corrupt, than the police. There might be hope for these girls. They were still shivering from their night in jail (it was March), although the weather outside was warming up by that time.

"Do you have anything left?" I asked the girls. They were still wearing the little dresses they had started out in the previous afternoon.

"We have out rucksacks at the youth hostel," said one. "We've got a change of clothes." She started to cry again. "But they took all our money. And they've got our plane tickets!"

"Judge, don't you think—?" I began.

"Well, what do you want to do, Theresa?" he interrupted, already expecting me to make the proposal that was on my mind. I had done it before.

"Let me sign an affidavit, saying I will take care of these girls and make sure they don't run away. Then they can come and stay at my house for the seventy-two hours."

It was done. The judge was a good friend of mine—that is, unless I was the one in jail. Then his hands were tied, usually by the ones who had arranged for me to be there.

We went for the rucksacks, and I paid the bill at the youth hostel. Their vacation had been ruined, but otherwise the girls were not in bad shape. I could tell they were starting to feel better again, when they announced that they were ravenously hungry.

"Girls," I said, once we were home and I had brought out a big pile of meats and cheeses, "I'll go into town and talk to the honorary American consul to see what we can do. We've got a small pool outside, but I promised you'd either be with me or stay on my property, so you can't use the beach. Sorry."

"That's OK, Terry. I think we've had enough of beaches for a while!" they all said at once.

They had a ball playing with my kids while I was gone.

The consul told me he was so backed up that it would be three weeks before he could get to their problem. So I drove back and took them downtown to the telephone company one at a time, to let them make a call to their parents. Two girls had return tickets in their hands within forty-eight hours. The parents of the third girl couldn't afford it, but they told me they could repay me in a couple of months.

On the fourth day I put them on their plane for America. They were wonderful girls, fun to have as guests. I hated myself for thinking, "Well, you can kiss the money for that plane ticket good-bye!"

I got the money back in two months, long after I had gotten nice, chatty thank-you notes from each of the girls. My natural trust in humanity had not been misplaced this time. It was not another emerald story.

I think I felt even more grateful to them than they did to me.

The next time I was called to help out, it was at the hospital. Doctor Calderón grabbed me, again off the street. "There's a woman who tried to kill herself, Theresa," he said. "She's at the hospital, and we can't understand what she's trying to tell us."

"I'll follow you back," I said.

When I walked into the room, I saw a huge mound on the bed, in a yellow flowered dress. The woman must have had some kind of competition going with fat Theresa, my lawyer's wife. Only this one had short greasy blonde hair, and she was ugly.

Her whole body was shaking.

"Cokes!" she yelled at me, when she heard me speaking English. "I've got to have diet Cokes!"

It was the damndest thing I ever heard. No wonder Calderón had trouble making it out.

She had come to Puerto Vallarta to stage a suicide, in order to get revenge on her husband and make an international scandal. He was a well-known physician in Chicago.

She had almost succeeded, by taking an overdose of drugs. She was found in the bathroom of her room, at one of the luxury hotels. But her shaking was not from a drug habit. Not the hard stuff, anyhow. She was addicted to diet Cokes. They were the only thing that would calm her body down.

I started to laugh at her, but she got mad, and swore she was telling the truth. She looked like a frog.

"You can't find diet Cokes in Mexico," I told her.

She started to get hysterical. The nurses rushed in, and Calderón escorted me out into the hall. I told him what the woman had said. He shook his head. "These crazy Americans," his eyes sparkled. But he admitted an addiction like that was possible.

"You go find some diet Coke, Theresa," he said.

"You can't—"

He grabbed me and hugged me close to his stocky body and whispered, "*¡Dios mío!* I've always wanted to go to bed with you!"

He already knew my reply, from years of trying.

"Oh yeah?" I laughed. "But I haven't with you, my dear. I like 'em young and skinny!" We were good friends, Calderón and I.

"OK, you win. Get me a speed boat, and I'll go through all the boats in the marina. I'll get some Cokes for the crazy bitch."

"Get several cases," he called, as I went out the door of the hospital.

I had struck out on several attempts, when finally I pulled up to the *Dulcinea* out of San Diego, a gorgeous yacht, all shiny teak and brass. It must have been worth about $3 million.

I called up, and the owner looked over the side at me. "You have any diet Cokes? I've got a sick lady who can only survive with diet Cokes."

He looked dubious. "Come on up," he said, grudgingly. These boat owners hate it when an outsider comes aboard, getting dust all over everything and scratching the varnish.

"Yes sir!" I said, and saluted. He didn't have much of a sense of humor.

I explained my problem again, and he seemed pretty skeptical, but he led me to the cabin. "I can give you two cases," he said, bending down to a low cabinet.

The ceiling was a beautiful silk velour. I reached up to touch it.

"Don't!" he yelled, but too late. I had made fingerprints on the material, by rubbing it the wrong way. It would all have to be brushed out again.

I started to correct my mistake (perhaps a little on purpose), and he got even more agitated.

"Hey, man," I said, "this is Mexico. This boat is to live in, isn't it?"

I still couldn't get a smile out of him. But I got the Cokes.

"You really gonna save somebody with these?" he said, still dubious.

"Yessir!" I saluted, and hurried back to the hospital.

I wrestled the boxes into the hospital room, and the woman drank off the first case without a pause, her chins bobbing violently in all directions.

She topped it off with a gallon of water.

"Ahhh!" she said.

"Now what did you want to go and do a thing like that for?" I asked, referring to her suicide attempt.

"My husband said he wanted to divorce me. I'll get that bastard!" she snarled.

I knew I should have had some sympathy for her, but it was difficult. She didn't seem the least bit grateful for my efforts. Still, I stayed with her in the hospital that night, on a little bench, and the next night too.

I gave up three days for that woman. We were all relieved to get her on a plane back to America.

I saw Jim, the owner of the *Dulcinea*, later, and I even got him to relax a little over a few lobster dinners. He turned out to be a nice guy after all.

When I wheeled back into Las Glorias, chewing myself out for wasting my time with the Chicago matron, I had more troubles.

Guilberto was bending over our prized quarter horse, Juana Gallo, who was lying on her side in pain. He rushed up to me.

"*Señora*, we saw you do it before, but we got into trouble this time," he said. His eyes had a look of fear I had not seen before.

"Do what? What are you talking about, Guilberto?"

"You remember the last time she got out? You gave her a douche with the garden hose."

"*¡Cómo no!*" I said. "Of course." She had jumped the fence and gotten herself screwed by a wild horse. She was only two years old, and I didn't want her to get pregnant, so Guilberto and Carlos and my maids beat off the stallion, and then got the hose, all the while calming down the mare.

By talking to her slowly and steadily, we managed to get the hose into her hind parts, and even to scrub them out with a bar of blue laundry soap. My arm was way up inside her, past the elbow, and I worked until I got her completely cleaned out. It did the trick. She did not get pregnant.

From Guilberto's face, I could not imagine what was coming this time.

"Well, you know how the girls up in the mountains give themselves a douche with a Coca Cola or a 7-up?"

My heart sank.

The horse had gotten out again. In my absence, they had started to douche her with the same hose and the laundry soap. Then, to make sure of the results, when Juana Gallo was all slippery inside, they had shaken up a bottle of 7-Up and inserted that too.

The poor horse was lying miserably on her side. They were unable to get the bottle out. Guests from Las Glorias were starting to mill about. We all tried harder, but it was stuck.

The 7-Up incident has a happier ending than the diet Coke incident. We rushed into town to the vet and brought him back, and he managed to extract the bottle without harming the horse. The doctor did not need to warn us about homemade remedies in the future.

Though Puerto Vallarta was growing fast, it still had the feeling of a small town. I had always been proud of how safe everyone felt there, not like in a big city. But things were beginning to change.

My mother came back that summer from an extended stay in Holland, and Espinoza and his gang moved out.

I guess they figured they had had a good look at Las Glorias and had calculated the damage they could do there. I only hoped it wouldn't cost me too much.

She arrived carrying a bottle of Scotch from the duty-free shop. Scotch was hard to find in Mexico, especially Johnny Walker black, and it was a real treat.

"Let's have a drink," I offered.

"No thanks. I'm tired. I'm going to bed," she said, and started off to her house next door.

"We'll save it for tomorrow," I promised, and left it on the kitchen counter. "I'm tired too. Good night."

The kids' fan had broken in their bedroom, so they were excited at the chance to sleep with me. Little Dido was already asleep in my bed when I went up. The boys were asleep on the floor. Lupe had fixed up *petates*, little woven straw mats, for them, and they were thrilled to be "going native."

Bob and I no longer even made an attempt to share a bedroom.

In the middle of the night, I felt something brush my face, like a mosquito or a piece of light cloth.

Suddenly my nightgown was up and he was on top of me.

A small, wiry little bastard, smelling of liquor and breathing hard in my face.

"*Necesito sólo un momentito,*" he whispered roughly in my ear. "I only need a minute. No noise, cunt."

I tried to wrench free, but he had pinned both my wrists together with one of his hands, and he held the blade of a small knife at my throat with the other.

My only thought was of my daughter lying beside me in the bed, and of the boys.

I screamed and screamed, but no sound came out.

The guy wormed out of his swimming trunks and started moving on top of me. He didn't have another hand to rip off my clothes, but he was slimy with sweat, and his cock slid easily between my legs.

He started lurching and groaning over me, but he wasn't having any luck.

I was always a proper Dutch lady. Though lately with Enrique, I had started sleeping in the nude, before that I always wore a cotton nightgown and panties to bed, much to the annoyance of my husband. That night, the little sonofabitch had caught me during my period, and I was wearing two kotexes and two pairs of panties.

There was nowhere to direct his ardor, which was growing.

He was grunting with pleasure, pumping as hard as he could. I felt vile.

He squirmed around, trying to find an entrance without letting go of my hands.

"*¡Mis hijitos!*" I screamed, my kids! But still no sound came out of my mouth.

Suddenly I was fully awake, and the adrenalin was flowing.

'Only a *momentito?*' That bastard had had his moment.

With both knees, I kicked him as hard as I could, and sent him flying right into the massive cedar headboard behind me. It stunned him.

I rolled onto the floor, and in an instant he was on top of me again, but he had dropped his knife. I don't know how I did it, but I wrestled him out of the bedroom and away from the children. I ran down the stairs, and he made a dive for me. He was strong, but I was too.

I kicked and scratched and shoved him against the wall by the door. He must have been frightened by the noise, knowing there were other people in the house.

He ran out into the night, and I locked the door behind him. I stood there panting, still unable to make a sound.

He needn't have been worried about the others. The kids, Bob, and the maids, further down the hall, slept through the whole thing.

I ran upstairs and woke up Bob, and managed to squeak out a few words.

He rushed to his dresser. "My wallet! He stole my wallet!" he yelled. He grabbed his revolver and ran downstairs, dragging me behind.

I blocked the door so he couldn't run out. Somehow I managed to convince him that the guy was dangerous.

My husband, who used to jump over the side of his Jaguar into the driver's seat, and had won trophies in several sports, was not as young as he used to be, whether he would admit it or not.

"He didn't do anything to me!" I pleaded.

"Then why all the hysteria?" he said, irritated. Then he got agitated all over again. "Kaiser! Where's Kaiser?" Bob yelled. The German shepherd was nowhere to be seen.

"Another bitch in heat, I suppose. Some watchdog," he sneered.

I sank down on the floor, nauseous. I had bruises all over my body.

"Look at this," he said. "The little Mexican motherfuck drank that whiskey your mother gave us!" Sure enough, he had helped himself to about half the bottle of Scotch, to fortify himself before he came up. And he had borrowed my own paring knife to hold at my throat.

Just then we heard a sound. There was someone walking on the gravel path in the garden. Bob dived down on the floor next to me. He lay on his back, aiming the pistol at the door with both hands.

My mother walked in.

"*Theresa, was ist los*? Why are all the lights on?" she asked. I squeaked out a few words, but she couldn't make it out.

"Do you know what happened to me?" interrupted my seventy-year-old mother impatiently. "Some guy just came into my bedroom with a knife and tried to rape me."

"You came over here to tell us that? You could have been killed," I tried to say, but few of the words could be heard.

"What'd you do?" asked Bob.

"Sonofabitch tried to kill me," she said, "but I grabbed the *machete* beside my bed and swung at him."

She had it still, gleaming darkly in her hand. She held it up proudly. "Nearly got him too!" she laughed.

"What a broad!" said Bob.

For once, I think he liked her.

Next morning when things settled down, she was able to describe the man to the police.

He was little over five feet tall, but muscular. And he had the large head of an Indian woman tattooed on his arm. Bob found his credit cards, strewn all through the garden, and finally his wallet, with only the money missing. About forty dollars. A bottle of rum in my mother's house was half empty too. The little shit had really helped himself, although not everything had gone according to his plan.

Our kids' clothes were gone from the ironing board. That one puzzled us.

A few months later, we saw his picture in the Guadalajara papers. He had attempted rape again, and he had been caught this time. An eight-year-old child had also been detained. The boy had been sent in first through the window, to let the rapist into the house.

The caption read, "I only need a minute."

23

Amidst great hullabaloo, the first big showplace of the *fideicomiso* was finally completed and ready to open.

It was a first-class hotel on the beach at Bucerías, a large building with sixty luxury rooms, and a huge, handsome *palapa* bar out by the swimming pool. The sons and daughters of the local fishermen and *rancheros* (the town is right next to Nuevo Vallarta) had been trained as hotel staff. President Echeverría came down for the inauguration, and we were all invited too.

The party was a real bash. There was lobster spilling all over the tables, and champagne flowing. We all had too much to drink.

On the way back home, we came across a gruesome sight on the highway. Rafael de la Cruz had left just ahead of us in his tiny Volkswagen. His friend Louie, a partner of Carlos O'Brian's, who took over the restaurant at his death, and a third friend were in the car. A horse had suddenly jumped out of the ditch in front of them, and they had smashed into it head-on.

I was driving in the station wagon with Rita and all my kids and maids. We couldn't believe our eyes, as we stopped, horrified, and got out of our car to help.

Blood was spurting everywhere through the car and onto the highway. Rafael and Louie were slumped in the front. They appeared to be dead. Three legs and most of the horse's body were inside the car with them, and its head, sliced clean off, was filling up the luggage compartment with blood.

The police were already there. One by one, everyone returning from the gala hotel party pulled over beside the highway. These two men especially were everybody's friends, two in Puerto Vallarta who could always be trusted.

The three bodies were lifted carefully out of the car and brought to the hospital in town. Doctor Soto, the "battlefield doctor" who lived in my mother's house, was already there to meet them. Rafael had cuts all over his body, but Louie was even in worse shape. His liver was smashed.

In those primitive hospital conditions, the doctor moved fast. He slit Louie open the length of his abdomen, took out a portion of his liver, made the rest of the needed repairs, and sewed him back up.

The volunteer Red Cross workers scattered everywhere throughout the town, requesting blood. A steady stream of us passed in and out of the hospital for three days and lay beside these men, giving them their life, drop by drop. Ironically, it was Rafael himself, the editor of the local newspaper, who had organized the Red Cross years before, after an Aeromexico plane crash up in the mountains above Yelapa.

Those who had already given blood spent more time picking splinters of glass, one by one, out of Rafael's face and upper body, for three days.

We dropped our households, we put our businesses on hold, the whole town worked together, and we saved them. It was a wonderful moment for Puerto Vallarta.

Shortly before this, when my mother Dido returned to Mexico, she had been furious to find Doctor Soto still living in her house. He had never paid her rent, never given her a slim peso for utilities. She started after him, cussing him out every time they met.

He tried to weasel out of it with his oily charm. He brought her cognac from the "love boats" in the harbor, where he had inspection duties. She took the maid's cleaning bucket, filled with dirty water, and dropped it on him from the balcony.

"You spend all my money on whores and liquor, you *bandido!*" she yelled. It was all in Dutch, but somehow she had picked up the word *bandido*.

"Mother, shut up!" I interrupted. "This is an important man. You'll get deported."

"This little so-an-so—"

"You foreigner!" yelled Soto. "You're the one who should go!"

"I'll call my Dutch ambassador. He'll get my money for me."

This went on and on until finally, after Rafael's accident and the doctor had become somewhat of a local hero, they made an arrangement.

"Look here at your legs, *señora*," he said, kneeling on the floor in front of her and examining them. "These varicose veins are serious. You cannot allow them to grow worse. A blood clot could develop and go straight to your heart. I will take them out for you."

I was translating for him. My mother was listening with close attention. She seemed interested.

But at this last suggestion, I drew the line. This wasn't an emergency, like Rafael's, after all.

"Are you crazy?" I said to my mother in Dutch. "He's right. You have to tend to your legs. But have you seen this hospital in Puerto Vallarta? You'll hate it. They've got no blood bank, no anesthetist, no lab—their equipment is fifty years old."

"Well, it's one way to get paid by the sonofabitch. Tell him I'll swap the operation for my rent money."

"Mother, you don't need the money. You're covered entirely by insurance in Holland. All the hospitalization and everything. Why didn't you have it done there?"

She was looking away, already bored with the subject.

"Why don't you go back and have it done there now?" I continued, choked with exasperation.

Soto was eager. "You tell your mother not to drink anything tonight. Not one ounce of liquor!" he said. "I'll see her in the hospital tomorrow at six in the morning, and she'll get the best operation she can get."

I relayed the message, adding that we'd better bring along a mattress from home, because those at the hospital were filthy with blood and urine.

Even that didn't put her off. She was determined to get her rent money.

Soto's eyes lit up. "I'll make the bill real big," he said, rubbing his hands. "You make up the price, and we'll send the bill to Holland so her insurance pays. OK? A deal?" He laughed heartily.

The next morning we showed up at the hospital, with the mattress hanging out the back of the station wagon. She was brought into the operating room, and then Soto stepped out to invite me in there with them, in case she started spouting off again in Dutch.

I love hospitals! I should have been a nurse. I put on the smock and the face mask, and watched everything. As he made his expert incisions, the blood started flowing everywhere. I must have replaced his gloves half a dozen times.

He cut into one leg near a vein and began pulling slowly, carefully. Yards and yards of blood vessels ended up in the stainless steel bowl beside the operating table.

"You want to try?" he asked.

"Sure!"

"Be careful not to break the vein," he said, as he continued checking her heartbeat and her pulse. "Very healthy. She'll live until she's a hundred years old."

After he finished with the other leg, he handed me the bowl. "Perhaps she'll want to have these for a souvenir," he said. I looked down at the bloody mass. "When she comes out, tell her I'll throw in the ambulance trip home for free."

By late afternoon, she was ready to go home, to skip the usual nine days' recovery period in the hospital. The open vent holes near the ceiling of each room did a good job of moving out the hot air in the place, but they also carried all the sounds of screaming children and the women in labor. She had had it.

The doctor was right. She was a tough old broad. She came through the whole thing beautifully, and soon she was out driving around through Puerto Vallarta again in her little Volkswagen, finding out where the action was.

Soto did not fare so well. Shortly after this, his days of grabbing onto the boobs of tall, blonde women were swiftly over. He chose the wrong woman. The wife of an American official at the consulate in Guadalajara accused him of raping her in his office, and he lost everything.

My mother finally got him out of her house, but not the way she had wanted. He had been an amusing adversary for her.

Enrique came through town again, and off I went. I stayed away even longer this time. Bob's remark about 'hysteria' after my rape attempt was really grating on me, and I had to get out.

We were on our way to El Paso again. "We've got some trouble with hoof-and-mouth disease," Rick explained.

There were several little crates in the rear of the plane.

"What's in there?" I asked.

"Well—" he hesitated. "It's better if you don't know."

That made me angry, and finally he told me. We were smuggling mercury into the United States.

"I get about $40,000 every time I make this trip," he said.

Mexico is a rich land, filled with valuable minerals. In Chihuahua, besides amethyst and other crystals, large quantities of mercury are to be found, dripping down and spilling out freely over the mountains. Enrique paid men to gather it, and then he "marketed" it up north. Mercury eats through metal, so it had to be carried in wooden cases.

We landed in El Paso without incident, and found our favorite motel with the water bed. Rick was feeling cocky. A waitress from the bar brought us drinks to the room, and he flirted with her outrageously, I thought. She was acting as if I wasn't even there in the bed beside him.

"Cut it out!" I yelled. "I'm here, aren't I?"

"Oh, Theresa, what does it hurt? A little harmless game—"

"I don't like it. You do that once more, and I'm out of here."

"What are you so upset about?"

I got up, still naked.

"You wouldn't dare. You're too Dutch to go out there like that."

I made a run for the door, and continued thirty or forty feet until I hit the swimming pool. I sat there in the water until he came over and begged me to come back.

I had wanted to embarrass him. It worked.

But I saw that our relationship was taking an odd turn.

Enrique got caught smuggling about a year later, and barely got his plane out in time. He was not allowed back in.

The next time he came through Puerto Vallarta, he needed a car for some business appointments. Bob was out of town, so I lent him his.

Bob flew in that afternoon from San Francisco, and immediately asked about his car.

"Oh God, I loaned it to a friend," I confessed.

I think my husband was actually more upset about the car than the friend. He stewed about it all afternoon, and when Rick drove in that night and started walking up the driveway, Bob tore out after him.

"You sonofabitch! What are you doing with my car!" he shouted. He wound up, and was about to hit him.

Rick was cool. "Hey, man, back off!" he said.

I ran between them. Bob was still shouting. And by then my lover was saying he was going to kill him.

When it was all over, I stood back and took a long look.

"What have I gotten myself into?" I thought. "I've got two men here fighting for me." (Well, that wasn't exactly right. Bob was fighting for his car.) "One I can't divorce because we're too closely tied together to this hotel thing, and the other one I can't marry."

I heaved a deep, bitter sigh. "And to tell the truth, I'm not so sure I want either one of them."

In December of '73, the vultures started to move in.

Miguel Salinas came by Las Glorias and explained to us that the Reys were getting too "heavy." The officers of our corporation had decided it was better if the hotel manager had some experience in law. They had appointed Licenciado García to take over.

That was it. Like a lightning bolt.

After seven and a half years, we were out of the hotel business.

I had designed it, built it, financed it, worried over every detail of it, and now our figurehead president had taken it away from us. I was sick. Miguel assured us that he was merely protecting the investment.

Investment! He hadn't contributed a penny toward Las Glorias. On the contrary, he had gotten weeks, even months of free rooms out of the deal. He had timed the take-over just before the big influx of tourists at Christmas time, when all the deposits were in.

Bob was actually kind of relieved. He was still to operate the restaurant, under the new agreement, which would give us a good income. We had our house and free utilities. We had the company truck, and meals at the restaurant. We could continue to live very well.

I consoled myself with the bigger plans we still had with Doug Walker. What else could I do?

Licenciado García was a large, repulsive man, with a pock-marked face, greasy hair and a sort of lumpy body. He was a second-rate lawyer in Miguel's entourage. He had no experience in the hotel business, and he quickly rubbed everyone the wrong way.

One day, Bear and Buster were out playing, climbing up to get coconuts in the trees near the office. García's new secretary came out and told them to get down. "Those are not your trees. You must stay on your property," she told them.

When they started to move toward the swimming pool, she informed them that the pool was off limits too.

They came running home, with our maids. Lupe was distraught. She told me everything that had happened, and I saw red.

I marched over toward the office. The slimy manager was standing in front, leaning against my arch, with a sly grin on his face. Something snapped inside me.

I lowered my head like a toro, and charged at him, hitting him so hard in his big gut that he fell over backwards.

"*Señora*, we have orders from señor Salinas—"

"You can screw your orders!" I screamed at him, my whole body shaking. "Nobody's going to tell me I can't use *my* pool."

I straightened my head as best I could—my neck hurt for weeks afterwards—and marched right past him with the boys and the maids, to the swimming pool. He just watched us through the louvered windows for the rest of the afternoon.

Miguel flew in the following day, but he avoided talking to me.

Hotel Las Glorias quickly began to slide downhill.

It's a lot of hard work to keep a place looking clean and trim in the tropical climate. We saw the evidence of decline everywhere. The bungalows were now only somewhat clean, instead of spotless. The sheets began to disappear. The grounds were becoming scruffy. The trees were no longer being repainted at the bottom with white lime, to ward off the beetles that bore to the center and killed them in no time. The planes no longer flew over with DDT, and the rats grew bigger.

We were sick to our stomachs. Not only because of our pride in the place, but because this new look would surely affect business in the restaurant as well. Customers were no longer thrilled to be staying there.

Alejandro, Ramón, Jesús—they all walked around the place with sad faces. They had been good workers since its opening. They must have felt a vested interest in the place as well.

We had never had a problem with them. In fact, once when an American tourist lost a very valuable watch, he stirred up trouble, accusing everyone of stealing it. But Guillermo, our youngest bellboy, found it buried in the sand, not a yard away from the door of the man's bungalow. The sand had worked it down a few inches already. With pleasure, the man gave him a large reward.

But now, our workers found themselves in trouble with every move they made. García claimed the staff didn't respect him.

Xavier left us. Others soon followed.

Bob was fit to be tied. He spent a lot of time flying back and forth to America, to talk to Doug Walker. He was our best hope. Until then, we were stuck in our house, in the corner of some property whose ownership was still under question.

I spent my time at the office of the *fideicomiso*.

I also got a job with Grubb & Ellis, a California real estate firm, which had an office in Puerto Vallarta. I was hired by my old friend Guillermo Wulff, who had built the set for *Night of the Iguana*, years before I came down, and many of the best houses in town since then. Once again I was working with builders and architects, and especially since it took my mind off Las Glorias, I was enjoying myself.

I was sitting in the Oceano one morning at a breakfast meeting with Bill Wulff and a couple of other hotel owners and builders, and some officials from the *fideicomiso*. The new D.A., Herrera de Cairo, was there with us. We had met through Ofelia's husband, and when we discovered how much we had both liked and admired Mel Melton, we became immediate friends.

I hadn't noticed that the D.A. had left the table, but suddenly I looked up, and he was coming back toward me from the entrance of the restaurant. He bent down and whispered in my ear.

"Look at me and tell me if you're in trouble with the law," he said, with a grave face.

I laughed. "Not as far as I know. I've been in jail a few times, but I guess you've heard about that."

He went back to the entrance and conferred with someone, then stepped inside and signaled to me. I went over.

"Please come outside with me, but don't run," he cautioned in a low voice.

"Run? Me?" I said. I still thought it was a joke.

"There are four *federales* here, who say I must take you to jail. I'm sorry."

"Don't worry about it," I shrugged. "I love to go to jail. I'm the cleaning lady in there!"

I walked through the door, and was immediately surrounded by four uniforms. We all followed Herrera de Cairo to his office.

These cops from Guadalajara looked disappointed. They thought they would be able to make a big scene, to nab a *gringa* in public in front of her friends and handcuff her, perhaps drag her away screaming. But I went calmly, almost cheerfully.

What could they possibly be charging me with now?

Silly question.

Herrera got on the phone with Juárez in Guadalajara, who was still my lawyer, believe it or not. Even after the emerald, even after the take-over at Las Glorias. I guess I just hadn't had the time or the occasion to find another one.

By listening to my end of the conversation, I made out the reasons I was sitting in that office, waiting to be led off to jail. They were possibly the most preposterous yet.

Back in 1969, I had engaged Adolfo Rey to take care of my documents, and to get me my official working papers, since by then I had been in Mexico for five years. I paid him by check in advance, six thousand pesos.

I've already mentioned how he, the brother of Ignacio, had had to flee the country in the middle of all that, leaving me without visa or working papers for several years. I thought I had explained that one enough—to the authorities in Puerto Vallarta, to the authorities in Mexico City.

But that wasn't the problem this time.

He had never cashed my check. Over the course of the next few years, I had forgotten about it.

Now, apparently, since I still had the gall to sit on a corner of my land and demand justice from the *fideicomiso*, he had cashed it—five years later—leaving my account 27 centavos short.

I was overdrawn by two American pennies, and I was back in jail.

Herrera looked sick, but there was nothing he could do.

I spent the first hour or so at the window, finding friends on the street and sending messages. I asked one of them to let Lupe know where I was, and gave her instructions for the children. I asked my pharmacist friend, don Conrado, to try to find Bill Wulff and tell him. I got a message to Ofelia.

On her own, she telephoned Enrique León, and he sent me $3,000 immediately from Mexico City. But of course, it didn't help me.

Seventy-two hours was the rule.

Nobody found Bill Wulff until nightfall. He came looking for me, when he discovered I hadn't come back to the office. Nellie, his fashionable wife, came along with him to the jail, bringing a hot seafood platter from the El Dorado. They stayed around and visited a little.

As they were leaving, he looked at me sadly, and said, "You can't win, Theresa."

He was shaking his head slowly from side to side. "Perhaps you should pack your bags. They'll shoot you if they have to."

I squeezed his hand in thanks for his concern.

Leave? Where? I had no place to go.

Herrera came back later with a burly guard, and said he thought I would be safer in the federal jail near his office, than in the city jail. But I took one look at the vicious face of the guard, and asked him to let me stay there. At least the city jail was a pretty lively place.

After my recent rape attempt, I was not spending the night alone with that guy. He agreed.

Within the hour, "lively" was hardly the word to describe it. At about eleven o'clock, as I was settling down to sleep on my usual top bunk, a small young woman was led in—or rather dragged in, kicking and screaming.

She was only about four-six, but she was feisty. She was a whore, who had been arrested for stealing money from one of her tricks.

"Hey! Nena! Nena!" called the male prisoners from the other side, as soon as they saw her. Apparently she was a favorite of theirs.

She gave them an obscene sign, which delighted them, and continued screaming at the cops who had wrestled her in, and cussing them out.

"*¡Cabrones!*" she screeched, leading off the attack. "You sonsofbitches! Don't you get enough at home?"

Then, "I want to make a formal complaint!" she said to the air. "These men tried to fuck me in the car before they brought me in here."

The men looked half sheepish and half proud, and started joking among themselves. She punched and jabbed at them, and finally got away from their grip, starting toward the bunks where I was.

A heel from her shoe was broken. She blamed the cops for that too. "Sons of whores!" she shouted. "Your mothers are no better than I am!"

The reference to their mothers got them all stirred up, but they soon forgot about it again, as they saw her walk across the room.

It was masterful, the way she moved her hips! She couldn't have been hurt too badly.

The men locked up on the other side were out of their minds, crawling up the bars of the cell like monkeys to try to get closer, and shouting "Nena! Nena!"

She sat down on the lower bunk and put her foot on the bed next to her, to get a closer look at her shoe, all the time squirming so that the guys across the room had the best possible view. Her skirt was already about as short as could be, but it fell back even farther, revealing everything.

The men were cheering deliriously, and rubbing their dirty underwear against the bars.

"You like that, huh?" she called over to them. "You want more, *hombres? ¿Eh?* You want a little smell? Come on over here and take it!"

She checked her face in a broken compact, put on another heavy dab of rouge, and then suddenly she was on her feet, squirming around to a rock beat in her head, and lifting her skirts up high, front and back. She was lost in her own world.

The men were clapping and humping in rhythm.

"*¡Andale, ándale!*" they screamed. "Give us a show! We love you, Nena!"

Hard-ons were popping out of underwear shorts at an alarming rate.

That only encouraged the girl to writhe more. She shook her long dark hair back and forth in front of her face.

I started to get into the swing of it myself. I grabbed onto my Tarzan rope, and jumped to the floor, to join in the clapping.

"Go for it, Nena!" I shouted. "Let's have some action!" It was a party!

The police looked positively torn apart. Their bodies were moving cautiously in rhythm. They were obviously enjoying it. They were only sons of *rancheros*, after all, with no training.

But their eyes were constantly darting about nervously, knowing that they were supposed to disapprove, checking to see that no one else saw them looking.

Nena crouched down and shoved her breasts together with her hands. Then she pawed the floor with one foot, and started to run toward the men, like a bull in a bullfight.

"*¡Toro!*" they all shouted, and screamed with delight.

With each pass, the night air of Puerto Vallarta's center filled with shouts of "*¡Olé! ¡Olé!*"

All at once the guards in the towers shot into the air with their machine guns. That brought the cops in the room around, but the men behind bars could have cared less.

I, however, dived back up to my bunk. Perhaps I had thought more about what Bill told me than I cared to.

The guy who seemed to be in charge, more or less, grabbed Nena and yanked her off to solitary confinement.

"Wait a minute, *hijo de puta!*" she screamed. "I've got to go to the toilet first!"

He left her alone for a minute, and the catcalls from the men got even louder. She had started to take off all her clothes, in full view.

The man grabbed her again and threw her into the small four-by-four cell, where she spent the rest of the night howling like a hyena. About four in the morning, the mayor came by and ordered them to give her a tranquilizer to shut her up.

I think we were all sad to see her disappear. It was the most fun I had had in a long time.

But not even Nena was enough to take away my uneasiness about being in jail again. Each time, the reasons for arresting me were getting slimmer, the charges more contrived.

At least in the past, it was true that I had hit Norma—though I was never charged with assault. And it was true that my papers were not in order—though certainly not for my lack of trying.

Now, within a year, someone had kidnapped Bob, and someone had gotten to my bank account, knowing that a check for 6000 pesos would make it overdrawn.

One night soon after I got out, we heard unexplained gunshots on the grounds near our house. I started to fear for my children, and I decided to make a move. I would take them to Canada.

Who knows? Perhaps the handsome Malcolm MacNeill was not so bad after all. With his money, he could protect us and give us a good life. I longed to join him in his dream, to sail the world for a year, where the kids and I would be out of everyone's grasp.

Bob was in favor of it. "That'll be good for them," he said. "Maybe they'll learn English." He agreed to stay on in Mexico to protect our interests. There wasn't a lot he could do, but at least our property would not be abandoned to the gangsters. Bear and Buster were excited about learning to ski.

So I packed up all our bags, about six hundred pounds over the limit, and we flew to Vancouver.

Rita had moved back there and found herself a man. Many of our favorite guests at Las Glorias over the years lived there too, senators, bankers, and lawyers. I had many contacts, and many friends. I stayed several months. It was a healthy, quiet time for me.

Malcolm and I resumed our relationship, and I continued to pretend that my feelings weren't, well, tepid.

Down in Puerto Vallarta, my mother traveled in and out of town from visits to Holland, and she and Bob learned to live with each other, or at least next door to each other, in a friendly way. It was while I was in Vancouver that I saw my buddy Candelario Ramos on television, being led off in handcuffs on marijuana charges. Later I learned that the charges were never proved.

I looked forward to life for the five of us at sea. But Malcolm had other plans.

One day toward the end of summer, he started talking about finding boarding schools for the kids. Bear was growing more and more jealous of him, in defense of his father. Nothing was working out the way I had hoped. Even Malcolm's life, though safe, was starting to seem dull.

Therefore, it was a relief in more ways than one, when Doug Walker telephoned me from Oklahoma.

The *fideicomiso* had finally come to a decision. After all of our efforts, they had finally agreed to let us buy Las Glorias and go ahead with the development. At last! I must have punctured his eardrums with my screams of joy.

Bob and I met Doug Walker in Mexico City on February 6, 1975, at the central offices of the commission.

Doug had a cashier's check along, in the amount of $265,000, as a downpayment on the property. Better yet, the acceptance of our money represented a guarantee from the government.

Salinas and the Reys could not screw us around any longer.

Miguel was also there, "protecting his interests," by which he meant that he wanted Doug Walker for himself.

The check was received, with handshaking all around. We had a grand celebration in Mexico City that night.

In less than twenty-four hours, we were again sitting there in the offices. The local head of the *fideicomiso* had been asked to deliver the message.

"Your check has not been accepted. You will not be allowed to buy the property at Las Glorias," he said in Spanish.

"You black son of a bitch—"

"Listen, *puta*, go home to Holland. Mexico is for the Mexicans."

I started to charge at him, but there were guards around him in an instant.

Bob and Doug hadn't understood the Spanish, but they knew from my actions that it was bad. I managed to kick the commissioner a good one in the shins before I was dragged away.

And the land? Did it belong to Cloro's family, who still held the lease? No way.

Overnight, the best beach property in Puerto Vallarta had been split down the middle. Half was purchased by the Reys, half by Salinas.

It was a fine day for Mexico. These mortal enemies had agreed on something, perhaps for the first time.

I refused to accept it. Doug went back to America with his check, and Bob went up there too, to look for a place to live. But I was determined to remain in Mexico City until I got some satisfaction from the big shots.

I made arrangements, for the times when I would be in town, to stay at the home of Racán, ironically—one of our *prestanombres*. He was the one who had mysteriously joined Juárez in the Guadalajara shoot-out at the Hilton.

Why did I still trust them?

For one thing, Miguel had now begun hinting that the commission would still hear our case, and was willing to pay us as they had been paying the others, for their expropriation of the property. He was going to help us. A figure was even named. $150,000. Though Las Glorias was worth millions by that time. I continued to hope.

Armando was crushed, for my sake. He offered to take my three kids home with him, to leave me free to travel back and forth. His mother, doña Luisa, fell in love with little Dido and took her to stay in the small village of Ameca, where she still lived.

The boys stayed on Armando's fabulous old *hacienda* in the mountains, which he had acquired through litigation. A huge, two-story house with tall columns, a swimming pool fed by a natural stream, and acres of ranch land and sugar cane, it was one of the oldest *haciendas* in Jalisco. The boys were in heaven. The place had its own church with a big bell from the 1840's, its own stables, and its own bull ring.

There's no point in describing in detail those long, dreary hours in the office in Mexico City. I made no progress.

The Racáns had a big luxurious home, with treasures acquired, who knows how? It was filthy. I spent the evenings cleaning it up, as any good Dutchwoman would, venting the frustration I continued to gather up during the day.

Every day, hundreds of us presented ourselves at the office and took a number. Then we waited. The office was filled with all sorts of people anxious to have their cases re-examined. We were all in the same boat. Many of the Indians had walked hundreds of miles. The stench was terrible.

I made copies of all my documents. My number moved slowly down toward 100. I went for other documents, and started over again with a new number. I talked to lawyers. My number moved down to 40. I had very little money. I was buying cigarettes one at a time, for 60 centavos.

Señora Racán had an extra car sitting at home, but she never offered it to me. I took the bus, or walked four or five miles every day. And I found out what I knew already. Las Glorias was not the only property in trouble.

We were hearing stories everywhere about retired Americans losing their homes and their land.

When my number finally reached the teens—18, I think it was—the top commissioner of the *fideicomiso* left the country for a trip to Italy and Spain. The whole office was put on hold.

I returned to Las Glorias from time to time, but it was too difficult for me to stay there. Word must have gotten out that Armando was helping me with the kids. He was a clever lawyer. Perhaps they were no longer sure which side he was on.

One morning, without warning, the bulldozers appeared and the *fideicomiso* began making "improvements" on the land.

One by one, I watched the bungalows I had built by hand, with concrete mixed to last a hundred years, crushed beneath their power.

I was desolate.

Cloro's heavenly angels toppled off their pedestals beside the big entrance arch. The original paintings that Daniel Lechón had done for each of the rooms had long since been stolen. The little stream that used to flow through the back part of the property was straightened until it all but disappeared.

In the front, a retaining wall was built, which resulted in cutting the luxurious, sandy beach down to less than a third of what it had been. The swimming pool, the restaurant, the tennis courts, all were torn out. All that was left was the original well that was there when I first talked to Cloro.

I could only watch. Until they settled my appeal in Mexico City, I was living on someone else's land.

They spent millions making a new entrance to the place. A long, broad road was graded and made ready for cobblestones. Some of the palm trees were knocked down. When the trunks of others were covered up with earth, they slowly began to die. The workers built a huge fountain in the center, with beautiful sculptures of horses' heads. Elegant lampposts were installed, with globes that appeared to come out of the mouths of fiery dragons. All this was done in a big hurry, while other projects, like the highway by-pass up behind the town, which could have relieved the impossible congestion in the center, languished half finished. At Las Glorias we had a huge fountain, while the Mexicans across the road didn't even have water lines.

"Now, what the hell are you doing to my land?" I asked a local official one day.

"Theresa, don't worry about it. You'll get your money from the expropriation. And you'll be buying your own, at 500 pesos per square meter, right? We are just going ahead and spending that money in advance, to improve the land. You'll have all the benefits for your houses."

Why did I listen to such doubletalk? Perhaps because some of it made sense.

We agreed, he and I, that Puerto Vallarta had grown too fast. It had never been planned properly, to accommodate all the thousands of people who had filled in the two miles between us and town, and by then had stretched out even beyond us. We needed bigger water lines, bigger sewer lines, bigger power lines. They were to be put underground, to keep Puerto Vallarta a tropical paradise. I could only agree with all of this. I had long since lost any hope of getting a fee, as promised, from each hook-up to the water line Bob and I had put in.

Then the construction started to slow down.

And then it stopped.

The *fideicomiso* was having trouble financially. The bills had started coming due for the high living of the officials, for their world-wide junkets to look at various engineering projects, and for the extravagance of their dreams at home. Huge water and sewer pipes were stuck around at random, half in the ground, half out. The cobblestones lay scattered in piles beside the new entrance, a prey to theft. The potholes grew. Kids came by with slingshots and took out the new light globes. I must admit I got some pleasure in taking a couple shots myself.

When the peso was devalued in 1976, there was no hope of continuing. The tourists continued to come down because the prices were good, but Las Glorias remained a desert for four more years after that.

I am sick to my stomach as I write this.

I loved the Mexican people. I still do now. They have beautiful, gentle souls that warm my heart.

A lot of them tell me they need a revolution. They need to throw out the crooks, to retrieve all the money that has been stolen, term after presidential term, from the treasury. But they are afraid. There is no leader. All firearms have been confiscated. Those who stir up the people soon disappear. They are trapped.

Perhaps they are trapped in their own traditions. Corruption began long ago, with Huerta and Carranza, earlier presidents who stole the treasury and made plans to take it out of the country—perhaps even before them. President Santa Anna, of Alamo fame, even sold his own people, the Indians of Yucatán, to Cuban slaveowners, at a few pesos a head.

Others are afraid of an uprising. The grandfathers and grandmothers still remember the horrors of the revolution at the beginning of this century, and discourage their sons and grandsons from becoming involved. Some others are still comfortable enough that they willingly put up with the *bandidos* in office, to keep things stable.

Now they are crushed by a staggering national debt. Inflation bleeds them daily.

A Mexican in a high position recently told me he had calculated that, if Americans were allowed to buy outright the coastline property they now hold on the Pacific, as foreigners are allowed to do in other lands, that amount alone would pay the national debt. Not to mention that a gesture of good faith like that could encourage an explosion of American tourism as never before.

I heard over twenty years ago from my Mexican friends, as soon as I arrived and steadily ever since, "You Americans, you could help us. Come on down with your soldiers. We will not fight. We are not revolutionaries. The only way we'll ever make it is for Mexico to become the 51st State!"

I don't think I agree with that solution. Mexico is its own proud land, with its own rich traditions. But I must say that my gentle Mexican people deserve better.

While I was in the capital in 1975, haunting the *fideicomiso* offices, the news came that Judge José María Macias, that dear gentleman friend of mine, had committed suicide.

He had returned from a trip to Paris with his secretary, the girl he taught to play tennis at Las Glorias, and found his position terminated as judge. Apparently he had refused one time too many to bend justice for those in power. He was thrown out in disgrace. He had no job, no retirement, no reputation. He took an overdose of sleeping pills.

He left seven children.

For the second time in my life that I can remember, I cried.

24

On Mother's Day of 1975, May 10, I was staying in Mexico City, when I got a frantic call from my husband.

About eight o'clock that evening, Bob, who insisted on strict rules for bedtime, had been moving the kids toward the stairway. Don Andrés, Cloro's old coconut man, who still had his shack at the entrance to our place across from El Infierno, came running into the house yelling. Several of his kids were with him. They all started talking at once in Spanish.

Exasperated, Bob waited for an explanation.

"It's grandma! They say she went right through the wall, and she's lying out there in her car!"

Because of the soft roar of the waves, they hadn't heard anything.

They all ran to the highway, and there she was, crushed inside, still conscious. She was framed by a VW-shaped hole in the brick wall beside the highway. The steering wheel was bent square.

She handed Bob her purse and started crawling out of the car. The ambulance and the police arrived shortly afterwards, and then Bob called me.

She had gone out to dinner with Dorothy Sparks. It was getting hard for Dorothy to get around easily, and she had moved into town. My mother dropped her off and was turning in from the highway to Las Glorias.

The curve in front of our place had never been banked properly. For years, people in town referred to it as *la muerte*, the "death curve."

A huge eighteen-wheeler coming in from the airport cut too far into her lane, and sent her little Volkswagen flying through the air. She surprised the hell out of a little man who was standing at the wall, taking a piss. He leaped aside just in time.

The truck driver apparently never saw it or felt it, and never stopped.

When I arrived the next morning, Calderón met me in front of the hospital.

"She's a tough old bird," he said. "She has twenty-two bones broken, but she'll be OK. We're flying in a bone specialist from Guadalajara."

I thanked him and went to the room. She was in traction, with both legs up in the air. Her arms were broken, several ribs, and her nose. She looked awful.

I was convulsed with pity for her. Here she was, an elderly woman in a foreign country where she didn't speak the language, flat on her back and completely helpless.

When she tried to speak, I saw that her new set of teeth was gone too. I couldn't make out a word she was saying, but she was insistent. She kept pointing toward the little closet next to her bed.

To humor her, I went over and looked in the closet. All I saw was a little brown paper bag. I shrugged and held it up. She seemed satisfied with that, so I looked inside.

And there, in the innocent-looking bag, were her choppers and her three-carat diamond ring. She had had the presence of mind to take them off and give them to a paramedic on the way into town, fearing they might be stolen if she waited until later.

Two days after that, she was home again with us, still in traction. She herself asked for no pity from anyone. That same toughness that had brought us through the war and the concentration camps was sustaining her now.

I had it too. It was that same strength that had gotten me through my recent battles.

But my life had become crude and strident, and I didn't like it.

My mother has never had any patience with pain. When I was little, she took care of my father's spinster sister for a time. She had been bitten by a snake in the concentration camp, and later in Rotterdam, she had finally lost the leg, at the age of seventy. She came to stay with us.

My mother could not tolerate all the complaints about the new wooden leg, and how sore her thigh was, and so forth.

One day my aunt was hobbling across the room and moaning as usual, and Dido got up and reached inside the woman's brassiere and yanked out one of her falsies. She fastened it between the stump and the wooden leg, and stalked out of the room without a word. The next day they got her a leg that fit better.

She seemed just as indifferent to her own pain. A while after the accident, when she had progressed to a wheelchair, Helen was bathing her. While lifting her out of the bathtub, she accidentally brushed her foot against a protruding nail, and made a nasty deep gash the whole length of her foot. Helen became hysterical. Blood was spurting everywhere.

I grabbed my mother and sat her down on the toilet, and closed the wound tight with my hands. I sat there and held it together for about fifteen minutes, and then I wrapped it tightly with bandages. My mother never made a sound. We never went to the doctor. Never needed to.

When she was still working in the pharmacy in Rotterdam, she fell from a high ladder, reaching up for one of the cabinets, and broke five vertebrae. She got up and drove herself to the hospital in her Mercedes.

Later in Mexico she broke several more vertebrae, and a hip at the same time. From then on, she has been confined to a wheelchair.

But during that time, she must have fallen again, perhaps trying to get out of bed. Her leg looked a little odd the next morning. I gave her an ice pack and a couple of aspirin. The next day the same.

Finally on the fifth day, I asked, "Mother, does your leg hurt?"

"Just a little bit."

The doctor, when we arrived, told me the leg was broken. He set it in a cast, while my mother watched, never complaining.

It was just at that time, of course, when my mother was in traction, that the *fideicomiso* decided to play their next trick. The utilities were cut off at both our houses. Water and lights.

It was not a temporary move, until we were put onto a new line. They simply stopped altogether.

We had three nurses there to help out. We had to bathe Mother and powder her several times a day, to prevent bed sores and gangrene. There was nothing else to be done: we started dipping water from the small pool in the garden. The kids and I bathed in the sea, and rinsed off briefly when we got back, as we had done long ago when they were babies.

For six weeks, I made all the bureaucratic rounds. Mario, the guy who had given me my water years ago in exchange for making all of his cedar furniture, was still in charge. He had become a friend. He used to spend weekends swimming at Las Glorias with his family. But what I didn't know was that he was also a childhood buddy of Miguel Salinas. A *honcho*—that is, a poor kid who grows up with the rich kids at the big house, sort of like Don Andrés' kids with mine. Mario was a good man, but in this situation he had no choice.

He started avoiding me.

Daily I stood in line for hours in the hot sun, along with all the people who had water and were paying their bills. Seventeen pesos, about a buck and a half a month.

Mario lived upstairs in that building with his family. For years, once a month, I couldn't get away from the place without joining them all for breakfast and a chat. Now I couldn't even get the time of day. Only he could give permission to hook me back up, and he was never around.

One afternoon I was sitting under the hair dryer in my favorite beauty salon. Several women, wives of the commission lawyers, and of various other officials, were sitting around with me, gossiping, having their fingernails and toenails done.

"*¡Ay!* Theresa, it's terrible what they're doing to you. How is your poor mother?"

"We'll make it fine," I said. "I'll get a damn 5000-gallon water tank and hook up my own gas pump, if I have to."

"But how do you cook without electricity?"

That remark shows how far our little Puerto Vallarta had progressed. Had they forgotten the wood-burning *comal* they all used to have in the corner of their kitchens?

"Well, I didn't have any electricity when I came down here eleven years ago, so I guess I can do it again," I vowed. Nobody was going to kick me out of my house.

They shook their heads. "*¡Ay!*" they kept repeating.

Mario's wife walked in, got a horrified look on her face, and turned to leave.

"COME ON IN!" I shouted. "I'm not mad at you."

She looked mortified, but she joined us.

"I know it's not your fault that I don't have any utilities," I assured her. "We can still be friends."

The next time I went to the water office, Mario was on his second-floor balcony waving at me. "*¡Pssst!*" he called, as if he was signaling a waiter. "*¡Pssst!*"

He gave me a wink and told me to come up the back way.

What he said was a masterpiece in avoiding the subject. But the message was that for a price, the work could be done. The reason I was upstairs and not downstairs was that if the *mordida* came to him privately, he would not have to share it with Guadalajara and Mexico City.

Meanwhile, I had decided that Armando was a much better choice than Juárez as my lawyer, so I had started him working on the problem. I don't know whether it was Mario's wife, or Armando's persuasion, or the ten thousand pesos I paid, but after six weeks we got some action. We went way up the line, far away from where anyone would think to look, and hooked on to city water again. The lights followed soon afterwards.

There is a dear man who stood by me all these years, whom I haven't identified in my story, for reasons that will become clear. He was a lawyer, and he tried to help me through these times, but he too was unable to do anything for me. He did everything he could to encourage me, though, and to bring my spirits up when I was down.

His name was Hilario López. He looked like a typical Hollywood Mafioso, smooth manner, short but powerful build, with a deep tan that gleamed through his thinning hair on top.

Once he told me, "I know, Theresa. I sympathize with your terrible stories of the concentration camps. When I was a boy, the *asesinos* from the Agrarian Reform came onto our land. They took my father and strung him up by the legs, and cut open his stomach in front of us. I was nine years old." This suave man shook as he was telling me his story. "All I wanted to do was find the men who killed my father and get them. It took me fifteen years, but I did it. The judge let me out of prison finally, because I was so young."

In fact the judge hired Hilario as his own private bodyguard from that point on.

One afternoon Dorothy Sparks and I were downtown. I was helping her do some shopping, and taking her arm as we stepped up and down the high curbs and over the rough cobblestone streets. We were preoccupied at the time with managing the high step at the corner where the *federales* had their offices.

All of a sudden López ran out of the building, not ten steps in front of us, jumped into his truck, and sped off.

"Isn't that odd?" I said to Dorothy. "Hilario always stops to joke around a little bit with us. I wonder why he was in such a hurry?"

She didn't have time to answer me. We were nearing the door of the office. It was wide open.

As we passed, we were scared out of our wits at what we saw.

One federal policeman was stretched out on the floor, contorted in agony. Another one was slumped over the desk, and slipping off of it as we watched. There was blood everywhere.

Other, younger *federales* were running around the room and out onto the street to see if they could discover which direction the truck went.

There was confusion everywhere.

"Help, them, dammit!" yelled a guy who was kneeling over the man on the floor. "They're dying!"

As close as we had been, we hadn't heard the shots. There were no windows, so the echoes of gunfire must have stayed inside the room.

"Let's get out of here," I said to Dorothy. "Fast! Those are *federales*!"

Then immediately I contradicted myself. "Just walk calmly. My car's in the next block."

How we made it without falling I don't know. My ankles seemed ready to give out at each step. I couldn't get that bloody picture out of my mind.

"Don't say anything about this to anyone," I cautioned Dorothy when we were in the car. "Ever!"

"Just bring me home," she agreed. "I don't want anything to do with it."

She heaved a deep sigh. "I don't think they noticed us. They were too busy running around."

"Right," I said. But I wasn't sure.

It was all I needed, to be witness to a double murder done by a friend of mine. And police officers, on top of that.

I was desperate to know what was happening to Hilario, but I promised myself to stay as far from the whole thing as I could.

I dropped Dorothy off, and started toward Las Glorias. Then I remembered my children. I wanted them around me.

The trouble was, I had kicked Bear out of the house, for insolence, and for staying in trouble constantly by running away from school to go swimming or horseback riding. He was twelve or thirteen years old. I just packed his bags and threw him out. Of course behind the scenes, I made sure he was getting along all right.

He could have cared less. He seemed happy to have found a job as a mechanic with a friend of ours, Eduardo.

But now I was shaken. Forget the school problems. I wanted to have my whole family with me.

"What kind of a mother are you?" I was chiding myself as I drove over to Eduardo's garage. When I pulled up in front, there was Bear, perfectly content and covered with grease.

"Your daddy's home," I lied. "Let's go."

"Yeah, OK," he said. "Just let me finish this."

A telephone rang in the shop. Eduardo had a little wrecker service, so he was one of the first in town to have one of those modern conveniences installed.

From his little office in back, he yelled, "Theresa, can you pick up the telephone?"

"Sure."

I answered it, listened to the message, and then called out to Eduardo. "Do you understand this? They want to talk to the commander of the military."

"Yeah. They're right across the street," he said, as if it were a perfectly normal request. "Theresa, would you do me a favor and run over there?"

"To get the police?"

"The military."

"They don't have a phone of their own?" I was grasping for reasons to stay away from law enforcement officers of any kind that afternoon. I was still shaking from what I had just seen.

"Not yet," he said. "It's just over there."

He pointed to the garrison across the way. "Would you mind?"

"OK," I said. Bear was still busy with the car.

The *comandante* was a friend of mine from our riding days in the *charreada*. I hadn't had much time for that recently, but we still saw each other at parties.

"Surely it's innocent enough to ask him to come to the telephone," I told myself. I felt as if everyone suspected me of something, with every move I made.

I walked into the office of the military headquarters. One of the sergeants told me, "The *comandante* is not here. He'll take the message," indicating a young boy with a very big Belgian automatic.

We crossed back over the street together.

The guy picked up the receiver, hanging down at the wall. I went over to see about Bear.

"Hello! Hello!" he said "*¿Qué pasó? Hello?*"

Only then did I look up to see that he had a funny, sort of retarded look on his face. He was twisting the receiver every which way in his hand. Nobody was talking to him on the other end.

The child with the automatic weapon had no idea how to make the thing work with his ears and his mouth at the same time.

"*Señora,*" he said with a pleading expression. "There's no answer. Can you help me?"

"*Así . . . así,*" I said, showing him, but he didn't want to look.

He had been completely defeated by the experience.

He shoved the receiver away toward me. I put it to my ear.

And then my blood went cold. I couldn't believe what I was hearing at the other end. I get chills when I think about it, even now.

"Tell him we found the truck of Hilario López. It's in a ditch on the way up to—" He named a town far up in the wilderness behind Puerto Vallarta.

"Tell the *comandante* to send all the soldiers up there in his fastest cars. We can still get him."

I must been white as a sheet.

The young soldier stood beside me, grinning from ear to ear—most impressed at my expertise with the telephone.

I gulped in a deep breath of heavy air.

It was, I guess, a small gesture of protest for all that I had been through, but I had to do it for my friend. Why else was I put in that place at that time?

"They found the truck of Hilario López. It's in a ditch—" And then I gave the soldier exactly the opposite directions from the ones I had heard on the telephone.

Three or four cars crammed full with soldiers sped out of the garrison on their wild goose chase.

I grabbed Bear, greasy hands or not, and took him back home with me.

I had given López the time he needed. He made it through the mountains and escaped to Spain.

A few weeks later, Rick flew into town on business again. He had four of his children along, and he invited me and my kids out to dinner with them.

We went down to the plaza, to the Venice Restaurant, and ordered steaks. My three kids tore into their meals and made short work of them. His four, who by then were calling me 'Mother,' picked at their food without interest.

"Those kids don't like their food," Buster whispered in my ear. *"Sssh!"* I cautioned.

"We'll take the meat!" shouted Bear, and grabbed at the plate. We were all laughing and having a good time.

But Enrique was suddenly furious. Not at my kids, but at his own.

"Your mother never sees to it that you get fed!" he stormed. "She spends all her time in and out of hospitals—"

He was getting angrier and angrier. "And you've all got too much money to spend! Look at you!" He was screaming. People were turning around and staring at us in the restaurant. "You're so skinny—"

He grabbed the oldest child and whisked him off to the jeep he had rented. He told his driver to take the kid to the hospital where he could see other children dying of hunger. "Maybe then you'll feel like eating," he said.

A pall hung over the table. It had been quite a display. My kids looked at him with wide eyes, not knowing how to react.

Enrique was back lowering over us at the table, panting. His other children had tears in their eyes.

Something in me snapped. "How could I ever subject my children to such scenes?" I asked myself. "Even if it happened that I could marry him some day?"

He had wanted me to come and live with him, but I saw then that it was impossible.

"That's it! It's over," I resolved. And it was.

Actually, the affair tapered off somewhat more gradually than that, but after that evening, my heart was no longer in it.

Looking back, that scene seems like a rather small thing to base such a large decision on. Perhaps it was. Perhaps I did not really love him. Perhaps I never had.

He had given me a certain amount of freedom at a time when I desperately needed it, and I was grateful for that. I wouldn't trade the fun we had together for anything. But I wouldn't stay with him either. I become a ferocious lioness when my children are concerned.

The last time I saw him, about a year later, was at the Hotel Del Prado in Mexico City. When I saw him in the lobby with his wife, I decided to take suite 602, next door.

I could hear them fighting through the wall.

"She's worth more than you'll ever be!" Rick was shouting. "She is a better person to your own kids! They already call her 'Mom'!"

I heard the door slam. I went to the window, shaking. At the hotel entrance, a limousine pulled up a moment later, and a frail woman about my age got into it. She had blondish hair, and she was wearing a very expensive mink. She had been pretty once.

There was a knock on the door. Rick walked in. *"¡Ay, mi amor!"* he beamed, looking confident and happy. "Where do you want to have dinner?"

I must have looked startled, not by his presence, but by his mood, so quickly altered.

"Don't stand there looking out the window," he said. "There's nothing of any interest out there."

I hesitated. Then I said, "I'll be ready in a minute."

I named a restaurant, and we had a farewell dinner, although he didn't know it at the time.

1975 was quite a year. I lost the hotel, I almost lost my mother, and I lost Enrique. The next to go was Bob Lewis.

In October, he got into a fight with one of the minor *fideicomiso* lawyers at Carlos O'Brian's. It wasn't anything serious, just trading insults about Las Glorias, with a "cocky Mexican sonofabitch" who had shelved document after document of ours without ever looking at them. Bob threw a glass of whiskey in his face, before Rafael pulled him off.

But after that, he got very jittery, and his ulcer was giving him a lot of pain.

"Terry, I can't take this bullshit any longer," he told me. "And I don't think the kids should have to put up with it either."

I agreed. I thought they would be safer in America. The possibility of kidnapping had even crossed our minds.

"I'll stay here and fight," I said finally. "You take them up to Sun Valley."

Idaho was too far away from Mexico, as far as I was concerned, but Bob had fallen in love with it, and when he described the small town and the mountains, I too was convinced that our kids would be happy there.

There was still a chance, I thought. The commission had re-evaluated the Las Glorias property. They were asking for millions from us, as we had ourselves estimated it long before. But I still thought I could get that amount from Walker, and that we could make far more than that on it, if the government would just accept our money.

In the meantime, I was still selling real estate for Grubb & Ellis. I could send some money to my family to live on. Bob was by then in his sixties, but he said he would find a part-time job too.

And so, after fifteen years of marriage, I no longer lived with my husband.

All our friends in Puerto Vallarta were sorry to see him go. He had always been a lot of fun at sports and at parties, even though his Spanish was horrendous till the end. He had taught many of the men to play tennis in our courts, and the women adored him—even the few he hadn't been to bed with. He had had several at a time, and managed to keep them all happy. An artist, really.

It's maybe easier to say that now than it was then, but when I see how much my children love him, I'm happy we stayed together as long as we did. I was still married to him, when he died recently.

But married, technically, or not, I was ready for a new life. A life without cares, I hoped, for the first time in years.

It was not going to be with Armando, though he must have asked me to marry him a hundred times already. I loved him a lot, but as a younger brother only.

He had troubles enough of his own, supporting his parents and helping all of his brothers and sisters, and managing the tough balancing act required in working with the Reys and still trying to live with honor. Every so often it got to be too much for him, and he just went off on a bender.

Soon after Bob left, Armando and I were having a night of it in Guadalajara. I had called on him at his office, and he had invited me out for a drink. Several hours later, near midnight, we were still drinking.

"*¡Ay, mujer!*" he slurred. "Don't worry. I'll take care of you when you're old. You can come and live with me, and we'll get stinking together!"

As a proposal, that didn't seem to offer much of a future, but I loved him for loving me in advance as a grandmother.

"I'm so afraid," I admitted. "I don't want you to end up like the *juez*, José María." I went straight to the core of it. He had admired the judge mightily himself.

"Don't worry. I'm tough," he said. He stood up, and changed the subject. "Whatta you say we have something to eat?"

It sounded like a good idea to me. We went out to his Mustang, and he drove the short distance to his office. There was a Denny's across the street. The car squealed into a parking lot next door, just as they were turning the lights off in the restaurant.

"Watch my car," he slurred to the man in the lot, and handed him his keys. The car had an official government sticker on it, and the man asked no questions.

"Come on, Theresa, let's go!" Armando ran over to Denny's and started yelling. Inside, they refused to open the door.

He shook a fist at them and shouted abuses, with no result. Suddenly he wound up, and sent his fist through the thick plate glass panel of the door, to the horror of the workers finishing up the night shift.

The cops were there in an instant. Armando's arm was gushing blood, but he seemed oblivious. When the police grabbed him, he said, "Theresa, get my wallet out."

I fumbled in his pocket and finally brought it out. It flipped open to the badge of a top government official. Immediately, we were treated as royalty. We were taken to the hospital in the police car, and he got instant attention from everyone.

Not even the sewing on his arm sobered him up.

"Where should we take you now, sir?" asked a policeman politely.

"Well, Theresa, where should we go?" asked Armando.

"Hey, man, let's get you some penicillin first," I said.

"No, I think we should have another drink," he said. "COME ON!" he shouted to his police escort. "Let's have another drink."

So we all went out and closed down the sleepy city of Guadalajara, cops and all. They brought us home at dawn, one of them even stopping off to get Armando's Mustang on the way.

And that's the man who's been like a little brother to me.

By now we had far more room than we needed at Las Glorias, my mother and I, so I decided to rent out some of our space to make more money to send to America.

A big old friendly bear of a man came up to the door one day and said he would take the bottom floor of my house for himself, and the bottom floor of my mother's for his secretary. It was John Huston.

He had just returned from Morocco, where he had been filming *The Man Who Would Be King*. He needed a place to rest and to write.

When he had started counting up all the unforeseen expenses that the film and his estate in Ireland had required recently, he saw that he was not so well off as he had hoped, at least for the moment. He came "home" to Puerto Vallarta again, where one could live well on very little. All the old-timers knew him there, and loved him.

Our houses were close together, the atmosphere easy, and we became friends. I especially liked his secretary, Gladys Hill, who was an old-fashioned woman about sixty years old, and totally devoted to him. They had been together since before *Night of the Iguana* days. They had written some scripts together, including the thriller, *The Kremlin Letter*, and she had proved herself indispensable to him.

John lived in my house with his young Mexican girlfriend, Maricela, who had previously been a friend of his ex-wife.

Every day from ten o'clock till two, he and Gladys wrote together on her little typewriter, and no one was allowed to disturb them. They may have been writing a screenplay, or perhaps he was beginning his autobiography, I'm not sure.

I'm sorry to say I didn't know much about motion pictures back then. I used to sneak away to a few when I was growing up, but my mother always dismissed them as "bad," and filled with people "kissing and making whores of themselves." I don't know why I listened to my mother about that—I didn't about much else. But I guess it stuck.

You can imagine how impressed Dido was with the eminent John Huston.

She would pop in on him—sometimes even in bed—as she used to do with Bob and me. John then flew into a rage, and they got into a tangle.

"Who in the hell does he think he is?" she would say, sulking.

"Please, Dido," Gladys chimed in, with her soft, ladylike voice, "you mustn't talk to our John that way."

"Well, now Dido," said John, teasing her in an authoritative growl, "don't you know who I am?"

"I don't give a damn who you are. You're bullshit, that's what you are! You just make movies. Those robes—"

She thought he put on airs, with the flowing robes he had learned to love in Africa.

Then Maricela would join in, and everyone started yelling at one another. Still, their battles were harmless. By Thanksgiving, John was playfully bouncing my mother on his knee.

Next she turned on Gladys. "You give that lady all your time," my mother complained to me. "You never see me any more."

"She doesn't like to drive that Safari by herself," I explained calmly. "She doesn't see that well to drive. I don't mind helping her."

But my mother, as always, wanted me all to herself.

Every day after writing, John liked to swim in the sea for an hour. Gladys, always worried about his health, asked if I would go out with him.

"Marvelous, marvelous," he would say, floating on his back endlessly.

Afterwards we used to sit on the beach and talk, and appreciate the crabs, and the sounds of the jungle birds. He really loved the Bahía de Banderas. He had decided to build a house across the bay, near Quimixto.

While he smoked on his long Cuban cigar, which I had helped him get into the country with a quick *mordida* at customs, he asked me to sneak him a vodka if the coast was clear.

"Send Gladys on some errand," he said slyly. She allowed him drinks, but only according to the clock. I managed to slip a few past her. Still, we were all watchful of his health.

Sometimes we made trips together up into the wilderness, as he had loved to do years before, in scouting locations for the Tennessee Williams film.

Life at Las Glorias began to be full of joy again, despite the little female arguments.

Gladys and Maricela were the worst. The girlfriend tried to protect him personally, and she took good care of him. The secretary tried to protect him professionally. Those interests often collided.

There could hardly have been two women more different from each other. Though John was very elegant, Maricela was a small Indian girl with no education. It was I who taught her to eat with a knife and a fork. (My mother had also recently taught Armando to quit shoving food with his tortilla!) Gladys had thick glasses and a studious manner. She was very fastidious, personally. Maricela often disagreed with her on principle, just to assert her power, and then the older woman, who had been with the man for fifteen years, had her feelings hurt.

One day I decided to console her by taking her out in the Safari for shopping and a little lunch at the El Dorado, on the "social beach." There we met Rebecca, a Mexican girlfriend of mine, and the three of us had a nice, relaxing meal on the terrace, with plenty of *margaritas*, while we watched the action on the Playa de los Muertos, just steps away.

We were completely mellow when, on the road back to Las Glorias, we saw three Americans walking along, loaded down with sacks full of groceries, mostly beer. Rebecca and I exchanged a jovial glance.

"Where you guys going?" I shouted. Gladys flinched.

"To the marina!"

"Well, jump in!" I said. So the three guys climbed into the Safari with all their packages. Gladys squeezed way over in the front seat, to make room for one of them. The car sank down on its tires—these were big men!

Gladys sat there shaking her head. You would have thought, after traveling around the world with John Huston for fifteen years, that she had seen everything. But she continued to be amazed at how carefree and unguarded I was. It was a change from her usual Hollywood associates, I suppose.

"I hope you don't mind if I give them a ride," I said. It was her car, after all.

"No, of course not."

The guys were bubbling over with plans for drinking and dancing that night, and they kept trying to get a commitment from us to join them. Dinner was mentioned occasionally. They were typical sailors on the town, though not in the military.

"Sure," we all said, "that sounds like fun." We kept it purposely vague.

As we passed Las Glorias on the way to the marina, Rebecca blurted out, "That's where they live!"

Gladys flinched again.

I let the guys off at the marina, and we said good-bye. I let Gladys off to work a while longer with John, and I drove Rebecca back to her place in town.

We had another couple of drinks there. It was a lazy afternoon.

When I pulled up in my driveway about eight o'clock, I heard an American voice from my mother's balcony.

"HEY, THERESA! Are you Terry Lewis?"

"Yes, I'm Terry Lewis."

I looked up, and all three of the guys were hanging over the railing of the balcony, looking as if they already had a good start on a party. My mother had been entertaining them for a couple of hours.

She hated to cook, but she always had a splendid spread ready to go, with lots of rum and beer and whiskey, with ham and cheese and snacks.

She was having a blast. She understood them some, but they couldn't make out much of what she was saying. In paradise in the tropics, that didn't matter much.

We ate some more and drank some more, and then went out dancing. Gladys begged us to find a friend of Rebecca's to take her place.

The one I liked immediately was Jim Goodell. That surprised me. I had never taken these big, beautiful Americans very seriously. I guess I like the hot-blooded, playful little Latins more. *'Sangre de atole,'* we used to call the straight *gringos*—they had cornstarch in their veins.

But Jim was different. He was *simpatico* , slow and easy, with a philosophical turn of mind. He didn't mention money or making money all evening, except to say that his wife was trying to bleed him for alimony.

He had gone out to Los Angeles from the Jamestown area of New York to try to patch it up with her one last time, and she had slammed the door in his face. He rented a car and just started driving south. At Cabo San Lucas, on the tip of Baja California, the road ended.

"What did you do then?" I asked.

"I had a hitchhiker along. A Mexican. Picked up this guy somewhere along the way, I don't know. I just handed him the keys and a note for the rental place, and asked him to drive the car back."

"Did he?"

"Hell if I know!" We all laughed.

"Well, you didn't drive over here to Puerto Vallarta. How'd you get here?" I asked.

"I was hanging around the marina in La Paz, and I met this guy with a trimaran. They had new outriggers made of metal, and they were sailing down to the Canal to test them out."

"So you went?"

"They needed some help on the boat."

"What did you know about sailing?"

"Not a damn thing."

We all laughed again.

Here was a free spirit, with no complications. Just what I needed!

Or perhaps what I really needed was absolutely no complications—not even Jim. I reserved judgment, while I studied him.

"Did you learn?" I asked.

"I learned that I don't like oatmeal. That bitch of a wife of his, that's all she serves to us. Trying to save money, I guess."

He took another long swig of beer. "And no drinking on board either. Now that's not the kind of trip I had in mind!" he laughed.

He raised his glass and we all toasted nothing in particular, with a lot of raucous laughter. "I'm blowin' off that tub," he added.

About three a.m., I called it a night. I had an early morning appointment to take John out fishing. Dino de Laurentiis was coming in, with some other Italian film producers, and he wanted to show them a good time.

At 7:30 in the morning, I drove up to the marina, and almost straight into the water when I suddenly found I had to duck down in the front seat.

The guys were out already, looking for me. Apparently they had decided to invite themselves along on our fishing trip. But I eluded them successfully, and met John and the others on his boat, the *Mary-ua-na*.

Besides the obvious, the name was a take-off on Maricela's name.

We spent a pleasant, relaxing day at sea, diving and fishing off Punta de Mita.

The next few days, I saw that these movie men were hard workers, not just talkers. Even though they appeared to be lounging around on the floor cushions at John's place, they were in fact conducting business. Million-dollar ideas floated tantalizingly in the air, above my black and white Dutch tiles. But that first day on the boat, these suave Italians showed that they also knew how to relax.

At about sunset, I drove back to check on my mother. She was drunk as a cuckoo. She had been entertaining the American sailors all day. They had made themselves completely comfortable in her house.

The maids adored them. Jim had even endeared himself to Gladys, and to my mother too, at that point. There was something very appealing about his openness and laid-back attitude. And, of course, she didn't yet feel any sense of competition for my time.

My mother had been so independent all of her life, it was sad to see her clinging to me so much now. I remember a time, not very many years before, when the Swedish consul had proposed to her.

"Now that you're alone, Dido," he said, "why don't you marry me and come to live with me in Stockholm?"

"Why don't you marry me and live all over the world?" she answered. "I'm not getting stuck up in that God-forsaken Sweden."

And now this evening, she was stretched out in our small pool, almost flat on her back, with three American sailors. They were in the same position, and almost as pickled. They looked like a flower formation in one of those water ballets.

To sober up the guys, I suggested dancing again. And I suggested to Emilia, the sweet new girl I had gotten to take care of her since the accident, that my mother might be ready for bed.

Gradually the guys started staying overnight at our place, instead of going back to the marina. There was plenty of room.

In about a week, the trimaran was ready to continue its journey down the coast. One of the guys said he didn't mind oatmeal so much, and he replaced Jim. The other one left soon afterwards.

Jim stayed on.

We had ourselves a ball. He was seven years younger than I, and he made me young again too. I started letting my hair grow longer, and highlighting it.

Occasionally, he got into a sad mood about his children (we could always tell, when he started playing my Barry White records at top volume, which drove Gladys crazy), but those spells happened less and less often.

He was a very gentle soul, not a physical type. I don't know how he ever thought he would be a good hand on a sailboat. If there was gardening to do around my place, he was perfectly happy to let me do that too.

One day we just fell into bed. He was cozy and warm to be with.

Of course, my mother knew the exact moment somehow. We had sneaked home, leaving my new Volkswagen parked across the highway. She crept silently over the balcony, which wrapped most of the way around her house, and peered in my bedroom window.

"Theresa! THERESA! Are you home?" she yelled. She knew very well we were in there, from the stifled giggles.

She tossed a beer bottle through the window. It landed at the foot of the bed, scattering glass everywhere.

"I'm going to kill that woman," said Jim, but of course we both thought it was funny.

On February 6, we planned a big party.

It was exactly a year since those bastards stole my hotel, but that was not the occasion. Sondra Cellini was in town to celebrate her birthday. It was also Rebecca's birthday, and Jim's birthday. All three. We were going to pull out all the stops, and have a real bash.

I was swimming as usual that afternoon with John Huston, and the others were all at Rebecca's place making preparations for the party. As we walked back from the sea, deep in conversation, I thought I noticed some movement in the yard by my mother's house. I said good-bye to John in front of my house, where he was staying, and continued on.

All of a sudden, three dark guys in suits popped out from behind the garden wall and grabbed me.

I guess I should have been more clever, but it was a total surprise. We hadn't had any trouble since we got the utilities turned back on. Besides, I didn't really think it was serious.

"Damn! Only four steps away from my gate," I thought casually. They knew it was illegal to arrest me inside, on my own property.

Later that struck me as being an odd thought. How many of these Mexican maneuvers of recent years had actually been legal?

"The mayor would like to see you downtown, with your papers," said one of them, with a very sober face.

"Well, it's already about 2:30. He won't be there now," I argued. "He'll be out for lunch."

"He's waiting."

I shrugged. As usual, they hadn't identified themselves, but I could see they meant business.

"Emilia," I called, "will you throw me a dress? I have to go downtown with these men."

She tossed down a light cotton muumuu, which I threw on over my bikini.

"Y tírame las llaves," I added. Since Bob had gotten kidnapped and taken to Guadalajara in someone else's car, I vowed I would never let that happen to me. So Emilia tossed down the keys.

"Are you going to be gone long?" she asked. My mother was waiting to have lunch with me.

"No. I'll be right back."

The men started heading toward their raggedy little Chevrolet (with California plates), and I went for my blue VW. When they saw that I was determined to drive, two of them jumped in my car with me.

I hadn't taken my shoes or my purse, of course. I was coming right back. And I didn't have any papers to show anybody. The mayor already knew that.

While we were stopped at the entrance to the highway waiting for the traffic, I saw Iris, a German girl I had gotten to know.

"Hey, Terry, are you going downtown?" she asked.

"Sure. Hop in!" I said.

She climbed aboard, in a very small bikini and a very large straw purse. The men loved that.

We bumped along toward town, talking about nothing in particular.

"Right here will be fine," she said at the Oceano Hotel, and got out.

We drove on to the municipal building, next to Our Lady of Guadalupe. I parked my car on the plaza and locked it. We walked down the hall to the office of the mayor, still my friend Luis Favela. He was out, as I had predicted.

"Well, that's it. I'll meet you guys back here at six o'clock," I said, turning to leave.

"Oh no, *señora.*"

The *federales* took me by the arm and steered me to the door of the jail, a trip I had made several early mornings with Luis or Rafael, when they had provided me a cot in the office. They shoved me inside.

I had not had a chance to call Armando. I had not even thought to ask Iris to tell someone where we were going. Stupid.

I was a Mexican jailbird again.

Not counting the bizarre episode with Bob at the Guadalajara Hilton, this was number six.

25

Once inside the jail, I realized it was Friday.

They had done it again. The judge would not be there, the mayor would not be back. I was again the victim of a *sabadazo*, a weekend holiday in jail. The bastards usually timed their arrests when everyone official would be gone.

Worse yet, I had heard the *federales* talking about flying me out that afternoon to Guadalajara. If I was going to the capital to prison, I was in real trouble.

Once again, I managed to flag down don Conrado, the pharmacist on the corner.

"Theresa!" he said in a hushed voice. "Are you in jail again?"

"Please go tell Rafael de la Cruz," I begged. As the editor of the newspaper as well as a friend, he had more contacts than anyone else I could call on to help me.

I wrote a note to my mother in Dutch, and handed it to Rafael when he walked in.

"Here are the keys to my car," I said. "I parked it on the square. Would you take it back to Las Glorias, and give this note to my mother?"

"¡Seguro!" he said. He was eager to help.

Before they left, the *federales* had made me a proposition. "For 40,000 pesos, you can be out in an hour."

In my note, therefore, I told my mother I'd be gone for a while, and not to give anyone any money.

Rafael was back in forty-five minutes. "I drove my own car," he said, "and I gave your mother the note. Was I supposed to tell her you were in jail?"

"No. I don't want to worry her."

"OK. Your car wasn't on the square. You must have parked it somewhere else," he said.

"Of course I parked it on the square," I insisted. "Go look again. It's right on the corner."

Somewhat impatiently, he went to look again.

No car. The sonsofbitches had stolen my Volkswagen.

They must have been tired of their beat-up Chevrolet. Or they had decided to take that, since they'd had no luck with the *mordida*.

Now they had their bribe—much more in fact—but I was not out in an hour.

Rafael offered to go find Rebecca and tell them where I was.

Their reactions to the news were interesting:

Sondra was distraught. "Now what am I going to do with all this food?" she kept repeating.

Jim was ready to go out and find a posse and some M-16's and storm the jail. That was more of an American reaction than I had expected from him. Rebecca went to find Gladys, who called me a lawyer.

She left Jim pacing back and forth, thinking of other Americans he had met in Puerto Vallarta and mumbling about firearms, and Sondra fluttering around behind him moaning, "This whole party is destroyed. Just destroyed!"

Before I knew it the *federales* had me in a jeep on the way to the airport. As usual, no charges had been mentioned.

"Where's my Volkswagen?" I screamed at them.

They just stared at me, with no expression at all.

When we got out of the car, they snapped on handcuffs, and led me into the terminal. At that moment a planeload of top *fideicomiso* officials arrived from Mexico City, and streamed past me one by one. Great for my image.

"Hello, Theresa," a couple of them said. I was no longer '*doña* Theresa.'"

Maricela came up from behind and shoved two thousand pesos in my hand, from John. That was a little over $160. I used all of it over the next nine days.

She also dropped a pair of sandals on the floor in front of me so that I could step into them.

"Can you get me a drink?" I whispered.

She went to the bar for a Coke with a double shot of rum.

Then Rebecca came up, and both of them started making trouble with the *federales.*

"*¡Oye, cabrones!*" they screamed. "We love this lady. Leave her alone!"

"*¡Cállense!*" they replied. "Shut up!"

"Shame on you! You could at least take off the handcuffs. She's a lady!"

"We're under orders. Move on."

The girls were sort of poking at them and irritating them, until one officer shoved Rebecca so hard he almost knocked me on the marble floor. I was still attached to him with the handcuffs.

But their diversion gave me time to sneak the drink, which would have been forbidden otherwise.

Rebecca told me that Gladys was at home crying, too afraid to come to the airport, but that she had called her lawyer. Unfortunately, she did not know about Armando, who perhaps could have been of more help. But I appreciated what she did.

"Don't tell my mother where I am," I said as I boarded the plane. "She'll get with Jim, and they'll shoot up the whole town."

And then I was inside the plane, in my bikini and muumuu, on my way to the mountain city of Guadalajara. It was February.

"Happy birthday, Jim," I sighed, "and Rebecca and Sondra!"

We arrived at about nine in the evening. Since there would be no one to receive me at the jail at that hour, they put me in a private car, still handcuffed, and took me to the federal building.

"I know this place," I thought, as we started up the stairs. Then it dawned on me. It was here that I had staged the scene for José María, with my tacky black wig. I got a small lump in my throat, thinking of my friend.

The men led me to a room guarded by two soldiers with pistols, and shoved me inside. The room was bare except for a small table and a couple of chairs. There were two windows looking onto a courtyard. Nothing to do but sit and wait. About eleven, I stretched out to sleep on the tile floor. I was shivering from the cold.

At around two a.m., there was a huge commotion out in the hallway. I heard a lot of boots scuffling, several dull thuds followed by groans, as flesh was being pounded by the butts of rifles. I couldn't see anything, and I was scared.

I grabbed one of the chairs and shrank as far back into a corner as I could, trying to be invisible.

The door burst open and three good-looking men about Jim's age came flying into the room and slid into the wall. Six or eight soldiers were right behind them, kicking them in the legs and stomach.

Then they turned around and left the room.

The men were bruised and cut all over. They sat on the floor and inspected the damage, talking quietly among themselves.

"How many did we get, three?"

"Four, I know it was four. *¡Hijos de puta!*"

They glanced over at me occasionally, but didn't say anything to me at first.

They were friends, ranchers in the Emerald Mountains near Guadalajara, and pretty well off, judging from their clothes and their boots. Squatters had come onto the land belonging to one of them, and there had been a shoot-out. I listened hard for the name of Ignacio Rey, but didn't hear it. They were strong, handsome guys, two of them rather short and wiry, but the third was tall, with curly, almost blond hair and a slightly pock-marked face.

After a while they decided I must be a comrade. *"¡Oye, güerita!* American? You?" said the blond to me hesitantly, clutching onto his big *sombrero.*

I nodded my head quickly. I felt I could protect myself better if they didn't know I spoke Spanish.

"Why —*aquí ?*" he asked, pointing to the floor of the room.

I shrugged.

That was the best answer I had. After all, I had been asking myself the same question.

"¿Marihuana?" he pressed on bravely.

I shook my head no. He smiled a genuinely friendly smile, and then shrugged himself. I think his English had run out.

I was in a bare room in the middle of the night with three murderers, and I felt completely at ease.

They went back to their conversation, while I sat there and shivered. This time I heard them say they were sure they had been framed. Just as the shooting had started, a helicopter appeared out of nowhere, with soldiers. It was too much of a coincidence.

Then suddenly one looked over at me. "Hey! *¡Mira a la pobrecita!* Look at the poor kid, she's cold."

He punched his buddy. "Give her your poncho," he said.

One of the darker ones stretched out his hand and offered me his thick, rich poncho. I accepted it gladly.

"Gracias," I said to him. ("That much Spanish won't give me away," I thought to myself.)

About five in the morning, we were all getting drowsy. The three men stretched out on the floor.

The blond, Manuel, raised his head slightly. "Here," he said in Spanish. "Come on over here." He pointed to the spot beside him.

I was really cold. I grabbed the warm poncho and curled up against him, with my head on his big bicep, and peacefully fell asleep.

At seven o'clock we were rousted out by six big, armed guards. I scrambled toward the wall again. I didn't think they would shoot me, but in a fight I could still be hit by a stray bullet.

They kicked the men into a standing position while I cowered in the corner. Then one of them grabbed me too, and shoved me out the door with the rest.

"Where could we be going at this hour?" I thought. The only people awake in Guadalajara at seven o'clock in the morning were the guys at the fish markets and the meat markets.

I didn't want to be with these *rancheros.* As much as I liked them, they were still so rowdy, that I was afraid I might be harmed by accident.

We were taken to an old black van with California plates. The hippie they stole it from must have been an original. It was all painted black, inside and out, including the windows.

The soldiers were brutally shoving the *rancheros* into the back. I hung back as much as I could. When they were all inside, I started toward the door. A guy grabbed me and pushed me into the front, next to the driver.

My three new friends were in the back of the van on their knees (there were no seats) with six guards, and I was shivering in front. I had kept the poncho, but it was freezing cold outside.

We drove for a while, when all of a sudden, one of the rancheros shouted, *"¡Cigarros!"* A couple of the guards snarled for them to be quiet, but they insisted.

"Me too!" I yelled. Out of gallantry for the lady, I guess, we stopped for cigarettes.

They all shouted out their orders and passed the money forward, including enough for me. I had hidden John's two thousand pesos in my crotch, and I didn't think this was the time to reveal that information.

The driver handed me the crumpled pesos.

"Me?" I indicated with a startled look. He nodded his head.

I ran into a corner store, my poncho flying, and bought cigarettes for everybody. There weren't enough the first time. *"¡Oye!"* they called from the back. *"¡Dos más!"* So I went back and got two more. And then they sent me back a third time.

The prisoners were now buying for the guards and the driver too.

We drove to the edge of town, and up along the huge walls of the prison, several blocks long. At the gate, they took us out and quickly handcuffed us.

We were hustled into a big entry room, M-16's poking us in the back all the way. The lawyers were in there, and all the families. Hundreds of people, everybody talking at once.

A door burst open, and a big fat woman in slacks, with tits spread out all over the front of her, walked up to me. *"Theresa Laao-is?"* she growled.

"Sí," I answered timidly. *"Soy yo. Soy yo."* She made me nervous. The Spanish just bubbled out.

"Theresa! *¡Hablas español!* " said my big blond friend with surprise. They all gathered around me, with the surly guards and the guns following close behind.

"Theresa, *adónde vas?*" they all asked. "Where will you go? What's going to happen to you?"

"I don't know," I said quietly.

They bombarded me with all sorts of questions that I couldn't answer. They were so concerned about me that they gave me a hundred pesos to help out in the women's prison, as the fatass woman with the keys shoved me toward the exit.

I was genuinely sorry to leave those guys. I never found out what happened to them.

The women's prison, about three blocks along the same wall, covered a much smaller territory than the men's. I was brought to a medium-sized office filled with books and papers. At the back, in the corner of the room was a large medicine cabinet with locks.

There were four girls there, being treated for serious wounds. One girl had been shot in the arm, another was missing an ear and much of her neck below it, and a third had a huge chunk of meat hanging off her shoulder.

They were completely stoic. They hardly flinched as rough fingers punched and jabbed at them.

I knew who they had to be. The papers were full of the story.

For eighteen days, old eighty-year-old Guadalupe Zuno, the former governor of Jalisco, and the father-in-law of Echeverría, had been kidnapped by socialist terrorists from Sonora. Just yesterday he had been discovered and rescued. There had been a desperate shoot-out, and some were killed. These, of the women at least, were left.

Recently also, the thirteen-year-old son of the president had been shot in Echeverría's own limousine.

The attempt had really been on the president. He was not a popular leader.

The prison matrons finished with the girls and led them off. I was alone in the office.

Late in the morning, *la directora* walked in. "Theresa Lewis?" she said sternly, in an educated voice. She even said my name in an English way. She was tall and well groomed, with a henna rinse on her hair.

"Your lawyer already called for you, but nobody knew who you were," she said, smiling. I was surprised—relieved—at the reception.

"He will be here between eleven and twelve this morning," she continued. "Would you like to make a telephone call?"

"No, thank you," I said quietly. I didn't know who to call besides a lawyer. I would wait and see.

"Don't worry about anything. It will take a couple of days, of course." She was looking me over closely. I wondered why. Thousands of women must have passed through this office.

"I have known about you for a long time," she said, a strange look on her face, "through my friend, Judge José María Macias."

"Ah!" I said and smiled. I knew I had a friend.

I didn't know if she would be able to do anything for me, but I knew she would be good to me.

She started asking me all about Las Glorias, and listened to the whole story with fascination, but without any specific comments. I went easy on the connection with the Reys and Salinas, less to protect myself than to avoid getting her in trouble.

"It's such a pleasure to meet you after all these years," she smiled. She stepped around the desk and shook my hand. "It's such an honor to know a woman who knows how to fight."

Then a grim shadow passed over her face. "But this is Mexico," she added. "You must never forget it. In Mexico you have no rights whatsoever."

She turned away, and then went back to her chair behind the desk.

"Do you need drugs? I can give you valium, or librium, to help you sleep."

"Thank you," I said. I didn't want them, but they might come in handy as a raw sort of currency for the days ahead.

"I hope your stay is as pleasant as possible, under the circumstances," she said, and ushered me into the open courtyard of the jail.

"If ever you want to sit in my office and read a newspaper or a book, you are welcome," she added. Then she turned and went back into her office.

It was eleven o'clock in the morning. I stood facing a sea of women, clutching a few pills in my hand, since there were no pockets in the muumuu, and pulling Porfirio's poncho close around me.

The federal prison had all the same rules and hardships as a local jail. Food and bedding, or even beds in this case, were not provided. If you had a lawyer, he could start to work on your case, but it was up to you or your family to find one.

In many instances, since telephone calls were not seen as a natural right, even the families of the prisoners did not know yet where they were. And often there wasn't a telephone at home anyway.

There were no public defenders. Armando took three or four cases a year as charity work, but only the ones that interested him. For common thieves there were few lawyers, unless they stood to gain from their work. So the family set about making arrangements to sell their land, or their car, or their turkey, whatever they had.

But first they had to be notified. Outside the steel bars of the windows, the street was crowded with twelve- and thirteen-year-old boys who ran errands for the prisoners. The women clustered around, all yelling at once.

"*¡He, muchacho!* Go find my mother and tell her I'm in here! She lives in—" She named a street in Guadalajara, and some rough directions.

The boy stalled. A couple of pesos came flying down to him. Several kids scrambled for the money, and the strongest beat off the rest.

If it was enough, in his opinion, and especially if there were hope for more money later, he delivered the message. Sometimes a kid stepped on the coin defiantly and said he couldn't find it. Then he held out for ten pesos instead. He had to go all the way on the bus, it would take several hours, and so forth.

Finally the negotiation was completed. If the women were lucky, the message got through. But only when he got around to it, sometimes three days later. Meanwhile, they waited.

There were some women who had waited for years. Their only hope of release was when the D.A. and the mayor finally got together because the jail conditions had become too crowded. Every few years they went through the lists, and let out the less serious offenders.

One girl I met, Elena, had stolen three thousand pesos, or about two hundred fifty dollars, from her boyfriend. She had been in jail already for three years. The boyfriend had turned her in to get her off his back.

I stood there and took in the whole scene.

A large, burly woman who resembled my earlier escort came up to me and shoved me behind bars. The door thundered shut.

"Now you've done it," I said to myself. "Now you're really inside." I started to sweat.

I shared the room with about two hundred fifty women, many with screaming babies and small children. They were all clustered in small groups. The kidnappers were huddled off in one corner by themselves. There was a hot plate with a dirty coffee pot in another corner. Long lines of laundry stretched through the courtyard.

The 'tough' who had put me behind bars was a trustee. There were four of them, all murderers who had been there for almost thirty years. They ran the prison. If you were on their good side, you could get anything: drugs, alcohol, food, medication.

You paid even for the little things. Hot water, for example, was five pesos a bucket. It took ten minutes to fill up a bucket at the faucet. Soap was another five pesos. Kotex a little less, a threadbare little hand towel a little more. But if you were not on the good side of those bitches, they stole from you.

Some of the richer women even had little apartments with television and ice boxes. Their husbands visited every day. But there were not many who could afford one of those.

While I stood there, three women ran up to me before I knew it, and wrestled the pills out of my hand. I'm strong, but they were desperate. They had slept very few nights in five months.

And they made it clear that when I saw the *directora* again, they wanted more.

I found a place against the wall and sat.

The lawyer that Gladys had arranged for me, with money from John Huston, came to visit at eleven.

"Why are you here?" he asked.

"I don't know. I thought you knew," I said, my heart sinking. I saw that it was going to be a long, complicated process.

Armando also came every day, his ardor warming with every visit. Did these conditions or my condition turn him on? There was nothing he could do officially since another lawyer had been named, but he promised to look into it, and do what he could behind the scenes. What he did mainly in those first days was give me comfort, which I desperately needed.

Suddenly I felt that my mother and I were alone in Mexico.

In the early afternoon the whole complexion of the place changed. It was nearing dinner time. The women were fixing themselves up, getting ready to receive their families. They buzzed happily among themselves, putting on elaborate make-up and inspecting their tattered dresses. Laughter started breaking out here and there.

Then the mothers and sisters and cousins began to stream through the doors with hot *tamales* and rice and beans. They stayed until it was time to collect the dirty plates when dinner was finished.

The Indian women, refugees in their own country really, stared dully at the others' food. They had been caught on street corners, selling the Quaaludes that they hid in their Kotexes. What little money they had made had been stolen by the police. Now they were preparing to fight for the vile-looking scraps for their children, when the time came.

And so the long afternoon wore on. Some prisoners went out onto the patio to the clacking sewing machines, to sew little pieces of underwear. They sold them later for a small price, in order to get money for food.

The girls who had kidnapped Guadalupe Zuno still stayed isolated in their corner of the large cell. I heard a stifled moan from time to time, but their faces betrayed no emotion, except enthusiasm sometimes for the study they were doing.

Well-educated, middle-class women, they continued to conduct impromptu seminars in socialistic thinking among themselves. The rest of us stayed away from them, afraid to make friends. The nurse, who had maintained the old man's insulin shots for eighteen days, was among them. She got off later with a lighter sentence.

Suppertime finally came and went, and then bedtime. Two hundred fifty women found their mats and chose their places on the floor. I had no mat or bedding, but there were filthy items piled up in a corner, left over from those lucky ones who had gotten out. I hesitated, not willing to try to fight for what were considered the choice spots.

Two of the women who had stolen my valium came up to me and made friends, inviting me to sleep next to them. I was pleased.

Alicia was highly nervous and ready to break, it seemed to me. She prayed constantly, day and night.

Why was she there? Her husband had spent a long afternoon and evening at the *charreada*. He had come home drunk and shot himself in the belly by accident with his own pistol. Now she was the one in jail. She didn't know where her seven children were. The other one was Elena, the girl whose boyfriend had sent her there indefinitely to get rid of her.

It was freezing cold. The long cell was open to the patio and the night air. I blessed Porfirio again for the poncho I held tightly against me. "At least I made two friends here," I thought.

When I lay down beside them, I discovered the reason why they wanted me there.

They were using my body as a shield against the stinking Indian women who nursed their babies on the other side of me. The stench was nearly unbearable. Their total diet, after all, was the inedible scraps from the others.

Nothing, not even that, prevented me from falling asleep.

The next morning, two hundred fifty women lined up for the seven toilets and showers.

What that meant was a small cell with a hole in the floor, to be used for both activities. There were a couple of slippery bricks to stand on, green with the slime. You soaped up your body with one hand and hung onto your clothes with the other, so that they didn't get stolen. You tried to ignore the rats and the cockroaches.

Still, there was an odd camaraderie about the whole affair.

A Mexican prison is a much more social place than its American counterpart, I would think. (Thank God I don't have a real basis of comparison.) There are no individual cells, except for the rich, and everyone shares in the life together. They share the food, more or less, they share the crises, and they share the good news along with the bad. We had a complete, close-knit little community there behind bars.

On Tuesday, my fourth day there, there was a flurry of special activity. All the women were nearly beside themselves with anticipation. That evening those on good behavior, as judged by the thick trustees, would receive a pink or a blue slip. 'Pink' meant that they could be alone with their husbands for a short time the next day, in a filthy little private cell in back. 'Blue' meant that they could receive other visitors privately on Thursday. Colored paper was used because many of the women were illiterate.

The excitement grew. Everyone shared in the joy of the favored ones. All night long, the huge cell buzzed nervously.

On Wednesday morning, the women were up early. All began making themselves as beautiful as possible. They had no way of knowing, of course, whether their husbands or boyfriends could actually get away to be with them, but all had hopes.

The chattering grew intense. Eager faces peered into dirty, cracked mirrors, as dozens of shaky hands tried to apply mascara and false eyelashes.

"Theresa, do you have a pink slip?"

I held it up.

"Who is coming to see you? Do you have family here?"

I shook my head.

"I wish I could trade you for my boyfriend," laughed one. "He's a real bastard. I think he's sleeping with my sister."

"Or his sister!" chimed in another. Everybody loudly appreciated the joke. The air was electric.

The time finally came. The women were crushed against the iron grill on one side of the patio, yelling to the visitors on the other side. They were jumping up and down, holding their pink slips high in the air. I climbed up on an old bench to try to get a good view of everything, but it broke under my weight.

The huge, tough women in charge stood at the gate on the men's side. One called out a name, and he fought through the mass of horny men to gain entrance.

Then he stood there, and submitted himself to a more than thorough frisking. These fatasses, whose boyfriends had probably all long since died, looked as if they had looked forward to that part all week.

"Hey, Ramona! Is that your little fucker?"

"He's cute! Send him over to me when you're through with him! He looks like he's got enough for two or three of us!"

"Don't make it too long, *chica*! You don't want to get another little brat in this place."

As the tough's hands passed slowly over the man's crotch, the cheers went up.

"*¡Chingaaa—!* Look at that! You better check again for weapons, girl. I think I see a big one hidden in there!"

When the burly trustees had finished their work, they tossed the poor guy into the women's part. He fought his way slowly to his girl, while several other women checked him out themselves, especially those who had not gotten pink slips.

Finally united, the pair made their way back to the tiny cells behind the chapel. There was a concrete bunk against the wall. A faded flowered curtain could be pulled across the entrance, for a little privacy.

I was surprised to see that Armando was there for me.

"*Mi amor,*" he said, "we don't have to wait for Wednesday. We can have one of those little cells any time you say." He threw out his chest and patted his wallet, where I had seen his top government badge. He was in his thirties now, still unmarried, but I knew he liked women. A lot.

The last time I had stayed with him at his house in Guadalajara with an American friend of mine, I found them in bed together the next morning.

"Theresa!" he panted when I discovered them. "*¡Ay! ¡Qué chichonas!* I love the big tits on this woman!"

My friend with the *chiches* just lay there in his king-sized waterbed with a stupid, satisfied smile on her face.

Now in prison, Armando pressed on. "I hear you have a new *gringo* lover. How is he, this Jim, where it counts?" he breathed in my ear.

"Well, that you'll never know, my dear," I said. "Or how I am, either."

There was still too much Dutch blood in me to think that there was anything sexy about humping in a dirty little cell.

He shrugged and laughed cheerfully, as if to say, "I thought so—but it was worth a try, at least."

Howls went up from the women whose men had not showed up. They continued the wailing all afternoon, yanking on their hair and ripping their nylons and tearing off their false eyelashes, until they wore down.

Or until the trustees couldn't stand them any longer, and hustled them off to solitary, to beat the shit out of them.

The system seems crude, it's true. But homosexuality in Mexican prisons is almost non-existent—far lower than in the more "civilized" countries of the world.

When the Wednesday ritual was over, the attention focused again on the lawyers.

Officials from the American consulate, sometimes the consul general himself, came by to see what they could do for the *gringas.* There were three American girls in prison while I was there, scared to death. None of them spoke Spanish.

One of them told me she had bought a used car in Arizona and brought it across. Near Guadalajara, the *federales* had stopped her and torn it apart. They found seeds from a marijuana plant under the floor mat in front. Only the seeds.

"Terry, I've never smoked pot," she told me. "If that's really what they found, it must have been in there long before I bought the car."

Her parents had borrowed on their house, and had already spent $25,000 on legal aid for her, and she was still there. Americans are all thought to be rich in Mexico. It could easily go on for a lot longer.

She consoled herself by visiting an American boy on the other side. They pooled their pink slips and had two afternoons together.

I started getting bored. One day I organized a make-shift basketball game in the courtyard. It came to an abrupt halt when an armed guard in one of the towers was hit by the ball. He accused me of doing it on purpose. Perhaps I did.

On the sixth day Armando was there again, this time to get me out. The trouble had been something about my check to Adolfo Rey. Again. Armando had posted a *garantía*, to allow my release.

Then I was disappointed just as quickly as I had been elated. The question of my papers came up with the *directora*. I still didn't have any.

I went back to prison for three more days, while Armando continued to work on it.

Nine days in all. I had spent the whole hundred and sixty dollars, mostly on tequila, and vodka and 7-Ups, to dull the pain and boredom of the long nights.

I could have checked into the Hilton for about the same amount of money.

On my way out, the women were grabbing me, some saying a friendly good-bye, some asking me to try to get towels or shoes or blankets back to them, once I was out.

I asked Armando to take me to Ofelia's place. She and her family had moved to Guadalajara, where Crisanto had taken a job selling shoes and boots. In Puerto Vallarta they had actually gotten prosperous enough to have one of the first telephones in town. But their Coca-Cola and mineral water business was ruined overnight, when one of his truck drivers turned over on a mountain road and killed three people.

There was no insurance. They lost everything. They had to start over again.

I knocked on the door at Avenida Guzmán, still shivering in my bikini and my pitiful muumuu.

"Theresa!" said their fifteen-year-old, one of my goddaughters. "Have you been to the beach?"

Ofelia came running up to me. "I've been dreaming about you every day this week! Where have you been?"

She reached out her arms and started to give me a big *abrazo*, but I wouldn't let her.

"Lice," I said. "The itching's been driving me up the wall. Just get me to a hot bath with some Lysol. And please—a good, strong tequila!"

I stayed with them for a couple of days, and got to enjoy again the life of freedom I had taken for granted.

After a day or so of rest, I was ready to go out on the town and do some shopping with Ofelia, to clear away my recent unpleasant memories.

In a dress shop, we got a glimpse of Lola Salinas, Miguel's beautiful wife.

We were friends. I had often stayed with her at their mansion when I came to Guadalajara. When she saw me then, she just put her face down and stared at the floor, utterly embarrassed.

There was nothing I wanted to say to her either. She fled at the earliest opportunity.

Back in Puerto Vallarta, we had a late birthday celebration. Jim and Rebecca and Sondra had all pitched in to help with my mother the whole time I was gone. I really appreciated what they had done for me.

I thanked John Huston and Gladys Hill for their help.

He was confused. "But what was the accusation against you, Terry?" he kept asking.

"There wasn't any," I said sadly. "Like the lady said, 'This is Mexico.'"

"Well," he drawled in his husky voice. "Let's try to forget about the politics." He patted me on the shoulder in consolation. "Living here is so fine. Let's forget about the rest."

I returned to Grubb & Ellis, but shortly afterwards they let me go. I suppose I was too big a risk for them.

Before my arrest, I had been involved in a project that John was also excited about. The Nuevo Vallarta people had invited him to build his house on their land. They offered to give him a free ninety-nine-year lease on three acres of property, in return for encouraging his friends among the movie colony to join him there. We all saw him on television, making an advertisement for PV. There was excited talk of Charles Bronson, Gene Hackman, and Stanley Kramer, who had all shown some interest.

This latest chapter in my own history had thrown a whole new light on the project. I could no longer push it with any enthusiasm.

And he had recently had by-pass surgery. He could get sick again. There would be no telephone there, perhaps for years. It was far away from the center of Puerto Vallarta.

But more importantly, this time I told him my whole story. Without frills. I told of all the harassment, all the times in jail or at the immigration office in Mexico City, all the worry and uncertainty, all the deceit among those who I thought were helping me.

John went back to his former plan of building a place near Quimixto, which he did later. He moved out of our house soon afterwards.

I was never bothered again after my time in prison in Guadalajara.

I began to devote my life to Jim and fun times.

I called Helen in San Francisco and asked her to come down and take care of our mother, while Jim and I took off for Europe. We spent a couple of months there, driving through the peaceful, well-ordered villages of England and Scotland and France. He grew a large mustache, so he would look closer to my age. The vacation was a tonic for both of us.

When we returned, we made the first of several trips through America, to try to find the ideal place to settle down, once I had received payment for Las Glorias.

We went north to meet his parents. We looked through several states on the east coast, but none seemed just right. Later, after we had driven up to put Helen's son Robby in a boarding school in Denver, we drove into Santa Fe. It was late September, already the grey, rainy season in San Francisco, but here the air was dry and the sun was bright. We both fell in love with the place immediately. We started negotiations to buy a ranch, about an hour out of town.

We camped, both of us for the first time, all along the Pacific coast of Mexico. On one of our trips, Jim had bought a big station wagon in San Antonio.

In no time, we were old hands at camping. I had a big mattress, which we threw in back. We drove until we found the tiniest road possible, leading off the highway through the jungle toward the sea. Invariably it led to a small, sandy cove that we had completely to ourselves.

Jim parked the car under a palm tree (he usually drove, since I had never gotten a driver's license), and then I scrambled up onto the roof to secure the mosquito netting. We had rigged a large stone in the center of the net, on a rope. I tossed it up and caught it on a palm branch above the car. In an instant, we had a tent ready-made.

We hoisted the mattress on top of the station wagon, and made love all night under the stars, listening to the iguanas *swoosh* through the palm trees, or sometimes tuning in to music on my short-wave radio, coming in from far away out in the Pacific.

We loved to snorkel in the calm pools, to hunt for lobster or crab, oysters or mussels along the shore. Each night there was a different delicacy at our camp fire.

Finally I had found the paradise I had come to Mexico to discover!

There were guavas and mangos and papayas for the picking, which we ate sprinkled with lemon and salt and chile powder, the way the Mexicans did. We could be completely independent from the village stores, once we had a small stock of salt and coffee. And rum and cigarettes, of course.

Occasionally we went into a restaurant for breakfast. Jim was working on his Spanish, but it was still rough around the edges.

"¿Tiene huevos?" he asked the waiter, looking up from his phrase book. An old joke, but he walked right into it.

And as many times as it must have happened to our waiter, the guy still snickered. Actually, the expression on his face was almost mean, probably because the *macho* guys in the kitchen were by this time roaring with laughter, and jeering at him.

"I thought I asked him if they had eggs here," said Jim. "What's funny?"

I was laughing too, and the waiter was becoming even more irritated with me.

"You did," I explained. "But there's a double meaning. What you actually asked him was whether he has balls—the important kind, don't you know?" I added, in my crispest Oxford accent.

We bartered for all kinds of little trash we didn't need. Jim was actually better at that than I was. He had developed a good Cary Grant imitation, and he could act nonchalant until the little storekeeper was salivating.

One afternoon we pulled up onto a beautiful deserted beach. We jumped out of the car and dived into the water immediately. It was a hot day. Then Jim settled down to finish off a bottle of tequila, while I took off down the shore to see what I could see.

Far off in the distance, it looked as if the beach was covered with huge black tarantulas. I don't particularly like the beasts, but just then the breeze took my hat, and I went running along the sand after it, in the direction of the big spiders.

I grabbed my hat, and suddenly screeched to a halt. They were not tarantulas at all. What I had seen was the pubic hairs of a couple of dozen German tourists, all spread out naked and oblivious on the sand. They hadn't made a sound or a movement.

Apparently sunbathing is a very serious business with Germans. They never even looked over at my gaping mouth.

I stifled a giggle and turned back. I was surprised they had gotten away with it. Nude sunbathing was illegal in Mexico, and it was one of the things the authorities loved to hand out citations for—long after they had gotten themselves a leisurely eyeful, from their hiding places in the dunes.

If we stayed closer to Puerto Vallarta, we usually went through town and down toward Mismaloya, where the set of *Night of the Iguana* still stands, decaying in the sun.

We sometimes met Richard Burton there, walking along the beach, as we were. By that time he was with Susan Hunt.

I liked him better than Peter O'Toole. After all the world's hysteria had centered on him for so many years, he still had the quality of a friendly country boy about him.

If we wanted to get way out of town, we drove down the Manzanillo highway to Tenacatita, a little past the Club Med where I had tried to run myself off the road after the fight with Bob Lewis. There we found a totally unspoiled beach, and the place had the added attraction of hot springs.

We met a Swiss couple there who had been keeping their discovery of the place a secret for years. Every winter they came for several months, and parked a VW camper in the same spot, next to a little patio area they had fashioned under a big *palapa*. They had their lawn chairs along, and everything they needed for writing and painting.

They fished and sunned, just like we did, and luxuriated in the tropical paradise. Then when spring came around, they went back for half a year to work in Switzerland. Every year when they returned, they loaded themselves down with secondhand clothing for the poor families at the nearby villages.

The water of the Rio Caliente was so hot you could cook a chicken in it, and we did. Where it became cooler, as it emptied into the sea, we used to sit for hours and take warm baths. There were a few houses up the river, with little plots of sugar cane or *coquitos*. There the Mexican women's social life on the river went on, as it had in Puerto Vallarta back in the early days. But neither of us bothered the other.

As much as I liked the grand hotels in the cities, I preferred camping like this with Jim. I don't think I would have stayed as long afterwards in Mexico as I did, if he hadn't been there with me.

One day he came up to me on the beach at Las Glorias and said, with great excitement, "Come on! We're starting a baseball team, and we need you to translate!"

"Baseball? I don't know anything about baseball."

"Well, I do. Come on. I'll tell you, and you tell them."

I still hung back. "It'll be fun!" he tempted me. "We'll make some extra money to buy us a lobster now and then!"

It sounded simple enough. We drove up the coast a little past Bucerías, where Jim had been watching the fishermen play in their little wooden soccer stadium. They too were excited about having a genuine American coach to teach them all about his national sport. Here in Bucerías, of course, it was *béisbol*.

The team was made up of the local fishermen. They started work around four in the morning, and were back home by noon. After dinner and a *siesta*, they mended their nets or whatever, went to the river for a bath, and then they were ready for some action.

They were tough, muscular little guys, who got right into the calisthenics Jim taught them, to warm up. I wasn't needed for that part, since they just imitated him. Then he started showing them how to pitch a slow ball, how to get their thumb just in the right place. And then how to slide into base. The mounds of cowshit dotting the field didn't deter them in the least.

Finally it was my turn to explain the game. The guys had built a little *palapa* for me, and I had had an easy time of it so far. I had gotten to rest all by myself in the Mexican "dugout."

To my surprise, some of the guys even had gloves. We decided they would be the outfielders. Jim instructed me, and I relayed the message. "Now it's your job," I said very precisely, "to go out there and catch flies." *Atrapar las moscas.*

They gave me a strange look. I shrugged my shoulders. Neither of us knew what we were talking about, but that was what Jim had told me to tell them.

They must have thought it was a pretty silly game, but they walked far out into the field and stood at attention. Then they started swatting and grabbing at the flies swarming around the cowpies.

Jim came running up yelling. "Now what did you tell them? What in the hell are they doing out there?"

I stuck my chin out belligerently. I was ready to resign my position as assistant coach already.

"You told me to tell them to go catch flies. Isn't that what they're doing?"

He fell down on the field, howling with laughter. I did too, though it took him quite a while to explain the joke, gasping for breath as he was. All the little dark fishermen gathered around us, scratching their heads.

Jim's career as a baseball coach ended shortly after it began.

26

Puerto Vallarta was no longer a small, sleepy town. It was becoming a city, which meant interesting restaurants, several new big hotels, and a lively night life. It also meant that the lost, the unfortunate, and the con men were finding us too. The beach boys from Acapulco had moved in, and many others too, with their scams.

After John Huston moved out with Maricela and Gladys, we had the Swift family. They rented my house, and we all moved next door to my mother's and spread out.

A prosperous family of four, they pulled up in a beautiful new gold Cadillac Eldorado. They had been vacationing in town for two weeks already at Hotel Las Palmas, and had decided to extend their stay for three more months. The man paid me by check. I knew it would take a month and a half for the check to clear, but I was impressed by Mr. Swift.

After about ten days, he went back to his business in the States. We didn't have much in common, and the woman and her children stayed pretty much to themselves.

Lupita told me one day that that our renter had borrowed a hundred pesos from my kitchen money.

"What for?"

"For food, I guess. She hasn't paid her maid yet either."

I made a friendly visit next door. I must say I was curious about how she intended to feed a family on a hundred pesos. I didn't learn much from the mother, except that her husband was "sending money."

Since she didn't speak Spanish, I quizzed the maid while I was there.

"They don't eat. They don't have milk. Only beans."

A week after that, they were gone. Birds flew out of my empty house. They hadn't stolen anything, but I was left with a check, when it finally cleared, for $1200. It was marked 'account closed.' I was furious. I had thought I was a better judge of character than that.

Jim calmed me down.

There had been a chance to rent the place to Penny Barker and her family, but I had turned them down because my house was rented to the Swifts.

In the early weeks that I knew Jim, he and I hung out a lot at the marina, and we met the Barkers first through their son Fred. That boy was a con man with the best of them. About eight years old, he spoke perfect Spanish and English. His skin was as dark as could be, but his hair was white—well, green actually, from all the chlorine in the hotel pools.

He would stand boldly on the swaying boarding planks of the big yachts, and sell small fish as bait.

"Those fish look dead, son," said the millionaires looking out at him over the side.

"Oh no, *capitán*! They are just sleeping. If you put them back in the water, they will come alive. Look!" He held the fish so that it appeared to squirm a little in his hand. "Bait! Good bait!"

It seemed there was always at least one who fell for it.

He acted as interpreter for the yacht owners when they wanted to have their boats washed down or their baggage moved. He was unofficial tourist agent at the marina, filled with information about all the sights to be seen. He rented out his bicycle by the hour to all the little Mexican boys who hung around, and he was a hustler for the parachute boys on the beach. The young man was becoming a real entrepreneur.

Gradually we got to know Penny too. She and her husband had actually been guests at Las Glorias a few years back, but I hadn't paid much attention to her. Just five feet tall, she was tough, and full of ingenuity, especially the mechanical kind. She had to be. She had left school about ten years before when she fell in love with Fred Barker during spring break at Guaymas, on the coast south of Tucson.

She had married him after a few days, and they took off right then. By this time now, ten years later, they had sailed the Pacific, all up and down the coast of the Americas, and as far off as Fiji and Samoa.

They had known nothing about sailing when they started, like Jim, but Penny took a couple of days' worth of lessons on the sextant, and off they went. Little Freddy and his sister were born on the boat. They grew up in a little crib in the stern. Their diapers were emptied and sloshed out in the sea. It was the only life the kids had known.

Romantic? Perhaps. But by the time we got acquainted, Penny's husband was in the advanced stages of alcoholism, and he had gotten to be an unbearable, foul-mouthed, repulsive man. He made some money at the marina by taking groups out on fishing trips. But he spent it all immediately on himself, on at least one bottle of tequila a day, and lots of smelly cigars. He ate garlic all day for his heart condition. Jim and I avoided him, but we admired Penny's guts.

After we got friendly at the marina, Penny started showing up every day at the house, with her two kids and a big black Labrador, who kept fouling up my pool in the garden. The girl seemed desperate for company, especially American company, and Jim enjoyed talking to her, so I bit my tongue and tried to calm down the maids.

"*Señora*, those little brats are at the refrigerator again!" Lupita complained.

"What's the matter? Don't they ever eat at home?" I asked, exasperated.

"No, they're not starving, exactly. They go for the cake and the sweets. And *señora*, they've been stealing guavas and breadfruit from the trees too."

"Well, just keep kicking them out when you see them," I said.

I'm afraid I wasn't much help, but I didn't quite know how to handle this. Perhaps once Penny put them in school, as she intended to do, everything would work out.

I learned that the kids weren't just stealing my food. They had been kicked out of every hotel pool and restaurant on the beach, after enjoying a meal and then signing the check with a fictitious room number.

One day out the side of my head I thought I saw flashes of white plastic in my big mango tree off the balcony. I looked hard into the shiny, dark leaves, but I couldn't make out anything. The branches shook again and I shouted at the movement, but I still couldn't see what was causing it. By the time I got downstairs, the tree was serene and peaceful.

When I drove out later to do some errands in town, all of Don Andrés' kids reported that the little *gringo* had been selling my mangos on the highway. He came dragging in about supper time, his pockets bulging with pesos, and an awful stomach ache. He had finished off the green ones that nobody bought.

"Serves you right, you little monster!" I yelled. "You were stealing from my tree. That's not your tree, it's mine!"

With an angelic expression, he looked up at me and said, "Oh, Aunt Terry, there are still millions of mangos on that tree. I've never seen a mango tree like that one. God will never let your tree stop making beautiful mangos!"

Well, I guess he had a point. But I drew the line when I noticed my table. Jim had painstakingly glued peso coins all around the edge of a Mexican leather table of mine. Then he varnished it to a high gloss, and we used it for cocktails on the balcony.

One evening at sunset, when we were sipping a leisurely tequila on the balcony with Penny, I noticed that there was a new look about the place: my table was ringed with dozens of clean, round, empty circles without varnish.

Penny and I looked at each other without a word and then ran to the balcony, screaming for her little *bandido*. But he had been too quick for us.

The little son of the storekeeper on the corner came by later with a message. "My father wants to know if it's OK, *señora*. The *gringo* is buying candy for all the kids in the neighborhood. But his pesos are so strange! They all have varnish on one side!"

With a father like his, I guess we were lucky to get by with minor damage. Fred Barker's latest project was selling shares in a silver mine, located high up in the mountains near Mascota. For a $25,000 investment, some lucky Americans could become part owners in an enterprise that would make them millions.

Several jumped at the chance.

Jacqueline and her husband were the first. They were perhaps typical. The money was nothing to them. They had a house in Tulsa, and a condo on Lake Chapala. Jacqueline was a striking woman in her fifties, aging well. She had a massage every day, before she went shopping. On many an afternoon I was with her when she spent over a thousand dollars on clothes, even though her closets bulged so much already, that she had trouble trying to find a place for them. What could a woman do in the Mexican tropics with seven fur coats?

"Oh, Tom! A silver mine would be fun!" she begged him.

Fred and Penny took them up into the mountains to see their new property. It was unusual in Mexico, but their Mexican partner did actually have the legal mineral rights, since the title to his place predated the revolution.

The trip to the mine involved eight hours in a bumpy truck. Then they all transferred to *burros*, for another several hours. After a while, it became a sort of hideous experiment to see whether the tequila or their rear ends would give out first.

But Fred's enthusiasm kept them going, and convinced them that they were having fun.

When they got to the mine, what they found was a small hole in the side of a hill. Two men were working there, ever so slowly, with their *burros*, some picks and a couple of wheelbarrows.

"Of course, it's not producing much right now," Fred explained, "but once we start developing it—"

The investors were perfectly happy, if exhausted. They stayed the night in a little mountain hut nearby, and rode back down the next day.

Then the two couples flew off to Las Hadas, a luxury hotel in Manzanillo, to discuss business.

Penny told me later that it could have worked. There was silver in the ground. But that almost wasn't the point, for them or for their investors. The Barkers needed money, their partners had it.

They continued to come down to Mexico to 'check on the investment.' They didn't feel the need of actually looking at the mine again, but they talked about it at all the best hotels. It was an adventure. Penny and Fred moved into an $800-a-month apartment at Los Tules. For a while, they were living high. But not even one-shot investments from a few Americans can support a life like that for long.

I couldn't have dealt with my investors like that. I couldn't have taken their money. Well, I could have. I could have disappeared in Guadalajara and never been found. But that wasn't what I wanted.

Penny and I got to know each other better later on, and we talked about it. She explained it the way she saw it:

"Those Americans had more money than they knew what to do with. Look at the guy who wrote that best-selling exercise book. He bought the Sherwood house for almost four hundred thousand dollars, the first day he ever saw it."

It was true. There were huge, luxurious mansions in Puerto Vallarta that were going for hundreds of thousands of dollars. Meanwhile, the rich Mexicans, like the man from Woolworths who dug up a chest of Spanish doubloons, was buying up half of Vail, Colorado.

"These guys were buying adventure more than anything," Penny said. "They came down here, and we showed them a good time. I translated for them all over the place. They were buying our time, and they got their money's worth. And what they lost here in Mexico," she added, "they gained on taxes at home."

"The rich are bored," she yawned. "They want to be amused."

Maybe she's right. They lost everything, but she and Jacqueline are still the best of friends.

Meanwhile, Carter put a stop to much of the careless profiteering in America, and the devaluation of the peso in 1976 finished off the job in Mexico. Wealthy Mexicans transferred millions of dollars out of the country secretly in the first days following it, to Switzerland if they were able to find the proper contact quickly enough. Those who weren't were crushed.

Shortly after that, ex-President Miguel Alemán reneged on Conrad Hilton's guaranteed option to renew his thirty-year lease. Together as friends, they had built hotels in Acapulco, Guadalajara, and Mexico City back in the late Forties.

That was quite a jolt. I asked myself if Hilton, with all his influence and all his money for the best lawyers, was booted out, what hope was there for *La Holandesa*?

One day I was at my favorite liquor store, and my friend behind the counter said, "Theresa, have you heard? The Swifts are back in town."

Aha! Now was my chance. I grabbed Jim and we made a long, careful inspection of all the hotel parking lots, looking for a gold Eldorado. We finally found it, right across the highway from Las Glorias, in fact, parked way back behind the Hotel Las Cabañas. By this time the man even had a personalized license plate that said "SWIFT."

"Now how am I going to deal with this?" I thought. "I'm always tripping over the police when I don't want to see them, but they're never there when I need them." They always had some excuse—a broken jeep, or an important investigation on the other side of town.

Then I hit upon a plan.

We waited until dark, and then Jim and I snuck back over to Las Cabañas. He boosted me up over the six-foot wall in the rear. I fell over the other side and nearly sprained my ankle, but I kept crawling on my stomach toward the Eldorado, and I let the air out of all four tires. You would think I had been raised on American television.

Very early the next morning I raced down to the police station. To encourage the interest of those sleepy guys in my project, I offered them half of the $1200, when we recovered the money. They stood to earn $600 in less than ten minutes. They were in their car before I was in mine.

The cop got Swift's room number at the office, and then said to me, "Stay back behind this column. When you see him, shake your head yes or no, if it's the man."

"Police!" they shouted, as three of them stormed the door all at once and kicked it in. Their revolvers were drawn.

A handsome, gray-haired American man, pale as a sheet, stood in the doorway, probably thinking Pancho Villa had struck again. A stranger. I shook my head 'no,' totally embarrassed, and ran off toward the office.

The cops caught up with me in front, angry as hell about their easy money. "Listen, *Theresa la Terrible*, just let us earn our $600 the usual way, after this, *¿de acuerdo?*

I invited them over to Las Glorias for a couple of pitchers of Bloody Marys (it was still early morning), to ease the pain.

That afternoon, Jim and I were swimming at one of the hotel pools nearby. In the pool he met a friendly American who came up and started warning both of us to be careful in Mexico.

"I'm getting the hell out of here," he said gravely. "They beat down your door whenever they feel like it. And they let the air out of all your tires!"

In earlier days, I would have invited the poor guy to stay for a week at Las Glorias, on the house. But I no longer had a hotel. I was sorry I had ruined his vacation, but I didn't dare to confess the truth.

My kids came down to visit me in Mexico during the school vacations. Little Bear and Buster had now become Alfred and Robert, as they were named, for my father and my husband. They were growing up.

They loved the water sports, tearing around the whole bay area parachuting, sailing, fishing, and deep sea diving. Once they caught a nine-foot electric eel, skinned it, and threw a party, with twenty-five people eating off of it. They told me they especially missed the fresh papaya in the mornings, and the *camotes* and *calabazas*, the candied sweet potatoes and squash, at the street stands.

Little Dido was ten years old then, still not of an age where she could move around much without a chaperone in Mexico, but she was content to be at home with Lupe's baby. It was the baby she had missed most of all.

My sons started bringing home girls.

Women, I should say. They looked as if they were twenty-five.

"Where did you meet?" I asked casually, when we were introduced. A friendly, noncommittal smile was glued to my face.

"Oh, we were all at the City Dump last night," said one of the pretty, empty-headed ones.

I pulled young Bob aside in the kitchen. "Now, don't you think they're a little old? What the hell do you do with these girls?" I asked. I looked at him hard. There was just a bit of fluff coming in, on his upper lip. He smiled a sly smile.

I gasped, "You're only—"

"MOM!" he interrupted, looking around to see if anyone was listening to us.

" —fourteen," I whispered.

"We dance, Mom. Come on!" He swore to me there was no drinking or drugs, and I believed him. These were really little Mexican boys, after all, and the Mexicans aren't much interested in drugs. They're smart. Everything they have, they sell up north to the Americans.

I backed off, and decided to relax and enjoy the show.

One day I was out with Rebecca, and she dropped me off at home rather late in the afternoon. Both my new VW and Jim's station wagon were gone. I waited in the house till about 10:30 or 11:00, getting angrier and angrier all the time.

Jim finally pulled into the driveway in the station wagon.

"Now where the hell have you been?" I asked. "You could have left a note at least."

"We—uhh—we've been out dancing," he said.

Jim was never a very good liar.

"Where are the boys?"

He hesitated. Then he said, "OK, Terry. Promise you won't get mad at me."

I took a deep breath.

"The boys have been begging me to take them to a whore house. They say that's the way everybody learns in Mexico. The fathers take them."

"So my little boys are downtown at—"

"They're not little." He started to laugh in spite of himself. "They guaranteed me, they're not little."

I couldn't help it. I started laughing too. My boys hadn't had much experience with whores since Cloro used to chase them away from the dugout canoes when they were babies. I guess the time had come.

"They didn't want to go downtown. They said they heard the Cadillac Bar is much better. Better *chiches*."

The place was a dive, way down a dirt road and up toward the hills behind the airport. There were always dozens of cars parked all around. It had a reputation for well-stacked girls in low-cut dresses, and dancing all night to the *mariachi* music.

The boys had my VW. They'd been driving since they were twelve, without a license. Helen's son Robby was with them too. Jim took them out there in his car and got them set up, and then left.

So he said. They'd been gone for hours.

"Well, we had a few beers and danced. They're having a great time."

What could I do? I backed off. Again.

At five in the morning I heard the rustle of a VW being pushed slowly into the driveway. As much as they worried about the noise of the car engine, they weren't able to stifle their giggles.

"They're home," I said, yawning.

"Go back to sleep. I'll take care of it."

Jim got up and met them on the stairway. They all tiptoed out on the balcony, giggling about the beer and the dancing, and how they looked down the dresses all night, at the big, juicy *chiches*.

First Bear—I mean Al—had disappeared with a girl, and then Robby. Poor little Bob was only fourteen. He had to wait. But finally Robby took pity on him, and brought him in to share the same girl. They were in a hilarious mood.

Every few moments a *ssssh-ssh* broke out, when they remembered I was still safely asleep.

Suddenly it got totally quiet on the balcony. "Now what the hell is going on?" I asked myself.

I snuck over to the window, and peeked out.

There they were, lined up in a row, with three little penises sticking out of their pants. Jim was examining them. Apparently he had gotten some sense in the meantime, and started worrying about disease. He was crouched on his knees, trying to get a good look without having to touch them. Their three little cocks in a row, all red with their recent work-out!

"OK. Now go wash off with alcohol," I heard Jim whisper. "And when you come back, I'm giving you a shot of penicillin, just to make sure."

We laid in a good stock of penicillin for the rest of the summer. This was the first "education" they had ever shown any interest in.

They also learned from Robby how to win drinks, playing backgammon at Carlos O'Brian's. There too, the women always seemed to flock around.

When Jim and I wanted to get away for a week to go camping by ourselves, we put them on a boat, the ferry to Cabo San Lucas, and sent them to Baja California, return trip. There wasn't much damage they could do on the boat, we figured, and Dido was safe with Lupita. I gave them each a hundred bucks to spend.

When we returned, the house was full of beautiful German girls in their twenties. Little Bob spilled the beans that time, by accident. And when the girls learned they were only fourteen, they left in a hurry. Al was pissed. But luckily for them, the girls couldn't make any arrangements to get out of town right away, and they were back by evening. They stayed for several days. My house was starting to turn into a youth hostel.

Helen's son Robby was turning into a real beach bum, strutting around the big bars with a gin and tonic in his hand, brown as a berry, and totally comfortable in both Spanish and English.

He was becoming a genuine Mexican *macho*, in all the unpleasant ways. But he was also developing an interest, and a real talent, for deep-sea diving. He proved it one Sunday when we were all diving off Mismaloya.

Helen liked to dive with Gabriel, the local expert, every weekend. The waters around Los Tres Arcos, 'the three arches,' were always a hub of activity. Large boats from California would anchor there with perhaps a dozen college kids on board, whose summer job it was to dive for exotic tropical fish. But Helen was more interested in the huge carp, which sometimes grew to a couple of feet in length.

We were all out one pleasant Sunday afternoon. It was nearing sunset. I had already picked up a couple of flounder for our supper, and was relaxing on deck. (The Mexicans do not touch flounder. Since they swim flat—that is, parallel with the surface—and both eyes are on the same side of their body, they are considered 'devil fish.' But in America and elsewhere, they're simply considered a great dinner!)

It was late, but the divers had decided to treat themselves to one last dive. Helen didn't feel like taking the time to put on her weights, so she jumped straight into the water. She had forgotten to take her knife too.

I was sipping a rum and Coke on deck, when out of nowhere, the sea started to come up strong and heavy. The waves grew wild in moments. Jim was on shore, not far off, building a campfire for our evening cook-out. He waved to us from the beach to come in fast.

Suddenly, Robby ran past me, yelling, "Stay with the boat! Mom's in trouble." He dove into the water and started swimming fast toward Los Arcos.

I ran to the railing. The boat was heaving, and the waves were crashing everywhere. In the distance I saw my sister, dashed cruelly against the rocks. There was blood streaming everywhere from her body. With speed and efficiency, Robby lifted her off the rocks and got her back onto the boat. Gabriel had already surfaced, and we all rushed Helen in to Puerto Vallarta to the hospital.

In the car, Gabriel told us the story. Helen just moaned. She plainly wanted to die.

They were at the bottom, near the end of the thirty minutes their tanks allowed them. She had spotted a huge carp, and shot out her line. It was only when the fish had circled her a couple of times and entangled her in her own line, that she realized their time was running out, and that she had forgotten her knife. She swam down to Gabriel on the floor of the sea, grabbed the knife from his boot, and cut herself free.

But without her weights, she shot up fast, from over a hundred feet deep. On the surface, she became completely disoriented. Her ear drum had burst, and the blood was pouring out.

When Robby spotted her, she was swimming toward the rocks instead of the boat. Then the big waves took her body and hurled it against Los Arcos. She was wearing her life jacket and tanks, which protected the top half of her, but her hips and legs were a mass of deep gashes.

When we lifted her up onto the deck, we saw she was covered with inch-long spines from the sea urchins attached to the rocks. They were burrowing into her body, and she was screaming out with pain.

Calderón put her up on the operating table at the hospital. Then the fun started. He took out a huge, flat paddle and started spanking her, beating her really, all over the lower body. I saw that Helen was suffering, but I couldn't help it: the whole scene looked so silly, that I snuck off to the side, where she couldn't see me stifling my laughter. She looked like a naughty child who was being punished.

The doctor's treatment may seem cruel or primitive, but actually it's the only effective remedy against urchins. He was popping the little spines out of her bruised flesh, so he could grab onto them. There's no way to cut them out whole, for they break off in the flesh too easily, and then continue to work their way through the body and into the bloodstream, sometimes with fatal results.

We picked out stingers for weeks afterwards. She was left with scars all over her lower body. One little devil did get away from us, and two years later, it had worked its way across and out the other side of her. She was lucky.

Meanwhile, our Emilia was proving to be a perfect addition to our family. It was her job to take care of my mother, who was by that time in a wheelchair, from her latest falls and broken bones. '*Mi gorda*,' we called her, because she was plump, good-natured, and easy-going. The term referred to her round figure, but in Spanish its sense is endearing, not mean.

My mother loved her too, though they squabbled constantly, as Dido liked to do with everyone.

To bathe her, it was easiest for Emilia to take off both their clothes, roll the wheelchair into the large shower, and soap her down with her fat arms. The water would start out too cold. My mother pinched her. Then the water was too hot. My mother pulled hard on her pubic hairs, which were right there at her level, within easy reach.

All of this was carried on at top volume every morning, my mother screaming bloody murder in Dutch, and Emilia trying to calm her down in her gentle, caressing Spanish. They understood each other, but not through their words—though the old lady did manage to pick up some colorful obscenities in Spanish along the way, too. It was a real circus. They had us all in stitches.

Once a week on Emilia's day off, I drove her over to her little village of Ixtapa, a short distance away on the Rio Ameca. We loaded ourselves down with several sacks full of mangoes and avocados, or whatever our trees were bearing at the time.

She lived in a run-down little *palapa* with her grandmother, a couple of sisters and some cousins, and her own eleven children. There were about twenty in all, sheltered by a few bamboo poles and a leaky roof of palm fronds.

As long as I had been in Mexico by now, I was still shocked by the contradiction. Puerto Vallarta was filling up with swank luxury hotels and condominiums. During the week at my house, Emilia was surrounded by the twentieth century, modern appliances, beautiful furniture, a complete bathroom with all new fixtures, and well-kept gardens.

When she went home, a few short miles away, she returned to the Middle Ages.

I had managed to rescue some of the materials from my carpentry shop when the bulldozers came through, and so in my last year in Mexico, I found myself in the building business again.

Once a week we started adding posts, and bricks, and pieces of asbestos roofing material to the sacks of fruits and vegetables we carried. And I built her a house in Ixtapa. Sometimes I brought a few workers along with me, and we also made her some built-in concrete furniture and an oven, in the Mexican style.

Her eighty-year-old grandmother watched our progress from her hammock off to the side. A frail woman, shriveled down to perhaps only seventy pounds, she spent her life now in that *hamaca*.

Her bladder and her runny bowels emptied out onto the dirt floor beneath. When the smell got too bad, some loving family member shoveled the mess out the back of the house, and replaced the floor with fresh earth from the front. To bathe her, they doused her with a bucket of warm water from the river. The poor woman never left her hammock. She would die there.

I hadn't seen anything like that since the concentration camp in Java, and I had hoped I would never have to be exposed to a scene like it again. It was pretty hard for me to take.

"At least I'm going to buy you a plastic sheet," I promised. "You can put it on the floor underneath, and it will be easier to clean."

"Oh, doña Theresa, a piece of plastic like that costs—well, my wages for two weeks. *Muchas gracias*, but we can do it this way."

I dropped the subject. Probably if I had bought them one, they would have put it away to keep it nice, and continued doing as they had always done, as their people had done for centuries.

Then my attitude about it all started to change.

"At least the woman is here at home, in the hub of the activity," I decided. I watched all the kids come to her all day long and kiss her and talk to her. They took turns carefully feeding her, bite by tiny bite. The woman was able to watch the youngest of her grandchildren grow up, swinging in another hammock right beside her.

She was not shunted off to an old folks' home, as many women her age are in America. She continued with the social life she loved, surrounded by her family.

Clean? Perhaps not. That offended my Dutch blood. But this woman had no lack of love.

Jim was beginning to get bored. He used to hang around the marina and meet new people, going out sailing with them sometimes, sometimes helping to wash down the boats or do other odd jobs.

There was certainly no possibility for him to pursue his legal profession in Puerto Vallarta. At the marina, he met an international group of people, who were always fascinating.

There was a couple from Chicago who had just bought a boat there, and invited us to try it out with them on their first voyage. He was a black man from some Caribbean island originally, with blond hair in tight curls, and blue-black eyes. His wife was beautiful, and wealthy.

I organized about a week's worth of provisions for us, and we four took off up the coast. The first night out, we met the *Pacific Princess*, the 'love boat,' all lit up like a fairyland. Dozens of faces peered down at us from the railing, possibly thinking that we envied them. But we were free to go anywhere on the high seas, and stop whenever we found our own private, jeweled cove. There was no place we wanted to be, rather than right where we were.

We sailed a bit past Punta de Mita, then turned around and headed south, to visit our favorite Tenacatita, where the springs bubbled hot into the Pacific. Large schools of Spanish mackerel and *bonitos* swam past, close to the surface. A giant manta ray, beautiful in its display of raw power, leapt out of the sea and landed on its back in front of us. We threw out a fishing line and caught the huge, poisonous tail of the beast and let him do the work of pulling the yacht for a time, until it got to be too dangerous. Its wing span was over twenty feet. We cut him loose.

Finally we anchored off Yelapa, at the south end of the Bay of Banderas. There we swam, fished, sunned, listened to good music, and drank a lot of *mezcal* on the beach. We watched the huge waves roll toward us in our hallucinatory state. We screamed with delight, as they threatened to wipe us flat in the sand. We pretended to be even richer than we were—or than they were, anyhow. We had a relaxing, thoroughly enjoyable time.

Sailing back toward the marina at Puerto Vallarta, we passed in front of my beach at Las Glorias.

I hadn't seen my mother for a week, and I was feeling a little guilty, so I told Jim, "Take my car keys and bring the guys back in my VW. I'm going to swim home. I'll meet you all there."

There was a good brisk wind for sailing. We were only about a third of a mile out from the shore, and I could easily get home.

I waved a cheery good-bye and dived into the clear blue waters. And straight into a huge, thick cloud of shit, hovering about three feet below the surface of the water, and at least three feet thick.

In a flash, I was coated with the international excrement of thousands of Mexicans and millions of tourists, who were enjoying their Pacific paradise at that same moment, oblivious to it all, only a few hundred yards away. I had dived in at the end of the *fideicomiso's* much-heralded new sewer line.

I fought my way to the surface. Brown filth streaked my body from head to foot, glued to my skin. I brushed at it, and succeeded only in spreading it around even more.

I screamed after my friends on the yacht, but they had already moved too far away in the direction of the marina.

I was choking, trying to keep the noxious stuff out of my mouth. But it was already in my ears, in my eyes, and matted all through my hair. My bikini was filling up with hundreds of slimy little turds.

I thrashed through the water to the shore, hoping the friction of the waves slicing past me would wash off some of my oozy brown coating. But when I stood up on the sand, I felt as if there was even more, if possible. Long, stringy turds drooled from my hair and into my face.

"EMILIA!" I screamed from the surf. "Emilia, get me the hose!"

"*¡Señora! ¿Qué le pasó?*"

She came running. "What happened to you? What is that stuff?"

"Never mind! Just turn on the hose! And get the alcohol."

In an instant, I was safely behind my garden wall. I pulled off my swimming suit. Soaking wet piles of shit fell off my body on all sides, and into the flower beds. I hosed myself off thoroughly, and included an impromptu ice-cold douche into the bargain. Anyone coming to our house for a visit would have had quite a show.

"Your goddam country! Just look what they did to me!" I yelled.

Poor, gentle Emilia, *mi gorda*. Somehow in that moment, it became all her fault.

"Get me some more rubbing alcohol! Grab the whiskey bottles if you have to! Goddam lying, stealing sonsabitches! *¡Corre , corre!*"

It was the *fideicomiso* who stole and lied and skimmed the top off thousands of payments from the *rancheros* along the coast. Emilia would never have dreamed of it.

For my bath, she brought some bourbon, which I don't particularly like to drink, and for my spirits, a good stiff rum and Coke. That girl knew her business.

"*Doña,* this is not good for your heart," she said, with huge eyes.

I calmed down relatively quickly. At least enough to get myself into the shower inside my house, and start bathing and rubbing down with alcohol all over again. I scrubbed every inch of myself three times.

"Well," I thought when I finished. "I'm covered with bourbon, now what do I do?"

My mind flashed on the erotic possibilities. "Jim would love this!" I giggled. I stopped short, remembering that I was supposed to be angry, but then started giggling again.

Emilia brought me another rum and Coke.

"*Gracias, mi gorda,*" I said softly. "*Sabes que te quiero.* I love you. You know that, don't you?"

"*Sí, señora,*" she smiled.

The explosion was over.

We talked often of how we wished that she could somehow follow me to America when I left, and stay with us. But with eleven children, we both knew that was impossible.

Still angry about my shit bath, I went to the mayor. I went to the newspaper. I screamed bloody murder at the offices of the *fideicomiso.* They all expressed deep concern. But nothing changed, for many years.

Now, finally, the sewer line goes out a mile and a half.

Gradually I noticed that Emilia was becoming more *gorda* than ever. She was spending a lot more time hanging around my refrigerator. Usually quick on her feet, even in the little spongy rubber sandals she liked to wear, she had started taking it easier, and I noticed her hand sometimes going to the small of her back.

"Don't you feel well, Emilia?" I asked, half knowing what the answer would be already. Plump as she was, she had several admirers. One *ranchero* in particular liked to ride past our house on his horse, and look longingly in our direction.

"*¡Ay, señora!* Don't be angry with me." Tears welled up in her big, brown doe's eyes. "I am pregnant again!" she admitted, and started to sob.

"Emilia, how could you let that happen? You already have eleven children! " I said, pointing out the obvious.

I could have added, "—from seven different men, and you're not married yet!" But I could see that she had enough troubles.

She looked shyly at the floor. "You remember my day off a couple of months ago? You had some business in town, and we didn't do any building that day."

"Yes," I said, impatiently.

"Well, I took all my kids' clothes to the river to wash them."

I could see the scene, as I've seen it hundreds of times. Washing at the river is a social affair. Scattered along the river bank, where the water flows more slowly, a dozen women crouch in their brassieres and panties. Each one has her favorite *palapa,* for protection from the sun. They bend over to soap the clothes and scrub them on a large, flat rock, and then they slap them hard on the surface, to let the river carry off the soap and the dirt. When it comes time to wash out their own underclothes, they simply wade in deeper, and let the river cover their nakedness.

Women who already had running water in their homes still preferred to go to the river, to catch up on the gossip.

"Panchito was there too, washing his horse," she went on.

A little smile came across her face, though she knew she should be serious. "Before I knew it, he was right there behind me. *¡Chingaaa—!* He tickled me good!"

"You were raped?" I was incensed. "But why didn't you stand up and yell?"

"What—in my brassiere and worn-out panties? In front of all those women?"

I sputtered at the logic of it all. "But they saw the whole thing anyway, didn't they?"

"Oh no, *señora*, the *palapa* fell on us and covered everything."

"That does it!" I fumed. "I'm going to have your tubes tied this time."

We had been through that before. The government had initiated several forms of birth control in Mexico, with little result. Industrialized nations sent down their latest contraceptives, using the women of the third world as guinea pigs.

But I had also explained to Emilia that a very small incision in the belly would get her fixed up. "No more children," I emphasized. "You can screw all you like. In the river, on the bed, under the bed, in the jungle, on the beach, and no more children!"

Emilia listened politely, but we both knew that she would not consider it.

"One more doesn't make any difference," she kept saying. There was always somebody at home to take care of another baby.

Abortion was equally out of the question. There were the ever-recurring stories about the country women who had tried it themselves with coat hangers, and gotten unbearable pain in return for their experiments.

And Emilia had already been working for us when we saw one day that Chacha, one of the hotel maids, could hardly walk. When she confessed that she had poured undiluted iodine into her vagina, I was horrified. I took her to my house, and shy as she was, I made her open up her legs and show me. The raw pink flesh, oozing with pus from dozens of inflamed blisters, made me sick.

I couldn't scold her.

"Just trust me, Chacha. I will take care of it," I assured her.

I put her in a bathtub with a solution of beer and cornstarch, and began the penicillin injections. I made her sit with a forty-watt light bulb between her legs, to dry her out. Within a week, she was cured.

But there was no way Emilia was going to submit herself to that, or an abortion of any kind.

"Who is this Panchito, anyway? Do you know him?"

"Of course, *señora*. He is from our village. He was washing his horse in the river."

"In his underwear, I suppose?"

She looked down at the floor again. "He is so handsome and *joven*!"

That was hardly an answer.

"So it wasn't exactly rape, Emilia?"

She hesitated. "Well . . . it was . . . fifty-fifty."

I swallowed hard and promised to take her to the hospital for this birth. She was nearing forty, and I didn't want her to take a chance on a midwife.

Seven months later, little Jaime (Jim's name in Spanish) was born. We were his *compadres*, which meant that we threw a big celebration for the child at its christening. For the poorer Mexicans, it's not always easy to find godparents who can afford to give a big party like that. Often, out of convenience, the godfather just happens to be the mother's next lover.

And the chain of birth continues.

"You won't let me go, will you, *señora*?" Emilia pleaded.

"Of course not, *mi gorda*. When your little baby is born, he can stay here in the house while you work."

She became her usual happy self again, humming all day long as she did all the household chores, and grew larger and larger.

She continued to help my mother exercise in her little pool every afternoon. At the end of it, she used to hand her something to read, to while away the long hours. Half the time, I found my mother sitting there in her wheelchair, studying the book upside down.

She couldn't see, and Emilia couldn't read, so nobody was the wiser.

I couldn't resist taunting her one more time. "You're pretty cheerful for a girl who's been raped," I pointed out.

"Don't think of it as rape, *señora*," she giggled. "It was heaven!"

27

The last camping trip that Jim and I enjoyed was at our favorite spot, Punta de Mita.

I had bought the ranch in Santa Fe. There didn't seem to be much point any longer in hanging around to collect my compensation from the *fideicomiso*, or the extra money that Miguel Salinas had promised me. They would either pay me or they wouldn't.

No amount of persuasion was going to encourage them, or hurry them. We needed to get on with our lives.

The camping trip proved a fitting way to say good-bye to Mexico, especially the humiliating ending of it.

We spent the whole day snorkeling along the beautiful white coral beaches of the point. We had pulled the station wagon up under a palm tree as usual, but that night, since we had seen a lot of scorpions in the area, we happened to be sleeping on our mattress inside the car.

Jim woke me out of a sound sleep.

"Look at those guys sneaking along the dunes back there. Wait—now look! You can see a little flashlight."

I tried to focus my eyes.

"Jesus Christ! They've got guns!" he said.

I was fully conscious immediately, and I saw dark pistols gleaming in the hands of two little runty Mexicans. They were coming toward us.

I dived into the front and struggled into my muumuu.

"Toss me the keys!" I said. "We're getting out of here."

"Shit! I can't find my shorts," screamed Jim. I felt around the front seat, and I spotted them by the light of the full moon. I took the keys out myself and threw Jim's shorts into the back. The car rocked back and forth in the sand, as we tried to get dressed.

The guys were upon us.

"Give us your money and your jewelry!" barked one of them in English, hitting the window on the driver's side with the barrel of his pistol.

I ducked and tried to start the ignition. He shot twice at the front tire, missing both times. But he convinced me to behave myself.

I turned off the motor.

"Out of the car!" he said, motioning with his pistol.

Jim was still struggling into his shorts, trying somehow to leave both hands free to grab some of the money out of his billfold and hide it. The flashlight shone into the back seat.

"All of it!" commanded the *bandido*. "And your watch too."

Jim handed them over.

Their English was surprisingly clear. They must have spent some time in America. But I began to cuss them out in Spanish anyhow. *"¡Hijos de puta!"* I yelled. "Is this the way you treat guests in your country? Fucking *pendejos!"*

His lips curled in a smile. Was it admiration for my command of the language? All he said was, "Open up the hood."

He stuffed four thousand pesos and the watch from Jim into a shopping bag of nylon net, and opened up another one. In the moonlight, it looked as if it was filled with giant tarantulas.

Jim got out of the car and swung at one of the guys. They were both leaning over the engine, looking for something.

"Slam the hood down on their heads!" I shouted to Jim. "Kill the bastards!"

"I wouldn't do that, if I were you," said a voice from the dark. "They won't hurt you. They only want your distributor wires." A tall, blond American hippie came into view. His hands were tied behind his back, and he was being shoved along by a third little runt with a pistol.

"Sonsabitches," snarled Jim.

The dark men took out our distributor cap and jammed it into the bag with the others.

The third guy opened up the back of the station wagon and looked under the mattress for more. "No jewelry, *señora? ¡Pobrecita!* Poor little kid," he taunted.

"Cabrón—"

He picked up my expensive Phillips short-wave radio, scrutinized it, and tossed it back contemptuously. "No tape deck," he sneered.

"¡Vámonos!" one of them said in an urgent voice.

He grabbed the good-looking American, still trussed up in back, and the three *bandidos* ran to the motorcycle they had stashed behind in the dunes. They all jumped on top and drove off slowly, dragging the poor hippie along down the beach as a hostage.

In a short time they saw that he was in the way, and they sent him sprawling onto the sand.

Within minutes he was back to us, and we were quickly joined by several more Americans, from four other vans. Six groups of campers had been parked on the beach, out of sight of one another, and they had hit all of us.

"Little shits," said one. "If they hadn't had guns, we couldda—"

It was true. Most of these beautiful Americans were a head taller and a lot stronger and healthier looking than the slimy little farts who had robbed us. It had made my heart sick to see the first guy, John, walk up, simply towering over the little Mexican monkey who held him hostage at gunpoint.

Since I could speak Spanish, I was gradually chosen to be the leader of the group.

"There's a military post in Bucerías," I suggested. "We could go there, but don't get your hopes up."

"We've got to get the distributor wires first," Jim pointed out. "Probably the little motherfuckers just dropped them beside the road."

John offered to go looking for them, while we calmed everybody down. At least the bastards had left us our rum. He returned in an hour, holding up the bag in triumph. He looked like Jimmy Stewart in one of his early movies.

It was just as they guessed. The bag was in a ditch beside the road, about two miles down.

"Well, it's only money," I said, trying for a cheerful tone. "They didn't harm any of us."

"Over two hundred bucks!" grumbled my lover.

One of the tall hippie girls was sobbing quietly. "We can't even get back home! We don't have enough money to buy gas," she said, thoroughly subdued.

"Well, let's try the military commander," I offered. "But I warned you not to expect anything. Those guys might have even been the police, for all we know. We've heard of that before."

We all sorted out the wires, and soon five vans were gathered around our station wagon. In a convoy, we made the trip back along the point, to the shoddy little concrete barracks of Bucerías.

A sleepy watchman woke up the *comandante*. He puffed out his chest and started issuing orders, yelling *"¡Corran, corran!* Run!"* to all the little *rancheros* in his command. They ran in and out a few times, looking helpless, the commander cussed them out a few more times, and then it was over.

I explained to the Americans that the guys couldn't get their jeep started. I had offered to drive, but they were insulted by the thought of it. It was like a scene from the Keystone Cops.

"Come on," I said. "You can all stay at my place. I've got plenty of room."

So my house became a campground for about a week, while the honorary American consul tried to get some money down for them, so that they could drive back to the States.

The day after they all left, Jim was sitting at a bar on the Malecón, when he saw the same little *pendejos* drive by on their motorcycle.

He jumped into his station wagon and took off after them. They ducked into one of the small side streets. He followed. Suddenly they found themselves at a dead end, stopped cold by the little Pitillal stream that goes through town. They plunged right into it, and roared across.

Jim went in after them, and knocked the stuffing out of the bottom of his car.

The repair bills were far higher than he could have recovered, even if he had caught up with them.

"Goddam Mexicans!" he kept repeating afterwards.

The symbolism of that experience did not escape me. Screwed in Mexico. One more time.

But there is an interesting coda that gives the other side to it.

One day, Jim and I were on our way into town. We pulled the car up near the little coconut shack of Don Andrés, to wait for the traffic. A beautiful American girl was in tears, sitting there on her luggage beside the highway. Her companion stood next to her, looking helpless.

"Can we help?" yelled Jim out of the window of the car.

"Perhaps," said Ed, a little sternly.

He explained that they had hitchhiked into PV, and that when they jumped out of the truck in front of our house, his girlfriend had forgotten to grab her purse. It was still in the back of the truck, with all of her valuables inside.

The girl's name was Charley Brown. She looked spectacular, even through the tears, and Jim invited them both for a drink at Carlos O'Brian's while we talked strategy.

We calmed them down over *cuba libres*.

"The guy probably had deliveries in town for several hours," I explained.

"The best thing you can do is to go back there beside the highway, and wait for him to drive by. Everybody has to use that same road out of town, to go back to Guadalajara."

They agreed that it was a slim possibility, but about the only hope they had.

"You can stay with us, if he doesn't come by tonight."

We drove them back, and they waited for several hours, with no luck. They came in after dark, and I fixed a big mess of crayfish, *langostinitos*, and that helped to cheer them up considerably.

Jim was in heaven. Charley Brown was a topless stripper from New Orleans, who charmed us all with her soft Southern accent.

Once they started feeling better, she agreed to give us a demonstration. We put on a record, and she started gyrating wildly all through my living room, her long dark hair flowing sinuously behind her, while we cheered her on. Without embarrassment, she took off her clothes, and finished the dance in her lace panties. Her breasts were large and firm. I was impressed too, if a bit jealous.

The next morning they were out on the highway again, and I'll be damned if the truck driver didn't pass by and recognize them—not too difficult, everything considered.

The purse was still tucked in a corner in the back of the truck. Charley Brown checked her passport and counted her money. Everything was there, except for a small bottle of perfume.

The truck driver was shocked that the perfume was missing, and apologized profusely.

I shook his hand, happy to be reminded of that other side of my Mexico, that I had loved so much.

Ed was a former philosophy professor from an American university, though not a typical stereotype. He was sporty and youthful, and he and Jim got along well. They stayed for a few weeks with us, while Jim prepared to leave for Santa Fe, to meet my kids and set us up on the ranch.

I made plans to follow him up shortly in Penny's truck with our belongings.

But first I drove to Guadalajara to say good-bye to Ofelia.

"You look as though you could use a good spiritual cleaning, after all you've been through," she said when she greeted me at the door.

She and I loved to visit the Indian healers from time to time, when we needed a lift. Crisanto just shook his head. I had never even found the nerve to tell Bob Lewis about it.

"I found a new one out near Tlaquepaque," she continued. "You have to be there very early in the morning. We'll get up around five."

I started to object, but she told me she thought my aura must be pretty black, with the devils I had been fighting. I'd better go with her.

I couldn't argue with that. "Where'd you hear about him?" I asked.

"It's an old Indian couple. My great-grandmother told me. They're famous in the area."

"OK," I agreed. Perhaps my aura was tarnished.

We got up early the next morning and drove outside the city. There was no one on the streets. But when we pulled up into the small village, we saw there were already several expensive automobiles parked outside the place, and there was a long line of people waiting to see the holy couple.

Ofelia and I stopped at a couple of road stands nearby, and bought two fertilized eggs and two carnations, as all the rest of them had done, and joined the line.

Once inside, I met two small, rather heavy Indians, with long, unkempt hair streaked with grey. They were middle-aged, and ordinarily they would not have been too impressive, except that here a kind light shone brightly from their eyes. It outshone even the candles that lit up the small grotto where they worked. The man had carved out this room himself from the yellow rock of the mountain, and it looked like what I had always imagined in Lourdes or the shrine in Fátima.

There was a peaceful hush in the room. Ofelia went first. We were still both clutching onto our two eggs and two carnations.

When it was my turn, the man beat me softly around the shoulders with a small bunch of herbs, and then with a large rattlesnake rattler. The whole time, he continued to repeat prayers to Jesus and to the blessed Virgin. He sprinkled pure spring water on my head, and then he made a circle of alcohol, and set it afire, as he had done with Ofelia. I stood in the center, while the burning circle cleansed the bad spirits from my mind and soul. Then I was led off to a small shrine to pray by myself.

I left the carnations and a small donation on the shrine, and then I was led back to the lady. She sat at a small table, and held out her hand for the eggs. She broke them into a goblet of water, and we watched as the yokes sank to the bottom, and the whites rose up into the magical fairy castle formation of a child's imagination. She shook the glass slightly, but the shape did not change.

"Oh! There's going to be a big accident," she said slowly.

"An accident?" My stomach sank.

"Yes, a terrible accident. Be very careful. You will suffer." She shook her head sadly from side to side.

"What do you mean? A car?"

"An accident," she repeated. "That's all I see."

Then it was over.

She put the glass with the eggs aside, and I was shown out. I was shaking all over.

Ofelia and I talked it over a bit, but we couldn't make anything out of it.   "At least my aura was healed," I thought. "Not much else I can do about the rest."

I forgot about it until a week later, when there was a major plane crash outside of Chicago. I wracked my brain to figure how I was related to that, but nothing came to me. I hadn't known any of the passengers who died.

Still, I was left with an uneasy feeling.

Penny had come to me and told me she was leaving her husband and taking her kids back to America. "But I haven't got any money," she confessed. Every dime from the silver mine investments was gone.

"If you'll pay for our trip, I'll drive your furniture up in my truck."

"A deal," I said.

As we started out, I discovered to my great distaste, that we were to be escorted by her husband Fred, in his silver Cadillac. I never did figure out why. Perhaps she hadn't told him her plans. Perhaps he hoped he could change her mind during the trip—though in reality, he didn't appear to care much one way or the other. As long as he had his tequila and cigars, he seemed satisfied.

Every once in a while, he would pull up beside us on the road, and yell, "Why don't you let the little fuckers ride with me in the air conditioning?" referring to his children.

Penny, who was driving about a hundred miles an hour down the straight-arrow desert roads of Zacatecas and Chihuahua, with her left leg hanging out the window to cool off, shouted some obscenity or other, and he zoomed past. It was an altogether chilling trip for me, but I was happy that I found some transportation for my things.

At one point the truck broke down, and Fred sped on ahead. Penny crawled up and all but disappeared under the hood. I was no help at all to her, but apparently she had been used to doing this for years on the boat. About a half hour later Fred came back, and there, in the heat of the summer desert, we were all treated to an ear-shattering screaming match, including several words that I had never heard in any language.

Penny slammed down the hood, asked me to take the children to a nearby farmhouse for some water, and sped away with Fred in the Cadillac.

I sat on the ground with her barefoot kids under the shade of a scrubby little tree, and waited in the dust. I wondered what had become of my cats, who had run off in that same desert about a dozen years before.

The idealism of my youth was shattered, but I was about to begin a new life with Jim. I was still happy, and undaunted.

When the couple returned, they were calm. I don't know what happened inside that air-conditioned car, but there were no more arguments. Penny and I crossed the border without incident, if you don't count the bedbugs at the motels Fred chose for us, and she said good-bye forever to her husband, while I made arrangements for a moving van to take my furniture to the ranch.

While in New Mexico, I got a call from Helen, who was still staying in my house in Puerto Vallarta.

"The vultures are closing in," she said. "You'd better get down here. There are bulldozers outside the house right now."

I flew down and was met at the airport by Armando. I was taken to the offices of the *fideicomiso*, but was not allowed inside the room while the lawyers conducted their business. I was furious, but Armando calmed me down.

I stepped outside briefly and made a call to Rafael de la Cruz at the newspaper. "Can you get a photographer over to Las Glorias? The bulldozers are there already."

"I'm sorry, Theresa," he said. "I'll see what I can do."

He told me that he had been shot at in his office recently, and kidnapped for a short time in Mexico City also, on account of some articles he had written about the activities of the *fideicomiso*.

He would not be taking the pictures personally. I understood.

I returned to the office, and then Armando brought me to a waiting car. We were escorted to Las Glorias in a convoy of four gleaming new limousines.

The Reys were there, with all their lawyers and bodyguards. Miguel Salinas and Antonio Juárez glowered from another side with their own toughs. Four soldiers stood by with M-16's.

As we rounded the curve at Las Glorias, I saw that the bulldozers had already leveled the little shack where Don Andrés lived with his ten children. In tears, they picked through the rubble, here and there holding up a dead chick or a little duckling, a broken dish or a photograph, a Christmas ornament, a baptismal dress. They stared at the convoy with hollow eyes, as we wheeled into the driveway.

There on the patio of my beautiful house, I was presented with a check for $32,000, my total compensation from the *fideicomiso*.

"Better take it, Theresa," said Armando gently at my side. "There won't be any more."

He whispered to me that Cloro's wife Nemecia had refused the $20,000 check offered to her privately by Miguel. She told him she wanted at least four times that amount. In fury, he tore up the check, and she got nothing. There was no further mention of the $150,000 Miguel had hinted to me about.

I reached out my hand. I was wearing a proper little hat and matching purse for the photographers. They didn't get there in time.

Later Rafael sent me a copy of the paper, with a picture of the rubble from Don Andrés' little shack.

Armando got me to the plane, mercifully, before the bulldozers began their final demolition of Las Glorias.

In Guadalajara, I stood at Ofelia's front door, as I had done so many times in the past.

"You got a telephone call from your son," she said.

I put a call through to Bear.

"Jim's dead," he said.

The blood rushed from my head and I sat down.

"He went to see his children. I think he was drinking," Bear went on, his voice shaking. "His car stalled, and he got out to push it. He slid underneath it as it started to roll, and it ran over him. I think he managed to walk back over to the car and get in, but the police found him dead at the steering wheel."

At the autopsy, they discovered that nothing was broken except a small chip of bone that had pierced the aorta. He was thirty-six.

I called Jim's parents in New York, and they began making the funeral arrangements.

I gave away most of my money, to my maids and to Ofelia, to be used for the education of her children.

Thirty-two thousand dollars was such a laughable sum, considering the millions that Las Glorias was worth, and the tens of millions that the property has made since then.

Besides, legally I was able to take only five thousand dollars into the United States.

I sat alone on the plane back to New Mexico. "I may be down, but I'm not out," I promised myself. "I've got my whole life ahead of me, with my kids."

I'm a survivor.

I took a taxi from the airport in Albuquerque to the ranch. On the interstate, we passed the hearse, which carried the body of Jim Goodell back east to be buried.